AS Applied Business for Edexcel – Double Award

Authors	Michael Fardon
	Frank Adcock
	John Prokopiw

Consultants	Edward Hughes
	Graham Williams
	Debbie Wilson

osborne
BOOKS

Published by Osborne Books Limited
Unit 1B Everoak Estate
Bromyard Road
Worcester WR2 5HP
Tel 01905 748071
Email books@osbornebooks.co.uk
Website www.osbornebooks.co.uk

Graphic Design by Richard Holt

Printed and bound in Malta by Gutenberg Press Limited

British Library Cataloguing in Publication Data
A catalogue record for this book is available from the British Library

ISBN 1 872962 39 4

Contents

Authors

Michael Fardon has had extensive teaching experience of vocational business courses at Worcester College of Technology. He now specialises in writing business and financial texts, and was lead writer for the highly successful 'GCSE Applied Business' from Osborne Books. He has also worked in a consultancy role for QCA and Edexcel and has been involved in planning and drafting units for vocational business courses.

Frank Adcock has had fourteen years experience in commercial marketing, working for four different businesses, including the Mars Group. Frank was also Marketing Director of New Education Press Limited for twelve years. More recently he has worked as a Business and Management lecturer in FE Colleges where he has taught marketing on a variety of vocational business courses.

John Prokopiw is Senior Lecturer in Management and Business Studies at Worcester College of Technology where he is Course Director for the Institute of Personnel and Development programmes. He has been a writer for Osborne Books for a number of years, having contributed the Human Resource Management content for 'Advanced Business' and 'GCSE Applied Business'.

Acknowledgments

Osborne Books is grateful to many people and organisations for helping towards the writing and production of this book. Particular thanks must go to Edward Hughes, Debbie Wilson and Graham Williams for their consultancy work for Units 4, 5 and 7 and also to Roger Petheram, Jenny Clarke and Jane Tait for reading and advising on the text, to Richard Holt for his designs and Robert Fardon for his photography. Thanks must also go to Haymarket Business Publishing and 'Personnel Today' who have kindly allowed reproduction of extracts from journal articles and to Thomson Holidays who provided their holiday questionnaire.

Case studies form an important element of this book and Osborne Books is greatly indebted to the businesses who generously donated their time and resources in compiling the text of selected case study material: Alton Towers, Cadbury, Land Rover, Tesco and World Cancer Research Fund UK.

Osborne Books would also like to thank the following organisations for illustrations used in this book: AC Selection, Action on Smoking and Health, The Advertising Standards Authority, Amazon.co.uk, American Adventure, Andrew Grant, Angelfire, Anything Left Handed, Apple UK, Auto Electric Supplies, Banking Code Standards Board, Boots Plc, British Airways, British Broadcasting Corporation, British Franchise Association, BUAV, Business Link, Cadbury Schweppes plc, Call Centre Focus, Call of the Wild, Cancer Research UK, Central Taxis, Checketts News and Food, Co-operative Bank Plc, the Co-operative Group, Department of Trade and Industry, Dell Computers, Easy Group, Edinburgh Bicycle Co-operative, The Environment Agency, Envirowise, Estron Signature, Exoticmeats, Experian, Fairtrade, First Choice Holidays, Ford Motor Company, The Garden Escape, Golden Wonder, Greenpeace UK, Harrison Clark, Health and Safety Executive, Heinz, Highland Water Ltd, Homebase, Honda Motor Europe Ltd, HSBC Holdings Plc, Hughes Media, the Information Commissioner, Investors in People UK, Jaguar Cars, John Lewis Partnership, Kelkoo, Kraft Foods, Land Rover, Lastminute.com, LloydsTSB, London Camera Exchange, Lynx, Mars, Merryck & Co, Morgan Cars, Microsoft, National Express, National Shoppers Survey, Net Jobs, New Deal, Nominet, Northern Ireland Electricity, npower, Office of National Statistics, OMSCo, Orange Plc, People Maps, Play.com, The Post Office, Prontaprint, Publicis, Recycle More, Rentokil Initial, Royal Bank of Scotland, St John's Sports Centre, Simply Gifted, Slater Menswear, Small Business Service (DTI), Spin UK Ltd, Stepstone, Subway, Tesco, Thomson Holidays, Total Jobs, the Telework Association, Toyota UK, Unison, Usborne Books, Virgin, Volvo Car UK Ltd, Worcester Bosch, Worcester Rugby Club, Worcestershire County Council, Worcestershire Royal Hospital, World Cancer Research Fund UK, Young Enterprise.

About this book

A note for teachers

AS Applied Business for Edexcel – Double Award has been written for the new Edexcel vocational 'Applied' GCE.

The text covers all seven units available for the Double Award AS. Units 1 - 3 and 6 are compulsory for completion of the award and two optional units are also required from Units 4,5 and 7.

The material in this book for Units 1 - 3, is reproduced from the Osborne Books text *AS Applied Business for Edexcel – Single Award*, which has been endorsed by Edexcel.

AS Applied Business for Edexcel – Double Award has followed in many respects the design of the popular Osborne Books *GCSE Applied Business*, which was written in response to the opinions and suggestions of focus groups of teachers and students.

This text is divided into seven sections reflecting the seven units of the course. Each section is divided into chapters, each with progressive activities, case studies, key terms and chapter summaries.

Wherever possible the activities have been designed to help students towards their assessments, whether internal or external.

A number of case studies in the book are based on real businesses, or have been written and contributed by real businesses.

Much use has been made of the internet in this text to provide practical examples and

illustrations. Website addresses have been integrated into the text where appropriate and website screens have been extensively used as illustrative material. Note that both can change without warning and so students should be advised as such.

The website constructed in the Case Study in Chapter 23 'Setting up a new website' can be found at www.edsperfectpizzas.co.uk. Its four pages are available for download from the Student Resources section of our website www.osbornebooks.co.uk and can be used as templates for the students' own designs for the Unit 4 internal assessment.

A Tutor Pack, containing guidance answers to the student activities and other supporting material, is available from Osborne Books (01905 748071).

Osborne Books likes to keep in touch with its customers and would welcome comments about this book – please write, telephone or email books@osbornebooks.co.uk with your feedback.

Michael Fardon
Frank Adcock
John Prokopiw

Introduction for students

AS Applied Business – the Double Award

The Edexcel AS in Applied Business is a double award, equivalent to two AS qualifications, and will be awarded a grade based on an A to E scale. It attracts UCAS points and will enable you to progress to higher education or direct to training in business.

The Edexcel Applied AS is a vocational qualification, putting you in contact with real businesses and requiring you to investigate areas such as marketing, employment of staff, finance and electronic commerce. You may also set up your own school or college-based enterprise scheme. Contact with business could include work placements, visits and talks from speakers. The course is very much student-centred and will enable you to acquire the knowledge and develop many of the skills that you will need in a business career.

Structure and Assessment of the AS Applied Business – Double Award

The Edexcel Double Award AS requires you to complete six units out of a choice of seven. The award involves a mix of external and internal assessment.

Unit 1   Investigating people at work (compulsory Unit)

This unit explains the aims and objectives, types and structures of business. It is also very much involved in investigating the 'people' aspect of business and explains how businesses set about recruiting staff and then keeping them.

This unit is externally assessed by a series of questions which combine analysis of Case Study material in the assessment and evidence from your own investigations into businesses.

Unit 2   Investigating business (compulsory Unit)

This unit investigates the way in which businesses plan, manage and review their resources, including their financial resources.

This unit is internally assessed and involves a group investigation into the setting up of a small business which provides a service to your local area. Your findings will be incorporated into a live presentation.

Unit 3   Investigating marketing (compulsory Unit)

Successful marketing is essential for the survival of any business. This unit requires you to investigate the ways in which you would market a chosen product or service.

This unit is internally assessed and involves producing a 'marketing mix', ie a plan of action for successfully selling your chosen product or service to the appropriate type of person.

Unit 4   Investigating electronic business (optional Unit)

This unit investigates the way websites are increasingly used by businesses to market and sell their products and services.

This unit is internally assessed and involves a detailed analysis of one website and the planning and possible construction of a new website.

Unit 5   Investigating customer service (optional Unit)

This unit explores the need for an organisation to monitor and constantly improve its levels of customer service in order to keep its customers.

This unit is internally assessed and involves making a presentation explaining how an organisation provides, monitors and improves customer service.

Unit 6   Investigating promotion (compulsory Unit)

This unit investigates the need for an organisation to use promotional techniques, such as advertising and PR, as part of its marketing policy.

This unit is externally assessed by questions based on given Case Study material and evidence from your own investigations into promotional campaigns.

Unit 7   Investigating enterprise (optional Unit)

This unit investigates the need for individuals who can demonstrate enterprise and encourage teamwork and innovation in setting up and running a business.

This unit is internally assessed and requires evidence from a class setting up, running and then disbanding a small business enterprise.

How to use the chapters

This textbook is divided into seven sections – one for each unit – and each section is divided into chapters. The chapters contain:

- an opening 'Starting Point' which introduces the subject matter of the chapter, followed by a summary of what the chapter covers
- a text with definitions and highlighted key terms
- activities which help you understand the concepts
- Case Studies – some of them contributed by real businesses
- a list of key terms at the end of the chapter – useful for note taking and revision
- a chapter summary – also useful for note taking and revision

How to use the internet for your investigations

The internet is a goldmine for the business student. With the help of search engines such as www.google.co.uk you can log on to the websites of businesses of all sizes, Government departments and pressure groups. You can also use business educational websites such as www.bized.ac.uk to search for information.

Website addresses have been incorporated into the text, but remember that these can change without warning – if in doubt, use a search engine.

Good luck with your studies!

Michael Fardon, Frank Adcock, John Prokopiw

Investigating people at work

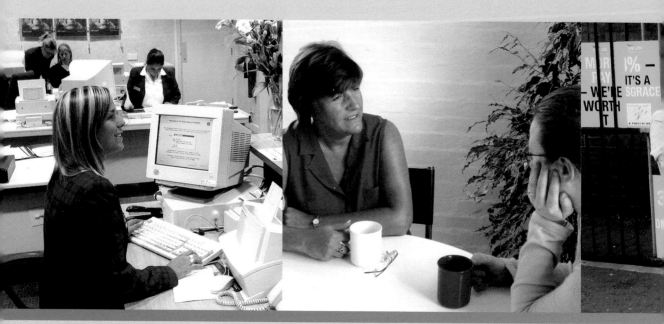

In this unit you will investigate a range of businesses and examine the way in which people and the management of people contribute to the success of business organisations. You will research:

- people working in business and people starting businesses

- the differing aims and objectives of business organisations

- different types of business and how they are structured

- the need to plan the workforce and recruit employees

- the training needed for people in the workplace

- the need to evaluate employee performance and to motivate employees

- the way people at work are affected by outside influences such as legal requirements, environmental and ethical pressures

Chapters in this Unit...

1 People and business – an introduction

Starting point

If you get a job in a business, you are dealing with people all the time. You deal with people at work on a daily basis – colleagues and bosses – and also with customers and other outsiders, over the counter, over the phone, through email and through written communications. Some people you get on with; others you may find difficult to deal with.

What all these people have in common is that they are essential to the business.

In a successful enterprise the people working inside the business provide customers with what they ask for and make them want to come back again.

What you will learn from this chapter

This chapter is a general introduction to Unit 1. It provides an overview of a number of areas dealt with in later chapters. It covers:

- what a business is and what it produces

- the variety of different types of business

- the importance of entrepreneurs who start and support businesses

- the range of people who work in a business

- the range of people and institutions outside a business – the external stakeholders – who affect the way the business operates and influence the people working in the business

A Business – Some Definitions

goods and services

If you ask the 'person in the street' what a business is, you are likely to be given an example: HMV, McDonald's, the sports centre, the local taxi firm, and so on. The person is most likely to view these businesses from the point of view of a customer – they are where you can get music, food, fitness and transport. He or she may also see them as places offering employment.

Businesses involve a wide range of activities which result in a **product**. The product of a business might be manufactured **goods** or it might be a **service** provided to customers.

Products are tangible (touchable) items such as cars and crisps, whereas a service is something that is done for you, eg being sold goods in a shop, being transported from London to Birmingham on a train, having your hair styled.

providing what customers want

Successful businesses provide products which customers want – whether they are products for basic needs such as bread and toilet paper, or whether they are products which customers can be persuaded to buy as the 'must-have' essential fashion accessory.

A **business** can therefore be defined as:

an organisation which provides goods or services for its customers.

Activity 1.1 – what businesses 'do'

The following organisations can be defined as businesses. Decide in each case:

■ whether they provide goods or services, or both

■ to what extent the products provided by them are really needed by customers

You may find it useful to access the websites of the businesses by carrying out a search using a search engine such as Google.

1	Thomson Holidays	4	Coca-Cola
2	Cadbury's	5	Ferrari
3	Direct Line Motor Insurance	6	Tesco

Varieties of Business

The main impression you will get from investigating businesses is the wide variety that you will find.

range of activity – industrial sectors

The activities carried out by businesses vary greatly. As we have seen, some businesses manufacture goods and others provide services, the general trend in the UK being for a decline in the manufacturing industry and growth in the number of service businesses. Traditionally, business activity is classified into three interlinking **industrial sectors**:

- **primary industrial sector – extracting natural resources**

    This involves the extracting of natural resources – raw materials for use in the manufacturing process. Examples of primary production are mining, farming, market gardening, fishing and forestry.

- **secondary industrial sector – manufacturing products**

    This is the next stage in the production process; it involves the processing of raw materials into the manufactured product: fruit into pies or juice, wood into paper, metal into cars, and so on.

- **tertiary industrial sector – providing services**

    This third classification involves a business providing a service rather than a manufactured item; examples include restaurants, shops, insurance, travel and advertising.

These three sectors link together to form a **chain of production**, as in the example of Honda Cars shown below.

primary sector (extracting raw materials)	secondary sector (manufacturing goods)	tertiary sector (providing services)
iron ore extracted from the ground is made into sheet steel	the sheet steel is used on a Honda car production line	the Honda car is sold by the dealer

differing sizes and localities of business

Businesses vary considerably in **size**. It may come as a surprise that over 99% of the businesses in the UK are small businesses employing fewer than 50 people. This contrasts markedly with the comparatively small number of large businesses with over 250 employees. The Activity below analyses these statistics in more detail and provides an interesting overall picture of the structure of business in the UK.

Businesses also vary in **geographical scope** – some are local and serve local needs (the taxi firm); some are known nationally within the UK (All:sports), and some are worldwide names (McDonald's, Coca-Cola, Nike).

Activity 1.2 – an overall picture of business in the UK

The Small Business Service (an agency of the Department of Trade and Industry) regularly publishes statistics relating to Small and Medium-sized Enterprises (SMEs). These are available on www.sbs.gov.uk. A report based on 2003 data for all UK businesses revealed the following (the figures are approximations):

Total number of business enterprises in the UK	4 million
Small businesses (0 - 49 employees)	3,968,000
Medium-sized businesses (50 - 249 employees)	26,000
Large businesses (250 and over employees)	6,000

National Statistics, a government agency (www.statistics.gov.uk), has published figures which relate to the turnover (total sales) of main types of business in 2002 and the comparative trend in sales from the previous year:

Production (manufacturing)	531.1 £bn	trend: – 2.4%
Retailing and services	1,402.5 £bn	trend: + 2.8%

1. Calculate the percentages of the number of small, medium and large businesses from the Small Business Service data. If you are able to, use a spreadsheet and produce a chart showing your findings. Why might these figures surprise you?

2. Calculate the percentages of the two types of industry shown in the National Statistics data. Explain the relationship between the two sectors and the trends shown by the figures. Do you see any evidence of these trends in your local area? Give examples of any businesses opening up or closing down you know of and see if they follow the trends shown by the figures.

the Importance of Entrepreneurs

being an entrepreneur

Businesses are about people. It is the enterprising people with ideas for new products who are willing to take risks who start businesses. These people are innovators and known as **entrepreneurs**.

As part of your Applied AS in Business you may be studying enterprise or you may devise and run your own business as part of your course. This will enable you to appreciate the personal challenges and problems involved in starting a business. You will then understand what fires up and drives the entrepreneur.

A survey on entrepreneurship by the Small Business Service (www.sbs.gov.uk) has shown that the main motivating factors for a person starting a business are:

- freedom to work in the way that you want and being your own boss
- needing a challenge
- making more money than you are earning now

The survey shows that the typical UK entrepreneur is a well-educated, middle-class male – which is clearly a challenge for enterprising females! The majority of entrepreneurs have already been in full-time employment and have taken the decision to go it alone for the reasons listed above – these can be summarised very basically as self-fulfilment and money.

why entrepreneurs are valuable

The entrepreneur clearly aims to create wealth for him/herself. This is often achieved when the business is a sole proprietor – 'one-person' – operation. Of the 4 million UK enterprises, no fewer than 2.9 million (ie over 70% of all businesses) do not employ anyone else – they are 'one-person' enterprises.

The value of a 'one-person' enterprise entrepreneur lies in a number of areas:

- wealth creation and personal satisfaction
- launching of new products and improvement of existing products

An entrepreneur becomes even more valuable to the economy when he/she:

- employs other people
- starts other businesses

As we will see in the Case Study which follows, some individuals have become well known for being 'serial entrepreneurs' – ie starting a whole range of new businesses and giving them a common 'brand' identity.

Case Study – Stelios: serial entrepreneur

easyJet

Stelios Haji-Ioannou is a 'serial entrepreneur' and the founder of the easyGroup of companies. He has founded a wide variety of companies, the biggest of which is easyJet, the leading low-cost airline. Launched in 1995, easyJet PLC listed on the London Stock Exchange in 2000. It is currently Europe's largest low-cost airline (by revenue) with an ever-expanding fleet of jets.

In 1998 Stelios formed the easyGroup, a holding company to explore new ventures to extend the 'easy' brand (which it owns) and capitalise upon the expanding use of the internet. All the companies described below are currently entirely or majority privately owned by Stelios. He is chairman of each one and remains very active in their day-to-day running.

The first such venture, easyInternetcafé, is the cheapest way to get online and started trading in June 1999. It has a growing number of franchised internet cafés across Europe and the New York area.

easyInternetcafé

easyCar

easyCar, a car rental service that sells 95% online, started trading in April 2000 and is now well established with offices in Europe, the US, Australia and New Zealand.

easyValue.com, impartial comparisons for online shopping, started trading in November 2000, the same month as the launch of the portal for all easyGroup companies www.easy.com which also offers a free web-based email service.

easyMoney, online financial services, launched with the world's first dynamically personalised credit card in September 2001 and easyCinema, low-cost movie theatres, launched in May 2003. easyBus, which offers low cost intercity travel, launched in August 2004.

easyCruise

easy4men

More recent additions to easyGroup companies include: easyMobile, easyPizza, easyMusic, easy4men, easyHotel and easyCruise.

useful websites accessible through the global portal www.easy.com

www.Stelios.com

www.easyInternetcafe.com

www.easyMobile.com

www.easyJet.com

www.easyCar.com

www.easyMusic.com

www.easyBus.co.uk

www.easyCruise.com

www.easyHotel.com

Activity 1.3 – entrepreneurs

1 What factors are likely to motivate an entrepreneur to set up a new business?

2 How many 'easy' companies has Stelios founded, and which is the largest? Visit www.easy.com for the most up-to-date position.

3 Give another example of a 'serial' entrepreneur who has created a brand name for a range of businesses providing a variety of products. List some of the products.

People in Business

We saw earlier in this chapter that the large majority of businesses – over 70% in fact – consist of an entrepreneur working on his or her own. When the business expands, either because the entrepreneur wants it to, or because the enterprise 'takes off' and requires more staff, the owner will have to take people on and become an employer.

This is a big step. The whole 'culture' of the business will change from one independent individual working on his/her own to an organisation, a team, which will require management, motivation and long lengths of 'red tape' involving payroll, employment law and Health & Safety at Work regulations.

Many business owners will then aim to keep the organisation small. Over 90% of businesses in the UK are classed as 'micro-businesses', employing fewer than ten full-time staff. The advantages of being small include containment of costs (staff are expensive) and ease of management. The phrase 'small is beautiful' has become a cliché, but remains very true.

As the business grows further, the owner (or owners) may decide to form a limited company and possibly bring in extra finance, in which case they will become shareholders and directors and, if the company is large enough, employ managers to oversee the staff. The business then becomes a three-tier structure: owners/directors, managers and staff:

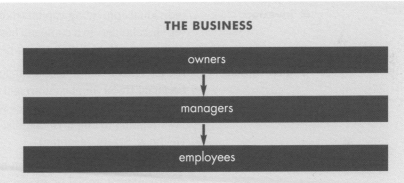

THE BUSINESS

owners

managers

employees

Business ownership will be dealt with in detail in Chapter 3 and business structure in Chapter 4. The point to be made in this introductory chapter is that in a business structure of this type the owners, managers and employees all take on roles and responsibilities: the owners to establish the aims of the business, the managers to motivate and control the staff, the staff to work as a loyal team.

People Outside the Business

No business works in isolation. In this section we will introduce the concept of how people and organisations outside a business affect the way in which it operates and how they influence the people working in it. This theme will be expanded in Chapter 2 'Business aims and objectives' on pages 20-23.

stakeholders

In common English a 'stakeholder' is someone who has an investment in an organisation or project. In business terminology 'stakeholder' has taken on a more general meaning:

a stakeholder is any person or organisation with an interest in a business

This is best explained by giving examples of stakeholders. Read the text that follows and study the diagram on the opposite page. Note that the word 'people' used below can equally apply to organisations.

- **customers**   people who buy the products of a business and are interested in customer service and product quality

- **suppliers**   people who supply the business with goods and services and are interested in being paid – on time

- **lenders**   financial institutions such as banks who lend money to the business – they want to be repaid and receive a good rate of interest

- **investors**   individuals providing capital (money) for a business (eg shareholders in a company business), interested in seeing the value of their investment increasing

- **government**   the interest of central and local government is both financial (receiving taxation) and regulatory (ensuring the business complies with the many laws relating to employment, discrimination, Health & Safety, planning)

- **pressure groups**   bodies such as Greenpeace who have an environmental, social or ethical interest in how a business operates

- **local community**   the interest of local people in issues such as getting jobs and not clogging up the roads with delivery lorries

As we will see in the next chapter, the pressures brought to bear by stakeholders affect not only the operation of the business but also the individual employees working in the business. These effects can be positive (Health & Safety, discrimination law) and negative (stress from dealing with customer service, personal threats from animal rights protestors).

STAKEHOLDERS IN A BUSINESS

Activity 1.4 – external pressures on business

Choose and investigate a business that operates in your locality. Answer the following questions:

1   Who are the stakeholders of the business?

2   Identify any *positive* effects that the stakeholders may have on the employees of the business.

3   Identify any *negative* effects that the stakeholders may have on the employees of the business.

CHAPTER SUMMARY

■ A business is an organisation which provides its customers with the goods and services that they need or can be persuaded to buy.

■ Businesses can carry out a wide variety of activities, ranging from the extraction of natural resources, through manufacturing to the provision of services (including the retailing of goods).

■ Businesses vary considerably in size, with smaller businesses being far more common than larger ones. The normal classification of size of business is:

micro-business	0 - 9 employees
small business (including micro)	0 - 49 employees
medium business	50 - 249 employees
large business	over 250 employees

■ Businesses also vary considerably in geographical coverage: some are local, some are national and some international.

■ Businesses are formed by entrepreneurs who have the resources and vision to establish an enterprise. They are also willing to take the risks involved. Some have the ability and energy to form a number of businesses in succession, and to oversee their management. Entrepreneurs are very valuable in being able to generate wealth and provide employment for others.

■ Most businesses are 'one-person' enterprises and do not employ staff. As businesses expand and take on employees, they are likely eventually to develop a three-tier structure of owners, managers and employees.

■ Businesses do not operate in a vacuum. The owners, managers and employees are all subject to influences from outside stakeholders. Stakeholders are people and organisations which have an interest in a business. They include:

- customers
- suppliers
- lenders
- investors
- local and central government
- pressure groups
- the local community

KEY TERMS

business an organisation which provides goods or services for its customers

product goods or services provided by a business

primary sector the sector of businesses that extracts raw materials

secondary sector the sector of businesses that manufactures goods

tertiary sector the sector of businesses that distributes and sells goods or provides a service

chain of production the linking together of the primary, secondary and tertiary sectors in order to provide the customer with a manufactured product

micro business a business that employs between 0 and 9 people

SME a Small and Medium-sized Enterprise is a business that employs up to 250 people

entrepreneur a person who has the idea and energy for starting a business and who is willing to take the associated risks

shareholder someone who has an ownership stake in a limited company business

stakeholder a person or an organisation with an interest in a business

2

Business aims and objectives

| Groceries | Finance & Insurance | Telecoms | Wine | Electricals | DVD, Video CDs, Games | Flowers | Books | Today at Tesco |

OUR CORE PURPOSE IS 'TO CREATE VALUE FOR CUSTOMERS TO EARN THEIR LIFETIME LOYALTY'. WE DELIVER THIS THROUGH OUR VALUES – 'NO-ONE TRIES HARDER FOR CUSTOMERS' AND 'TREAT PEOPLE HOW WE LIKE TO BE TREATED'.

Starting point

We have seen that a business is set up to provide its customers with the goods and services that they require. In order to achieve this it establishes long-term aims – its 'mission'. The 'core purpose' of Tesco, for example, is to earn the lifetime loyalty of its customers by providing good value in terms of its prices, quality, choice and service.

These aims will be supported by specific objectives which include making a profit, helping the community and caring for the environment. In providing goods and services a business such as Tesco is answerable to its 'stakeholders'; these include customers, shareholders, employees and society at large, all of whom in one way or another are affected by the business and influence its operations.

What you will learn from this chapter

■ the overall aim of a business is set out in a Mission Statement

■ the objectives of a business are the goals it sets to enable it to achieve its aim

■ a stakeholder of a business is an individual or group that has an interest in the business; stakeholders can be:
  - internal: managers and employees
  - external: customers, suppliers, investors (shareholders), lenders, the local and worldwide community, environmental pressure groups

■ businesses have a 'corporate responsibility' to the interests of stakeholders representing community, environment, marketplace, and workplace; they often adopt a corporate responsibility policy and publicise their achievements in these areas

Business Aims

business aims and the Mission Statement

An **aim** – or 'purpose' – is what you set out to do.

An aim or purpose for a business is the overall direction in which the management wish it to develop over a period of time. Examples include:

> *"I want this company to be the biggest supplier of home-delivered pizzas in the UK."*

> *"I want this travel agency to provide the best level of customer service in the town."*

The small business owner is likely to have a reasonably clear idea of the main aim of the business and will work hard to achieve it. The management structure of a larger business will be more complex and will have to deal with many more staff. It is the job of management to identify common aims and to motivate the employees to work together to achieve those aims – to maximise sales, to provide the best service, and so on. The 'core purpose' of Tesco PLC shown on the previous page therefore broadly reflects the 'people in business' concept developed in the last chapter.

A business will often set out its aims in a published 'statement' in the form of a Mission Statement or Vision. In the example below, Boots the Chemists states its main aims – concentrating on its customers and its market share.

> Boots aims to be the place for health and beauty customers. We want to secure market leadership in the UK and build on our brand's growing success internationally.

Activity 2.1 – Mission Statements

1   Use the internet and other resources (eg printed company reports) at your school or college to collect examples of business Mission Statements. If you are online, you may find these on the 'about us' section of the websites. Also make use of the educational websites www.bized.ac.uk and www.tt100.biz

2   Comment on how brief or long the statements are and how successful they are in telling you what the aim of the business actually is (some Mission Statements are very bland and vague).

3   Make up a Mission Statement for your school or college.

Business Objectives

An **aim** or **purpose** expresses in general terms what the business sets out to do in the long term.

An **objective** is a specific goal the business wishes to achieve.

A business will succeed in its aim through the achievement of a variety of objectives, including profitability, growth, quality and social responsibility.

making a profit

The **profit** of a business is the income from the sale of its products less its running costs. All businesses, whether they are large companies like Tesco PLC or small one-person enterprises, need to cover costs. An important business objective is to maximise sales, which will in turn lead to creation of a profit.

Profit provides resources for business expansion and for rewarding the owners – the shareholders in the case of a company such as Tesco PLC.

The extract from the Tesco Annual Review and Summary Financial Statement shown below illustrates this point. Note that overall sales of the Tesco group were £33.6 billion and profits £1.6 billion. The dividends are the profit that is distributed to the shareholders and are calculated as a number of pence for each share held. If you visit www.tesco.com, you will see the share price quoted and get an idea of the current return on investment.

	2004 53 weeks	2004 52 weeks pro forma	2003
Group sales (£m) (including value added tax)	33,557	32,989	28,280
Underlying Group profit before tax (£m)	1,708	1,684	1,401
Group profit before tax (£m)	1,600	1,576	1,361
Underlying diluted earnings per share (p)	16.31		13.98
Diluted earnings per share (p)	14.93		13.42
Dividend per share (p)	6.84		6.20
Group enterprise value (£m) (market capitalisation plus net debt)	23,866		16,896
Return on capital employed	10.5%		10.2%

non-profit making organisations – making a surplus

A profit-making organisation such as a business has profit as one of its main objectives, largely because the owners (eg the owners of Tesco shares) will expect to make a return on the money that has been invested. A non-profit making organisation, on the other hand, will not have profit as a main objective, but will still want to cover its costs and, in some cases, make a surplus. Examples include:

■ a **charity** such as Cancer Research UK – raising money for a worthy cause and providing a benefit to society

■ a **public corporation** such as the BBC, providing quality programming and other services in return for a licence fee

Study the extracts from their websites below and identify their objectives.

AIMS AND OBJECTIVES OF NON-PROFIT MAKING ORGANISATIONS

Our objectives

What we aim to do

Cancer Research UK will work alone and in partnership with others to achieve the following objectives:

1. **To carry out world-class research into the biology and causes of cancer**
   Cancer is a highly complex disease that is still only partly understood. Only through a better understanding of the disease will the improved treatments, diagnostics and prevention strategies of the future be developed.

2. **To develop effective treatments and improve the quality of life for cancer patients**
   Research will be carried out to accelerate cancer cure rates, aiming to translate our understanding of the disease into effective treatments. Research will also be directed at improving diagnosis of cancer, and at prolonging the life and improving the quality of life of those patients whose disease cannot be cured.

3. **To reduce the number of people getting cancer**
   Research will be carried out into the influence of lifestyle, individual risk, environment and interventions such as vaccination on cancer, and into how people can change their behaviours to reduce their risk of the disease. We will make the wider public aware of cancer risk factors and the options available to them to reduce that risk.

4. **To provide authoritative information on cancer**
   As a leading international research organisation Cancer Research UK will provide authoritative cancer information to the public and promote the best treatments and prevention strategies to governments, commercial organisations, those responsible for cancer care, and the media.

www.cancerresearchuk.org

(Image courtesy Cancer Research UK and correct as at May 2005)

About the BBC

Purpose & values

"to inform, educate and entertain"

"to serve everyone and enrich people's lives"

"to be the most creative, trusted organisation in the world"

BBC purpose

The BBC exists to enrich people's lives with great programmes and services that inform, educate and entertain. Its vision is to be the most creative, trusted organisation in the world.

It provides a wide range of distinctive programmes and services for everyone, free of commercial interests and political bias. They include television, radio, national, local, childrens', educational, language and other services for key interest groups.

BBC services are hugely popular and used by over 90% of the UK population every week. The BBC also runs orchestras, actively develops new talent and supports training and production skills for the British broadcasting, music, drama and film industries.

The BBC is financed by a TV licence paid by households. It does not have to serve the interests of advertisers, or produce a return for shareholders. This means it can concentrate on providing high quality programmes and services for everyone, many of which would not otherwise be supported by subscription or advertising.

www.bbc.co.uk

growth – increasing sales and market share

For some businesses, beating the competition is one of the main objectives because the survival of the business often depends upon it. A weak business can be a prime target for a takeover by another business. Beating the competition can often be achieved by growth – a policy of expansion to increase sales and market share (market share is the percentage of the market taken by the products of a business).

In the extract from the Tesco Annual Review and Summary Financial Statement shown below growth is shown in terms of expansion of geographical coverage, increased sales and profit, and increased return to the shareholders of the company.

AROUND THE WORLD

UNITED KINGDOM · CZECH REPUBLIC · HUNGARY · POLAND · REPUBLIC OF IRELAND · SLOVAKIA · TURKEY · JAPAN · MALAYSIA · SOUTH KOREA · TAIWAN · THAILAND

FINANCIAL HIGHLIGHTS

GROUP SALES	+ 18.7%
UNDERLYING GROUP PROFIT BEFORE TAX[†]	+ 21.9%
GROUP PROFIT BEFORE TAX	+ 17.6%
UNDERLYING DILUTED EARNINGS PER SHARE[†]	+ 16.7%
DILUTED EARNINGS PER SHARE	+ 11.3%
DIVIDEND PER SHARE	+ 10.3%

survival

For businesses operating in a competitive environment, growth and establishing market share can be critical objectives. Without growth and the achievement of a significant market share, both small and large businesses can fail to survive. One method of achieving growth is price cutting. You will be aware of this happening in a number of industries: supermarkets, airlines, online retailers. The problem here of course is that cutting prices can also cut profits and this can result in the policy backfiring and threatening the survival of the business. The lesson here is that objectives can work against each other. It is all a question of priority – should the business be the biggest player in the market or should it be the most profitable? The most successful business can be both.

Activity 2.2 – survival of the fittest

A number of types of business are cutting prices (and consequently profits) in order to increase sales and market share.

1 Find out the lowest price of a sliced loaf of white bread from a supermarket and the price charged by a local 'corner' shop.

What is the difference?

Why is there this difference?

What might happen to the businesses as a result of this difference in price?

2 Can you think of any other businesses which carry out price cutting like this? What are these businesses aiming to do?

providing quality

A business which provides a quality product and quality customer service keeps its customers. Quality products – which can be manufactured items or services – are often the result of a policy of quality which extends to every person and procedure within the business. This policy is known as Total Quality Management (TQM). Many businesses apply for and are granted a quality certificate in line with ISO 9000, an international standard for quality systems.

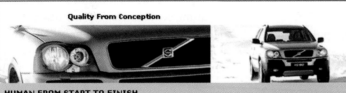

Quality From Conception

HUMAN FROM START TO FINISH

At Volvo, human beings come first. We start with who you are and what you need from your Volvo, and then work out from there. Along the way we insist on quality at all stages of development–from the establishment of these functional requirements, to the development of virtual models and life-size prototypes, right down to materials, fabrics and colors. All of which are determined, in a very real way, by you, the driver, and your passengers.

Our designers conceive an aesthetic that must meet these functional requirements determined by consumers. These designs then pass through a veritable gauntlet of scrutiny and assessment as improvements are sought, identified and implemented–down to the size and shape of cupholders. Which will suit you best? What kind of liquids will you carry? And how can you access them safely? Again, the human being is fundamental to every detail.

If a business adopts quality as a major objective, it will need to ensure that the workforce is involved in the quality process. It will implement stringent standards of quality control.

This quality objective has become important for Volvo Cars which links it firmly with the theme (also adopted by Tesco) which makes 'people' central to the company philosophy, as seen here on the company website: www.volvocars.co.uk.

Corporate Responsibility Objectives

the needs of stakeholders

We saw in the last chapter that stakeholders are individuals or organisations that have an interest in a business.

Many stakeholders are **external** to the business:

- customers
- suppliers
- investors
- lenders
- the local community
- central and local government
- pressure groups (environmental, social, ethical causes)

Other stakeholders are **within** the business itself:

- managers
- other employees

It matters to a stakeholder what the business does and it matters to the business what the stakeholder does or thinks. It is the responsibility of the owners and management of a business to formulate business objectives to keep the majority of the stakeholders happy for the majority of the time. This may not always be straightforward. Cutting costs to maximise profit may not always be popular with stakeholders – for example, importing goods produced using cheap overseas labour, using overseas call centres, or forcing suppliers to bring their prices down.

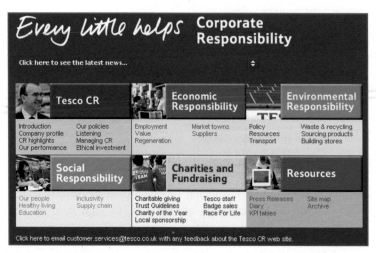

corporate responsibility

This overall responsibility has become known as **corporate responsibility**. The term 'corporate' simply means 'relating to the organisation'. Businesses are becoming increasingly accountable for their corporate responsibility. Most large companies now regularly publish some form of corporate responsibility report, either in paper format, or in a special section of the website, or both. Many are listed on a Corporate Responsibility Index (see www.bitc.org.uk). This index looks at four main areas of corporate responsibility:

- community
- environment
- marketplace
- workplace

The illustration on the previous page shows the Tesco website corporate responsibility home page, with the catchphrase 'Every little helps'.

serving the community

Tesco supporting the 'Race for Life' to beat cancer

The term 'community' refers both to the local community in which the business operates and also to the wider community in the UK, usually referred to as 'society'. There is a need in both for financial support for charitable causes, sports events and artistic events. There is, of course, a publicity spin-off for businesses helping in these areas.

It is useful for a business to support the community in this way because it is likely to provide not only the customers of a business but also its employees. Why do businesses support the community? A business that is seen to be socially responsible will retain the respect of customers. A business that advertises its good works is likely to gain new customers.

serving the world community

The term 'community' can be extended to the worldwide community of different countries, some of which are richer and more prosperous than others. Some businesses adopt the objective of sourcing their products from economies which will benefit from this support. Products which carry the label 'Fairtrade' indicate this policy in action – coffee from Costa Rica, for example. Visit www.fairtrade.org.uk for more information.

"If it wasn't for Fairtrade with prices so low...we would get deeper and deeper into debt" Isabel, coffee farmer.

caring for the environment

It is common knowledge that the earth's resources are being depleted and damaged by business on a worldwide scale. Not only are resources running out, but it is likely that pollution is damaging the balance of gases in the atmosphere, leading to global warming. It is claimed that the production of genetically modified food is also disturbing the balance of nature.

Businesses are under increasing pressure to carry out a policy of **sustainability**. This means adopting objectives such as:

■ cutting down on pollution

■ not wasting natural resources

■ using recycled materials wherever possible

■ using energy efficiently

Businesses like to be seen to be helping to save the environment. If they are thought to be socially responsible, consumers are more likely to think well of them and therefore more likely to buy their products. The ban in some supermarkets of the sale of genetically modified food is a case in point. Also, savings on the use of resources such as energy can mean savings in costs; this directly helps to boost profits.

These environmental objectives of a business are partly driven by **pressure groups** which represent public opinion about environmental issues. Members of Greenpeace (www.greenpeace.org.uk), for example, protested against the oil company Esso by dressing up as tigers (the Esso 'mascot') and surrounding EU energy ministers at a meeting organised by Esso. Greenpeace claims that Esso is sabotaging the fight against global warming.

Image supplied courtesy of Greenpeace / Cobbing

Local pressure groups can often have significant influence on business decisions – blocking planning for new business projects, for example, when they threaten the environment through noise and emissions.

The **government** as stakeholder has an interest in and influence over business. Laws cover areas such as planning, environmental hazards and Health & Safety at Work.

looking after the marketplace

Many businesses are **customer**-focused – in other words they aim to keep their customers happy by looking after them, listening to their views and meeting their needs. With businesses in keen competition, a customer that is ignored is a customer that is lost.

Suppliers are also important to businesses because they provide the quality goods and materials which customers demand. A business needs to build up a long-term relationship with its suppliers to ensure continuity and quality in the supply chain.

internal stakeholders – the workplace

The **owner** of a business is a stakeholder who looks for a return on the capital (money) put into the business. In a larger business, such as a limited company, there is a distinction between the owners, the management and the employees. **Managers** and **employees** are stakeholders in a business because the success of the business in terms of making a profit and the employees working together with the same aim (see 'culture' below) ensure job security and job satisfaction.

One of the primary objectives of businesses is to look after the workforce. This reflects on the 'culture' of the business. Tesco states, for example (Annual Review and Summary Financial Statement) that:

> All our people benefit from training and we are committed to sharing knowledge and giving everyone the chance to progress through the company . . . Our industry-leading benefits package lets our staff share in the success they have helped to create.

'corporate culture' in the workplace

There is little point in setting objectives if the whole workforce is not dedicated to achieving them. If you go into a shop and find the sales staff indifferent and the goods in poor condition the business is failing in its objectives because the employees and the internal systems are not geared up to a common aim. The attitude to work is all wrong. The business lacks a 'corporate culture'. This may be defined as:

the attitudes, values and beliefs that are shared by the people in a business

If a business is to succeed in achieving its objectives, it is vital that its people (owners, managers, employees) share a belief in those objectives. It is up to the management of a business to instill that belief in the employees – to promote a common 'vision' involving:

- the business objectives
- a common code of behaviour for the employee

Activity 2.3 – identifying and balancing objectives

This chapter has shown that there are many different types of objective that drive businesses: profit (or surplus), survival and quality. There are also the 'corporate responsibility objectives which support the local and worldwide communities, environmental protection, customers and suppliers, and people in the workplace.

In this series of Activities you will:

■ identify business objectives and the stakeholders which they affect (questions 1 – 3)

■ assess and suggest solutions for situations where there may be a conflict between objectives (question 4)

The next page reproduces extracts from Tesco's Corporate Responsibility Report and Annual Report and Annual Statement (both available for download on www.tesco.com). Study these extracts and carry out the following tasks:

1 Read the Corporate Responsibility Highlights 2003/04 and describe what Tesco PLC has achieved in terms of providing benefits to:

    (a)   the community in the UK

    (b)   the overseas community

    (c)   the environment

    (d)   suppliers

    (e)   the workplace

2 What evidence can you find elsewhere in this chapter or at www.tesco.com about the way in which Tesco PLC views and treats its customers. Explain why customers are given so much importance in Tesco's 'main purpose'.

3 Read the Tesco PLC Group (Financial) Summary and:

    (a)   Comment on the Group's sales and profit performance. What does this tell you about the success of the Group and whom will it benefit?

    (b)   Draw up a chart showing the sales and profit for the Group's UK, European and Asian divisions. Comment on the trends shown and suggest whom they will benefit.

4 What stakeholder issues are likely to be discussed by the management of a supermarket chain if:

    (a)   the site for a proposed new 'open all hours' store is next to a local nursing home, and is also the cheapest to develop?

    (b)   a pressure group protests about the stores selling a make of trainer which it claims is produced using cheap overseas labour?

    (c)   it is offered a supply of plastic carrier bags which are 30% cheaper than the bags it currently uses, but are not guaranteed to be degradable?

Corporate Responsibility Highlights 2003/04

- creating 30,000 jobs:
- distributing £57 million of free shares to staff under a new Shares in Success scheme;
- launching our own-brand Fair Trade range;
- building on our work with the Ethical Trading Initiative (ETI) by training more of our buyers and suppliers in labour standards, via the 'Buying With Your Eyes Open' and 'Supplying With Your Eyes Open' courses;
- working with our peers to set up a global database of supplier ethical audit results (SEDEX);
- recycling 80% of cardboard and 85% of plastic used in our operations;
- introducing degradable carrier bags;
- using brownfield sites for 96% of new developments;
- giving £7 million of computer equipment to schools, bringing the total to £84 million since 1992;
- raising £2.5 million for the Tesco Charity of the Year, Barnardo's;
- sponsoring Cancer Research UK's Race for Life, in which 300,000 women, including over 12,500 from Tesco participated, raising £17.5 million;
- conducting our first audit of corporate responsibility processes.

GROUP SUMMARY

	2004 £m	2003 restated £m	Change %
Group sales (including value added tax)	33,557	28,280	18.7
Underlying profit on ordinary activities before tax[†]	1,708	1,401	21.9
Profit on ordinary activities before taxation	1,600	1,361	17.6
Underlying diluted earnings per share (p)[†]	16.31	13.98	16.7
Diluted earnings per share (p)	14.93	13.42	11.3
Dividend per share (p)	6.84	6.20	10.3

UK PERFORMANCE

	2004 £m	2003 restated £m	Change %
Sales (including value added tax)	26,876	23,101	16.3
Underlying operating profit[†]	1,526	1,297	17.7

REST OF EUROPE PERFORMANCE

	2004 £m	2003 restated £m	Change %
Sales (including value added tax)	3,834	3,007	27.5
Underlying operating profit[†]	184	141	30.5

ASIA PERFORMANCE

	2004 £m	2003 restated £m	Change %
Sales (including value added tax)	2,847	2,172	31.1
Underlying operating profit[†]	122	71	71.8

[†] Excluding net loss on disposal of fixed assets, integration costs and goodwill amortisation.

CHAPTER SUMMARY

■ The aim of a business – what it sets out to do in the long term – is often summarised in a Mission Statement.

■ Objectives are goals that the organisation sets out to achieve as part of its overall aim. They include:

- making a profit (businesses) or a surplus (non-profit making organisations)

- survival – beating the competition

- increasing sales and market share

- providing quality goods and services

■ A stakeholder of a business is an individual or a group that has an interest in the business.
Internal stakeholders include owners, managers and employees.
External stakeholders include investors, customers, suppliers, lenders, the local community, the government and pressure groups.

■ Stakeholders are directly affected by the objectives adopted by the business because they are influenced by what the business does.

■ Some objectives show a business displaying a 'corporate responsibility' to individual stakeholders and society in general, for example:

- helping the community both locally and on a wider scale

- caring for the environment

- looking after the workforce

■ Business objectives can conflict, for example maximising profit and benefiting suppliers. Businesses must therefore balance the demands of its stakeholders in its adoption of business objectives.

■ The 'culture' of a business – often referred to as 'corporate culture' – describes the 'way of thinking' within the business, for example the workforce 'thinking' total quality, customer focus, social responsibility.

■ If a business is to succeed in achieving its objectives, it is essential that these are built into its culture – they must be adopted by the entire workforce. This is a task for the management of the business.

KEY TERMS

aim	an aim is what a business sets out to do
objective	a goal which a business aims to achieve, for example profitability, growth in market share
Mission Statement	a written statement setting out the aim (and sometimes objectives) of a business – also sometimes known a s a 'core purpose'
Vision	an overall view stating how a business sees its main aim
business profit	the difference between the income from the sale of products and the running costs of a business
surplus	the difference between the money raised and the running costs of a non-profit making organisation
market share	the percentage of the market taken by the products of a business – growth of market share is a common business objective
TQM	Total Quality Management (TQM) is a policy which aims to ensure a high level of quality in an organisation's products and procedures
stakeholder	an individual or group which has an interest in a business and is affected by what the business does
corporate responsibility	the responsibility of a business to society in general and its stakeholders in particular
sustainability	a policy of conserving natural resources and preserving the environment
pressure group	an organisation which promotes and campaigns for the rights of stakeholders
corporate culture	the attitudes, values and beliefs that are shared by people in an organisation such as a business

3

Types of business

Starting point

Some of the questions asked by a person looking for a career in business include:

'What type of business should I go for?'

'Does size matter?'

'Will the job stay local?'

'What is the difference between the public sector and the private sector?'

'Can I set up my own business?'

'If I do, will I be able to expand?'

The answers to all these questions require a knowledge of the very wide range of business types.

What you will learn from this chapter

- businesses can be classified according to 'sector':
    - public sector businesses which are wholly or partly state-owned
    - private sector businesses which are owned by individuals
    - voluntary sector – made up of non-profit making organisations

- businesses can be also classified according to ownership:
    - sole trader – a 'one-person' business
    - partnership – a business owned by a group of individuals
    - limited company – a separate body owned by shareholders (either the smaller 'private' company or the larger 'public limited company' whose shares can be traded on the Stock Markets)
    - co-operative – a business owned and run by its members
    - franchise – a licence to use a well-known business name
    - charity – set up to help society rather than to make a profit

- the type of ownership of a business will dictate the size of the business, the way in which it operates and the range of job opportunities that it offers

Business Sectors

Businesses are divided into **private sector** businesses and the **public sector** enterprises. There are also organisations which form the **voluntary sector**.

the public sector

public corporation

This sector comprises government-owned or government-controlled bodies including:

- public corporations such as the Post Office and the BBC
- government departments (the Civil Service)
- local authorities such as County or District Councils

Some local businesses are public sector. Your local leisure centre may well be owned by the Council and either run by the Council itself, or run by an independent company which has tendered for the business.

The way in which businesses in the public sector operate will be restricted by governmental guidelines and the need to provide 'value for money' rather than to make large profits. They will offer a wide range of job opportunities and relative security of employment.

the private sector

This sector comprises businesses which are directly or indirectly in private ownership. This sector accounts for most businesses operating within the UK. Private sector businesses include:

private sector enterprise

- sole traders (one-person businesses)
- partnerships (groups of people in business)
- limited companies (bodies owned by shareholders)
- co-operatives (groups of people 'clubbing' together in business, eg the Co-op stores)
- franchise operations (where a trader can 'buy' a name and set up a business which is already established and used by other independent operators, eg Subway)

The way in which businesses in the private sector operate will depend on their size, their ability to raise finance and their main objectives. Generally, they will aim to maximise sales and profits and market share. They offer a very wide variety of jobs and careers, and the opportunity for the entrepreneur to start up a new business.

non-profit making organisations – voluntary sector

Non-profit making organisations make up the **voluntary sector**. They include charities such as Oxfam and Cancer Research UK, and educational and arts organisations such as many independent schools and the National Trust. Although they are not businesses in the strict sense of the word, they are often run on business lines so that they can make a surplus. The larger organisations offer a variety of jobs and career openings to suitably qualified employees.

Sole Traders

definition

A sole trader is an individual trading in his or her name, or under a suitable trading name.

sole trader

If you are interested in working in a small business, you can be employed by a sole trader or, if you have the money and initiative, you can set up as a sole trader.

If you set up in business, you may do so for a number of reasons: you have redundancy money, you are fed up with your present job, or you have what you think is a brilliant new business idea. In other words, you are both enterprising and innovative.

Most people setting up in business do so on their own. The sole trader is the most common form of private sector business. As we saw in Chapter 1, the majority of businesses in the UK are sole traders. As a sole trader expands the business, he or she may take on any number of employees. A sole trader does not always have to be a 'one-person' business.

why become a sole trader?

There are a number of advantages of being a sole trader:

- **freedom to make decisions** – you are your own boss and can decide on your own objectives, for example making a large profit, achieving a target market share, expanding into other localities and products
- **job variety** – you can end up doing everything – managing sales, marketing, doing the banking, making the tea – but you can of course employ other people to take on those roles if you want
- **simplicity** – there is little legal 'red tape' required before you can start trading – there is less form-filling than there is in larger businesses

problems of being a sole trader

There are also disadvantages to being a sole trader:

- **risk** – you are on your own, with no-one to share the responsibilities of running the business or taking over if you are ill or on holiday; if you get badly into debt, you could be taken to court, become a bankrupt and lose many of your possessions, including your property – this is because a sole trader has **unlimited liability** (total responsibility) for his/her debts

- **finance** – you may not find it as easy to raise capital (money) from the banks and other investors as you would if you were a limited company

- **time** – you may need to work long hours to meet tight deadlines

- **expertise** – you may have limited skills in areas such as finance

sole trader – is it the right decision?

Setting up in business as a sole trader involves total commitment in terms of capital, time and the risks involved. You have freedom to establish your aims and objectives – to do exactly what you want – and will experience a wide range of job activities.

Activity 3.1 – being a sole trader

Lisa operates a fresh fish stall in the local city centre street market. She says:

"I saw an opportunity here because all the fish shops were closing down and the supermarkets were taking over. People always like fresh fish, especially as it is so healthy. I get my supplies from a wholesaler in Billingsgate. The market here is crowded every day with office workers and other shoppers buying speciality foods. I make a comfortable living from the business as I keep my expenses low and I have a lot of repeat customers for my quality produce."

1 Draw up a list of what you think Lisa's business objectives might be.

2 What are the advantages to Lisa of operating as a sole trader?

3 What are the risks to Lisa of operating as a sole trader?

4 What other types of business supply fresh fish? What advantages do you think Lisa's market stall might have over these other types of business?

5 How would Lisa's pattern of work vary from that of an assistant at the fish counter of a large supermarket?

Partnerships

A partnership is a group of individuals working together in business in order to make a profit.

Partners
David R. Harrison
N. G. Hill
Jonathan Brew
Keith Mills
Andrew Caldicott
Andrew M. James
Guy C. Salter
Rod Thomas
Dawn E. Oliver
Robert Sprake
J.H.T. Hooke
Brenda V. Spain
Consultants
S. Driver White

a 'firm' of solicitors

A partnership is simple to establish and involves two or more people running a business together, the objective being to make a profit. Examples of partnerships include groups of builders, dentists, caterers, solicitors, computer consultants, musicians and accountants.

A partnership – often known as a 'firm' – can either trade in the name of the partners or under a suitable trading name. For example, if H Simpson & B Gumble set up an escort agency, they could call themselves 'Simpson, Gumble & Co.' or, more interestingly, chose a name such as 'Springfield Escorts'.

Like sole traders, partners operate as individuals in the business, and like sole traders they have **unlimited liability** for **all** the debts of their business. This could be quite a serious problem for a partner if the business became bankrupt.

As far as business **objectives** and **operations** are concerned, a partnership will potentially have more resources for increased sales, expansion and development. The larger number of individuals concerned will mean that jobs will be more specialised: there may be a managing partner, a marketing partner, an accountant, and so on. Partnerships will, of course, be able to take on employees to carry out various functions and will generally be able to offer a wider variety of **job opportunities** than a sole trader.

partnership agreements

Just as newly married couples sometimes draw up a marital agreement, some partnerships operate according to the terms of a Partnership Agreement, a document usually drawn up by a solicitor. Not all partnerships have a Partnership Agreement – it is optional, but it does come in useful in resolving problems if there is a dispute between partners.

limited partnerships

Some partnerships operate as **limited partnerships** which are set up very much like limited companies (see page 34). Partners in a limited partnership are protected because they have **limited liability** for the debts of their business. This is very useful if the partnership goes 'bust' (bankrupt).

why form a partnership?

There are a number of advantages in forming a partnership:

- **finance** – there is the potential to raise more capital than a sole trader is able to: there are more people to contribute funds
- **job specialisation** – there is more potential for expertise and specialisation: one partner may be a technical expert, another a salesperson, another a financial expert
- **opportunity for expansion** – because of the extra resources and expertise available, a partnership is more able to expand its operations

problems with partnerships

- **disagreements** can and do occur among partners (as they do in marriages) because people fall out with each other – occasionally this can lead to the break-up of the partnership and the business
- **unlimited liability** – each partner is usually liable for all the debts of the partnership and may be made personally bankrupt if the business fails
- each partner is also liable for the **business deals** of the other partners (this could cause a problem if a deal went badly wrong)

Activity 3.2 – forming a partnership

Jo and Ben have both worked in the recruitment business for a number of years, but want to leave their present jobs and set up a specialist recruitment agency for sales and marketing staff. Jo is an excellent communicator and likes interviewing; Ben is good on the management and finance side. An estate agent has given them details of a variety of offices, both in the town centre (expensive) and also out of town (cheaper). They want some advice and ask the questions set out below. How would you advise them?

1 "What can we call the business? We need it to sound good."

2 "What do you think our main business objectives should be?"

3 "Do we need a solicitor to set up the business?"

4 "Can we borrow from the bank to help set up the business? We are worried about our position if we get into debt."

5 "Where do you think we should operate from? It is a lot cheaper to rent premises out of town."

6 "How should we split up the jobs we do? What if there is too much to do?"

Limited Company

If an individual or a group of people wants to set up a business, another option is the formation of a limited company.

A **limited company** is a business:

- owned by shareholders
- run by directors
- set up as a body which is separate from its owners (the shareholders)

A limited company is very different from a sole trader or partnership business. The sole trader or partner is the business; if the business goes 'bust' then so does the owner. The shareholder owner of a limited company stands apart from the business, which is a body in its own right. If the company goes 'bust', the shareholder is protected by limited liability and does not lose all his or her money – just the money invested.

Study the diagram below which shows how a limited company differs from a sole trader and partnership.

TYPES OF BUSINESS OWNERSHIP

the owners <u>are</u> the business

the shareholder owners are <u>separate</u> from the business

private and public limited companies

A limited company will either be:

■ a **private limited company** (abbreviated to Ltd) or

■ a **public limited company** (abbreviated to PLC or Plc or plc)

a private limited company

Most small or medium-sized businesses which decide to incorporate (become a company) become **private limited companies**; they are often family businesses with the shares held by the members of the family. Private companies cannot offer their shares for sale to the public at large, and so their ability to raise money may be limited.

It should be noted, however, that some famous business names are also private limited companies, for example Debenhams, John Lewis, Virgin Atlantic.

A private company may, however, become a **public limited company**. A public limited company can offer its shares for sale on the Stock Market in order to raise finance, but not all PLCs take this step, as the cost of a company 'flotation' can run into millions. This type of public limited company is know as a 'quoted' company.

a public limited company

There are many examples of public limited companies in the last chapter, for example Tesco PLC. Public limited companies have very defined aims and objectives, often balancing well-developed plans for sales growth, profitability and expansion with well-publicised policies of corporate responsibility – charitable giving, environmental policies and helping the community.

PLC's also offer a wide variety of job opportunity and career progression. They also offer a wide variety of jobs as they are normally structured into different departments and operating divisions (see next chapter).

shareholders as owners

Shareholders own a limited company and appoint directors to control the management of the company and plan for its future. In the case of a private limited company, the directors may be the only shareholders, and so the shareholders can be said to control the company directly. The chief director is the managing director.

In the case of a public limited company, directors often hold shares, but there are likely to be many more shareholders who take no part in the day-to-day running of the company.

working for limited companies

As you will appreciate, working for a company is very different from the relative informality of working in a sole trader business or a small partnership. Working practices and processes in a company are highly regulated and formalised. This can have the effect of making a 'go-ahead' employee feel less significant as he or she will be a small fish in a large corporate (company) pond. As mentioned on the previous page, the functions of companies will normally be concentrated into separate departments or operating divisions. Job opportunities will therefore be in more specialised areas than those offered by smaller businesses.

the danger of takeovers

Working for a public limited company has its dangers because a quoted company is open to takeover if someone buys a majority holding of its shares, either with or without its consent. Sometimes this can be for the good, sometimes it can lead to widespread job losses.

Activity 3.3 – Pilgrim Computing Ltd: a new company

A group of ten people in the computing business are setting up a new computer company to be called Pilgrim Computing Limited. They will all be directors and will contribute £50,000 each as share capital. They hope eventually to 'go public'.

They plan to take on 50 employees and sell their computers to PC Universe, a large chain of computer superstores.

1 What type of company will Pilgrim Computing Limited be initially? What is the main financial restriction placed on this type of company?

2 What is the amount of share capital of the new company?

3 What type of liability will each shareholder director have, and what money amount can each director stand to lose if the business fails?

4 Why do you think Pilgrim Computing Limited is not being set up as a sole trader or partnership business?

Co-operatives

You may find yourself investigating or working for a **co-operative**. The term 'co-operative' refers to two types of business:

- a retail Co-operative Society – which sell goods and services to the public
- a workers' or trading co-operative – a group of people 'clubbing' together to produce goods or to provide a service

retail Co-operative Societies – the background

Retail Co-operative Societies date back to 1844 when a group of 28 Rochdale weavers, suffering from the effects of high food prices and low pay, set up a society to buy food wholesale, ie at the same price as it was sold to the shops. This food was then sold to the members at prices lower than the shop prices, and the profits distributed to the members in what was known as a dividend. These societies developed into the present 'Co-op'.

a co-op store

the Co-op today

A well-known example of a retail co-operative is the Co-operative Group, a collection of companies, known as 'the Co-op'. It operates a wide range of businesses, including over 1,000 food stores, the insurance company CIS, the Co-operative Bank (including internet banking), the UK's largest funeral business, car dealerships, pharmacies, travel services and opticians. Visit www.co-op.co.uk for full details of this group of companies.

Working for a Co-op company will provide you with similar conditions and opportunities to those provided by any other company.

a co-op dividend card

who owns the Co-op?

A retail Co-operative Society is owned by its members. You can become a member by filling in a form obtainable from your local Co-op store and buying a share, normally for £1.

As a member you have voting rights (one vote per member) and can often obtain discounts at the Society's retail shops and the use of other facilities such as funeral services.

other co-operative ventures

The term 'co-operative' also applies more loosely to co-operative ventures. At the time of writing there are around 2,000 co-operatives which fulfil a number of different functions:

trading co-operatives

Groups of individuals, such as farmers, who do not have the resources in terms of capital and time to carry out their own promotion, selling and distribution, may 'club' together to store and distribute their produce. They may also set up co-operatives to purchase machinery and equipment.

workers co-operatives

A workers' co-operative may be set up by its members, or it may be found where a business which is about to shut down has been rescued by its management and workers. They step in and take over the ownership and running of the business with the aim of 'making a go of it' and at the same time safeguarding their jobs.

Activity 3.4 – investigating co-operatives

Carry out a search on the internet on the word 'co-operative' using a search engine such as www.google.co.uk, confining the search to UK sites.

1 Identify and list sites which represent:

- manufacturing businesses

- service businesses (including retail)

2 Who form the membership of the two co-operatives illustrated above, and what objectives do the two co-operatives have in common?

Visit www.edinburgh-bicycle.co.uk and www.omsco.co.uk

Franchises

a Subway franchise outlet

The franchise system was first established in the USA and is now an integral part of the private sector in the UK.

A franchise is an established business name – eg Subway (healthy sandwich outlet) or Prontaprint (instant printing shop) – which is 'sold' to someone setting up in business. A number (but not all) of McDonald's are franchises. Many car garages operate as franchises for the car manufacturers.

Log onto the sites: www.subway.co.uk, www.prontaprint.com and wwwbritish-franchise.org

The two people involved in a franchise deal are:

- the **franchisor**, the person who has developed a certain line of business, such as clothes retailing, hamburgers, drain clearing, and has made the trading name well known
- the **franchisee**, the person who buys the right to trade under the well-known trading name

In return for an initial fee, the person setting up (the franchisee) receives full advice and in some cases the necessary equipment. As the business trades, a 'royalty' percentage of takings is paid to the franchisor.

franchises as employers

There are many employment opportunities within franchises. Either you are the franchisee – you pay your money and you take the name – or you are employed by the franchisee, in which case you are subject to standard employment terms and conditions. You will be bound by the business aims and objectives set by the franchisor, eg Subway's goal 'to be the number one restaurant chain in both consumer rankings and location count in every market it serves.'

advantages of a franchise

- the business has been tried and tested in the market
- the business may well have a household name such as Burger King
- you are more likely to be able to raise finance from a bank for a franchise
- you receive training and, in some cases, tried and tested equipment

disadvantages of a franchise

- the initial cost of going into the franchise – the payment to the franchisor
- a proportion of your takings also goes to the franchisor
- you are less independent – you cannot develop the business as you wish and you cannot change the name or change the method of doing business – your objectives are set by the franchisor

Activity 3.5 – working in a franchise business

Read the extract from www.prontaprint.com shown below and answer the questions that follow.

reducing the risk

Starting a new business is daunting. Starting a business that is based upon an established and successful formula is much less so.

A Prontaprint Franchise offers the opportunity to enter into an exciting and rewarding market, offering customers a proven high quality product with unparalleled levels of service. As part of an established and highly successful nationwide network of modern business service centres, the risks associated with a typical new business are significantly reduced.

The success of the Prontaprint Franchise is a result of the support available and the quality of the people it attracts, their hard work and initiative. Prontaprint Limited's support is all-encompassing, with intensive initial training and effective, ongoing support in all aspects of centre management and operations. A Franchisee has the benefit of assistance from experienced teams at the Network Support Centre, from centre location and acquisition, shop fitting, equipment sourcing and installation to supplies and consumables, and sales and marketing.

As a founder member of the British Franchise Association, with over 30 years of successful Franchise operation, there are few organisations with greater knowledge of providing a successful business formula.

1 What are the advantages to a person wanting to set up in business of entering into a franchise agreement with Prontaprint?

2 What business objectives can you identify from this extract?

3 If you were an employee of a Prontaprint outlet, what advantages would the franchise arrangement bring you?

Private and Public Sector Collaboration

At the beginning of this chapter we made the distinction between:

- the public sector (government--owned or controlled organisations) and
- the private sector (businesses in private ownership)

There is some overlap between these two sectors, as we will now see.

local authority enterprises

Local authority enterprises include a wide variety of commercial activities, including swimming pools, sports centres, golf courses, local bus services, car parks and local lotteries. Local authorities often use private sector businesses for supplying services such as waste collection and catering, and also for running leisure facilities. This gives private enterprise new opportunities, but it can also mean that the local community may end up getting the cheapest rather than the best service.

Public Private Partnerships (PPP)

The Government has introduced a scheme in which private sector companies have been encouraged to provide resources and improve public sector businesses. The arrangement is that the private sector raises the money for projects and the government then leases the facilities provided. Examples include the upgrade of the London Underground, refitting of prisons and barracks and the building of hospitals (see the example below). This initiative was started as the Private Finance Initiative (PFI), although new projects are now known as Public Private Partnerships (PPP).

Worcestershire Royal Hospital

The new £95m 550-bed Worcestershire Royal Hospital offers a modern, high-quality medical environment. It is one of the biggest Private Finance Initiative (PFI) projects ever undertaken in the health sector and has been built in partnership with a PFI consortium (including banks and construction companies) under the overall title of Catalyst Healthcare (Worcester) plc, which has financed the building and will lease it to the Trust for 30 years.

The Trust is responsible for all clinical services and will pay a fixed monthly fee to Catalyst to cover the 'mortgage' on the hospital as well as maintenance, equipment and support services.

CHAPTER SUMMARY

- The public sector comprises government-owned or government-controlled bodies. Many of these are run on business lines, including public corporations such as the BBC and local authority enterprises.

- The private sector comprises businesses which are owned by private individuals and organisations.

- The voluntary sector comprises bodies such as charities and arts organisations which aim to be 'non-profit making' but which use business techniques to promote themselves and raise money.

- The size and the type of the business or organisation will affect the way it operates, its ability to raise finance, its objectives and job opportunities.

- Smaller businesses such as sole traders or partnerships offer a wider range of activity to the owners and employees, and greater freedom to formulate business objectives. Business owners who are sole traders or partners also have unlimited liability for the debts of their business and could be made bankrupt if the business fails.

- Private and public limited companies are owned by shareholders who have limited liability for the debts of the company. They tend to be larger businesses with very defined objectives offering more in the way of specialised job opportunities. They also have greater opportunity for the raising of finance.

- Co-operatives are businesses which were originally 'self-help' societies set up for the mutual benefit of their members. Some have now grown and amalgamated to form the retail 'Co-op'. Other co-operatives exist on a smaller scale either as groups of traders or as workers' co-operatives.

- A franchise arrangement allows an entrepreneur to trade under a trading name developed by the franchisor. He or she pays a fee and a share of profits to the franchisor and in return receives training and, in some cases, equipment. The business will be operated and staff employed along strictly laid down guidelines.

- The private sector and public sector sometimes combine in large-scale projects known as Public Private Partnerships (eg hospitals) and on a smaller scale in the provision of local authority services.

KEY TERMS

public sector	businesses that are controlled or owned by the government
private sector	businesses that are in private ownership
voluntary sector	non-profit making organisations run on business lines
Public Private Partnership (PPP)	a collaboration in which private sector businesses fund and provide a public sector facility which is leased to central or local government
sole trader	an individual setting up in business on his or her own
partnership	a group of individuals working together in business in order to make a profit
unlimited liability	the requirement to repay all the debts of the business if the need arises
bankruptcy	being taken to court for non-payment of debts and having your assets (belongings) sold to pay off the debts
limited liability	the obligation to repay all the debts of the business restricted to a certain amount – normally the amount of the investment
limited company	a business owned by shareholders and run by directors set up as a body separate from its owners
private limited company	a limited company whose shares are held by the directors and are not for public issue, it must have 'limited' in the name
public limited company	a limited company which is authorised to allow its shares to be sold to the public through the Stock Exchange
co-operative	a group of people 'clubbing' together to form a business for their own benefit; this may be an association where the business is owned by the members or it may become a limited company
franchisor	the owner of a business idea and name
franchisee	a person who buys the right to use a business idea and name

4

Business functions and structures

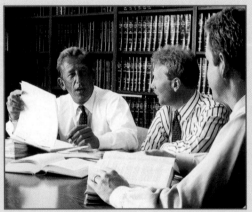

Starting point

If you ask anyone in business 'What is the key to getting what you want done in an organisation?' they will probably reply 'good communication between departments'. However large the business, people have to work together to achieve the objectives of the business. If a product does not look right, word has to get from Customer Services to Product Design and action has to be taken. If nothing happens, sales will decline and so will profitability.

When you are investigating a business it is important to get a clear idea of how the business is structured and how its various departments work together and support each other to achieve common objectives.

What you will learn from this chapter

- businesses operate through the co-operation of a number of different functions – finance, production, human resources, marketing and sales, administration

- business functions need to operate efficiently together in order to achieve the objectives of the business, for example growth or profit

- businesses are structured in different ways with different levels of management – some have many layers of management, others have very few; these structures are likely to vary according to the type of market in which each business is

- the current trend is for fewer levels of management – for what are known as 'flatter' structures – decentralisation – which allows more decision-making for people lower down in the organisation

Functions in Business

the functions

Whatever the size of the business – whether it is a sole trader or a public limited company – the same basic functions will need to take place. These include:

- **production** – using business resources to research, design and produce a manufactured product (eg a canned drink or car) or a service (eg a holiday, a haircut) – this is a basic function of any business
- **finance** – the control of money and the recording and reporting of money transactions – a central function in any business
- **marketing and sales** – finding out what customers need; promoting and selling the products
- **human resources** – the management of people in the business – even the sole trader with no employees has to manage him/herself!
- **administration** (also known as facilities management) – providing all the back-up needed by the business, for example, catering, office machine maintenance, security, reprographics (photocopying and printing)

management of business functions

All the functions listed above have to be co-ordinated by the management of the business to achieve the objectives of the business. For example:

- the type of products that are to be sold and to whom
- the amount of finance that will be needed
- the resources that will be needed – premises, people, equipment

This all requires careful operational planning. The success of the business will largely be determined by the quality of the planning and how the management co-ordinates the way the functions work together. We will look at business planning later in this book in Chapter 10.

Remember that the functions listed above apply equally to any size of business – a sole trader or a large company. The sole trader will have to carry out most of the functions him/herself and so will need to be highly organised and focused. The management of a larger business will need to ensure that all the functions operate smoothly and in a co-ordinated way by motivating staff to achieve the business objectives described in Chapter 2.

We will first examine in more detail the more important business functions and see how they inter-relate.

Business Functions

functions and departments

Business functions remain the same, whatever the size of the business – sole trader or PLC. In the descriptions which follow we look in more detail at the functions carried out by departments in a typical company. The range of activities carried out by the departments will, of course, vary according to the type of business. The descriptions here are fairly typical, but you will find variations in your investigations.

In each case we will see how the departments need to co-operate with each other. Frequently, other departments are seen as **internal customers** of the business and are treated with the same respect and level of care as the **external customers** who are needed to bring in the profits.

The main departments in a business can be summarised as follows:

TYPICAL DEPARTMENTS IN A COMPANY

SENIOR MANAGEMENT
- production/operations department
- finance department
- marketing and sales department
- human resources department
- administration department

the Production/Operations Function

If a business is manufacturing a product, there must be a **production department**. This will vary in size from the workshop of a small business (eg a furniture maker) to the worldwide factories of a large car manufacturer. But the activities carried out will always be common to both:

- maintaining quality of the product(s)
- keeping to production targets – the cost of production, the number of items produced
- monitoring the efficiency of production methods, making sure the best use is made of manpower, materials and energy resources

Toyota: modern car production

- research and development of new techniques and new products
- purchasing raw materials from the right supplier, at the right price and of the right quality

If the business is providing a service, the role of the production department will be taken by an **operations department**. Obviously, the products of, say, an insurance company or a holiday company do not come off a production line and end up wrapped in packaging, but they are subject to design and development, quality control and effective sourcing. A holiday company, for example, will need to choose quality resorts, 'buy' flights, hotel rooms and excursions. Some are better at it than others!

production/operations – areas of co-operation

There are a number of areas in which the production or operations department will need to co-operate closely with other departments of the business, for example:

- with the **marketing department**, to produce new products that market research shows that the customers want; to rectify any design faults that customers report with existing products; to adjust production volume in line with what customers are actually buying
- with the **finance department**, to ensure that funds are allocated for new product development; to keep to financial budgets (targets) set for production (eg use of power, spending on overtime, making sure that the business is not being 'ripped off' by suppliers)

If all this co-operation is carried out effectively, it will ensure that the right quantity of 'product' – be it a car or a holiday – is produced to the right level of quality and to a design that the customers want. The result will be the fulfilment of many essential business objectives – contented customers, a motivated workforce, sales and profit maximisation and growth in market share. That, anyway, is the ideal.

the Finance Function

It is money which 'oils the wheels' of a business and keeps it running.

The finance function of a business is central to the success of that business, be it a sole trader or a large company. The finance function involves a wide variety of day-to-day activities and also planning for the future.

Nominal Ledger	
N/C ▽	**Name**
0010	Freehold Property
0011	Leasehold Property
0020	Plant and Machinery
0021	Plant/Machinery De
0030	Office Equipment
0031	Office Equipment D
0040	Furniture and Fixture
0041	Furniture/Fixture De
0050	Motor Vehicles
0051	Motor Vehicles Dep
1001	Stock

recording financial transactions on computer

The finance department is responsible for:

- financial record keeping – this involves keeping records, either in manual form or on computer file, of money received and paid out
- organising the banking arrangements – paying in and making payments
- paying suppliers, chasing customers for money
- payment of wages and the handling of cash
- the management accounts of the business – these are figures produced for the management of a business showing how well the company is performing in terms of income and expenditure in comparison with budgets prepared in advance

The finance department will also be closely involved in the planning process as it is responsible for raising the finance needed by the business. The financial records maintained will be used to produce the financial statements of the business which are required when the business is applying for finance.

finance department – areas of co-operation

There are a number of areas in which the finance department will need to co-operate closely with other departments of the business, for example:

- in the **planning and budgeting** process the manager of the finance department will have to liaise with the managers of the other departments to establish targets and budgets for areas such as sales, production costs, other expenses, staffing, purchase of equipment and so on – he/she will also have to monitor these budgets and report any area that fails to meet its target
- in the **financial record keeping** process the finance department will provide the marketing and sales department with data such as sales figures and details of any customers who are slow in paying up
- in the **preparation of financial statements** process the finance department will draw up profit statements and balance sheets which show how well the business is achieving objectives such as maximisation of sales and profit

the Marketing and Sales Function

Marketing is a process which identifies what products the customer needs and then supplies them at the right price. Marketing is covered fully in Unit 3 of your course and Chapters 18 to 21 in this book.

customer service - the direct link with the customer

Selling, on the other hand, involves persuading the customer to buy the products the business has already produced. The sales function will co-ordinate the selling programme, using a variety of techniques – sales representatives, telephone sales, mailshots, emails and website coverage. In a business the marketing and selling functions are closely linked.

An important function in any business is the **customer services** section (or department) which answers customer enquiries and deals with customer complaints.

Some products may need to be delivered. This is carried out by **distribution**. In a manufacturing business, this is likely to be the responsibility of the production function; in a retail business it is likely to be the responsibility of the sales function. Efficient distribution ensures that the customer gets the product on time and in perfect condition. Distribution involves warehousing and storage, packing, despatch and transport. This is often known as **logistics**.

marketing and sales – areas of co-operation

There are a number of areas in which the marketing and sales functions will need to co-operate closely with other departments of the business, for example:

- in communicating **customer feedback** about the products of the business to the production or operations department – feedback may relate to design or quality and is essential if the business is to continually improve its products
- in setting a right level of **pricing** for the business's products the marketing function will discuss the possible pricing strategies it may adopt with the finance department – can it, for example, afford to cut prices to encourage sales and beat the competitors?

the Human Resources Function

The human resources (or personnel) department fulfils a critical function because it supplies and looks after all the people in a business. It is responsible for:

- recruiting and retaining staff
- disciplining and dismissing staff

- training, developing and promoting staff
- maintaining good working conditions
- dealing with employer/employee relations and Trade Unions

The work of the human resources department is covered in more detail in Chapters 5 to 8, which follow this chapter.

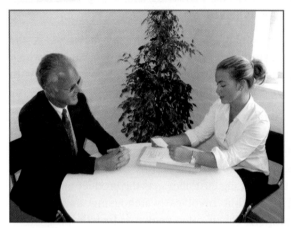

human resources – staff appraisal

human resources – serving the business

The work of the human resources department directly links with all the other functions of a business because it supplies and looks after the people working in them. In this sense the other departments are very much **internal customers** of the human resources department. The 'services' it supplies include:

- recruitment of staff
- maintenance of staff records
- payroll processing
- staff training
- staff appraisal

Administration (Facilities Management)

Administration and support services are also essential in keeping the 'wheels' of the business turning. They include maintenance of the business premises and equipment, reprographics, in-house printing (forms, stationery, newsletters), catering and computer services, mail handling and data storage. The department which provides these services is traditionally known as the administration department. Larger businesses are increasingly turning to specialist businesses to carry out a number of these functions, a process known as 'outsourcing'.

administration – serving the business

The administration function, like the human resources function, serves the whole business, which it treats as a group of internal customers. For example:

- providing security for the premises
- printing in-house forms and notices
- looking after the toilets and washrooms

Case Study – Zephyr PLC: co-operation of departments

Tornado 201 – a quality problem

Zephyr PLC manufactures vacuum cleaners in Bristol. During the course of the year it encounters a quality problem with one of its new products, the Tornado 201. A large number of customers have complained about its tendency to drop dust when the power is turned off. A feature about the problem has appeared on a TV consumer programme and sales have started to decline.

How do the functions within the business communicate with each other in order to deal with the problem? Examine the flow chart below and the actions listed on the right.

Activity 4.1 – co-ordinating business functions

A number of different business functions will be involved in any business activity. Identify the functions which are likely to be involved in the following situations, and explain how they connect with each other.

1 A customer returns a carton of milk to a supermarket. The milk has gone 'off' before the expiry date on the packaging. He wants a refund.

2 A production supervisor in a chocolate factory finds that one of her quality control operatives has been to the pub at lunchtime and gone to sleep on the job. As a result a number of faulty strawberry creams have gone forward on the production line and have been identified in the packaging section. Being found under the influence of alcohol at work is a serious offence under company disciplinary regulations.

3 The finance department has noticed that an important customer, who owes the company over £15,000, is in serious financial difficulties. The sales manager is due to go and see the customer tomorrow to discuss a new deal.

Organisational Structures

When looking at businesses it is common practice to illustrate the organisation by means of a structure chart. Look at the structure of a family – the most basic of organisations – set out below. Note in particular:

■ the levels of control and authority

■ how communication flows both horizontally and vertically

If you then compare the family with a business (as some Japanese companies do) you will see how an organisation should function, and can go wrong. Any failure in communication routes or in control could result in serious problems and inefficiencies – just as it does in a family.

Hierarchical, 'tall' Centralised Structures

A hierarchy is a series of levels of people, each level controlled by the level above it.

Large organisations, public limited companies or Civil Service departments, for example, may have thousands of employees. They are likely to have an elaborate, **tall** and **centralised** organisational structure, possibly based in one location, which has:

- a number of levels of hierarchy
- division into functional areas such as sales, finance, human resources

The structure chart below is that of a manufacturing company.

HIERARCHICAL STRUCTURE OF A MANUFACTURING COMPANY

responsibility, authority and delegation

Each level of the hierarchy has **responsibility** for the actions of the people in the levels below it. Each level has **authority** over the levels below it. Without this authority the organisation would not function properly – it would be anarchy! Each level can, however, **delegate** its powers to a lower level: a manager on holiday may delegate to a supervisor.

communications in an organisation

Communications pass up and down the hierarchy: instructions are passed down; problems and complaints are passed up; discipline is exercised by a higher level over a lower level. Good communication is important here.

job roles and responsibilities

Each horizontal level represents a step in the level of importance and responsibility of the staff:

- the **managing director** is responsible for communicating company policy and objectives and making sure they are carried out, and the other **directors** are responsible for making decisions affecting their function areas (eg sales, finance, production) and communicating those decisions to the people working in the function areas; the company secretary is the director responsible for the administration of the company

- **managers** are in charge of the departments; it is their role to:
  - organise their staff
  - plan and set targets for their staff
  - motivate their staff to achieve company objectives
  - delegate tasks to supervisors and support staff as necessary
  - control and monitor what the staff are doing
  - take corrective action if necessary

In some businesses managers are 'autocratic' – they tell their supervisors and staff precisely what to do. In businesses which encourage teamwork among staff, managers are 'democratic' and consult their staff when making decisions. Teamwork is a popular way of working because it motivates employees who feel that they are an important part of the decision-making process.

- **supervisors**, also commonly known as **line managers**, are in charge of the day-to-day running of the departments and normally work alongside their staff; they may be delegated responsibility by their manager and in turn may delegate responsibility to their staff

- **production**, **administrative** and **support staff** carry out the day-to-day work of the company

Flat Structure

A simple horizontal or 'flat' structure is in complete contrast to the 'tall' hierarchical structure. Here there are few layers in the organisation. The example below shows the simple flat structure of a sole trader shop which employs four assistants: three in the shop and one in the stock room.

You will see from this diagram that:

■ the structure is flat in shape; there is only one level of command – Ron himself tells the assistants what to do

■ Ron has a span of control which extends over the four assistants; if he had more assistants, it would extend over those as well

■ Ron presumably carries out the main functions of the business – finance, administration, human resources, marketing; his assistants do the selling

The flat structure is not confined to sole traders. Your own class is a flat structure with many students and one tutor in charge. Your school or college is also likely to have a flat structure, with independent departments.

centralised and decentralised organisations

The trend for 'flattening' organisations is popular. The management of large hierarchical organisations finds it advantageous to make functions, product divisions and geographical areas more independent of the senior management. They are in effect turning a **centralised organisation** into a **decentralised organisation**. A centralised organisation tends be 'tall' and does all its major decision making at higher levels of management – 'from the top'. A decentralised organisation is a collection of independent operating units which ultimately answer to top management – decision-making has been delegated to lower levels of management. It is often also known as a **divisional structure**, because it consists of many divisions. This can be seen in the diagram on the next page.

EXAMPLE OF A DECENTRALISED 'DIVISIONAL' STRUCTURE

advantages of a decentralised organisation

- there can be specialisation in the separate parts of the organisation, eg different products, different geographical areas, different functions (eg sales, production, finance, marketing)
- there is more motivation for the management of the individual units, who are rid of the bureaucracy of a hierarchical structure, and are able to take more decisions without reference to a higher level

disadvantages of a decentralised organisation

- poor communications across the organisation – the 'left hand' not knowing what the 'right hand' is doing
- weakened control from the top management which has a greater span of control to sustain and a wider spread of resources to manage

Activity 4.2 – tall (centralised) v. flat (decentralised)

1 What type of organisational structure would you be likely to find in the following organisations?

   (a) an organic ice cream producer, set up as a public limited company, based in one location and producing one main type of ice cream

   (b) a local authority

   (c) a sole trader shopkeeper employing five people

   (d) the easyGroup (see the Case Study on pages 7-8)

2 A recording company which has expanded rapidly to produce a wide range of music – pop, folk, jazz – is considering 'flattening' its tall structure, reducing its middle management ('de-layering'), and decentralising to form a loose group of operating companies. Explain the advantages and disadvantages of doing this.

Matrix Structure

Another form of structure is the matrix or 'project team' structure. The word 'matrix' (as in the American films) means a grid which operates in two directions.

Sometimes in an organisation it is necessary to take people out of their specific function areas – finance, sales, production – to form teams to work on specific projects. The project team or 'matrix' concept originated in the aerospace industry where new projects were essential to keep manufacturers in business. Project teams needed to work quickly in order to launch a new product first, before competing businesses brought out their version.

The matrix concept involves a different form of organisational structure chart. Look at the example below which sets out a traditional functional structure extended to staff two project teams. The 'matrix' operates in two directions – to the project management and to the departmental management.

A MATRIX STRUCTURE

| Sales | Finance | Production | Marketing |

PROJECT 1 MANAGER — Project Team 1

PROJECT 2 MANAGER — Project Team 2

Activity 4.3 – matrix structures

Hurricane Aerospace PLC manufactures military aircraft. It wants to set up a project team for a new design of fighter, the Raven. The company needs to use staff from the research and development, marketing, finance and production departments.

Draw a suitable matrix structure chart showing how the project team could be set up.

CHAPTER SUMMARY

- A business – whether small or large – operates by combining a variety of functions which include: production, finance, marketing and sales, human resources and administration. A successful business management will co-ordinate these functions so that the business runs efficiently and achieves its objectives.

- It is common for individual functions (departments) in a business to view the other functions as 'internal customers' who should be treated with the same level of care and consideration as external customers.

- The production department is an essential part of a manufacturing business, producing the product(s) and ensuring quality, efficiency of production and meeting production targets. In a service business the production function is normally referred to as the operations department.

- The finance department also fulfils an essential role in any business – planning, providing funds, recording and reporting all aspects of finance.

- Marketing and sales researches customer needs and provides and sells the products which fulfil those needs and generate a profit for the business.

- The human resources department provides the people a business needs – recruiting, training, paying, promoting and disciplining as required.

- The administration function provides all the necessary 'housekeeping' a business needs – premises, maintenance, catering, photocopying.

- Businesses are structured in different ways with different levels of management – some have many layers of management, others have very few.

- A hierarchical – 'tall' – structure involves many levels of management and is likely to be divided into separate functional areas (departments). It relies on a strong chain of command from top to bottom and good communication channels. This type of structure is often known as a centralised structure.

- A 'flat' structure involves fewer levels of management, but the span of control of the top management is likely to be wide. This type of structure is often known as a decentralised structure.

- A flat structure may represent a 'divisional structure' – showing independent divisions of an organisation – for example, functional, product and geographical divisions. These decentralised structures are often the result of 'delayering' (removing levels of management).

- A matrix structure is a 'project team' flat structure which operates in two directions – to the functional management and to the project team management.

KEY TERMS

function of business	an area of activity within a business
external customer	a person or organisation that buys the product (goods or services) produced by a business
internal customer	a function or department within a business that is provided with a product (often a service) by another function within the business
outsourcing	using an outside supplier to provide goods or services used within the business
span of control	the people or areas of responsibility over which a person in a business structure has control
hierarchical structure	an organisational structure characterised by a series of levels of people and command (a hierarchy)
tall structure	another name for an organisational structure which has many layers of authority
centralised structure	an organisational structure where senior management has close control and does not delegate much authority
flat structure	an organisational structure which is flat in shape – it has few (possibly only one) layers of management
divisional structure	a flat structure representing independent operating 'divisions'
decentralised structure	a flat organisational structure where senior management has delegated authority to independent operating units
delayering	the process of stripping out layers of management from a hierarchical structure in order to improve efficiency and at the same time 'flattening' the structure
matrix structure	an organisational structure which is based on a matrix grid and which operates both horizontally (eg to project management) and vertically (to functional management)

5

Planning the workforce

Starting point

Human Resources (HR) – the people employed by a business – are as important to it as its financial and physical resources.

A business will need to plan for its workforce – to decide on the quantity and the quality of the people that it is going to recruit. It will need a workforce that is flexible in what it does and when it operates.

What you will learn from this chapter

- Human Resources (HR) planning is concerned with making sure that the organisation has the right number and quality of employees

- the main problems for the HR planner are skill shortages, competition for employees and labour turnover

- organisations try to keep sickness and accidents as low as possible by the use of effective Health & Safety policies and good occupational health services

- succession planning (finding replacements) must be used to ensure that the organisation has a steady supply of new managers available to fill posts left by resignation or retirement

- in many organisations HR planners operate a flexible workforce, which is a workforce that has numerical, financial and functional flexibility

- a flexible workforce is composed of core and peripheral employees with differing pay levels, conditions of service and job security

- the purpose of a flexible workforce is to create a more competitive organisation which has a better long-term future for all of its employees

Human Resources Planning

Human resources planning used to be called manpower planning. It has been defined as:

the activity of management which is aimed at co-ordinating the requirements for and the availability of different types of employee

the reasons for human resources planning

There are four main reasons:

1 It encourages employers to develop clear links between their business plans and their HR plans so that they can integrate the two more effectively, for all concerned.

2 Organisations can control staff costs and numbers employed far more effectively.

3 Employers can build up a skill profile for each of their employees. This makes it easier to give them work where they are of most value to the organisation.

4 It creates a profile of staff (related to gender, race, disability) which is necessary for the operation of an Equal Opportunities policy.

If HR planning works properly, the outcomes will be:

- staff employed are fully utilised to the benefit of the organisation
- staff do challenging work which motivates and stimulates them
- overtime is only done when vitally necessary
- staff are properly qualified to do the job allotted to them

the Process of Human Resources Planning

Essentially, there are four key stages involved

- 'stock taking' of the available staff
- forecasting the supply of labour
- forecasting demand for employees
- implementation and review

We will deal with each of these in turn.

Stock Taking

This asks the question 'What is the quantity and quality of staff available in this organisation?' It uses the following techniques:

what skills are needed in your workplace?

jobs analysis

This means gathering together all the information available about all the jobs in the organisation. What are the duties in each job and what are the skills required to do each job? The most important tools to do this are the job description and the person specification for each job. These are dealt with on pages 87 - 93.

skills audit

This is a survey of the skills, qualifications and experience of all existing staff.

performance review

This involves looking at the performance of all employees in order to:

■ identify staff potential
■ identify where staff have more training needs

Forecasting Supply

This asks the question 'How many employees will we have in the future?' It therefore means looking at internal and external sources of labour.

When looking at the total supply of labour in the organisation it is very important to examine **labour turnover**. There are three main ways to calculate employee turnover.

annual labour turnover index =

$$\frac{\text{leavers in a year}}{\text{average number of staff employed during the year}}$$

This is sometimes called the 'percentage wastage rate'. It tells you what percentage of the workforce left in a year.

The two main problems with this method are:

■ It tells you nothing about the length of service of the people who left. Some could have left after four weeks and others could have retired.

■ It also does not tell you if, for example, ten people left the same job or ten people left ten different jobs. Obviously, the action needed to deal with these two situations would be completely different.

stability index =

$$\frac{\text{number of staff employed with one year's service on a certain date}}{\text{number of staff employed exactly one year before}}$$

This is a more useful indicator. It gives a good idea of how long employees are staying with the organisation. If employees are not staying very long in certain departments this can be pinpointed and investigated.

This method still does not deal with the second problem listed above.

Bowey's Stability Index =

$$\frac{\text{Length of service in months over a two-year period of all current staff added together}}{\text{Length of service in months over a two-year period if all staff had worked for the full two years}}$$

This looks at actual length of service and calculates a stability percentage.

For example, if there are 50 staff they could have worked a total of 1,200 months (ie 50 x 24 months = 1,200).

Suppose one woman left during the two years. She is excluded from the data because she is no longer 'current'.

The 49 remaining staff have service as follows:

40 with 24 months each*

2 with 18 months

4 with 10 months

2 with 3 months

1 with 1 month

* Note that some of the 40 could have been there far longer but we only count the last two years' service.

The total service is 1,043 months so the formula becomes:

$$\frac{1,043}{1,200} \ \text{x} \ \ 100 \ = 87\% \text{ stability (ie a very stable workforce).}$$

Although the Bowey Stability Index calculates stability very effectively it still cannot tell if, say, 10 people left 10 different jobs or 10 left the same job during a given time period. Therefore it is no use for identifying if particular departments in an organisation have particular retention difficulties (eg if they have an unpopular manager who staff find hard to put up with).

High staff turnover can result in the following:

- high recruitment and selection costs

- high costs for induction training

- poor quality work during the training phase of a new employee

- it creates a bad image to people looking for a job – they will ask 'why are people always leaving this company?'

Activity 5.1 – levels of staff turnover

1 Identify reasons why a department in a large organisation might have:
(a) a high level of staff turnover
(b) a low level of staff turnover

2 Describe how these levels of turnover can be measured and explain the shortcomings of these methods of measurement.

3 Identify ways in which you could reduce the level of staff turnover in an organisation.

staff turnover – cohort analysis

A further method of examining the turnover of staff in an organisation is through **cohort analysis**. A **cohort** is a group of staff made up of a similar type of person who has joined at the same time – for example, a group of apprentices or graduate trainees. They can be followed throughout, say, a two-year period to find out what happens to them and, hopefully, the reasons for any problems.

For example, university graduate turnover is often quite high. In many organisations perhaps half of a cohort of graduates will leave soon after appointment due to disillusionment or because they have a better offer elsewhere. By contrast, due to the shrinking manufacturing sector most of a cohort of apprentices may stay with a particular employer for many years.

Other Influences on the Internal Supply of Labour

sickness

A high level of sickness absence affects the supply of labour very badly. If it is all genuine (eg a flu' epidemic) then there is not much that can be done in the short term. In reality, quite a lot of sickness is bogus and employees 'throw sickies'.

If this is not tackled, it causes poor morale among the employees who are coming to work. They will, understandably, feel that the managers are 'wimps' for letting people get away with it.

Sickness absence needs monitoring against:

■ performance in the previous year

■ trends in other organisations in the same industrial sector

■ national sickness absence figures

Ways of controlling and monitoring sickness and bogus sickness include:

■ keeping proper records of sickness for all staff

■ a policy of 'sick visiting' by the personnel manager or by the company nurse

■ return to work interviews after one day of absence; this puts pressure on people who regularly have the odd day off 'ill' but do not want the embarrassment of an interview each time

■ a clear statement to staff that regular periods of unexplained sickness could lead to a disciplinary procedure or even dismissal

absenteeism – the lost time rate

One commonly used indicator to calculate absenteeism is the 'lost time rate'. The formula for this is:

$$\frac{\text{Total hours lost in absence} \times 100}{\text{Total hours scheduled}}$$

So, if the number of hours of planned work is 4,000 and staff are off for 200 in total, the calculation is:

$$\text{lost time rate} \quad = \quad \frac{200 \times 100}{4,000} \quad = \quad 5\%$$

This is useful for calculating which departments have bad absenteeism although again it has the same problem as the Bowey index (see page 63). Read the article on the next page and answer the questions that follow.

Case Study – attitude to sickness absence

Managerial training is key to crackdown on 'sickies'

Measures to crack down on sickness absence in the public sector will only succeed if line managers are given extra training, experts have warned.

Last week, the Government's taskforce for health, safety and productivity – led by minister for work Jane Kennedy – announced plans to cut public sector absence figures from an average of 10 days per person to 7.5. This would equate to the output of an extra 7,000 employees.

Under the proposals, civil servants would have to make daily phone calls to the office, when off sick for short periods. Managers would challenge staff who certify themselves as ill for more than five working days at a time, and make checks on those who regularly take Fridays and Mondays off as sick leave.

Ben Willmott, employee relations adviser at the Chartered Institute of Personnel and Development, said that civil servants need to make sure absence is managed in a co-ordinated and consistent way to ensure the targets are met.

"Managers and employees need to be clear about the procedures to go through, and managers need to make sure these policies are well communicated," he said. "This will require appropriate training for managers to meet their obligations and to take responsibility for managing absence."

AVERAGE WORKING DAYS LOST (per year)	
Public sector average	10.7
Private sector average	7.8
Civil Service (male)	8.5
Civil Service (female)	11.3

The National Audit Office, the public spending watchdog, said that managers were aware of their responsibility for implementing attendance policy. However, managers were not clear about the roles and responsibilities of other line managers, senior managers and HR teams. The report recommended increased monitoring of management actions by HR to ensure that managers could fulfil their roles, with mentoring and straightforward guides for new managers.

It also said managers needed more training in how to deal with personal issues and raising staff morale, and about what to expect from occupational health.

The Public and Commercial Services Union insisted that staff in the DWP were not work-shy, but faced stressful working conditions, such as job insecurity and IT failures.

Article reproduced by kind permission of *Personnel Today*.

Activity 5.2 – views on absenteeism

Read the article on the opposite page and answer the following questions:

1 What are the main ways in which managers in the Civil Service will try to cut sickness absence?

2 Why has sickness absence management been so badly handled till now?

3 Why do you think public service absenteeism is significantly worse than in the private sector?

4 Why is female absence in the Civil Service so much higher than for males?

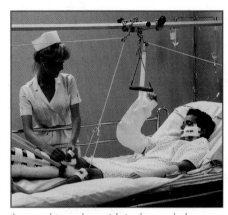

the need to reduce risk in the workplace

reduction of accidents

Better Health & Safety procedures and the use of EU regulations (eg on lifting and manual handling) have reduced the level of accidents in the workplace and consequently the number of employees who are likely to stay with the employer. A big factor has been the closure of many unsafe, old-fashioned manufacturing plants, steelworks and coal mines.

providing skills and training

Another important aspect of human resources planning is ensuring that employees are given the right skills and training. This subject is covered fully in Chapter 7.

succession planning

Succession planning means planning to make sure that when an employee leaves there is someone suitable available to take his/her place. This really only applies to employees at supervisor/line manager level and above.

A proper system of succession planning should include:

■ an estimate of what managerial jobs will be available in the future

■ an analysis of what skills and other abilities those jobs will require

■ a review of the strengths and weaknesses of existing staff who might fill some of those jobs

This enables the organisation to ensure that staff with the potential to fill top jobs are given extra training or wider experience so that when the time comes they will be able to fill those positions. Showing this kind of interest will improve employees' motivation and morale. If there is no succession planning then good employees will leave for better opportunities elsewhere. This will make it harder to fill gaps in the organisation at a later date.

This topic is dealt with in more detail in the next chapter.

External Sources of Employees

A number of factors can provide fresh sources of labour for the employer:

- **closures of other workplaces locally**

  If a large manufacturer or services company closes down, other local companies will find it easier to recruit skilled people from the redundancies that occur.

- **transport developments**

  When new high-speed train links open and further motorways are built more people are prepared to travel longer distances to work (there are now 'Eurostar' train commuters to and from Paris every day).

- **'output' from the education system**

  Schools will provide a local supply of employees and universities will provide an increasing number of graduate entrants.

using local and national statistical resources

When planning its workforce and operations a business may need to look at the local area or it may be faced with a choice of location. It might want to move out of London; it might want to open up a new office or factory for a new product. The choice of location will depend on a number of factors, but the cost of labour will be an important one. The cost of labour can be found from local and national statistics.

Local statistics can be obtained from the relevant Local Authority and Chamber of Commerce who undertake employment surveys in the area. The 'Economic Assessment' published on a regular basis by Worcestershire County Council, for example, compares local and national data such as employment by occupation, employment by gender and average earnings levels. This data is available online (www.worcestershire.gov.uk)

National statistics are carried out by the Office for National Statistics and are available online (www.statistics.gov.uk) as well as in paper format from libraries and resource centres.

Useful figures include unemployment levels and average earnings in the regions. Some sample figures for earnings are shown on the next page.

LOCAL, REGIONAL AND NATIONAL AVERAGE WEEKLY EARNINGS – BY GENDER

Worcestershire County	Economic Assessment 2004-2005		

Area	Male Earnings (£)	Female Earnings (£)	Overall Average Earnings (£)
Worcestershire	524.90	389.60	478.60
Herefordshire	431.40	325.00	396.80
Shropshire	500.00	367.30	451.00
Staffordshire	494.10	361.30	444.40
Warwickshire	565.60	390.80	506.10

Source: www.worcestershire.gov.uk

Average weekly full-time earnings in the UK regions (Autumn 2004)

	male (£)	female (£)
North East	420	348
North West	460	336
Yorkshire & Humberside	438	327
East Midlands	466	358
West Midlands	453	359
East of England	535	410
London	618	496
South East	561	403
South West	450	346
Wales	438	339
Scotland	455	345
Northern Ireland	403	344
UK	493	379

Source: www.statistics.gov.uk

Activity 5.3 – regional differences

1 Explain, using data from the statistical tables shown above, why levels of pay might vary so much between different parts of the country.

2 How does the region in which you live compare with the national average? What implications does this have for employers in your area?

3 What is the general difference between male and female average earnings? What do you think is the reason for this?

Forecasting Demand for Employees

This means asking the question, 'How many people will we need? Today? In five years?' This is the most difficult question of all in human resources planning. Managers have to look at factors such as the following when forecasting demand for employees:

- the business's trading and production patterns
- the demand for its products
- technological and administrative changes
- capital investment plans
- mergers, acquisition of new businesses, selling parts of the business
- product diversification

For example, new technology often means fewer jobs need filling but there will be more demand for skilled people. Mergers will mean that many head office jobs are made redundant, but if the merged company is now more efficient, there may be new jobs in other areas.

Implementation and Review

Businesses must undertake regular reviews to ensure that their human resources planning process is effective. For example, has a new recruitment drive been effective in recruiting the right number and right quality of people?

The business must also look at all the various environmental factors which might affect the supply and demand for labour. This involves collecting information on social, political, industrial, legal and technological changes. It also means finding out what the competition is doing. The Activity and article that follow show how the NHS can usefully review the current labour market for nursing staff.

Activity 5.4 – the changing labour market for nurses

Read the article from *Personnel Today* on the next page and answer the questions below.

1 Why is there an NHS skills gap for nursing staff?

2 Why have refugee nurses found it so hard to get nursing jobs in the UK?

3 What particular benefits would the NHS gain from employing more refugee nurses?

NHS taskforce to tap into refugee talent

A taskforce is being launched charged with recruiting experienced refugee nurses to plug the NHS skills gap.

It aims to make it easier for the thousands of professionally qualified nurses living in the UK as refugees to work, rather than recruiting staff from overseas.

"Employers continue to find it hard to recruit nurses throughout the UK and yet there are many refugee nurses who are finding it impossibly difficult to get back into work," says Patrick Wintour, director of the Employability Forum.

Guy Young, deputy director of nursing at Homerton Hospital NHS Trust, agreed there is a real need for the taskforce.

"We are aware there are trained, experienced nurses in Hackney (London) who are sitting at home doing nothing," he says. "We see that as a wasted resource and talent. The skills they could bring to our department could be immense."

Young said the hospital has been filling posts with expensive agency staff because there are not enough experienced nurses available.

"Refugee nurses have a valuable role to play in treating ethnic minorities and overcoming language barriers," he added.

Article reproduced by kind permission of *Personnel Today*.

the Flexible Workforce

The term 'flexible workforce' means that many employers now use their employees in a 'flexible' way so that they can get the most value from them. Employers argue that without this flexible approach their businesses would close down.

In the UK, employment practices have traditionally been inflexible and this has made employers inefficient and uncompetitive compared with businesses in other countries.

Examples of inflexibility include:

- permanent contracts of employment for most staff
- full-time contracts of employment for all staff
- no flexibility in working hours
- Union opposition to employees doing anything outside their contract of employment – eg an electrician does electrical work and nothing else
- Union opposition to 'distancing' (see next page for an explanation of 'distancing')

'the flexible firm'

The theorist Atkinson devised the 'flexible firm' model. His argument was that organisations need several types of employee flexibility to be really efficient. His 'flexible' approach has become extremely common and, whereas it only used to be found in private companies, it is used a great deal in the public sector as well (eg in local government) in order to save money. Flexibility takes a number of different forms:

- **numerical flexibility**

  'the ability to adjust the level of labour inputs to meet fluctuations in output'

  This means either altering hours worked or changing the total number of staff.

- **functional flexibility**

  'the firm's ability to adjust and deploy the skills of its employees to match the tasks required by its changing workload, production methods or technology'

- **financial flexibility**

  This means that the employer can increase or decrease levels of spending on HR as business conditions require.

subcontracting provides flexibility

- **distancing** (also known as 'outsourcing')

  This means that more and more services inside an organisation are carried out by other companies on a contract basis. These other companies employ their own staff to carry out these services. The most common examples these days are catering, cleaning and security – some very large subcontracting firms, such as Rentokil-Initial, can offer several of these services as one complete package (visit www.rentokil-initial.com). The aim of this strategy is to cut costs because the subcontractors can usually do the jobs more cheaply than the organisation can. This offers extra numerical flexibility.

Atkinson also explains that flexibility means the workforce is divided into two distinct groups: core and peripheral workers.

core workers

These are highly paid workers who offer 'firm-specific' skills which are hard to acquire from anywhere else. Often such skills will have been acquired within the organisation itself. They provide functional flexibility because they do a range of tasks. Because they are so 'firm-specific' they have high job security.

peripheral workers

There are two types of these:

■ **first peripheral group**

These are quite well looked after but less so than with core workers. They have reasonable security since they carry out skilled jobs, and are therefore sought after by many employers, but the key difference is that they do not have 'firm-specific' skills. Good examples would be customer services skills or a wide range of computer-related skills.

■ **second peripheral group**

This group mainly provides 'numerical' flexibility. They are easily hired and fired as required. They will be on lower pay rates, usually have poorer working conditions and job insecurity.

Some of them may be very highly skilled but are unable to get better jobs, perhaps because of family commitments.

Second peripheral group workers include:

■ full-timers on short contracts

■ part-time workers

■ teleworkers and other kinds of home workers

■ people employed on government schemes

■ subcontractors for cleaning, security etc

■ agency temps

Apart from the financial and numerical flexibilities noted above there are other real benefits derived from employing peripheral workers:

■ Because the workforce is broken up into several groups it becomes harder for them to unite in a common cause against management. On the one hand, 'core' workers are well looked after and, on the other, many peripheral workers will not cause trouble for fear of losing their contracts or because they hope to get a 'core' job in the future.

■ Human Resources and Accounts departments have less work to do because many staff are no longer the organisation's own employees.

■ If the core workforce is well looked after, it will be highly motivated and will increase its output.

Many organisations are now adopting flexible firm policies to some degree and the number of part-time workers and temps has increased dramatically, eg the big increase in the number of temp agencies. Subcontracting has increased as well – some of the providers (eg Rentokil Initial plc) are now far bigger than many of the organisations for which they provide services.

Now read the Case Studies that follow and carry out the Activity.

Case Studies – the advantages of flexible working

HR plays vital role in Toyota's working-life revamp

A major revamp of working life at Toyota's vehicle manufacturing plant in Derbyshire will lead to around-the-clock production, an extra shift, and will create 1,000 extra jobs.

It is the first time Toyota has operated a third shift at a vehicle manufacturing plant. The move will boost annual production of some models from 220,000 to around 270,000.

Toyota's general manager of HR, Clive Bridge, told *Personnel Today* that HR is playing a major part in the change. He said HR staff are working to ensure the existing shifts are properly maintained, and pulling together the necessary elements to integrate a three-shift pattern.

Toyota is using external consultants to recruit production supervisors, maintenance and production team members. Most of the supervisors will be promoted internally, and the team is developed on the shopfloor.

Existing staff will form the backbone of each shift to ensure a balance of skills, and staff will work on a weekly rotating shift pattern.

"Members were enthusiastic about the move to three shifts," Bridge said. "The hours of work are more attractive and their basic shift premium goes from 17.5 per cent for two shifts, to 24.5 per cent for three."

Council revamps flexible working

Nottingham City Council has introduced a new flexible working policy in a bid to boost staff recruitment and retention and reduce traffic in the city centre.

The policy has been developed following a six month, £80,000 pilot scheme involving approximately 50 staff from across the authority who tested home working, going to work on-site and a combination of the two.

Staff on the pilot reported feeling less stressed, more in control of their workload, more trusted and more motivated. They also reported they were better able to balance operational and strategic job demands and were more productive.

Andrea Shea, an HR consultant working in the authority's central personnel team, who led the pilot scheme, said there was also evidence that the initiative will help recruitment and retention.

Two workers withdrew requests to resign after taking part in the flexible working pilot.

Shea said the new policy also helped the council to comply with the Employment Act, which came into force in April, giving workers with young children the right to request flexible working arrangements.

"We are offering all employees the right to ask to work at home and have the request considered. But obviously there are some jobs you just can't do at home," she said.

Articles reproduced by kind permission of *Personnel Today*.

Activity 5.5 – the advantages of flexible working

The two articles on the previous page clearly demonstrate the clear benefits of introducing flexible working. Study them and answer these questions:

1 Explain why staff are happy about the changes being introduced in the two organisations.

2 Explain why there could be some resistance to these changes.

3 In what respects are the concerns of Toyota staff

(a) different from, and

(b) similar to those of Nottingham City Council staff?

Methods of Flexible Working

annualised hours

Under this scheme an employee has a contract to work so many hours per year. The way that the hours are spread across that year depends on the needs of the business. This arrangement is only valuable where an organisation has a fluctuating demand for their products or services.

The employee gets the same weekly or monthly salary throughout the year but hours per week could be, for example, up to 55 or down to 25.

This means that employees are only at work when they are really needed. In a traditional business with standard weekly hours employees can sit around doing very little at certain times of the year but they still get paid. When they are busy at other times they get generously paid overtime. By contrast, annualised hours reduces much of the overtime bill. Not surprisingly, it is not popular with employees, although they do get more days off at certain times of the year.

zero hours contracts

This is where the employee is 'on call' to come into work whenever they are needed. If they are not needed, they earn no money. This is not unusual in retailing where staff requirements vary during a week or even within one day. Some employees like it because it gives them flexibility as well – after all, if they do not want to come in on a particular day, they need not do so. However, for people wanting a secure job with reliable weekly pay it is not ideal.

job sharing

This means that two employees share a job. This could be a divided week or a divided day. The advantage is that the employer has an extra source of labour from people who could not work full-time. Job share requires that the sharers work well together because they have to overlap to pass ongoing work between them and to discuss any problems arising from that work. Even very senior management jobs can be 'shared'.

teleworking and telecottaging

Increasing numbers of people work at least part of their time from home or, increasingly, from a telecottage or telecentre (visit www.tca.org.uk).

The introduction of the laptop computer and, more importantly, the advent of email and the internet, has made teleworking very easy in practical terms. For example, salespeople can email their sales direct to the office and receive emailed instructions directly from there. Reports can be written in Aberdeen and emailed directly to the office in London or New York.

Working at home for part of the week has big advantages in terms of the reduction in travel time and travel costs. There is also the reduced stress and

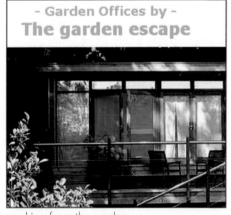

working from the garden

the ability to work at the best time of the day to suit the person involved. However, employees can feel cut off from the workplace and therefore forgotten by their managers. This could affect their promotion prospects. Also telework can be an intrusion into the employee's private life with computers and paperwork tying up spare bedrooms or even the living room.

Telecottaging, where employees meet at a dedicated telecottage with proper computer links and office facilities a few miles from home, is a better alternative because it separates 'work' from 'home'. Teleworkers can even build a 'telecottage' in the garden, as in the illustration on the left (www.thegardenescape.co.uk).

A recent report called 'Teleworking Britain' showed that around 30% of office-based staff are teleworking either full time or part-time. In 1997 one million people in the UK teleworked full or part-time. By 2004 the number was 1.28 million, a growth of 28% in just seven years.

The report concluded that many people who said they could not telework were overestimating the difficulties because they were frightened of new technology or had never had its benefits properly explained to them.

A further issue was that businesses were slow in recognising where the opportunities for teleworking existed.

family friendly policies

Employers are now required to put the quality of working life at the top of their priorities for their employees. In a 'tight' labour market, where it is very hard to find people to fill job vacancies, it is the employers who 'look after' employees who will find it easiest to attract people and – equally importantly – to retain them.

Brent Council (in London) currently offer their staff remarkably flexible working conditions. One female manager says that her director is happy for her to juggle things around so long as the work she does is on time and up to standard. She can work from home and she also has a laptop so she can pick up emails from work any time of night or day. The HR director in Brent says that they need to become an 'employer of choice' since it is so hard to recruit people in London. Equally importantly, they need to be able to persuade them to stay for more than a few months.

the Problems of Flexible Working

More enlightened employers are unhappy about some aspects of operating 'flexibly'. They consider that:

- the use of short-term contract employees actually increases costs because new people are being recruited very frequently and this increases the amount of basic training required
- if unemployment is very low, flexible contracts will look less attractive and employees will look for something more secure and better paid – this will increase staff turnover
- treating employees differently clashes with the harmonisation of conditions (harmonisation means that all employees have to have the same basic conditions of service)
- many employers want to get 'Investor in People' status (see page 121) and this requires that employees are treated properly on a long-term basis

legal aspects of flexible working

On the one hand, flexible working can work to the employer's advantage: employers can require employees to carry out a wider range of duties or change their hours of work. They can also offer employees fixed-term and temporary contracts which give the employee very little security.

On the other hand, a number of new laws and regulations have made it harder for employers to operate 'flexibly'. Most of these laws and regulations originate from the European Union. They are discussed in detail in Chapter 8 (pages 137-139).

CHAPTER SUMMARY

■ Businesses have to plan carefully to ensure that they have the right number and right quality of employees to meet their requirements.

■ Human resource planning is affected by factors such as employment trends, skill shortages and competition for labour.

■ Employers should take note of local or national employment statistics when carrying out human resource planning.

■ Managers need to know how to measure labour turnover using wastage and stability rates. They also need to keep absenteeism in the workplace to a minimum.

■ Organisations need good occupational health services and Health & Safety systems to keep accident and sickness levels as low as possible.

■ Proper succession planning will ensure that the organisation always has the right people at the right time to fill vacant posts.

■ Employers should be aware of the various sources of labour in their locality and also (where appropriate) nationally.

■ Organisations should carry out regular reviews of their human resource planning to assess its effectiveness and to see if it needs changing.

■ A flexible workforce is normally divided into two distinct groups: core workers (more permanent and more skilled) and peripheral workers (less permanent and often less skilled).

■ While it is chiefly for the employer's benefit, flexible working also suits many employees who could not work under any other arrangement.

■ There is a wide range of flexible working options available to suit different organisations in different situations, eg annualised hours and zero hours contracts.

■ Advances in technology have made teleworking and telecottaging more popular.

■ It is relatively easy to introduce flexible contracts of employment, often to the advantage of the employer.

■ On the other hand, there are a number of laws and regulations which protect employees' rights in employment contracts and make it more difficult for employers to impose total flexibility.

KEY TERMS

human resource planning	how to ensure that the organisation always has the right number and the right quality of employees
labour turnover	a measure of the recruitment into and the resignations from an organisation
stock taking	finding out the quantity and quality of staff available in an organisation
the annual wastage rate and the stability index	formulas that are used to calculate labour turnover
jobs analysis	an analysis of the duties involved and skills required for every job in an organisation
flexible workforce	a workforce unrestricted by permanent contracts, full-time working, fixed hours – a workforce that can adapt to changing conditions in workflow
skills audit	a survey of the skills held by all employees in an organisation
succession planning	a process of ensuring that vacant posts can be filled with the minimum of difficulty
core workers	the key employees in an organisation with the best pay and conditions and the highest level of job security
peripheral workers	groups of employees who are employed under a range of contracts with differing terms, pay rates and job security
job sharing	where the same job is divided between two people
zero hours working	where the employee is only called into work when the organisation really needs him/her
annual hours working	hours worked are spread across the year according to the needs of the organisation and can therefore vary considerably from week to week

6

Recruitment and selection

Starting point

One of the most important tasks for the human resources function in a business is the recruitment and selection of new employees.

Without the right employees the organisation will be unable to operate efficiently, serve its customers properly or make any profits. Using the proper recruitment and selection techniques, organisations can make as sure as possible that they can achieve these objectives.

What you will learn from this chapter

■ the ways in which recruitment procedures are used to attract good quality job applicants

■ how job descriptions and person specifications match applicants with vacancies

■ how to produce and evaluate letters of application for clarity and quality of presentation

■ how to produce and evaluate a curriculum vitae for clarity and quality of presentation

■ how to practise and appraise interviewer techniques

■ how to practise and appraise interviewee techniques

■ there are a number of important legal considerations to take into account in the recruitment process

the Process of Recruitment

filling a vacancy

Vacancies for jobs exist in organisations for one of several reasons:

■ A new job is available because of the expansion of the organisation.

  When the economy is growing and people are becoming better off organisations take advantage of that and expand their operations. To do this they may take on extra employees. This is more likely if they believe the economy is going to continue to grow for some time. If they expect economic growth to be short-lived, they are less likely to create new jobs, preferring instead to use other methods listed below under 'Alternatives to filling a vacancy'.

■ Someone in the organisation has retired.

■ Someone has been dismissed.

■ Internal promotion(s) occurred – the vacancy arises because the previous holder has been given a better job either in the same establishment or the same organisation. This is dealt with below under 'Filling the Vacancy – Internal Applicants'.

■ Someone has died – sadly there are some employees who die during their working lives, and with increased stress and the growing incidence of heart disease this is becoming more common.

■ There is a restructuring of the business, which means there are gaps to be filled in the organisation.

■ Someone has left because they do not like the job or have found a better job elsewhere.

alternatives to filling a vacancy

Human Resources Management departments are under constant pressure to justify the filling of a vacancy because it will save the organisation money if they do not. There are several alternatives to filling a vacancy, all with benefits and all with disadvantages too:

■ overtime by the remaining employees

■ restructuring of the work

■ employing part-time staff

■ more use of machinery/technology

At this stage it is important that the Human Resources Manager looks critically at the job description and person specification for this vacancy. From these documents (examined later in this chapter) it will be possible to assess how far it is practical to rely on these options instead of filling the vacancy.

Filling the Vacancy – Internal Applicants

If the Human Resources Manager, after consideration of the alternatives examined above, decides that the vacancy will need filling, then the next stage will be where to look for candidates. There are only two sources of candidate – **internal** and **external**.

internal candidates

identifying a possible internal candidate

Unless a vacancy is for the lowest grade job possible, there will be internal candidates who are interested in the vacancy for promotion, for example:

■ if they are temporary or part-time and want either a secure or full-time job (or both)

■ if they want to expand their range of work experiences – this is sometimes called lateral (ie sideways) career development

Internal promotion is an important method of motivating employees and is identified by several writers as a feature of a 'best practice' employer (ie a 'good' employer who tries to do everything properly).

the main benefits to the employer of internal appointments

■ an organisation with a reputation for internal advancement will find it easier to motivate staff, whereas in organisations where internal advancement is rare, staff will be less committed to the work and may be preoccupied with external job applications

■ the organisation will attract better candidates if they see there is a future career in it

■ many candidates will be local people who have bought homes there, have children at local schools and husbands/wives in other local jobs

■ internal candidates know the business and what will be expected of them, and they can become effective in the new job very quickly

■ although there is bound to be bitterness from other internal applicants who do not get the job, they will at least feel that there will be other career opportunities in the organisation and that they will get promotion later on

- the organisation will not need to rely upon external references when choosing from internal applicants – accurate information will be available from departmental heads and other colleagues

the disadvantages of appointing internally

- the successful candidates may suffer role conflict in that they are now senior to people with whom they worked as equals – there may be a problem for them in asserting their authority
- a person promoted internally may be expected to pick up the new job in an unreasonably short space of time
- filling a vacancy internally leaves another vacancy to fill

Note also that where an employer is practising 'equal opportunity' policies (see below) they cannot favour internal candidates when filling vacancies. Also, internal candidates must be required to carry out exactly the same recruitment procedures as external ones.

Recruiting External Candidates

There are clear **advantages** recruiting external candidates to fill a vacancy. These benefits are:

- a much wider range of people from which to choose
- newcomers to the organisation will bring in new ideas
- newcomers are not associated with the old policies of the organisation – for this reason it is always a good idea to bring in people from outside if a change in the organisational culture is planned
- newcomers are likely to be more mobile than existing staff and in a multi-site business this can be very useful
- newcomers may bring skills and management techniques from their former employers which your organisation might also adopt

There are also **disadvantages** to filling a vacancy with an external candidate:

- it is far more expensive than internal recruitment
- it takes time for a newcomer to get used to his or her new employer, and therefore the newcomer will not be performing effectively for the initial period
- people who move between jobs have a better idea of their market value than people who stay with the same organisation for a long time, and they make the best use they can of this by threatening to leave unless they get high pay rises or rapid promotion

■ employers have to rely heavily on the references of other employers, and in reality these can be quite unreliable – people are sometimes given good references by their employers simply to get rid of them!

sources of external candidates

Assuming that the advantages of external recruitment are judged more important than the disadvantages, where would an organisation go to find external applicants? It will depend on the type of job an employer is trying to fill. The main sources and the particular jobs they specialise in are as follows:

■ **School Careers Services**

These provide school leavers for a wide range of jobs and traineeships such as the government-financed 'New Deal'.

■ **Job Centres**

These provide a wide range of jobs but chiefly semi-skilled, unskilled and clerical workers.

■ **University Career Services**

These provide graduates and postgraduates (eg people with further degrees).

■ **Employment Agencies**

They will find applicants in virtually all areas of work although their busiest areas are clerical, secretarial and unskilled manual employees.

Agencies also employ their own staff and hire them to organisations on a weekly (or even daily) fee basis – this is mainly for short-term, unskilled manual and basic clerical work.

■ **Recruitment Consultants and Executive Search Agencies**

These are the 'head hunters' for people to fill senior management and professional jobs.

high-tech options for finding external candidates

■ **Internet**

Jobseekers are now using private, portable and updatable CVs that they can send to employers by email. Organisations such as recruitment agencies can also register CVs from a group of job hunters (eg a group of graduates) and individuals online and make them available to employers, also online.

Visit www.stepstone.com and www.netjobs.co.uk

recruiting externally

INTERNET RECRUITMENT SITES

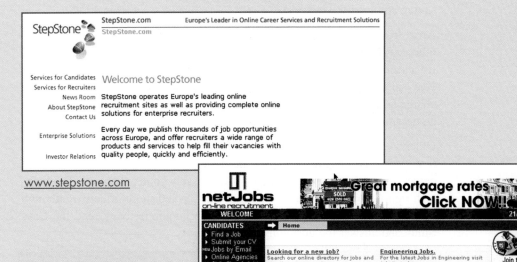

www.stepstone.com

www.netjobs.co.uk

■ **Voice recognition shortlisting**

More and more organisations are using this as a way of shortlisting when they need to recruit large numbers of staff (eg retailing and hospitality). Potential applicants ring an 0800 number and are told what vacancies are available. If they wish to continue, they then answer a set of questions. A computer scores the answers, based on a series of criteria, then automatically prints out a letter of rejection or an invitation to a job interview within a few hours. Visit www.resumix.com

■ **Digital interviewing**

The job applicant is filmed with a digital camera while answering questions set by a potential employer, who then views all the applicants remotely. This takes a far shorter time than the usual 'first interviews' would take. Final shortlisted candidates are then interviewed in the traditional manner.

which source of external candidates to use?

In a typical organisation with a mixture of jobs – skilled and unskilled, secretarial and clerical, professional and managerial – there will be a need to call on most of the above services at some time. Agencies can find staff to fill short-term contracts and can supply ready-made work teams to organisations for as little as one week (or even one day) for a fixed fee (this means the employees do not go onto the organisation's own payroll, thus saving administrative work).

Apart from the Careers Service and the Job Centres, which are both free, the other services are quite expensive. Using an Executive Search Consultant to fill a senior management job can cost the equivalent of 20 to 30% of the first year salary for that manager. Agencies supplying short-term labour will charge hourly rates that are far higher than the standard pay rates offered by an organisation. Convenience costs money!

Other sources available include notices on premises (such as supermarkets), newspaper and radio advertising, and word of mouth. These all take a lot of departmental time to sort through to find the few good applicants. The high-tech options mentioned above are far quicker and more effective although they are probably unappealing to older job enquirers. Now read the Case Study and answer the questions that follow.

Case Study – using internet-based recruitment

Sparkling results for jeweller from web-based recruitment

Jewellery retailer Signet is hoping to improve the speed and consistency of its recruitment by launching a career website for management applications. A new central recruitment team will manage the online applications, which should ensure all jobseekers have a uniform experience, wherever they are based.

Signet, which runs Ernest Jones, H Samuel and Leslie Davis, hopes the move to web-based recruitment will reduce the burden on HR, which currently has to manually sift through applications.

Each brand will have its own site and the recruitment team will be able to post vacancies from any of its 607 stores directly onto the relevant web page.

Resourcing manager Sheena Macdonald said the move would speed up the selection process and enable candidates to be dealt with efficiently, while giving the company a better overall system.

The system, which was designed by Workthing, will also enable the team to monitor the status of the entire recruitment process across the country.

"The technology will give the team visibility on the recruitment process throughout the UK at the touch of a button, which is particularly useful for us to keep track of nationwide store recruitment," said Macdonald.

The process also includes an integrated questionnaire to judge applicants' motivation and a CV talent pool so Signet can match any future vacancies.

Article reproduced by kind permission of *Personnel Today*.

Activity 6.1 – web-based recruitment

Read the article on the previous page and answer the following questions:

1 What should all jobseekers to Signet expect by 'a uniform experience, wherever they are based'?

2 What are the main benefits to Signet of online recruitment?

Further task

Carry out a search on the phrase 'online recruitment' on the internet using a search engine such as Google. What benefits are stressed by the recruitment providers?

Job Descriptions and Person Specifications

Before an organisation goes any further in the recruitment process it needs to examine the job description and the person specification for the post.

We will now examine what these two documents contain.

job description

A job description lists the main tasks required in a job. More and more organisations have job descriptions for every job they have – from the caretaker to the managing director.

In drawing up a job description the personnel department has a number of alternatives. These are:

(a) the line manager can draw up a description of what the job entails

(b) the existing job holder can do it

(c) the Human Resources Manager can interview the job holder and the line manager to find out what the job involves

In most cases it is probably best to combine approaches.

Clearly approach (b) may produce a biased view of what the job involves. After all, most people are likely to exaggerate the importance of what they do and the effort and ability that is required to do it. Moreover, the job holder may overemphasise those duties they prefer to do rather than their most important ones. Also, since they are leaving, they may not bother to do a very thorough job of it anyway.

On the other hand, in approach (a) the line manager will probably miss out many small but important tasks which are only obvious to the job holder.

The aim of the exercise is to itemise all the tasks involved in a job and to try to allocate a proportion of the working week to each task. The list of tasks, and the relative importance of each one, are vitally important for several reasons:

- In carrying out appraisals of employees – a manager cannot appraise his/her employees if he/she does not know what the job involves.

- When analysing the job for training needs the manager must be able to see what tasks a job involves so that he/she can determine what training may be required.

- In planning the size of the workforce for the future, it will be necessary to know exactly what tasks each job involves in case the reallocation of tasks between jobs is required. For example, three people may be required to share the work of a fourth post which is being made redundant – this cannot be done fairly without a detailed knowledge of the tasks involved in the fourth post.

- For pay determination – analysis of, and comparisons between, job descriptions mean that each job can then be allocated a pay rate. This process is known as 'job evaluation'. A simple example is where clerical jobs which include the responsibility for handling money get a higher ranking, and therefore higher pay, than clerical jobs which do not.

Clearly, none of this is possible without good quality and detailed job descriptions.

drafting the job description

From all the information collected, by whichever method is chosen, it will then be necessary to draw up the document itself. Most people applying for jobs will be sent a job description along with an application form and a person specification (explained below).

The main features of a job description are:

1. the job title
2. the location of the job
3. a brief outline of what the employing organisation does
4. the main purpose of the job
5. a detailed list of the main tasks required in the job
6. the standards that the job holder will be required to achieve
7. pay and other benefits
8. promotion prospects
9. the person to whom the job holder reports
10. the person(s) who report(s) to the job holder

Nowadays, employees are expected to be more flexible and to be able to do a wider range of work. This means that job titles (point 1) tend to be broader than they used to be. Point 3 is important in that a go-ahead, successful organisation will find it easier to attract applicants of an above-average quality. Points 4, 5 and 6 are the essentials of the job description, so that anyone interested in applying will know what they would be required to do if offered the job. Points 7 and 8 are needed as attractions to draw in good quality applicants. Finally, points 9 and 10 give the applicant a clear idea of the position of the job within the organisation.

In summary, the job description has a number of roles, not least of which is to turn enquiries from capable people into real job applications. Therefore, presentation of the job description is very important, although, regrettably, this is often forgotten by many employers in the selection process.

Now study the sample job description shown below.

Three Valleys District Council

HUMAN RESOURCES DEPARTMENT

Job Title	Personnel Assistant
Post Reference	43/789
Section	Human Resources Department
Employer	Three Valleys District Council is a 'second tier' authority in Wiltshire. Apart from the main town, Wereford, it is mainly rural and is an attractive area in which to live and work.
Grade	£15,225 - £16,968. The successful applicant will be placed on the point appropriate to his/her previous experience and qualifications. The position has been job-evaluated.
Aim and purpose of the job	To carry out a wide range of personnel administration work in a busy department consisting of three personnel assistants, two personnel officers and a personnel manager. This role is chiefly involved with personnel issues in the Council's Finance and Legal departments (employing a total of 97 staff). The postholder may be expected to carry out other duties when required (eg cover for colleagues on holiday).

Responsible to	Personnel Officer (Legal and Finance)

Duties

- To assist the Personnel Officer (Legal and Finance) in a wide range of personnel work.
- Administration of recruitment and selection processes and organisation of job interviews.
- Organisation of induction programmes for new staff.
- Appraisals administration.
- Maintenance of absence and holiday records.
- Administration of employee training programmes.
- Liaison with Finance department on pay/benefits.
- Handling general enquiries from staff in the two departments.

Job prospects

This is a compact department which offers ample opportunity to gain a wide range of personnel experience. This will provide a firm foundation for a successful career in local government personnel management.

The Authority will encourage, and support financially, the postholder to acquire professional personnel management qualifications (CIPD) through study at Wereford College.

Contact

Mrs Fiona Mellor, Personnel Manager, The Personnel Department, Three Valleys District Council, Hardy Street, Wereford WR1 3HN.

Direct line: 01876 567345

For an informal chat about this post ring Sue Stephens, Personnel Officer (Finance and Legal departments) on 01876 567333

Application deadline

Application forms must reach the Authority (address shown above) by March 15, 2005.

person specifications

A person specification sets out the qualities of an ideal candidate whereas a job description defines the duties and responsibilities of the job.

The best-known method of drawing up person specifications is called the Seven Point Plan originally devised by **Alec Rodger**. This bases the person specification upon seven separate groups of characteristics:

1 **Physique, health and appearance** – this includes grooming, looks, dress sense, voice, hearing and eyesight as well as general health matters.

2 **Attainments** – this includes educational qualifications such as GCSEs, A levels and degrees and vocational qualifications such as NVQs and job experience.

3 **General intelligence** – this is estimated by IQ tests and by assessment of general reasoning ability.

4 **Special aptitudes** – what special skills does a person have? These include skills with words, with numbers, with musical instruments, with artistic technique and with mechanical equipment.

5 **Interests** – are they intellectual or practical or social or a mixture of them all?

6 **Disposition** – this is an assessment of the person's acceptability by other people, leadership qualities, the person's emotional stability and self-reliance.

7 **Circumstances** – factors such as age, whether single or married, whether mobile or not.

Rodger's Seven Point Plan usually requires managers to distinguish between essential and desirable qualities under each of the seven headings. For example, five GCSEs at grade C or above might be an essential 'Attainment' to do a particular job whereas two GCE 'A' levels might be desirable but not essential.

An alternative approach is one used by **John Munro Fraser**. He proposes five headings rather than seven:

1 Impact on others

2 Qualifications and experience

3 Innate abilities

4 Motivation

5 Emotional adjustment

Activity 6.2 – person specifications

Draw up a person specification for the job advertised by the Three Valleys District Council (see previous page).

Use Rodger's Seven Point Plan, remembering to identify essential and desirable characteristics.

Now examine the Job Description below. It is for a job as a Personal Assistant at SunActive Ltd, a company in the travel and tourism industry.

SUNACTIVE LIMITED

Job description

Job title	Personal Assistant
Further information	Tania Patel, HR Manager (01675 453421 x 564)
Responsible to	The Managing Director, Andrew Jackson
Responsible for	Two Administrative Assistants
Job location	SunActive Ltd, Head Office, Reginald Road, Chester CH2 7KB
Duties	Acting as Secretary at business meetings
	Producing Agenda and Minutes of meetings
	Making travel arrangements for the Managing Director and for other Executive Directors.
	Accompanying Mr Jackson on business appointments in the UK and abroad.
	Organising hospitality/accommodation for business visitors to SunActive Ltd.
	Supervision of duties of the Administrative Assistants.
Previous experience	Good secretarial and P/A experience at a senior managerial level is essential.

The organisation	SunActive Limited provides a range of specialist activity holidays, operated in the Swiss Alps. Winter activities include skiing and snowboarding, while summer activities include mountain hiking, cycling , kayaking and white water rafting. The Head Office is in Chester and an office is maintained in Interlaken, Switzerland.
Pay and conditions	Working hours 09.00 to 17.00 Monday to Friday.
	Salary is negotiable.
	There is a generous company pension scheme.
	Because the job involves foreign trips, a travel allowance is paid.
General comments	This job calls for organisational abilities and personal qualities of a very high order.

Activity 6.3 – person specifications

1   Compare the SunActive Limited job description with that for the Personnel Assistant in Three Valleys District Council.

In what respects are the job descriptions similar?

How do they differ?

2   How does the SunActive Limited example meet the key requirement which is to attract 'good quality' applicants?

Advertising the Job

Unless an organisation pays a Recruitment Consultancy or an Executive Search Consultant to find potential recruits, it will have to design its own advertisements to attract people. Specialist consultancies have sophisticated advertising departments which place large and expensive adverts in the 'quality' press such as *The Times*, *The Guardian*, *The Sunday Times* and *The Independent*. Most businesses, however, will not have such facilities and they will have to draw up their own advertisements. The newspaper will typeset the final version.

writing the advertisement

Before writing the advertisement the employer must determine exactly what is wanted from the job being advertised. To ensure this, the employer, before writing the advert, must look carefully at the Person Specification – the type of person that is required – and the Job Description – what the person will be required to do in the job.

When drafting the advertisement the key points to consider are:

- **job description**

  The advert should specify what the job requires the person to do. Obviously, this can only be fairly general but the key duties do need outlining.

- **type of person**

  The advert should then say what kind of person is required. It is illegal to specify a particular sex or someone of a particular racial origin, except in a few quite rare situations (eg you could advertise for a person of Chinese origin to work as a waiter or waitress in a Chinese restaurant). You will also need to look at issues such as experience and qualifications.

- **pay and conditions**

  Depending on the nature of the job, state what the pay and conditions are, eg holidays, hours and pension arrangements (where appropriate). Flexible hours ('flexitime') is an attractive feature of a job for some people, while for others the opportunity to earn overtime pay will be very appealing.

- **place of work**

  The job location should be made clear. Some organisations are multi-sited: for example, most Councils have offices at various addresses. The location of a job may be awkward for some potential applicants, eg if they have to deliver children to school before 9 am. The advert should also say if travel is required as part of the job, and if so, how it is dealt with financially – is a company car or a mileage allowance provided?

- **how to apply**

  The advertisement should say whether applicants should write in or telephone for an application form. It needs to be borne in mind that it will take up more staff time dealing with telephone requests than dealing with enquiry letters.

SALES ADVISORS
IMMEDIATE START

A national company requires good communicators to work from its Manchester sales and customer services office. Applicants must possess a good telephone manner and customer services skills and be self-motivated.

Shifts Mon-Fri 5pm - 9pm, Sat 10am - 3pm.

Temporary and permanent contracts with good pay rates.

Successful candidates will undergo 2 weeks' training.

For more information and an immediate interview call Sasha on 0161 428 2060

newspaper job advert – traditional and effective

◾ depth of detail

An advertiser should not give too much irrelevant detail on the background of the organisation, although its 'guiding principle' or 'philosophy' could be mentioned if it helps to attract good candidates. For example, Body Shop Plc stresses its commitment to being environmentally friendly, and this will be an appealing feature to many people looking for work.

◾ ethics and honesty

Be honest about the job being advertised – it is no use giving an over-attractive picture of a job in order to attract very good candidates because if the job does not measure up to what they expect, they will soon leave – remember that very good candidates can find other jobs quite easily.

◾ placing the advertisement

Finally, where and when is the advert to be placed? This will depend on the type of job, how many vacancies there are, the budget available, and how quickly the job needs filling. For example, the Government advertises on TV to encourage recruits into the armed forces, teaching and nursing. A factory with a sudden order may need extra people, so an advert in the local evening paper will be essential (and usually over two or three consecutive evenings). If a business needs a chief accountant or a personnel manager, an engineer or a solicitor, then the best place is a specialist magazine for that particular profession. Some newspapers run specialised job supplements on particular days of the week.

hi-tech options for filling vacancies - internet job boards

Increasingly, organisations are using new technologies to help them to short-list job applicants. A number of 'job boards' now appear on the internet. The biggest advertises 60,000 jobs at any one time. Interested net users can enquire about the jobs online and send their CVs via email should they wish to do so. Visit www.totaljobs.com. Companies also recruit on their own websites to fill specific vacancies.

an internet job board

In a typical job recruitment exercise using manual systems and traditional advertising, the process from beginning to job offer can take around 30 days. Some commercial internet recruitment services can give a job applicant a first interview via the job board's online facility, followed up with a 'traditional' interview and job offer – taking a total of 15 to 17 days.

Letter of Application, CVs and References

Having attracted a number of candidates, the next stage will be to reduce them to a small enough number to invite for an interview. For high-level posts such as Chief Executive of a large Plc there will be very few serious candidates and so a lot of time can be spent on investigating all of them. For most jobs, depending on the general economic situation, there are many applicants and a simple and quick process is needed to sort them out.

The three main documents assessed in this sorting process are:

- the letter of application
- the curriculum vitae (CV)
- the application form

All organisations ask applicants to send in at least one of these documents. We will now examine all three in turn.

the letter of application

This is a letter (handwritten or word-processed) asking for the job and explaining why the writer is suitable for it. The letter will be structured in any way the writer thinks is appropriate, and this very fact makes it a useful selection method. If the letter is badly structured, poorly expressed and full of spelling mistakes, it could indicate that the applicant is not suitable for an administrative job which requires neat, well-structured work and a 'tidy mind'. On the other hand, a poorly-structured letter which is nevertheless imaginative and interesting could indicate that the applicant may be suitable for other jobs.

Human Resources staff may have to read hundreds of application letters so it is in a writer's interests to pay attention to doing it properly. Key points for the writer to bear in mind include:

- Keep the letter brief. Handwrite it, unless the handwriting is hard to read.
- Check grammar, punctuation and spelling.
- Structure the letter in paragraphs as follows:

   Paragraph 1 should explain how the writer found out about the job and why they are applying for it.

   Paragraph 2 should give the applicant's basic details – but most personal detail should be in the application form or CV.

   Paragraph 3 will give the particular reasons why the applicant wants the job and why they want to work for that organisation.

   Paragraph 4 will say that the writer is available for interview at most times. This will enable the organisation to fix an interview.

disadvantages of letters of application

The disadvantages of letters of application as an assessment method are that:

- Applicants taught to write letters well at school or college will stand out even though their other qualities might not be so good.

- Letter writers may miss out information which is important, and may concentrate on factors which they think make them look better – the only way around this is to ask applicants to supply a CV (see below).

Despite these shortcomings, letters of application are quite often used and increasingly it is specified by employers that they should be handwritten.

The science of graphology (the assessment of a person's character by the analysis of his/her handwriting) is becoming more commonly used by recruitment and executive search consultants (see page 107).

A LETTER OF APPLICATION

23 Trent Road
Tackworth Estate
Denby
DE2 6RG

4 June 2005

Dear Sir or Madam,

I am interested in applying for the job of HR assistant advertised in last night's 'Denby Evening Telegraph'.

I am studying at Denby Technical College for the Applied GCE in Business, which I will complete at the end of this month. My qualifications and educational details are in the curriculum vitae attached.

I am very interested in Human Resources work and I did one week's work experience in the personnel department of Hoyoda Cars in Darlford in November last year. I am also studying an HR unit as part of my course.

I am available for interview at any time convenient for you, apart from the dates of May 11 and May 17.

Yours faithfully

Deborah Smith

Deborah Smith

Activity 6.4 – letter of application

Study the letter shown on the previous page.

Give four reasons why you would be likely to invite the applicant for a job interview.

the curriculum vitae

'Curriculum vitae' means the 'course of your life' – the story so far.

The written curriculum vitae (the CV) is a formal description of an applicant's life and achievements. It will normally accompany a letter of application as an alternative to the application form when the advert asks 'please apply in writing'. It is essential that it is well presented.

Nowadays, there are plenty of specialist agencies that can prepare CVs for people in a professional manner. If you have access to a computer and printer you should have no difficulty in producing a well-presented CV using a word-processing program.

The next question is what goes into a CV? The simplest rule is to include anything which would normally be asked for in an application form. The basics will therefore be:

- name and address
- telephone number (preferably both landline and mobile)
- email address
- date of birth
- marital status
- education and qualifications
- training (where appropriate)
- employment history in chronological order (school and college leavers should include part-time employment)
- hobbies and interests
- references

When listing employment in chronological order, start with the most recent job. This principle also applies to education and qualifications. Attached to the letter of application for Deborah Smith on the previous page was her curriculum vitae, shown on the next page.

CURRICULUM VITAE

NAME   Deborah Smith

ADDRESS   23 Trent Road
                            Tackworth Estate
                            Denby DE2 6RG

TELEPHONE   01332 565678 (home) 0774368948 (mobile)

DATE OF BIRTH   3 February 1987

EDUCATION   Tackworth High School, Marlborough Road
                            Denby (2000 - 2004)
                            Denby Technical College
                            Denby (2004 - present)

QUALIFICATIONS   GCSEs:
                            English (A)
                            Maths (C)
                            History (B)
                            Business Studies (C)
                            Geography (A)
                            German (C)

PRESENTLY STUDYING   Applied GCE in Business (Double Award)

EMPLOYMENT DETAILS   Store Assistant, Sainsway Superstore,
                            Tackworth Centre
                            Saturdays only

                            Work experience at Hoyoda Cars (November 2004)

INTERESTS   Foreign travel, music, amateur dramatics with
                            college drama group

REFEREES   Mr A Chapman,
                            Headmaster, Tackworth High School
                            Marlborough Road
                            Denby DE1 4GH

                            Mr T Poole
                            Staff Manager
                            Sainsway PLC
                            Tackworth Centre
                            Denby DE1 9DF

Activity 6.5 – practice job application

You are required to write an application letter and a curriculum vitae for the job advertised below.

Use your own details, existing qualifications and experience (eg part-time jobs you may have had). Unless your tutor says anything to the contrary, draft the letter in your own handwriting and then use a word-processing package to set out a curriculum vitae.

THE JOB
Chorospan Limited
HR ASSISTANT

Chorospan is a major producer of throat lozenges and other medical products with two factories in Britain and a distribution centre in France. In 15 years we have doubled our sales volume and have increased our workforce in our UK factories to approximately 450. Expansion plans will take this to 550 within two years.

Our Human Resources Department, which is based at our head offices in Norwich, is seeking an assistant to help provide our first-class personnel service to all staff. Experience in all areas of HR work will be provided and it may include some travel to our other operating units in the UK and France.

We intend to appoint someone with good experience and qualifications but the most important factor is enthusiasm to do a job which deals mainly with people rather than routine office work. People of all ages are very welcome to apply.

The salary offered will reflect the successful person's experience and qualifications. Other benefits include a contributory pension scheme and BUPA membership plus five weeks' holiday.

Please apply in writing to
John Carrow-Rhodes,
HR Director,
Chorospan Ltd,
Canary Road,
Norwich,
NR2 7KB

the application form

This is a far more commonly used method of selection. Consultants devote hours to designing new and better forms which will extract even more accurate information from people. A typical form will require details on addresses, next of kin, education, training, qualifications, work experience, non-work interests and the names of referees from whom the organisation can collect personal recommendations. Look at the example on this and the next page.

BASSETT CONSTRUCTION LIMITED

application for post of _____

personal details

surname	forename(s)
Mr/Mrs/Miss/Ms	date of birth
permanent address	
postcode	telephone number
nationality	marital status

education and training

school/college/university	qualification	grade	date

employment history

employer	job held, duties and responsibilities	dates

additional information

Describe your present state of health.
Please give details of any serious illnesses or operations over the last 10 years.

Do you have a criminal record or criminal charges pending?   Yes/No

Do you hold a clean driving licence?   Yes/No

Where did you hear of this vacancy?

When are you *not* available for interview?

references

Please give the names and addresses of two referees

name	name
address	address

interests

Please give details of your interests and hobbies, any positions of responsibility held, and any other information which you would like to support this application.

DECLARATION

I declare the information supplied by me in this form is, to the best of my knowledge, correct.	
signature of applicant	*date*

benefits to the employer of application forms

The HR staff will have identified specific requirements from the job and person specifications. They can then compare these with the information on the forms. They need only shortlist for interview those people who have met those requirements, eg a particular qualification.

The forms can act as a framework for the interviewer to use should the applicant get shortlisted. For example, the interviewer can query gaps in the employment record, or ask about poor examination results, or about relevant non-work interests.

The organisation can keep all the forms for the shortlisted candidates for the vacancy and draw on them again if another vacancy arises.

The form from the successful applicant will become a very useful part of his/her initial personnel records.

references

For most jobs it is usual for the prospective employer to take up references provided by the job applicant. There are several types of reference:

- **Testimonial** – a letter, usually from a former employer or teacher, which will say very positive and kind things about the applicant. As the applicant has been given this letter it is unlikely that the writer will make anything other than positive and helpful statements. (Clearly, if the writer did say something critical, the applicant would tear the testimonial up and look around for someone else to write one!)

- **Reference letters** requested by the prospective employer – this is the most usual type of reference. The letters are confidential so that the referee can be completely honest without embarrassment, but it may not tell the prospective employer all he/she needs to know. Employers can learn to 'read between the lines', and often the omission of information can be a telling factor.

- **Reference forms** – some organisations, the Civil Service being a good example, use a structured form which asks specific questions about the applicant. These include assessments of effort and ability, and opinions about their honesty and health.

- **Telephone references** – some organisations telephone the people given as referees. The main benefit is that the recruiter can assess the tone of voice of the referee, and this can often say far more about an applicant than a letter can. They can also question the referee far more searchingly.

- **Medical references** – most employers will carry out some kind of medical check-up even if it is only the completion of a form asking a few simple questions about health problems in the past. Such a check is necessary because:

- the employer needs to safeguard the health of other employees
- the job itself may require specific health standards (eg perfect colour vision for a train driver, because of the need to be able to distinguish railway signals)
- if an employee is to join a company pension scheme, a medical check-up will be needed (again only the completion of a simple form may be required)

Interviewing

interviewer and interviewee techniques

The final stage in the process will be an interview, and – increasingly common these days – some form of test or assessment. Interviews are arranged for almost every kind of job. The process of sifting through forms or letters and the examination of references will mean that only a few of the applicants for the job will be interviewed. This is because interviews take up the time of senior managers who have to carry them out, and this will be costly for the business.

planning the interview

■ The interviewer must ask 'What are my objectives? What am I looking for? How will I phrase the questions I am going to ask?' It may sound obvious, but one key objective is to fill in all the gaps which are left after all the information from the application forms, CVs and references have been assembled. Another objective is to explore in detail and in depth some of the points raised in the application forms which you consider to be of importance.

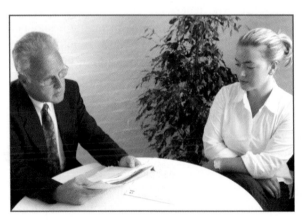
single interviewing – the dangers of bias

■ Decide if the vacancy requires just one interviewer or two, or even a panel of four or five. There are advantages and disadvantages to either approach.

'One to one' interviews put applicants at ease so that they will talk more naturally. The problems are that a single interviewer lacks the range and depth of knowledge of a panel of experts and is more likely to suffer from bias and can be highly prejudiced. A single interviewer is more likely to suffer from mirror imaging (favouring candidates who are like them) and 'halo' effects (favouring candidates who have particularly attractive characteristics – even if those characteristics have little bearing on the job applied for).

carrying out the interview – the interviewer

- As a general rule the 'talking split' in a job interview should be around 20% for the interviewer and 80% for the interviewee. The interviewer learns far more from the applicant if he/she listens than if he/she talks! However, 'listening' is not just 'not talking' – listening is the art of conveying to the applicant that you are interested in what they are saying, together with an ability to make the occasional comment which encourages them to say a lot more.

- The interview should always begin with a few friendly questions to put the candidate at ease – ones about the journey or the weather – before asking more detailed questions. Most interviewers will ask a mixture of questions. Some will be about the application form itself, eg asking for more details about work experience or about qualifications. It is usual to follow up with deeper questions such as how the candidate might handle a difficult situation at work.

- Finally, there should be a question asking the candidate if they have any questions.

carrying out the interview – the interviewee

The person being interviewed also needs to use communication skills to the full in order to create a good impression. Often interviewers make a decision very soon after the interviewee has walked into the room. For example:

- to appear relaxed and friendly – but not too casual
- to use eye contact – but not to overdo it
- to answer questions as fully as possible, but not to talk too much
- to prepare questions to ask in advance

EFFECTIVE INTERVIEWEE TECHNIQUE

the Use of Tests

It is increasingly common for employers to expect job applicants to carry out tests to give a fuller picture of their ability to do the job applied for. These are usually referred to as Aptitude Tests. They are appropriate for manual work where there is some skill involved and also in office work where applicants might be required to take a word-processing test. For professional posts such tests are less usual because it is felt that the candidate's qualifications, references and experience are sufficient evidence. In more recent years new developments in testing have included psychometric testing, assessment centres and graphology.

pyschometric testing in action (www.peoplemaps.co.uk)

psychometric testing

Psychometric tests assess the intelligence and personality of applicants. They are much more sophisticated than aptitude tests and the employer must have properly trained staff to analyse the test results properly. Such tests are particularly valuable when assessing intelligence, interest in the job applied for, motivation and personality. The producers of such tests (there are dozens available) argue that they are completely unbiased and extremely accurate. They are supposed to be particularly good at assessment of personality – for example, they can show if a candidate would work well in a team or would be more effective working alone.

assessment centres

Job applicants are subjected to a wide range of assessments over a whole day or sometimes two days. They are required to participate in group exercises (with all the other applicants), psychometric tests, aptitude tests and traditional interviews. By using a mixture of assessment this process is claimed to produce more accurate results. The applicants are given longer to prove themselves and therefore become more relaxed and more 'natural'.

Recent developments now mean that these assessment centre exercises can be videoed and then sent to a team of independent experts to be properly analysed. This reassures the candidates that their performance will be assessed objectively.

graphology

Graphology is the analysis of a person's handwriting to find out about the character of that person and suitability for doing a particular job. Although some people are wary of using it, graphology is becoming more commonly used in UK selection processes.

Much handwriting analysis is actually common sense. For example, if handwriting slopes forward, it is said to show people who are positive about life and where writing slopes backwards, it shows a person who is shy and 'inward' in reacting to other people. Large handwriting with big loops shows a 'feminine' and artistic side to a person's character. Scribbly, unreadable handwriting shows a person who probably has a large ego (a 'bighead').

Visit www.britishgraphology.org for further information and some analyses of well-known handwriting.

after the Interview

After interviewing all candidates and carrying out whatever tests may be necessary, the final stage is to select one or more of them. Interview panels often find it very hard to choose between the final two or three applicants. Although applicants will need to know the outcome within a few days there should be a thorough analysis of all the information that has been collected on each of them. It is fairly easy to devise a list of the key points. These will include:

- attainments
- experience
- disposition
- personal circumstances
- reference letters
- results from the medical check-up
- results from any essential tests/assessment centres
- and, finally, comments from the interviewers themselves

The job and person specifications make it a lot easier to do the final selection. From these documents a list of selection criteria will have been devised for the job. Every member of the interview panel can then mark each candidate out of ten for each of these criteria. The panel can then compare their results, see where they have similar marks and where they differ significantly. They then need to discuss the differences and come to a final result. The successful applicant should be notified first of all.

Employer Legal and Ethical Responsibilities

Always remember that there are legal obligations and ethical responsibilities which the candidate and the interviewer should abide by throughout the entire recruitment process. All employees are protected by a variety of laws that have been introduced over the last few decades. Some of the more important ones are described below. There are a number of websites which provide up-to-date information about employment law – visit, for example, www.dti.gov.uk/er

Equal Pay Act 1970

This requires employers to pay the same rate of pay to men and women if they are doing the same job. Prior to this Act many jobs paid lower rates of pay to women. The chief problem with the Act was that a job where most job holders were women could be badly paid while in a similar job where most job holders were men pay rates could be a great deal higher. For this reason the government introduced the Equal Value Amendment (1983) which requires men and women to be paid the same rates of pay if women can show that their jobs are of 'equal value' to a range of specifically named jobs held by men.

Sex Discrimination Act 1975

This law states that employers may not discriminate on grounds of gender. It makes it illegal to discriminate against a particular sex when:

- advertising to fill jobs available
- appointing employees for those jobs
- promoting staff into better jobs
- determining the terms and conditions of the job
- offering employees opportunities for training and development

There are a number of examples where the Act does not apply. These include:

- the armed forces – recruitment of women is restricted to specific areas – there are now female personnel on board Royal Navy ships and a number of female fighter pilots
- acting roles – eg actors required for the role of Father Christmas

Race Relations Act 1976

The 1976 Race Relations Act makes discrimination on grounds of race illegal in the same areas as described above under the Sex Discrimination Act 1975, ie advertising jobs, appointing staff, promoting staff and providing staff benefits.

Again, there are a few exceptions to the Act including:

- ethnic restaurants can specify they want people of a particular race to work as waiters/waitresses to make the restaurant look more authentic
- social work departments can specify they want to appoint staff of a particular race where they have to deal with social problems of people of the same race
- acting roles will sometimes require people of particular races – for example, a Chinese actress is unlikely to make a convincing job of playing the role of Queen Victoria

direct and indirect forms of discrimination

Both the Sex Discrimination and Race Relations Acts state that there are two ways in which employers could break the law:

Direct discrimination means that there is a positive decision to discriminate either against men or women.

Indirect discrimination involves situations where the employer creates certain conditions of employment which make it harder for a particular racial group or for women or men to get the jobs advertised. Such a practice is only legal if the employer can show that the condition was a 'genuine occupational qualification' of the job. For example, a minimum height requirement might make it harder for large numbers of women (or for certain racial groups) to apply for a job. If there were safety or health reasons for this height limit, this would be a 'genuine occupational qualification'. Therefore, it would not be indirect discrimination.

Disability Discrimination Act 1995

This Act updates the protection for disabled persons. It does not cover organisations employing under 20 people. The Act requires that:

- Employers must not discriminate against disabled people when:
  - advertising jobs and inviting applications
  - offering jobs after interviews have taken place
  - determining the terms and conditions of the job

  Once appointed, a disabled person must be treated the same as everyone else when training, promotion or any other benefits are on offer. If five people are applying for a promotion and there is only one post vacant, the disabled person cannot expect favourable treatment.

■ The employer must take reasonable steps to ensure that a disabled person can work on the premises. This includes making arrangements such as:

- modifying the buildings (entrances, ramps, lifts etc)

- changing working hours to suit the disabled person

- allowing time off for treatment or rehabilitation

- allowing extra training so the disabled person can carry out the job

- providing a reader or an interpreter

- putting a disabled person in a different, more convenient workplace (eg on the ground floor rather than three floors up)

Employers only have to do what is reasonable. If modifications are very expensive then this would be thought unreasonable.

Activity 6.6 – discrimination at work

Here are some examples of adverts for job vacancies and situations which might occur at work. Look at each of them and suggest whether they discriminate against certain people or not.

1 Advert: 'Barman required for Zone999 Club'

2 Advert: 'Young English woman required as live-in Nanny to three children'

3 Advert: 'Indian man required as waiter in Indian restaurant'

4 Three women have been appointed as supervisors in a factory. The manager explains "there were too many men supervisors – we wanted to even things out between the sexes".

5 Three women take a case against their employer to court complaining that men employed in a similar job by another company are paid more than they are.

equal opportunities and managing diversity

Employers are increasingly involved in using both of these policies to recruit, retain and motivate their employees.

Equal opportunities involve the removal of the barriers which are faced by minority groups in the workplace. The concept is based on the fact that certain groups have been disadvantaged in the past (female workers, older people, ethnic minorities, disabled people). It is about removing those disadvantages.

For example, equal opportunities means that jobs are advertised as widely as possible so that everyone who might be interested in them gets to know about them.

By contrast, **managing diversity** is based on the idea that people from different backgrounds and minority groups can bring fresh ideas and experiences into an organisation. This will make the organisation more efficient and improve the quality of its products and services, and also eventually its profitability. An example of managing diversity is where an organisation offers opportunities for flexible working (see Chapter 5) so that people from a wide range of backgrounds can consider applying for available job vacancies.

Activity 6.7 – managing diversity

Read the following article reproduced by kind permission of *Personnel Today* and answer the questions that follow.

Computer giant puts employees in the driving seat

The computer giant IBM, which employs 22,000 staff in the UK, has set up more than 150 diversity group networks, where staff with 'common philosophies' can meet and share knowledge and experience that will make IBM more competitive.

The voluntary groups, representing women, Asian staff and those with disabilities, meet locally to discuss the sensitivities of workers, customers and competitors. They are organised by a core of 500 employees, but are open to all staff. The information and views collected are sent to HR, which can then 'champion the networks'.

The company also hosts annual national forums, where respective local groups can share concerns and ideas. This includes an IBM women's conference, where more than 300 female staff discuss how they can be role models and play an active part in the growth of the company.

Dave Heath, HR director at IBM, said the networks were the company's main driver towards a diverse workforce and gave everyone in the business a voice.

"The networks are more than just talking shops," he said. "They focus the population of IBM on diversity and on how our competitors operate. This can only enhance business success."

1 What minority groups are represented by the diversity group networks established by IBM in the UK, and what happens to the information and views which they generate?

2 Describe the role played by the national forums organised by IBM in the UK and explain what they achieve.

3 What do the diversity group networks achieve within IBM in the UK both for the groups they represent and also the company as a whole?

CHAPTER SUMMARY

■ Businesses recruit staff for a number of important reasons – these include business growth, resignations, retirements, dismissals and changes in job roles.

■ Businesses recruit staff from internal candidates and external candidates. Each source has its advantages and disadvantages.

■ The basic documents required before recruitment and selection take place are the job description and the person specification for the job concerned.

■ It is vital to plan carefully how and when to advertise jobs.

■ Online job advertising and recruitment are becoming more popular.

■ Other important documents are the letter of application, the curriculum vitae (CV) and the application form.

■ Interviews must be carefully planned in order to recruit the right person for the job and to show fairness to all the candidates concerned.

■ A variety of tests and assessment techniques, including psychometric tests and graphology, are used to give a more accurate picture of the job candidate than an interview can provide on its own.

■ Employers must understand that there are legal and ethical responsibilities relating to recruitment and selection of new employees. Important legislation includes:

- Equal Pay Act 1970

- Sex Discrimination Act 1975

- Race Relations Act 1976

- Disability Discrimination Act 1995

■ Employers are working hard to implement equal opportunities in the workplace and to encourage policies of diversity management – making the most of the fact that there are differences and minorities within the workforce.

KEY TERMS

job description	this lists the main tasks and responsibilities in a job
person specification	this lists the qualities of an ideal candidate for a job
curriculum vitae	usually known as a CV, this presents the career and educational background of a jobseeker
testimonial	a supporting letter from a referee which is supplied by the job applicant
Internet job board	an online noticeboard provided by employers and recruitment companies
job references	these can be provided in a number of ways – their purpose is to provide more information about job applicants so the interview panel has a better idea of their experience, ability and character
psychometric testing	specialist tests which assess the suitability of a job applicant to carry out a job successfully – psychometrics is the systematic measurement of intelligence, aptitudes and personality
assessment centres	specialist centres where job applicants carry out a series of exercises to give a fuller picture than an interview alone could ever provide
graphology	the study of handwriting as a means of assessing personality
direct discrimination	preferring one job applicant or employee over another
indirect discrimination	creating conditions of employment or entry to employment which makes it harder for certain groups of people to work or obtain work
equal opportunities	the removal of barriers faced by minority groups in the workplace
managing diversity	using the inherent differences between minority groups to provide a source of ideas and impetus for the business as a whole

7

Employee training

Starting point

Employees are like athletes. Unless they are fully trained in the relevant skills, kept fit and motivated, they will not develop and achieve their full potential.

This chapter examines the process of employee training and development and its value to employers and employees.

Employee development is linked to employee performance – a topic that will be explained fully in Chapter 8 'Employee performance and motivation'.

What you will learn from this chapter

- training and development are vitally important for the overall efficiency and competitiveness of an organisation

- some skills and competences learnt in the workplace are non-transferable and others are transferable

- there are several types of training and development designed to fulfil a variety of organisational needs. These include induction, updating and multi-skilling training

- the Government has established various initiatives such as the New Deal and Employer Training Pilots

- all training is either 'on the job' or 'off the job' – both are equally important and valuable

- regular evaluation of its training by an organisation is an important process which ensures that the training remains worthwhile

Training Employees

'Training' can be defined as:

the acquisition of a body of knowledge and skills which can be applied to a particular job

In the last century it was the tradition that young people left school and found a job which provided them with sufficient initial training to enable them to continue to do the same job indefinitely. This was true whether the job was unskilled or semi-skilled, requiring only very basic training, or skilled where an 'apprenticeship' of several years was required. It was not unusual to be given an apprenticeship in, for example, a shipyard, a coal mine or a newspaper printing works which would provide a steady, secure and well-paid job from the day of joining the company until the day of retirement 50 years later. The training provided in that apprenticeship would be expected to be sufficiently thorough to ensure that very little extra training would ever be required.

Today there are very few 'traditional' apprenticeships, and people can no longer assume that any job will be a 'job for life'. Even people who do keep the same job for a long time are required to update their skills regularly, or face redundancy because their old skills are rapidly made useless by the advance of new technology.

For most people it is now assumed that they will change their jobs several times in a lifetime, often switching to completely different types of work.

The significance of this is that training is much more central to people's lives as an ongoing process rather than just something they do at the start of their careers.

training programmes

Nowadays, most larger organisations employ professional training officers to run training programmes for employees. In a large manufacturing or services company, for example, the training manager will have teams of training instructors to teach all kinds of courses to employees. Even in small businesses several types of training will be necessary.

Training can be divided into two main categories: 'on the job' training or 'off the job' training.

'on the job' training

This means that the employee acquires his/her training or development in the workplace itself. Many people enjoy the direct link with their job and can see more clearly how relevant the training or development is to job performance.

'off the job' training

This means attending courses which may be in a college or a training centre away from the workplace (or one situated inside the workplace). This type of training is important to an employee's career development as well as being an integral part of a training programme.

non-transferable skills and transferable skills

Skills acquired by employees can be either **non-transferable** or **transferable**. All the types of training and development described below fall under one or other of these headings.

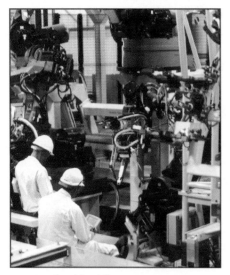
non-transferable skills

non-transferable skills

These are skills that are extremely specific to the job held. They are of little use in any other job. Training to work on a particular machine in a factory may provide the employee with not only a skill that is non-transferable but also one that causes 'negative transfer'.

This means that when the employee switches to a newer machine they have to 'unlearn' the skills acquired on the old one. This takes time, and time costs an employer money.

transferable skills

These are skills that can be used in a wide variety of other jobs later on. In the economy today, where people are changing jobs far more frequently than 20 years ago, non-transferable skills are of little use to a jobseeker. In looking around for jobs, people must have a selection of 'transferable skills'. People with transferable skills are more useful to employers because they learn a new job quickly and they are cheaper to train. This ability to use skills more widely is called positive transfer. An example is the skill of interviewing. This is transferable to a whole range of interviewing situations, eg a disciplinary interview.

transferable skills

Many larger organisations provide open learning or self-learning centres where their employees can study a range of skills in company or in free time. These can be work-linked topics such as time management or business communications, or general interest topics such as 'foreign languages for holidays'. The aim is to get employees to realise the importance of keeping up-to-date with new developments in industry and in their own particular areas of work.

Activity 7.1 – using IT to develop employee skills

The two articles below from *Personnel Today* are both very positive about employees wanting to acquire new skills. They also show how important training is for the organisations concerned. Read the articles then answer the questions that follow.

In-store computers boost staff skills at retail giant

Supermarket giant Tesco is installing computers at its stores around the country as part of a drive to give workers technology skills that could help them in their working and home lives.

All 200,000 staff will be given the opportunity to learn basic IT skills such as word processing, emailing and efficient use of databases.

In a separate move Tesco is also opening its first learning centre which will give staff access to training PCs and allows them to choose from a range of courses, from reading and writing to foreign languages and guitar lessons.

Clare Chapman, HR director at Tesco, said the move would help establish the group as an employer of choice and drive up the skills of the workforce. "Tesco is committed to supporting our employees both inside and outside work," she said.

Energy company bids to generate online learning

ScottishPower is providing its 15,000 employees and their families with access to online learning in their homes.

Employees and their families can choose from a wide range of courses which include IT skills, and business and professional development skills such as finance, marketing, communication and leadership.

"Home learning is a natural extension of our open learning initiative," said UK HR director Steve Dunn. "I believe this initiative will enrich the employment experience and provide valuable development opportunities to ScottishPower employees and their families."

Paul McKelvie, director of ScottishPower Learning, said the scheme was part of the company's commitment to investing in the skills of local people.

1 What specific skills are being developed by both these company schemes? Are they transferable or non-transferable?

2 Explain how the PC training in all 780 Tesco stores will benefit:
   (a) the employees and
   (b) Tesco
   Give examples of specific benefits in both cases.

3 Explain how the ScottishPower online learning scheme will benefit its 15,000 employees.

4 Why is ScottishPower extending this access to all employees' families?

Types of Training

induction training for new employees

Induction is the process of introducing new employees to the organisation and its way of life and 'culture'.

A successful job applicant should be provided with induction training of some kind. As might be expected the larger, well-resourced organisations do this more thoroughly than poorly-resourced, smaller organisations.

What does an induction programme include? Most will involve:

■ a tour of the buildings to show the newcomer all the important areas – the sick room, the canteen, the pay office, toilets, car parking etc – and to introduce them to the important staff such as the pay and personnel staff and the person in charge of Health & Safety and First Aid

■ an introduction to their new workplace – the specific office or factory area or shop department – where they will be working

■ some background detail about the organisation – the easiest and best way to do this is to show them a DVD about the organisation

Activity 7.2 – induction programmes

Work in groups and draw up a plan for an induction programme for new entrants to your college/school.

Plan it around their first day at the college/school and base it on the course that you are doing.

Give a short presentation briefing the new entrants when they first arrive at your college/school.

initial training for new employees

This is to ensure that the range of activities the employee will have to carry out in the first week or two is done competently and safely. All new employees must be given training immediately after the induction procedures have been carried out.

updating training

Increasingly, employees are required to learn new skills in place of skills that are becoming redundant. For example, in the newspaper printing industry the traditional printing skills have virtually been replaced by completely different work requiring completely different skills. Printers either had to learn the new skills or lose their jobs.

Most importantly, there is now a 'culture' of training in which employees are increasingly expected to update knowledge and skills on a regular basis.

multi-skilling training

Multi-skilling means that employees are trained to do several jobs rather than just one. Employers gain from this because:

- an employee can do the work of somebody who is absent through illness or holidays

- employees are more motivated because doing several jobs is usually more interesting than doing just one; where an employee is able to do several jobs it increases their value to the organisation and makes them feel more appreciated and more secure

- the flexibility gained from multi-skilling means the total number of employees can be cut down

Government Employment and Training Schemes

UK governments have traditionally financed training programmes to help people find work. Although the emphasis has been on finding younger people jobs, older and disadvantaged people have also been helped by a series of employment and training programmes.

Schemes at the time of writing include New Deal, Modern Apprenticeships and Employer Training Pilots.

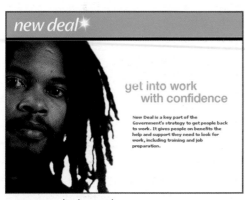

www.newdeal.gov.uk

New Deal programmes

New Deal programmes are designed to find work for people receiving state benefit. There are two schemes for people who are on Jobseeker's Allowance. These pay subsidies to employers who take on jobseekers. These schemes are:

- New Deal for Young People (18 - 24)
- New Deal 25 plus

In addition, there is a range of voluntary programmes:

- New Deal 50 plus
- New Deal for Lone Parents
- New Deal for Disabled People
- New Deal for Partners of Unemployed People

Figures from a recent four-year period show that 414,200 people aged 18-24, 135,900 people aged 25+ and 98,040 people aged 50+ were given jobs under New Deal.

Modern Apprenticeships

These enable young people to achieve higher level vocational qualifications and skills. They are available mainly for 16 and 17 year-old school and college leavers, but may be offered to people aged 18 and over who can complete the apprenticeship before the age of 25. Modern apprentices are normally employed by the organisation with which they train and are paid wages. The training employer receives government assistance towards the training costs. Visit www.apprenticeships.org.uk

Employer Training Pilots

Employer Training Pilots (ETPs) are government-funded schemes set up in selected areas of the UK which encourage employers to train low-skilled employees and give them paid time off work to be trained. Their target is employers (particularly small organisations) who traditionally do not train their staff and employees who would not normally be trained. ETPs benefit both employers and employees. Employers get skills gaps filled thus improving productivity and employees benefit as they improve their skill level and value to the organisation. Visit etp.lsc.gov.uk

---

Employer Training Pilots – some relevant facts and figures

- UK industry loses £4.8 billion a year because of poor literacy and numeracy skills. The cost to the country could be as high as £10 billion each year.

- 7 million adults in England lack basic skills, having an enormous impact on small businesses.

- Output in the US, France and Germany is around 30% higher, per hour, than in the UK.

- Up to a fifth of the gap with Germany and France is a direct consequence of lower skill levels in the UK.

- 7,500 employers and 35,000 employees signed up to ETPs in 18 months.

- Employer Training Pilots successfully reach employers who have never previously engaged in training their workforce.

Source: etp.lsc.gov.uk

Activity 7.3 – government assistance for training

Study the text on the previous two pages and then answer the questions below. You may find it useful to access the websites quoted in the text.

1 What is the problem that the Employer Training Pilots (ETPs) are attempting to solve? What is the actual cost of this problem to the UK economy?

2 What difference might the ETPs make to the competitive position of the UK in relation to its European neighbours, and why?

3 What is the success rate of ETPs? (See if you can get up-to-date information online.)

4 What difference will New Deal make to the ETP initiative, and why?

5 What difference will Modern Apprenticeships make to the ETP initiative, and why?

Investors in People UK (IIP)

This is known as 'a national standard for effective investment in people'. It sets out a range of targets which employers should achieve. For example, there must be a regular review of the training and development needs of all employees and resources clearly identified for this purpose. All employees should have a clear vision of where the organisation is going and be encouraged to contribute to the achievement of that vision.

Where an organisation achieves the specification laid down by IIP it is given the accreditation of 'an Investor in People'. This is not just a nice certificate to hang on the wall. More and more companies take the view that their suppliers should be IIP accredited since it reflects the fact that the organisation has a committed workforce who do a good job. Not having IIP may therefore mean less business in the future.

Visit www.investorsinpeople.co.uk for more information.

INVESTORS IN PEOPLE UK

WELCOME TO INVESTORS IN PEOPLE UK

Everyone agrees that people are an organisation's greatest asset, and we all know that for an organisation to succeed everyone has to perform well. It doesn't matter what size or type of organisation you are, the Investors in People Standard is there to help you improve the way you work.

What? ▸   Why? ▸
How? ▸   Next Steps? ▸

Source: www.investorsinpeople.co.uk

National Vocational Qualifications (NVQs)

The aim of NVQs (SVQs in Scotland) is to create a national system of approved competency-based qualifications.

QCA (Qualifications and Curriculum Authority) and SQA (Scottish Qualifications Authority) are the bodies that accredit NVQs/SVQs set up by the occupational bodies and the industry training organisations. These organisations have established sets of standards or 'competences' known as National Occupational Standards (NOS). These set out the skills and also the underlying knowledge which employees need in the workplace to do their jobs properly.

The main principles behind this initiative are these:

- qualifications are workplace-based, reflecting real workplace needs
- workplace requirements are now a far bigger influence on what is taught in further education colleges
- the Single European Market means that these new qualifications will eventually become part of a common system of Euro-qualifications

NVQs/SVQs qualifications are in five bands – NVQ 1 being the lowest level and NVQ 5 being the highest level – associated with managerial skills. The basis of assessment is reaching a performance standard laid down by the industry concerned. Assessment is mainly 'on the job'.

There is no time period set to complete any particular NVQ stage. People proceed at the rate which suits them. As long as a person is competent for a particular level NVQ, he or she will gain the appropriate Award. In essence, these qualifications are based on results, not just on how people learn.

For more information on NVQs, visit www.dfes.gov.uk/nvq

Training Courses

We will now examine the main types of training course that organisations run.

'in-house' training courses

This is where employers run courses inside their own organisation. Courses might be held in an ordinary office room or in a smart training centre owned by the organisation. Courses run 'in house' will be ones where it is impractical and unrealistic to offer any other alternative – an obvious example would be the organisation's induction programme. Other examples include training staff to use equipment which is specific to that organisation and customer care programmes.

The main benefits of using in-house courses are:

■ they are fairly cheap – there is usually no need to employ outside trainers and lecturers

■ course content is tailor-made for your organisation

■ references and examples to highlight points can be related to your own organisation

■ everybody knows one another, so there is no time wasted in having to get to know people

external courses

Sometimes it is necessary to send staff to do courses elsewhere. This may be with another employer or at a specialist training centre or at the premises of an equipment supplier. When an organisation buys new equipment the supplier will usually run training programmes at its own premises to get employees accustomed to using it.

The benefits of using external courses are:

■ they bring together specialist trainers/tutors who would never be available to an 'in-house' course chiefly because of the high cost

■ course members get together from several organisations, and this enables them to 'network' and learn more about each other and how their respective organisations operate

■ trainers place great value on the benefits of being away from the workplace – the course members are in a comfortable and peaceful environment away from any distractions

External courses are generally quite expensive because they include fairly luxurious accommodation in lavish surroundings and the guest speakers are highly paid. This means employers have to think very seriously about the value of such courses to the organisation and they have to carefully identify which staff would get the most personal benefit.

an NVQ accounting evening class

college courses

Internal and external courses often have to be reinforced by courses provided by local colleges and universities. These courses provide the essential knowledge to support what is learnt in the workplace and on internal courses. College courses include vocational courses and professional courses, such as the NVQ Accounting course shown on the left.

vocational courses

These provide training in job-related skills, eg IT skills. The Qualifications and Curriculum Authority (QCA) approves standards for workplace competences which can be assessed both in the workplace and at college by examining bodies such as Edexcel (BTEC), OCR (RSA) and AQA (City & Guilds).

professional courses

All the professions operate professional training schemes which enable people to acquire qualifications for their career development; these include the various Accountancy Institutes, the Law Society, and the Chartered Institute of Personnel and Development. Colleges are given permission to run these courses and the students sit exams which are usually set by the professional bodies.

Evaluation of Training in the Organisation

Good employers will continually evaluate the effectiveness of their training programmes to ensure that they are worthwhile and remain good value for money. The key points to consider are:

how have trainees reacted to the training given them?

Typically, training officers will have a review session at the end of a training course to assess what participants thought about it. A questionnaire asking for individual comments may also be used. It is important to stress that a training course might have been a lot of fun with a great deal of personal interaction between the participants, but in fact they may have learnt very little of direct use to their jobs.

what have they learnt and what skills have they acquired?

The simplest way of checking this is through a test. Trainers should stress that the test results are to assess the effectiveness of the training course not to assess how particular individuals have performed.

how has their job performance improved?

Over the first few months after the training the participants' work performance could be monitored to see if there has been any improvement.

how has the training benefited the organisation as a whole?

Training is not done just for the employees' benefit. The organisation will have established a budget for training, and management will want to know that it is money well spent. This is particularly important in the public sector (eg government departments, County and District Councils) where 'value for money' has become as much of a priority as profit is in the private sector (eg PLCs quoted on the Stock Markets).

The organisation will aim to achieve specific benefits from running training courses, and if those benefits are not achieved then the training needs looking at again.

A good example are 'customer care' programmes – more and more organisations are training employees how to deal with customers in a more sensitive, helpful and friendly manner. This has obvious benefits in terms of increasing customer loyalty and increasing sales.

Activity 7.4 – evaluation of training

Read the article below from *Personnel Today* and answer the questions that follow.

HR frustrated by failure to measure value of training

The public sector is failing to properly evaluate its training despite the huge costs involved – and as a result, has little evidence of its effectiveness or return on investment.

New research finds only 36 per cent of HR departments in the public sector bother to map training effectiveness against job performance.

This inability to accurately appraise the value and quality of training is leading to serious funding problems.

The focus of training has also been called into question, with one in three HR professionals imposing courses on staff based on the perceived, rather than the actual needs of the workforce.

The findings, taken from a survey by consultant LogicaCMG, also highlight HR's difficulty in gaining senior management buy-in for training budgets.

"Accounting for the return on training investment is paramount in the public sector. There is a definite and immediate need for change in the way training is defined, deployed and evaluated," commented Keith Scott, LogicaCMG's director of training.

1 What is meant by 'return on investment' in the first paragraph? Why should this be so important in the public sector?

2 What is the main problem highlighted by the article? What is the extent of the problem in percentage terms?

3 In small groups in your class discuss how you would try to solve these problems. Each group should compile a list of action points.

CHAPTER SUMMARY

■ Proper training and development are essential if an organisation is to retain its employees and remain competitive. An organisation should draw up a co-ordinated training programme for its employees.

■ Training can be divided into two categories: 'on the job' (workplace) training and 'off the job' (away from the workplace) training.

■ Training and development involve non-transferable skills (specific to the job being done) and transferable skills (which can be used in other jobs).

■ A number of different methods are used to train and develop employees including in-house and external courses and open learning.

■ Induction training is the process of introducing new employees to the organisation and its culture.

■ Multi-skilling training ensures that employees are trained to do several jobs rather than just one.

■ Government schemes such as Labour's New Deal exist to help people to acquire a range of transferable skills.

■ A business accredited by Investors in People UK means that the workforce is committed and does a good job.

■ National Vocational Qualifications (NVQs) have been set up by the government to create a framework of competence-based qualifications, largely assessed in the workplace.

■ Evaluation of training on a regular basis by an organisation is an important process which ensures that the training schemes remain worthwhile.

KEY TERMS

training	the acquisition of knowledge and skills in order to do a job properly
development	providing opportunities for employees to widen and deepen their skills and knowledge so that they are more motivated and of more use to the organisation
on the job training	training received in the workplace
off the job training	going on courses held in locations away from the workplace – eg at a college
transferable skills	skills that can be used in a wide variety of jobs and working environments
non-transferable skills	skills for which there is little use outside the job and organisation where the employee presently works
induction training	introducing the employee to the organisation, its geography and its 'culture'
multi-skilling training	training an employee to carry out a variety of jobs rather than just one
New Deal	government-backed schemes for long-term unemployed jobseekers and a range of voluntary programmes for people claiming benefits who want to work – the schemes provide financial incentives to employers who employ jobseekers on these schemes
Investors in People UK	an organisation which sets a range of nationally-established standards which ensure excellence in the workforce and management of the workforce
NVQs	National Vocational Qualifications (NVQs) are a national system of approved, competence-based qualifications in a variety of vocational areas

8

Employee performance and motivation

Starting point

Employees who are treated well will perform better than employees who are taken for granted and are not motivated in any way.

Employers need to understand exactly what it is that makes employees perform well and beome motivated.

Employees who are not motivated will detract from the whole organisation and are also more likely to leave.

A motivated employee will bring efficiency and a general feeling of well-being to the organisation.

What you will learn from this chapter

- there are a number of ways in which employees can be developed and encouraged to perform more effectively in their jobs

- employers need to ensure that they will retain their best employees

- both employers and employees benefit from the appraisal process

- the law helps to protect employees and encourage them to work more effectively, but it can also add to the cost of employing them

- a motivated employee works better than an employee who is not motivated – an understanding of motivation theories will therefore help employers get the best from their staff

Employee Development

Employee development may be defined as:

a course of action designed to enable the individual to realise his or her potential for growth in the organisation

In other words, the employer does not just train people for now, but for the future. How is this done? A good employer will have a system of identifying career potential in an employee. If there is no system to do this, the result will be that employees stay in 'dead end' jobs which may make them frustrated and bitter. Often they will leave for a better job where their potential is more likely to be recognised. This means that the employer will lose people who could have been a very great asset to the organisation, had their potential been realised.

A system to identify potential could include:

- an **appraisal system** – an analysis of employee performance (see the next section of this chapter)
- the use of **assessment centres** – arranging a series of practical tests to assess employee ability in handling the kind of work which more senior jobs might involve (see page 106).

Developing Employees who have Potential

Several techniques can be used to help promising employees to develop their abilities and give management a better idea of exactly where the employees' future may lie:

job rotation

Giving people a range of jobs in rotation widens their experiences and increases their skills.

job enlargement

Giving people extra tasks to do gives management a better idea of the employees' true capacity, ability and stamina.

job enrichment

Adding more interesting and more difficult tasks to the job. This might be done with a person of very great potential (often known as a 'high-flier') to see just how capable he or she really is.

understanding

Here an employee will be attached to a very senior manager to act as an assistant. This gives the employee insight into what senior managers have to do, and is often used to groom very able people to move rapidly into a top job. Many top business people acted as understudies in their early careers.

'acting up'

This phrase means that a promising employee gets a temporary promotion and if he/she performs well, the promotion may become permanent. It also increases the likelihood that they will get further advancement.

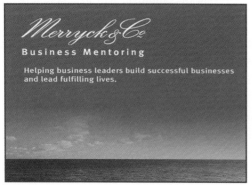

business mentoring

mentoring

A 'mentor' is an advisor. In HR 'mentoring' involves an experienced senior manager being allocated to a young employee in order to help him/her to structure career development within the organisation. Mentors pass on the benefits of their experience, insight and wisdom and will advise the employee how to deal with a wide variety of managerial problems. Mentoring works best when the employee being advised is starting a new job or has just been promoted or is making a sideways move. Visit www.merryck.com

coaching

This is rather similar to mentoring but the key difference is that coaching involves helping the inexperienced employee to acquire high quality skills in a number of specific management areas. Such skills include communication with staff, budgeting, appraisal of staff and how to carry out disciplinary procedures. It is similar to coaching in a sporting sense where, for example, top tennis or golf players are coached to improve particular aspects of their game. Like mentoring, coaching is best suited to employees who are determined to learn more. Visit www.coachingfutures.co.uk

project work

Giving a promising employee a specific investigative project enables them to get to appreciate many aspects of the organisation and it helps them to get to know senior managers. A typical project might involve the employee devising ways of saving the organisation money by proposing redundancies or by restructuring the workforce. How the employee handles people in this sensitive area will give an accurate picture of their potential to take on a very senior post later in their career.

internal and external courses

Potential managers will be sent on a wide range of courses to help them and the organisation to develop their skills and other abilities. Some courses will

give them the detailed knowledge they will need to be able to take on more responsible jobs (eg courses in law and accountancy). A type of course, which is now extremely popular, is the 'survival weekend' in which a group of managers or potential managers (sometimes from different organisations) are brought together and given tasks to perform in a hostile environment. Tasks might include building bridges across streams or rock climbing or canoeing – in most cases the aim is to get the participants to work together as a team and to develop leadership skills.

Visit www.callofthewild.co.uk

management training with Call of the Wild

studying for further qualifications

Many employers encourage able employees to study for advanced qualifications. This not only improves their knowledge for use at work, but it also demonstrates they possess the stamina to complete courses which may be two or three years long.

Activity 8.1 – training and workforce planning

Read the article below from *Personnel Today* and then answer the questions that follow.

Fast-track manager scheme fills staff shortages at Tesco

Supermarket giant Tesco has undertaken an accelerated leadership training scheme in a bid to plug skills gaps. Tesco decided to put 50 people through leadership training – which normally takes a year – in just 12 weeks.

"We needed a radical approach because of our vacancies," said Judith Nelson, Tesco's UK stores HR director. "We had to find 50 people to start the course in six weeks, and needed a robust assessment process to get the right people." Tesco assessed 200 candidates at a half-day assessment centre, and then put 47 successful applicants through a 12-week residential programme at a cost of £1.5m.

From an idea first presented at Easter, Tesco managed to have the managers in place by September.

However, Nelson said, they did make one mistake – not asking them to be mobile. Some locations now have more trained managers than stores. The danger of this, she said, is that those without stores may become bored and move to the competition.

1 Referring back to what you studied in Chapter 5 (Planning the workforce) explain what might be the causes of the shortfall in store managers.

2 What are the main problems when you shorten a one-year management training course to just 12 weeks? What training methods were used in this case and what was the cost per trainee?

3 What will Tesco look at when deciding whether the investment in this case was actually worthwhile or not?

4 What problem occurred with the scheme which might make Tesco lose some of its investment?

Performance Management: Appraisals

This section examines how and why employees are appraised (assessed). This process is welcomed both by managers and by employees so long as it is done fairly, managers are properly trained in it, and the process is fully explained to everyone concerned.

This **performance appraisal** is normally carried out by the job holder's immediate superior. The person who appraises is called the 'appraisor' and the person being appraised is the 'appraisee'. The usual procedure is:

Firstly, the appraisor writes an appraisal report of the appraisee. This can be done using different techniques:

- a blank sheet of paper – this gives the appraisor freedom to write what he or she likes
- a form with questions and spaces to complete – this makes sure that all issues are covered
- a rating form – for each heading the appraisor simply gives a mark out of, say, ten or a grade (A to E)

The best choice is probably a mixture of all three.

The essential features of an appraisal report will be as follows:

- an examination of the strengths of the employee
- an examination of the weaknesses of the employee
- the advice given to the employee in relation to future performance; this should include:
  - praise for strengths
  - helpful criticisms of the weaknesses the manager has identified
- an action plan for the next few months until the next appraisal; this will list the key objectives which the employee will be expected to have achieved by then

Secondly, the report is discussed with the appraisee at an interview. There are several options available:

- **open appraisal** – this is where the appraisee can discuss the appraisal with the manager as the interview takes place
- **two-way appraisal** – some organisations ask the appraisee to do an appraisal of himself/herself – this means that they fill in an identical form to that filled in by the appraisor – the forms are then compared and where there are clear differences there must be more discussion between them; for example, if the appraiser rates the appraisee's work effort at 5 out of 10 and the appraisee rates it at 8 out of 10 they need to discuss why there is such a big difference of opinion
- **360 degree appraisal** – this is the most modern approach – it is sometimes called 'peer appraisal'

In **360 degree appraisal** the appraisee is appraised by some of the people they deal with. Therefore, a 'middle manager' would be appraised by staff working for them, by fellow managers and by their boss. The opinions of their customers will also be collected (for example, through 'customer satisfaction surveys'). This gives an extremely thorough picture of an employee and it pinpoints strengths and weaknesses very well. Problems that might arise with this method include:

- managers do not like to hear criticism from their own staff
- employees may not be honest about their bosses

how often does one get appraised?

Appraisal normally takes place once or twice a year. In some organisations it happens every three months. The more often it is done the better.

the benefits of performance appraisal

- it helps to identify training needs
- it may reveal other problems – for example, there may be workplace difficulties with other staff (caused, for example, by sexual or racial harassment)
- it may untap useful new skills
- it improves communications between employees and managers – a few words of encouragement and praise for doing a good job are often highly motivating
- it provides disciplinary documentation – if the employer needs to dismiss somebody, the existence of thorough appraisal records which identify the person's inabilities or lack of effort will be very useful
- it helps to fix pay rises – increasingly, people get performance related pay which is based upon the appraisal

Performance and Pay

Every year or every six months managers should interview their staff and review their pay. This gives managers a chance to reward employees and to thank them for doing a good job.

Reviews are often associated with the system of **performance related pay**. This means that managers must examine the individual's performance by reference to performance benchmarks (ie what the typical employee can be expected to achieve). This will enable them to see how far above or below that benchmark an employee is performing. This then determines what pay rise the individual will get.

Some organisations will only give a rise in the individual review for above average performance. Other organisations will give all staff except the poorest performers something in their individual review. This is for morale reasons – after all, even those who are only 'adequate' are still making a positive contribution to the organisation.

There is often a problem with managers who try to be kind to everyone so that poor performers get very little less than good ones. This is because the manager sees the employee every day and may not want to create bad feelings that would damage their working relationship.

It is important to note that in many organisations Trade Unions negotiate a pay deal with the employer. In such cases the pay deal agreed will apply to all employees, except for senior managers. In these organisations individual pay reviews will only apply to senior managers.

Employee Retention

Employee retention – stopping employees leaving – is vitally important for an organisation, particularly when unemployment is at a comparatively low level and it is a lot easier for people to leave workplaces in which they are not very happy. High staff turnover means:

- higher recruitment and selection costs and higher costs of induction of new staff
- work quality suffers
- training costs are wasted because employees often leave soon after they have been trained
- the employer gets a bad image locally. Jobseekers will ask themselves, 'What is wrong with this organisation if people are leaving so quickly?'

The *Personnel Today* article in the Activity below shows how good management can help to reduce staff turnover, thus reducing many of the above problems. Good managers will try to make sure that:

■ the pay and overall reward package is good

■ there is a wide variety of work arrangements to suit as many jobseekers as possible, eg hours to suit 'working mums' or weekend shifts to suit university students

■ attention is paid to what really motivates employees

Activity 8.2 – the effects of poor management

Poor management causing underperformance of staff

Ineffective managers are fuelling high staff turnover and causing widespread employee under-performance, a new survey claims. The survey by HR consultancy Cubiks shows that 60 per cent of the 450 survey respondents said they had been forced to leave a company or a role specifically because of the actions of their manager.

Barry Spence, chief executive of Cubiks, said poor managers can wreak havoc in organisations, causing problems that extend way beyond their own personal sphere of influence.

"This survey demonstrates that when people are asked to assume full managerial responsibilities without receiving the appropriate development or training, they can have a major negative impact on individual motivation levels, team morale and, ultimately, the bottom line," he said.

When asked to identify the factors that separated the most effective line managers from others, respondents listed honesty, loyalty, and the ability to both give and receive personal feedback consistently as the most positive managerial traits.

Nelson Mandela was identified as the best managerial role model from public life for his ability to inspire people to work towards a common goal. Other leading figures named by respondents included Richard Branson, Bill Clinton, Jack Welch, Gandhi and Winston Churchill.

Assume that you are in employment. Read the article above and answer the following questions:

1 Make a list of the sort of things your manager might do which would encourage you to look for another job.

2 What do employees look for in a good manager? What do you look for?

3 What common features do you think the role models listed here have in common – Gandhi, Richard Branson, Nelson Mandela, Churchill?

the Law and Employee Performance

A number of laws have been introduced in the UK to protect the rights of employees to receive a fair wage and reasonable working hours. Some of these derive from European Union Directives which influence new legislation in the UK (see the next page for further details).

the arguments for new legislation – employees and employers

There is an ongoing debate between those who support this legislation and those who do not. Those who support it include the Work Foundation (a not-for-profit public company which exists to improve workplace performance through improving the quality of working life) and the Trade Unions. They argue that the rights offered to employees in the UK are still fairly poor compared to countries like Germany and France. UK employees also work longer hours than employees in some EU countries. Better rights make employees more effective and more productive.

By contrast, employer-led groups such as the Confederation of British Industry and the Institute of Directors argue that new laws add to costs and make it very hard for UK businesses to compete against overseas producers.

Activity 8.3 – UK and overseas working conditions

Take a good look at the clothing you have bought in the past year or so. Check the labels and find out what proportion are made in the UK. You may be very surprised how low it is.

Then have a look round your house at the electrical goods, the kitchen equipment, the washing machine, cameras, mobile phones – the list is endless – and you will probably get very similar results.

1 Give reasons why so many products are sourced from overseas producers.

2 Explain how this trend affects workers in the UK.

3 Describe what effect it would have on UK workers and your own financial position if the government insisted on a certain percentage of clothing being manufactured in the UK.

Employee Rights and the Law

In this section we explain the legal framework which exists to protect the rights of employees working in the UK.

the working time directive

This sets limits on the hours an employee can be asked to work. It prevents people from working for too long and suffering from stress – and it helps to promote safety. It affects, for example, drivers and pilots. Note, however, that it is possible for workers to **opt out** if they want to. The main provisions are:

- a limit of an average of 48 hours a week which a worker can be required to work (though workers can choose to work more if they opt out).
- a limit of an average of 8 hours' work in 24 which nightworkers can be required to work and the right for nightworkers to receive free health assessments.
- a right to 11 hours' rest a day
- a right to a day off each week
- a right to an in-work rest break if the working day is longer than 6 hours
- a right to 4 weeks' paid leave per year

the minimum wage

The government sets a minimum hourly pay rate known as the National Minimum Wage. The projected rates from October 2005 are:

- workers aged 22 and over   £5.05
- workers aged 18 to 21   £4.25
- workers aged 16 to 17   £3.00

These rates are regularly reviewed. Visit www.dti.gov.uk/er/nmw for further information.

maternity and paternity leave

Mothers of young children have traditionally been able to take **maternity leave**, both while pregnant and also after the birth, and receive state benefit.

A more recent development is **paternity leave**. All new fathers now have the right to claim two weeks' time off work following the birth of their baby. However, the 2005/06 rate of payment is only £106 per week, ie far below what most people earn today, and many fathers cannot afford to lose this much money, even for two weeks. Research has shown that if fathers got their full pay, 87% would take the two weeks off; at £106 only 46% would be prepared to stay at home.

Health & Safety regulations

The Health & Safety at Work Act 1974 states that an employer must have a 'written statement' of its Health & Safety policy. This must be available for all staff to read – a good employer will give personal copies of it to all new staff when they have their induction. What will be in this statement?

- an explanation of how all accidents must be reported by staff
- a list of all staff trained in first aid and details of where first aid boxes are located
- a list of all Safety Representatives – their job is to ensure that the employer is carrying out safety policies properly and they are required to carry out full three-monthly safety checks
- the name of a senior manager responsible for Health & Safety policies

As well as the 1974 Act more recent legislation has brought in further protection for employees. For example, the COSHH regulations (1988). This stands for 'Control Of Substances Hazardous to Health'. They lay down very strict rules on how dangerous chemicals are to be handled, stored and recorded. In 1992 a number of new regulations were introduced by the European Union, including:

- The Health & Safety (Display Screen Equipment) Regulations introduced tight controls on the use of visual display units on word-processors and computers. This was due to the problems they were known to cause (particularly eyesight problems). The regulations now require free eye tests for all 'habitual regular users' of VDUs.

- Repetitive strain injury (RSI) is now covered by the Workplace (Health, Safety and Welfare) Regulations. This also requires workplaces to be properly lit and ventilated.

the dangers of using a VDU

Activity 8.4 – legal protection of working conditions

1 What are the two main benefits of the working time directive?

2 You are running a small business such as a local shop. Identify two arguments for having to pay the minimum wage and two arguments for not paying it.

3 Explain why the new paternity leave arrangements may be unattractive to new fathers. Why should 13% of new fathers not want to stay at home even on full pay?

4 You are employed to input data on a computer for most of the working day. You start to get bad headaches, eyestrain and aching wrists. What regulations exist to protect you in this situation?

flexible working arrangements

Any employee who works for more than six months for the same employer now has the right to ask to work 'flexibly' (Flexible Working Regulations 2002).

For instance, if parents have a problem getting in to work for 9.00, because of taking children to school, they could ask for a 9.30 start instead. Such a request has to be seriously considered by the boss and it can still be turned down on 'business grounds'. It could be quite difficult for an employer to reject such a request from an office worker but for a teacher or a factory worker, where attendance at specific times is usually an essential part of the job, it would be much easier to turn it down.

part-time employee rights

Part-time workers must now be treated in the same way as full timers (Part-time Workers Regulations 2000 – see www.dti.gov.uk/er/ptime). This means they should get:

- the same rates of pay
- the same rights to pensions
- the same training and development opportunities
- the same holidays (on a pro rata basis – if a full-timer working five days a week gets 30 days' holiday, a part-timer working two days per week will get 2/5ths of 30 days, ie 12 days)

disabled employees' rights

The introduction of the Disability Discrimination Act has given disabled people the same rights as other employees. Employers must make reasonable adjustments to help disabled employees. These might include:

- altering premises, for example fitting a ramp or a lift for wheelchair users
- installing special equipment such as special reading equipment for partially sighted staff
- reallocation of duties, for example allocating tasks to a disabled person in a ground-floor office rather than upstairs
- alteration of working hours to suit disabled employees – for example an employee who has to have kidney dialysis for several hours per week at the local hospital

By contrast, it would not be unreasonable for an employer to refuse to fit a lift for a wheelchair user who was only working for the business on a six-month contract. What the employer would be expected to do is rearrange duties so that the disabled person can work on the ground floor.

Activity 8.5 – employer and employee rights

What are the rights of the employee and the employer in the following situations?

1   Sasha, a working mother who has a three year-old child at a local nursery, asks her boss if she can come into work at 9.15. What difference does it make if she is:

   (a)   a telesales operator in an office which employs people on a shiftwork basis?

   (b)   a business studies teacher?

2   Sophie is employed as a part-time assistant in an insurance broker's office. During the induction training she is told that:

   (a)   she will be paid £6.50 an hour, but if she goes full-time she will get £7 per hour

   (b)   as a part-time employee she is not entitled to a pension from the employer

3   Andy is disabled and confined to a wheelchair. He is also a qualified accountant and gets a job with Fiddlit and Fujitt, a firm of accountants. He is first asked to work in the taxation department, but finds that it is on the first floor and there is no lift. What difference does it make to the situation if:

   (a)   the job is permanent?

   (b)   Andy is only on a three month contract?

Motivation Theories

Frederick Taylor and scientific management

Taylor (1856-1915) worked as a factory superintendent in a locomotive axle factory in the USA. From his studies of how people worked making axles he concluded that:

Employees got jobs there because they were friends or relatives of the managers, not because they were any good at the job.

Employees did not work hard because they thought it would throw some of their friends out of work.

Employers paid employees as little as they could get away with.

Employees got very few instructions on how to do their jobs so they did them badly. The amount produced and the quality of output was often poor.

Taylor said that the following ideas would improve matters:

■   only money would motivate employees to work hard – therefore they should be paid on a piecework system, ie each item made would earn them a certain amount of money – this would encourage hard work

- properly trained managers should run organisations and supervise employees effectively with firm but fair disciplinary methods
- employees must be properly trained, through what he called 'scientific management', to do specific tasks efficiently – this was the beginning of what we today call Organisations and Methods Study or Work Study
- employees should be properly selected through tests and interviews to make sure they are right for the job; Taylor was one of the first people to see the need to do this
- employees, if motivated by good pay, would work efficiently without questioning what they were required to do

Many organisations still operate Taylorism, even in rich countries, but there has long been a recognition that employees want more from their jobs than job security and good pay. Other writers have developed more complex theories about what motivates people at work.

Abraham Maslow and the 'hierarchy of needs'

Abraham Maslow (1908-1970) said that all motivation comes from meeting unsatisfied needs. He stated that there was a ranking of needs which must be achieved in the correct order – from the bottom to the top of a 'pyramid' (see diagram below). Basic physiological needs (eg food, water) are at the bottom and self-actualisation is at the top.

the need . . .	which is achieved by . . .
self-actualisation	personal growth and self fulfilment
Esteem	Recognition
	Achievement
	Status
Social needs	Affection/love/friendship
Safety needs	Security
	Freedom from pain and threats
Physiological needs	Food, water, air, rest, sex

Once one need is satisfied it ceases to motivate and the next higher need 'up the pyramid' comes into play. This implies that higher level needs have more value than the ones at the bottom.

Only an unsatisfied need can motivate behaviour, and the dominant need is the prime motivator of behaviour.

From a manager's viewpoint, Maslow is saying that:

- employees need to be paid adequately so they can at least provide their basic physiological and safety needs (paying for food, mortgages, life insurance)

- employees need social contact through friendship with colleagues; working in teams helps to encourage social contact

- esteem can be provided where an organisation offers prospects of promotion; at the very least there should be an opportunity for employees to show that they are capable and they are winning the respect of other employees; organisations can raise employees' esteem by giving higher managers better cars, smarter offices and more generous pensions

- self-actualisation is far harder to achieve – it really means that an employee has the chance to become everything he/she ever wanted to become – for example, the employee might always have dreamt of becoming 'the boss' of the company he/she has worked for all his/her life

Two significant problems arise here:

Firstly, an employer simply cannot offer such opportunities to all employees. That would be unrealistic.

Secondly, writers like Maslow and Herzberg (see below) seemed to think that everybody is self-actualised by work. This is not true – many people are self-actualised by aspects of their private lives (bringing up their children, for example) and work is just a means to pay the bills.

Douglas McGregor and theories X and Y

McGregor (1906-64) said that many managers made sweeping generalisations about the people who worked for them. They would either put all their employees into a theory X category or a theory Y category. They would then manage their organisation using a theory X or a theory Y management style.

theory X

This states that all employees are lazy, unambitious and dislike extra responsibilities. They will always resist change of any kind and are totally uninterested in the future success or otherwise of their employer. They are not interested in how the organisation works and just prefer to be told what to do.

theory Y

This is just the opposite. Employees are interested in their work and want to be asked for their opinions on how to improve things. They want to be given more responsibility and will naturally work hard without having to be told what to do all the time. They are also prepared to accept change because they understand it is in everyone's best interests to move with the times.

The manager who takes a theory X attitude about their employees will need to supervise them very closely and introduce methods to control their behaviour (eg tight controls on absenteeism and lateness). There will be a lot

DOUGLAS MCGREGOR AND THEORIES X AND Y

'X' OR 'Y'?

of very specific rules and regulations with serious consequences for employees who break them. Frequent inspections of work will be needed to ensure that output is of adequate quality.

Naturally, there will be no attempt to get employee views on how to improve the running of the organisation.

A theory Y manager can be very positive about his or her employees. He/she can leave them to do their jobs virtually unsupervised (which also saves a lot of money) and can rest assured that the work will all be well done. Again this saves money because quality inspections will not be needed very much. It will be easy to find people who are willing to work over their normal hours, and often for no extra money. They will also be happy to take on more responsibilities because they hope it will improve their long-term career prospects. Because absence and lateness will be unusual, costly supervision will not be needed.

McGregor's ideas have meant that to this day people will still describe an organisation as 'theory X' or 'theory Y'. The trouble is that no organisation is completely full of theory X people nor of theory Y people.

This means that in theory X organisations many good employees are handled in a way that they do not really deserve and in theory Y organisations many people are getting away with things that they should not. Even inside the same organisation there are theory Y departments where good employees resent the fact that other colleagues can get away with doing very little. By contrast, in a theory X department good employees will often leave if they are constantly supervised and not trusted by their managers.

Frederick Herzberg and the Two Factor theory

In 1957 Herzberg (born 1923) devised his 'motivation-hygiene' theory which stated that two groups of factors affect employee motivation.

Herzberg said that certain elements in a job motivate people to work harder. He called these elements **satisfiers**. They include:

achievement, recognition, responsibility, advancement and personal growth . . . and the actual work itself

Other elements do not motivate people to work harder. These are called **hygiene factors**. They include:

pay and conditions, status in the organisation, job security, benefits (pensions, company cars etc), relationships with fellow employees, the quality of the organisation's managers

Herzberg's key point was that hygiene factors do not motivate but if they are not very good then the satisfiers will not motivate either. A simple example will explain this. Even if a job is interesting and gives people a substantial sense of achievement, it will not motivate them properly if they are not earning enough money to live in a reasonable house and cannot feed themselves and their families properly.

Activity 8.6 – motivation theories

Design, in groups, a short questionnaire to assess what factors motivate employees.

Write eight questions, based on the writings of the four theorists Taylor, Maslow, McGregor and Herzberg (ie two questions for each writer). Ask your tutor to discuss the questions with you.

Try the questionnaire out at work if you have a part-time job, or at a work placement, or with friends and family.

IMPORTANT – you MUST get the permission of the management of any workplace you work in or visit before carrying out the questionnaire.

When you have got the answers to your questionnaire, analyse and write up your findings, making reference to the theories of the four writers in your analysis.

Here are some suggestions for the type of questions you might ask:

"What factor do you consider to be more important in your working life, (a) or (b)?"

(a)	the level of pay	(b)	the job itself	(Taylor)
(a)	good working conditions	(b)	recognition for what you do	(Maslow)
(a)	lack of responsibility	(b)	having an input into what you do	(McGregor)
(a)	job security	(b)	promotion prospects	(Herzberg)

Activity 8.7 – training and workforce planning

Read the two articles from *Personnel Today* then answer the questions that follow.

Big Brother is watching you

UK office workers face the threat of increasing control, monitoring and surveillance, according to findings of a long-term study. The report – The Future Role of Trust in Work – is based on a year-long study by the LSE and Microsoft. It argues that outdated command and control management culture is causing managers to misuse technology, over-scrutinising worker performance. This means staff are reacting to communication from employers rather than interacting with customers – ultimately damaging UK productivity. Carsten Sorensen, from the LSE, said that UK business needed to find new ways of managing people in the face of changing technologies at work.

Asda helps staff to create healthy minds

Employees of supermarket chain Asda are on their way to becoming one of the fittest workforces in the country.

Asda's belief in the saying that a healthy body creates a healthy mind has led to the company adopting a new approach to keeping its staff productive. For just £1 a week, workers at Asda's Chepstow distribution centre are using a new gym, equipped with the latest in cardiovascular and resistance technology. And there's no excuse for not exercising due to awkward shift patterns, as the gym is open 24 hours a day, seven days a week.

Almost 1,000 people working at the New House Farm industrial estate base will also have the chance to check how their fitness is developing. Asda has taken on employee well-being company BodyCheck to give staff an induction in using the machines, with the option to have their individual health and fitness needs assessed and progress monitored.

"We listened to what our colleagues have to say, and this is about providing a service they requested," said people manager Sue Brewerton.

1 Describe the main management problem outlined in the 'Big Brother' article. What is management doing and how is it affecting the workforce?

2 What external damage to the operations of a business can be caused by the 'Big Brother' approach?

3 In what way can the Asda fitness scheme improve the efficiency of their Chepstow distribution centre?

4 Where did the idea for the fitness scheme originate? What does this say about the way in which Asda treats its employees?

CHAPTER SUMMARY

■ Development of employees is essential if an organisation is to retain those employees and remain competitive.

■ Employers need to develop employees who have potential. Methods include job rotation, job enlargement and job enrichment.

■ A number of different methods can be used to train and develop employees including understudying, 'acting up', mentoring, coaching, internal and external courses and open learning.

■ Appraisals should be used on a regular basis to assess employee performance and to encourage employees to work more effectively. They can take the form of an open appraisal, a two-way appraisal and a 360 degree appraisal.

■ Employee performance should be reviewed on a regular basis and linked to levels of pay of the employee.

■ Employee retention is important in maintaining the image, quality and profitability of an organisation.

■ Employment law has an important part to play in maintaining the rights of employees and ensuring a fair working environment; this law can, however, reduce the profitability and competitiveness of businesses.

■ This legal framework includes regulation of:
  - hours worked, flexibility of hours and pay rates
  - maternity and paternity leave
  - Health & Safety at Work.

■ Employment law also protects the rights of part-time and disabled workers.

■ Employers need to understand the relationship between the main motivation theories and the way in which they manage their own organisations. The main theories include:

  - Frederick Taylor and scientific management

  - Abraham Maslow and the 'hierarchy of needs'

  - Douglas McGregor and theories X and Y

  - Frederick Herzberg and the Two Factor theory

KEY TERMS

training	the acquisition of knowledge and skills in order to do a job properly
development	providing opportunities for employees to widen and deepen their skills and knowledge so that they are more motivated and of more use to the organisation
acting up	a promising employee receiving a temporary promotion which may become permanent if the employee does well in the post
mentoring	where a more senior employee provides advice and counselling to junior staff on their development inside the organisation
coaching	where a member of staff receives specialist training in particular aspects of his/her job
appraisal	the regular assessment of an employee's progress by that employee's manager
360 degree appraisal	where a number of people appraise an employee to provide a fuller picture of the employee's progress
scientific management	Taylor's definition for the accurate measurement of the main elements of a job so that the employee can then be trained to do it efficiently
hierarchy of needs	Maslow described this as a pyramid of needs which motivate employees throughout their working lives
theory X and Y	McGregor said that all workplaces fell under one or other of these two headings – theory X means that employees are lazy and must be forced to work hard; theory Y takes a more positive view and assumes that employees will naturally work hard and are highly motivated
the Two Factor theory	Herzberg argued that certain factors called 'satisfiers' motivate people to work hard whereas others called 'hygiene' factors create the basic environment in which they work

9

External influences on the workplace

Starting point

Take a typical day in the life of an employee of a local business – there will be many situations in which actions taken are affected by outside influences rather than by the individual decisions of managers. Some may seem relatively unimportant, some are very significant. For example:

- making sure all the lights are turned off at the end of the day in order to save energy
- suggesting that all the old, obsolete computers are collected by a recycling company
- going to a meeting to discuss whether the business will open on a Sunday
- passing on a circular from the Trade Union encouraging employees to take industrial action next week

What you will learn from this chapter

- managers and employees are affected not only by internal issues such as working conditions and motivation but also by external issues over which they have no control
- these external issues include:
  - environmental pressures such as energy saving and recycling
  - social and ethical issues such as animal testing
  - external regulations affecting issues such as consumer protection, Trade Union membership, Health & Safety at Work

Environmental Issues

People working in business are affected on a day-to-day basis by issues relating to the need to protect the environment. We saw in Chapter 2 (page 22) that one of the aspects of corporate responsibility is **sustainability**. This involves adopting a number of objectives such as reducing pollution, reducing wastage of materials, encouraging recycling of materials and using energy efficiently.

reducing pollution

Pollution involves producing harmful and unpleasant emissions such as smoke, fumes, oil and chemical spillages, raw sewage, noise and vibrations which adversely affect the environment and the people in it.

Clearly, some businesses run more risk of polluting the environment than others – abattoirs and chemical works, for example. Other less obvious polluters include restaurants (smelly dustbins) and night clubs (noise).

STOP PRESS: On 5th November...remember the environment

Businesses which carry out processes such as incineration, metal manufacture, printing, asbestos handling, and treatment of animal and vegetable matter are required to obtain permission to operate under Integrated Pollution Control (IPC) or Pollution Prevention and Control (PPC) Regulations. Owners and managers of any business that needs to control pollution in any form will obviously have to be mindful of the appropriate regulations and communicate them to employees. Employees in turn will need to comply with instructions given – eg burning materials in the yard, dumping chemicals down the sink, operating noisy machinery at unsociable times. Visit www.environment-agency.gov.uk for general information about pollution and www.environment-agency.gov.uk/netregs for information about pollution regulations.

waste and recycling

Waste is anything that you throw away, intend to throw away or are required to throw away. People working in business need to be aware of what they do with what is thought of as 'rubbish'. This includes:

- ordinary rubbish that has no further use
- items which can be recycled – eg paper, drinks cans, plastic bottles
- items which are hazardous and have to be disposed of, eg paint stripper, lead-acid batteries, fluorescent tubes, medicines and pills – these are covered under the Hazardous Waste Regulations

A responsible business should therefore introduce a **waste-management policy** which will:

- minimise waste
- reuse or recycle waste where possible
- dispose of hazardous waste
- train staff in the skills of waste disposal

One regulation which affects most businesses is **WEEE**. This stands for the **W**aste **E**lectrical and **E**lectronic **E**quipment regulations which require makers and users of electrical and electronic goods such as computers to dispose of unwanted equipment safely. Dell Computers, for example, will arrange to pick up its old computers for recycling free of charge.

Dell Recycling

Commitment to Customers, Commitment to the Environment
As personal computers have become common in most homes, there is a growing concern about the environmental impact of old computers, computer parts and other electronic products. When you are ready to dispose of your old PC and computer-related devices, Dell is here to help.

www.dell.co.uk

For further information about waste and recycling visit the websites illustrated below.

welcome

Welcome to recycle-more.co.uk, the one-stop recycling information centre. You will find help and advice on all aspects of recycling at home, at school and in the workplace right here! Simply click on the links below to explore the site or try our brand new search facility.

PLEASE RECYCLE

| homepage | bank locator | household | schools | business | local authority | resources | media centre | partners | recycling specifics |

site search — Search >>

recycling near you! UK postcode — Search >>
Just type your postcode into the above form and find out where you can recycle your waste!

www.recycle-more.co.uk

Waste minimisation

Cutting waste can be a really effective way to increase your profits, and you'll be benefiting the environment at the same time. You've made it this far: showing you're interested in taking this further. Congratulations — it's a sound business idea.

- But where do you start?
- What are the practical steps to take?
- How can you make this work?
- Where can you get support and further information?

www.envirowise.gov.uk

energy saving

A further aspect of sustainability is the saving of energy. A reduction in the use of any form of energy will not only reduce damage to the atmosphere from the burning of fossil fuels, it will also help business profitability by reducing running costs. Examples of energy saving by businesses include:

- turning off lights and electrical equipment where possible
- using energy-efficient light bulbs
- keeping heating to sensible levels
- using company cars with low emissions and low fuel consumption

Saving Energy

Quick Navigation

Tips for saving electricity - Lighting

- Encourage staff to turn off lights when leaving a room
- Label light switches so that staff can choose only the light that relates to their area
- Make sure lights are switched off at the end of the day and when premises are not occupied
- Make most use of natural light - its free and most people prefer it!
- Clean your light fittings each year to ensure maximum efficiency

www.nie.co.uk

Read the energy-saving tips from the NIE web page shown on the left.

Activity 9.1 – environmental issues at work

People working in business may be affected by environmental issues in a number of different ways:

- pollution of the environment
- dealing with waste
- recycling
- energy saving

The extent to which these issues affect employees will depend on the nature of the business and also the nature of the work carried out by the employee.

Describe the environmental issues which could affect employees working in the following situations and suggest ways in which they could help to protect the environment.

1 a butcher's shop

2 a travel agent's office

3 a taxi firm

4 a company that sells and maintains office computers

5 a night club

6 a school or college classroom or IT centre

Social and Ethical Issues

People working in business are also affected to a greater or lesser extent by **social** and **ethical** issues. These are brought about external pressures such as the demands of stakeholders (eg the 'community'), pressure groups and required codes of practice.

social issues – helping the community

Businesses which have a well-developed sense of corporate responsibility will set objectives for helping the local and wider communities. They may, for example, help to arrange sponsorship of a local school sports event, or they may sponsor a student to work on an educational project in Tanzania in a 'gap year'. Clearly, decisions to support these types of project will be taken at managerial level, but the idea could well be introduced by less senior employees who know about the need of the local school or schemes to help the Tanzanian educational system.

ethical issues – pressure groups

'Ethical' issues are those that involve a moral judgement, deciding whether a course of action is morally right or morally wrong. For example, some would say that it is morally wrong for a business such as a football club to accept sponsorship from a tobacco company or for a pharmaceutical manufacturer to sell drugs developed using animal testing. These two examples are likely to be highlighted by the campaigning of pressure groups, eg the anti-smoking ASH and the anti-animal testing BUAV. Intentionally shocking and distressing images from their websites are shown below.

IMAGES FROM PRESSURE GROUPS

Founded in 1898, the British Union for the Abolition of Vivisection (BUAV) is the world's leading anti-vivisection campaigning organisation. The BUAV is dedicated to using all peaceful means possible to end animal experiments, both nationally and internationally. The BUAV opposes all animal experiments on both ethical and scientific grounds and our campaigns cover issues such as cosmetics, household products, pet food, medical research, EU chemicals & genetic engineering. We are Chair of the European Coalition to End Animal Experiments and a founder member of the International Council for Animal Protection in OECD Programmes.

An animal dies in an EU lab every 3 seconds

anti-smoking (www.ash.org.uk)   abolition of vivisection (www.buav.org)

As far as employees of a business are concerned, ethical policy making and decisions will normally be taken at senior management level, but it has been known for employees to 'whistle blow' (ie tell the press) in the case of bad practice, or for journalists to infiltrate the offending business.

codes of practice – industry standards

Codes of practice are sets of externally set rules, normally laid down by different areas of industry, which dictate the way in which a business operates. They set standards for the carrying out of work by that business.

Industry-specific standards are set down, for example, to cover the safety and environmental requirements and best practice for businesses that deal with:

- agriculture, mining and quarrying, deep-sea fishing
- chemicals and explosives
- radioactive materials

So, if you work as a manager or employee in a fireworks factory, you will be bound by the appropriate external code of practice covering explosives. This will cover issues such as manufacture, storage, packaging, transport and security.

codes of practice – advertising standards

If you work in the marketing function of a business and are involved in the placing of adverts in newspapers, magazines, posters, the internet, TV and radio, you will be bound by the Committee of Advertising Practice Code (CAP Code) administered by the Advertising Standards Authority (www.asab.org.uk). This should ensure that your advert is legal and is not:

- socially irresponsible
- unreasonably offensive or distressing
- showing unsafe or anti-social behaviour
- encouraging people to break the law

You will no doubt be able to think of TV adverts or posters which stray near the limits of these requirements!

Activity 9.2 – social and ethical issues

1 Your school/college has been approached by a tobacco company with an offer to sponsor a student for a three-year sports management degree course. What social and ethical issues would be raised by this offer and how do you think the school/college should respond, and why?

2 Study the TV (or any other) adverts over the space of a couple of days and make a note of instances where they might break any of the four requirements of the CAP Code listed on this page. If you felt strongly enough about the advert, to whom could you complain?

Legal Influences

People working in business are affected on a day-to-day basis by a wide variety of legal requirements. These include simple matters such as complying with Health & Safety regulations – stocking up the first-aid box, for example – to more complex issues such as dealing with customer queries about faulty goods and refunds.

1.—(1) In section 14 of the [1979 c. 54.] Sale of Goods Act 1979 (implied terms about quality or fitness) for subsection (2) there is substituted—

(2) Where the seller sells goods in the course of a business, there is an implied term that the goods supplied under the contract are of satisfactory quality.

(2A) For the purposes of this Act, goods are of satisfactory quality if they meet the standard that a reasonable person would regard as satisfactory, taking account of any description of the goods, the price (if relevant) and all the other relevant circumstances.

(2B) For the purposes of this Act, the quality of goods includes their state and condition and the following (among others) are in appropriate cases aspects of the quality of goods –
(a) fitness for all the purposes for which goods of the kind in question are commonly supplied,
(b) appearance and finish,
(c) freedom from minor defects,

grappling with the small print of the law

external and internal regulations

Sometimes the regulations are formally set out in law – the Sale of Goods Act, for example – and sometimes the law requires that the regulations are set down by the business itself, as in the case of the Health & Safety at Work Act which requires that businesses draw up an internal Health & Safety manual (guide) for its employees.

the role of managers and employees

Business owners and managers should clearly have a firm grasp of all the complexities of the various laws which affect the way in which the business operates, even if they complain of the increasing burden of 'red tape'. Employees, on the other hand, should be aware from their training of the way in which laws and regulations affect them, but they would not be expected to quote the law itself!

what you need to know

You will not be expected to know all there is to know about business law for your investigation – it is material for a book in its own right, and relevant aspects of law are covered elsewhere in this text. This section will, however, outline some of the main areas which will help direct you in identifying external legal and regulatory influences in the types of business you are studying.

The main areas we will deal with are:

- competition law – price fixing
- consumer protection – the rights of consumers buying goods and services
- the influence of Trade Unions in the workplace
- employment protection law
- Health & Safety

competition law

The law aims to promote free and healthy competition between businesses. How would consumers react if it was revealed that certain products were overpriced because the producers had got together and between them 'fixed' the prices at an artificially high level. Suppose that the airlines, instead of aggressively cutting air fares as part of healthy competition, decided to fix prices at a high level. This would constitute an anti-competitive agreement.

London-Paris
only £150 return!

Special Offer!
London-Paris £150 return!

Cheapest deal in town!
London-Paris
£150 weekend special
fare

price fixing – a consumer 'rip-off'?

The **Competition Act** makes it unlawful for businesses to make anti-competitive agreements between themselves, for example:

- fixing prices and price rises
- sharing out the market with competitors (each agreeing to deal with certain groups of customers)
- taking advantage of a dominant market position (a taxi firm charging high prices because it is by far the largest taxi firm in town)

The **Enterprise Act** can prevent mergers between two businesses which both have a major market share. For example, if two major UK supermarkets or two banks wanted to merge, they may be prevented from doing so because they would then totally dominate the market and prevent free competition because they have formed a monopoly.

Because of the level of seniority within a business at which prices are fixed and negotiations with competitors carried out, competition law is most likely to affect owners and managers rather than their more junior employees.

consumer protection law

People in businesses which sell goods or services – whether they are managers or assistants – deal with consumers and inevitably have to cope with complaints from people who are not happy with what they buy.

Customer service employees – at all levels – must be trained to have a sound knowledge of what is required by consumer protection laws.

The **Sale of Goods Act**, for example, requires that goods are of 'satisfactory quality', 'fit for the purpose' and free from defects. Employees will not have to quote the Act (see previous page!) or even know its name, but they will have to know what to do and say when a customer brings in faulty goods and complains about them.

Services are covered under the **Supply of Goods and Services Act** and must be carried out with reasonable skill and care and at a reasonable price. 'Reasonable' here means the way in which another supplier would be expected to provide the same service. Businesses which provide a service are also likely to have well-trained customer services staff.

Trade Unions

A **Trade Union** is an independent organisation that represents the interests of employees. In a business where Trade Union membership is at a significant level, the influence of the Trade Union on employees is strong. It can provide support in the case of management/employee disputes, representing employees at hearings and tribunals. The Trade Unions are most commonly seen in the public eye and are most influential in the workplace when they call for industrial action.

employment protection

The interests of employees are primarily protected by employment law, for example the **Sex Discrimination Act**, the **Disability Discrimination Act** and the **Race Relations Act**, which protect employees being discriminated against on the grounds of gender, disability and race. Employees who are Trade Union members will expect support in cases where these laws are apparently being broken.

People working in business – whether managers or junior employees – are therefore very much influenced by external legal regulations in their everyday behaviour towards their colleagues. The whole issue of discrimination can become a legal minefield!

Health & Safety at Work

The principal law covering this area is the **Health & Safety at Work Act**, which states that an employer must provide a healthy and safe workplace for its employees, including, for example:

- safe equipment and machinery and systems of work
- training to ensure that staff work safely
- a Health & Safety poster prominently displayed (see extract above) which explains employer responsibilities
- a system of recording accidents in an 'accident book'
- a 'written statement' of the Health & Safety policy of the business

This 'written statement' must be circulated regularly to staff and given to all new employees to read as part of induction training.

Note that the obligations laid down by the Health & Safety at Work Act do not just apply to management – every employee has a duty to keep the workplace healthy and safe. For example, filing drawers should not be left open and banana skins should not be left on the floor.

The law also influences the way in which computer equipment is operated: the **Health & Safety (Display Screen Equipment) Regulations** exercise tight controls over the use of visual display units on word-processors and computers, to help prevent headaches, eye-strain and related symptoms.

screens can damage your health

Activity 9.3 – legal influences on employers

1 There are two home-delivery pizza businesses in your town, each employing between five and ten people. You work for one of them. After a period of cut-throat competition during which prices have been slashed, your employer calls a meeting of employees and suggests that your business approaches the competitor with two suggestions that would help profitability:

■ the two businesses should decide on a fixed (higher) price for their pizzas

■ the two businesses should concentrate on certain areas of the town

What would be your response to these suggestions?

2 You work on the customer services counter of a major DIY store in your area. A colleague of yours loses her cool one day after a customer has returned a plant which he claimed was going brown and dying. You have given a refund. 'What else does he expect - he probably didn't water it!' What would be your response?

3 You work in an office in which the line manager constantly makes remarks about women members of staff such as 'I hope her work is better than her parking'. Other employees also remark that men get quicker promotion than women. What can you do about a situation like this?

4 You get a new job in telesales. This involves sitting in front of a computer screen most of the day and using a headset telephone. After a week or two, you get bad headaches and your back aches. Your colleagues say, "Don't worry, it happens to everyone here. You'll get used to it.' Would you accept this advice? If not, why not?

CHAPTER SUMMARY

■ People working in business are affected in a variety of ways by external pressures from stakeholders and pressure groups campaigning for the protection and conservation of the environment.

■ This need for supporting sustainability is an important objective and part of the corporate responsibility of a business.

■ The reduction of pollution is a legal requirement of certain types of business and is controlled under pollution regulations. Employees too have a responsibility not to create harmful emissions.

■ Businesses are also controlled in the type and amount of waste that they produce (Hazardous Waste Regulations). Recycling is the answer to some areas of waste disposal. This extends to computers and other electrical equipment under the WEEE regulations.

■ Energy saving is also an important aspect of sustainability. People working in business can take personal responsibility for efficient use of electricity and other forms of energy.

■ People working in business are also affected by social and ethical issues. Social issues relate to helping the local and wider community (eg by sponsorship) and ethical issues relate to dealing with situations where there is a moral choice between courses of action (eg avoiding sponsorship by tobacco companies).

■ People working in business are also governed by codes of practice which regulate the way in which a business operates. These can either relate to specific industries (eg safety requirements for firework factories) or affect the way a business advertises its products in order to avoid offending the public.

■ The operation of businesses and their employees is regulated by legal requirements – either by Acts of Parliament or through internal regulations required by law.

■ Competition law prevents businesses from price fixing and unfairly exploiting a dominant market position by merging with other market leaders to achieve a monopoly. This law mainly affects the owners and managers of businesses.

■ Consumer protection law is an important constraint on all levels of employees in a business and particularly on the customer services function.

■ Business employees are affected by external pressures in the form of employment law and the operation of the Trade Unions.

■ Employees at all levels are also affected by Health & Safety legislation which requires the organisation to regulate and maintain conditions in the workplace.

KEY TERMS

sustainability	a series of objectives which help preserve the environment
pollution	production of harmful emissions into the environment – including gases, liquid spillages, noise and vibrations
waste	anything thrown away, intended for disposal or required to be thrown away
WEEE	the Waste Electrical and Electronic Equipment regulations which require the safe disposal of old equipment by businesses
social issue	an issue which involves a business helping the local or wider community
ethical issue	an issue which involves a business taking a moral stance on the way it carries out its operations
pressure group	an external group (stakeholder) which exerts pressure on businesses to act in a morally responsible way
code of practice	externally set rules which regulate the way in which a business operates – either for safety reasons or for ethical reasons (in the case of advertising)
competition law	statutes such as the Competition Act and the Enterprise Act which promote free competition in the marketplace, preventing price fixing and mergers of market leaders
consumer protection law	statutes such as the Sale of Goods Act and the Supply of Goods and Services Act which protect the rights of consumers and influence the operation of the customer services function in business
employment protection law	statutes such as the Sex Discrimination Act, the Disability Discrimination Act and the Race Relations Act which influence employee management and behaviour
Health & Safety law	legislation such as the Health & Safety at Work Act and regulations such as the Health & Safety (Display Screen Equipment) Regulations which help to improve and ensure the safety of working conditions of employees

Unit 2

Investigating business

	A
1	DVD EXPRESS
2	CASH BUDGET for
3	
4	
5	
6	
7	RECEIPTS
8	Sales
9	Bank Loan
10	Capital
11	TOTAL RECEIPTS
12	PAYMENTS
13	Purchases
14	Equipment
15	Rent
16	Insurance
17	Electricity

This unit requires you to plan the setting up of a small business. This will involve you in assessing the need for various type of resource and will enable you to develop some specific financial skills. You will investigate:

- the business planning process

- the need for different types of business finance

- the importance of profit as shown in a profit and loss account

- the techniques for calculating break-even so that you can assess if a business project is viable

- the different types of business budget, including the cash flow forecast and the importance of cash flow to a business

- the use of ICT as a resource for business

B	C
NUARY	FEBRUARY
£	£
10,000	10,000
8,000	
12,000	
30,000	10,000
5,000	5,000
14,500	15,250
575	575
50	50

Chapters in this Unit...

10

Planning and managing a business

Starting point

Planning a business is like planning an extended holiday for a group of friends. You set objectives – deciding where you are going – and co-ordinate resources: raising finance, getting the right people together and acquiring equipment which will enable you to get where you want.

But things may go wrong and you may have to change your plans; you may realise that things are not working out. You will need to be flexible. You will need to decide how you move on from the point you have reached, making the most of the lessons that you have learnt on the way. Planning is a continuous journey – in any context.

What you will learn from this chapter

- business planning requires you to set realisable objectives

- planning a business involves monitoring your performance – identifying problems and learning from them

- planning is equally important both for a business start-up and also for a business that has been operating for a number of years

- planning a business requires a knowledge of the legal implications of running a business and knowing where to get advice

- planning a business involves planning for sales and marketing, the management of resources and in particular the management of finance

- a business plan is a formal document, normally presented to a potential lender, which sets out the details of all these processes

Introduction to Business Planning

business planning and business plans

It is important at this stage to distinguish between the concept of **business planning** and the formal document, the **business plan**. You will encounter them both – they have similar aims, but are very different.

the formal business plan

The **business plan** is a formal written document compiled when a business wants to raise finance, either when it is starting up or when it wants to expand. It is presented to a lender such as a bank or a potential investor and sets out the reasons why lending to or investing in the business is an attractive proposition. You may well be studying or writing a business plan as part of your course. Drawing up a business plan is a very useful exercise as it clarifies business objectives.

business planning

Business planning, on the other hand, is an ongoing, month-by-month process. It involves the setting of objectives by all areas of the business – eg levels of sales, market share, product quality – and then measuring how successful the business is in meeting those objectives. The overall 'plan' can then be altered if necessary. For example, if a computer games manufacturer launches a new game in the autumn and finds that it has a winner on its hands, it will have to move rapidly to maximise its sales for the Christmas market. It will need to allocate more resources for production, marketing, sales and distribution. It may have to take on more staff, but it will receive a boost to its sales and profits. Business planning is never static.

the planning cycle

A business should constantly be planning ahead. For example, it may look at the coming year in order to calculate staffing needs and estimate sales. There are four distinct stages in the planning process which form a **planning cycle**:

1 **set objectives** – for example, to increase sales or market share by 25%
2 **collect information** – assess the situation: can the business increase sales by 25%? how much will it cost? is the target realistic?
3 **make plans** so that objectives can be achieved – expand operations, take on more staff
4 **monitor progress** – see how the business is getting on: the business can look at its sales figures each month, see if it is achieving its target, and try to do something about it if it is not

The four stages in the planning cycle are illustrated in the diagram below.

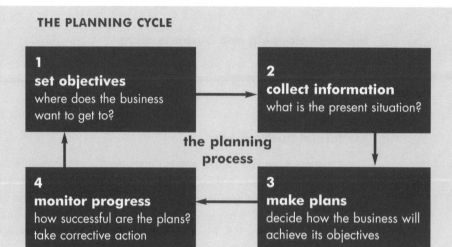

THE PLANNING CYCLE

1 set objectives where does the business want to get to?

2 collect information what is the present situation?

the planning process

4 monitor progress how successful are the plans? take corrective action

3 make plans decide how the business will achieve its objectives

Levels of Planning

Planning by a business takes place at three distinct levels:

Mission Statement and Vision Statement

Planning can be said to start in general terms with the Mission Statement. This is a public statement by the business setting out in a succinct way what the business does, what it aims to achieve, its values and standards. A Vision Statement is a more general statement of how the business sees itself developing in the future – a 'vision' of what it wants to be. This is planning on a conceptual level.

corporate plan – long-term objectives

A corporate plan (the term 'corporate' means 'company') sets out the long-term objectives of a business – up to five years, for example. It involves all areas of business activity: profitability, market share, product range, staffing, environmental policy. A corporate plan produced by a larger business will be a formal document as it will need to be consulted by a large number of people. In a smaller business the same planning process will take place but will be more informal. A sole trader is likely to have an idea of where his or her business will be in five years' time, and may discuss it with colleagues and the bank manager, but that idea my well be stored in his or her head!

operational planning – short-term targets

The operational planning process in a larger business follows the setting of objectives and normally sets targets for one year in areas such as sales, marketing, production, finance, human resources and administration. Plans are constantly reviewed and monitored by the people responsible for them. Towards the end of each year, new plans will be drawn up for the following year, taking into account all the developments during the current year.

If the business is a smaller one, this planning process will still take place, but will be more informal because it will involve fewer people. Again, in the case of a sole trader, the planning may be in the person's head or even on the back of an envelope. The important thing is that it exists.

The remainder of this chapter looks at the process of planning for resources in more detail.

Planning and Managing Resources

In this chapter we focus on the **planning** which takes place when a business first starts up – because this is the basis of your Unit assessment.

The sections that follow cover the areas of:

- the **legal form** of the business – whether to operate as a sole trader, partnership or limited company
- **sources of assistance** for business start-ups and business in general
- the important **role of the entrepreneur** and innovation – the new and different business idea
- setting **business objectives** and identifying relevant **stakeholders**
- defining the product and the market and drawing up a **marketing plan**

The chapter concludes by examining the way in which resources are managed to ensure that the performance of the business is meeting its targets. The two main areas covered are:

- **managing resources**, including people, premises and equipment
- maintaining **product quality** throughout the organisation

You will see that we have not mentioned **finance** in this list. The raising and management of finance is, of course, central to business planning. This subject will be covered in detail in later chapters which will cover areas such as calculating how many products will need to be sold before the business breaks even (covers all its costs) and working out the month-end bank balance to make sure that the business does not go 'into the red' (a 'cash-flow' forecast).

Deciding on the Legal Form of the Business

In Chapter 3 'Types of business' we described in some detail the legal implications of forming different types of business. The summary below describes the main features of the three main types of business. For further detail please read pages 30-36.

THE MAIN LEGAL FORMS OF BUSINESS

sole trader

A quick, cheap and easy way to set up in business – you trade on your own – you take the decisions, the risks, the profits, the losses; you are responsible for all your debts and may lose your possessions if you go bust. But you can be your own boss.

partnership

Two or more people setting up in business, sharing profits (or losses) and being responsible for all the partnership debts and the dealings of the other partners, but sharing the management. If it goes well, it goes well, but if there is a dispute there can be major problems.

limited company

Owned by shareholders and run by directors (who can also be the shareholders if the company is small). Shareholders have a limited responsibility for company debts, but a company is expensive to set up and can involve a lot of time-consuming 'red tape' in its running.

Sources of Advice for Business Start-ups

There are many organisations which will advise people who want to start a business. Firms of accountants and solicitors are very helpful, but will charge for their services, whereas free advice can be obtained from:

- banks
- government bodies such as the DTI (Department of Trade and Industry)
- government-supported organisations such as Business Link

Advice may come in the form of 'starter packs' which contain case studies and templates for business plans and financial projections. The internet has become a rich source of advice. Carry out a UK search on the phrase 'business advice' with a search engine such as Google and you will find a great deal to look at.

Some useful sites are shown below.

WEBSITES PROVIDING INFORMATION ABOUT BUSINESS START-UPS

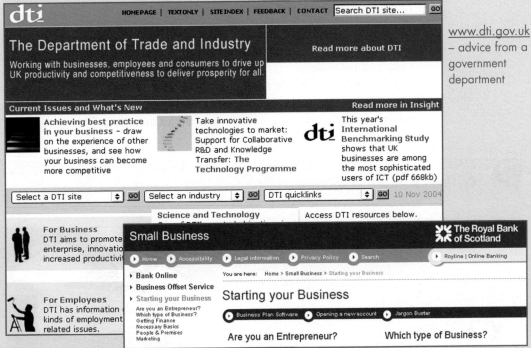

www.dti.gov.uk – advice from a government department

www.rbs.co.uk – a very useful source of business start-up information from the Royal Bank of Scotland

www.businesslink.gov.uk – advice from government-supported local centres

Business Ideas, Objectives, Stakeholders

the entrepreneur – enterprise and innovation

Most people starting up in business do so because they have a good idea which they think will catch on. The true entrepreneur (see Chapter 1, page 7) will have any number of ideas and the energy and drive to follow them through. These may well be innovative new products or new ways of marketing existing products.

If you are a student of business and have to set up a small enterprise, either for real, or just as a planning exercise, you will have to put yourself in the place of the entrepreneur. You may have to brainstorm for business ideas – for example, if you are required to plan for a service business serving the local area. These ideas could involve either a brand-new product, or an existing product which you think you can improve upon.

Activity 10.1 – brainstorming the business idea

This Activity should help you to get some ideas for a product for your business. It can be used for the assessment work for this Unit and for helping you formulate ideas for a Young Enterprise or mini-business scheme.

- Divide up the whole class into smaller groups of around three students.

- Elect a secretary and a spokesperson for each small group.

- Conduct a 'brainstorming session' for ideas for services which the business could provide.

- The secretary should record the suggestions, and the group should select a shortlist of, say, the three favourite ideas.

When the groups have come to the end of their discussions (or arguments!) the class should reassemble and the spokesperson from each small group should present the ideas. This can then provide material for further discussion.

objectives and stakeholders

An important part of the planning process is the formulating of business objectives. These will depend on:

- the character and ambitions of the business owner(s)
- the pressures exerted by the stakeholders of the business

The entrepreneurial nature of the business owner(s) will dictate to what extent the business will aim to:

- expand its market share
- maximise its sales
- maximise its profitability
- provide 'value for money' to its customers
- increase the size of the business and the number of its products
- stay small and manageable
- take on more staff and look after them well
- keep staff to a minimum
- stress the quality of its products
- produce its products as cheaply as possible
- support local suppliers
- support charitable causes and the local and wider community

Two main points arise from this list of business objectives:

1 it is clear that some of these objectives are contradictory
2 the objectives relate directly to the demands of the stakeholders of the business, ie the people who have an interest in what the business does

For example, there is a trade-off between sales maximisation and profitability – which benefit the business owner – and a number of other objectives which favour the stakeholders. This happens if costs are cut to achieve these objectives, as you can see in the diagram below.

an increase in	can be achieved at a cost to
sales	product quality if cheaper materials are used
	staff wage levels and benefits
profitability	support of local suppliers if they are more expensive
market share	support of charities

The main stakeholders who are likely to be affected by a new business setting up in a locality include:

- local **customers** who are likely to buy the products of the new business
- local **suppliers** of goods and services who will increase their business
- the local **workforce** which will receive the benefit of new jobs
- local **charities** who may receive donations and sponsorship
- local and national **government** which will receive revenue from rates and taxes levied on the new business
- **pressure groups** who may be concerned about the effect the business will have on the community in terms of noise, waste and litter

Remember that it is the nature of the business and the nature of its objectives which will determine whether or not the interests of the stakeholders are well looked after.

Activity 10.2 – objectives and stakeholders

You live in a town in which there are two home-delivery pizza businesses. One is very expensive, but the pizzas are good; the other is cheap and cheerful, but the choice of toppings is limited and the delivery times are unreliable.

You and two friends want to set up another home-delivery pizza business in competition. You are going to call it 'ProntoPizza'.

Form groups of three in your class and:

1 Draw up a list of business objectives for your new business. These can relate to areas such as price, profit, market share, level of service and product range.

2 Write a Mission Statement for the business, based on the objectives you have listed.

3 Identify the main stakeholders who will be affected by your business. Explain to what extent your business objectives look after the interests of the stakeholders.

Marketing Planning

If you are starting a business, you will need to collect marketing information which will help you in your decision-making. If you are considering manufacturing a product or providing a service, you will therefore need to look at a number of critical questions:

who are your customers?

is there a demand for the product?

There is no point launching a new product for which there is no demand, or for which you cannot create a demand. Many new businesses fail because their owners think they have a good idea but fail to carry out sufficient research to see if consumers are equally enthusiastic.

who are your customers?

Another aspect of marketing policy is to decide which group(s) of customers your business is going to target. This will in turn enable you to calculate how many customers you will be selling to, and whether you think they will be repeat customers who will buy from you again.

what is the competition doing?

If you are going to market a product, you will need to research the competition, examining its products and its pricing. As you will know from your marketing studies, it is always more difficult to launch a new product in a market which is already congested with existing products.

what are the financial implications of this?

The financial aspects of business planning are covered in detail in the chapters that follow, but it is worth noting at this point that when you have worked out the number of customers to whom you will be selling, and have assessed the market, you can then:

- fix a price for your product
- estimate the number of items you will be able to sell in a year
- estimate your annual sales figure (turnover)

how do you fix the price?

Pricing is notoriously difficult to get right. You need to know:

- what the competition are charging

- what the market will bear
- what your costs are

You can then set a price.

There are a number of different pricing strategies:

- **market-led pricing** – pricing your product at the same level as your competitors; this is the price consumers expect to pay
- **penetration pricing** – cutting the price as low as you are able below that of your competitors in order to penetrate the market with a new product
- **destruction pricing** – starting a price war with the object of knocking the competition out of the market entirely
- **added value pricing** – you may be able to charge more than competitors by providing some 'added value' to the product in terms of extra quality or additional features

The strategy that you will adopt will depend very much on the nature of the product and the competition.

Activity 10.3 – ProntoPizza: marketing planning and pricing

The previous Activity in this chapter was based on the scenario of three friends wanting to set up a home-delivery pizza business in a town in which there are already two other competitors – a 'cheap and cheerful' supplier and a more 'upmarket' provider of home-delivery pizzas.

Form groups of three or more students and discuss the ways in which you are going to plan your marketing for the new business. You should decide:

1 the methods you are going to use to obtain information about the demand for pizzas in your town

2 the information you are going to need about your competitors and how you are going to obtain it

3 what pricing policy you are going to adopt – and why – explaining the likely effect this will have on your sales and profitability

Managing Human Resources

You may already have studied and investigated the ways in which businesses recruit and motivate employees so that they stay with the business (see Chapters 6 - 8). In Unit 2 you will need to appreciate how a business manages its human resources – its people – effectively. In your assessment you will need to show how the business you are planning will recruit and motivate its staff so that they provide a quality output. 'Quality output' for staff means a high level of customer service.

So what is needed at the planning stages?

setting objectives for human resources planning

A business will need to choose and employ people so that:

- the productivity and output of the business is efficient
- the profit is maximised
- people working in the business are motivated and satisfied

These objectives will inevitably result in a compromise!

the skills that will be needed

A business start-up will involve one or more entrepreneurs (people who get businesses going) who have to provide skills in a number of areas:

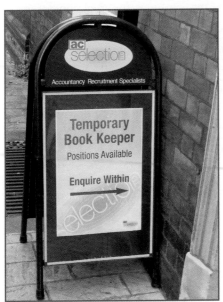

employing the right staff

- administration and management
- marketing and selling
- finance/book-keeping/payroll
- production and operations
- research and development – the 'ideas' person

It may be that the sole trader has all these talents, or the partners/directors share these abilities between them. It is more likely, however, that the business starting up will have to 'buy in' help in one or more of these areas.

This can be done by:

- bringing in a new partner/director with a particular skill who may be willing also to put in capital and share in the success of the business
- using self-employed specialists (eg for accountancy services or marketing) on a contract basis
- employing temporary staff from an agency

- employing one or more general assistants who can be on the permanent payroll of the business

The first option (new partner/director) can be a risky proposition. There may be personality clashes between the people involved: can the new director get on with the existing management? Hiring self-employed specialists or agency staff can be expensive, but it is also flexible: a business only pays for what it wants done. A general assistant may cost less in terms of £s per hour, but there is little flexibility in terms of hours worked, and the employee(s) may need training.

the practicalities of human resources planning

As far as business planning is concerned, the owner(s) of a new (or expanding) business ought to bear in mind:

- manpower planning – what are the staffing requirements likely to be?
- what training is needed?
- what employee benefits and facilities need to be arranged?
- have the wage levels been fixed?
- have Health & Safety requirements been planned out?

legal aspects of human resources planning

Unit 1 (Chapter 5) covers this area in detail. It explains how the law requires the employer to:

the importance of Health & Safety planning

- take note of the age limits for employment
- pay at least the Minimum Wage
- issue written terms and conditions of employment
- avoid discrimination on the grounds of sex, age, race and religion
- be guided by the Health & Safety at Work regulations
- keep payroll records

employer's liability insurance

This type of insurance covers the employer against claims from employees who have been injured at work.

'Employees' can include outside consultants and even students on work experience – you may have come across this problem!

Activity 10.4 – planning and managing people

You are starting up a pizza home-delivery business with two other partners. You are the 'admin and finance' partner and will manage the day-to-day running of the business. One of the others will specialise in sales and marketing and the third is a skilled pizza and pasta chef. The pizzas will be delivered, either by van or by motorbike.

1 What staff would you need to take on?

2 What skills would you be looking for in those employees?

3 What legal aspects relating to your employees would you need to get sorted out before you start trading?

Premises Planning

premises – work from home?

Many small businesses operate very successfully from home. These businesses are mainly sole traders who either provide a service to the public by travelling from home, or who deal with the public on the telephone or on the internet. Examples include electricians, photographers, designers and insurance sales representatives. Business owners who use the home as a base can charge a proportion of their expenses (telephone, electricity, heating) to their business – ie the business will pay rather than the expense falling on the household budget. A major disadvantage is keeping business and private lives separate!

the e-commerce dimension

In an age where many service businesses are trading online, 'premises' can become virtual – in other words, a website on a computer server can replace commercial premises. The 'shop-front' is being replaced by the website home page. This enables the services business owner to work wherever he or she can get online, including from home. The practicalities of selling goods (rather than services) by e-commerce still require, however, that the product is stored and despatched – so premises will still be needed for handling the goods.

obtaining the right premises

buy or rent?

If the business manufactures a product or needs to deal with the public face-to-face as part of its everyday operations, it needs premises – commercial property. Information about premises can be obtained from:

- local Business Link offices
- the commercial property offices of estate agents
- commercial property pages in the local press

The main question to ask when choosing premises will be whether you wish to buy or rent the property. If you have the capital, you may wish to buy the premises, possibly with the help of a commercial mortgage. If, as is more likely, you do not have much spare money to invest, you will plan to rent a property and pay a regular 'rental' to the owner of the property.

what does the law say about premises?

If a business plans to operate from premises, there are a number of legal obligations that the owner(s) of the business must consider:

- **planning permission** from the Local Authority for the type of business carried on at the premises (if it is needed)
- **licences** needed to trade, for example: restaurants, food manufacturers, ice cream and mobile food stalls, sellers of alcohol and tobacco, nursing homes, child nurseries and scrap metal dealers
- **environmental restrictions** – the law places strict controls on the emissions which a business can make into the atmosphere, into drainage systems, and into rivers and streams

insuring premises and their contents

Insuring a business can be expensive, but it is well worth it if anything goes wrong.

- **fire cover** insures premises and its contents against damage by fire and other disasters such as lightning, explosions, aircraft, riots, vandalism, earthquake, storms and floods
- **theft insurance** covers the removable belongings of the business, eg machinery, computers, office machines, stock and money
- **business interruption cover** provides funds if the business comes to a halt following a fire or any of the other disasters covered under fire insurance – because presumably it will have to stop trading for a while

Planning for Machinery and Equipment

When a business plans to acquire machinery, equipment or vehicles a number of critical decisions will have to be made, including:

- should they be bought straightaway
- should they be bought or leased?

Other factors affecting the choice will be the supplier chosen; this will depend on the supplier's quality, payment terms (ie when payment can be made), technical back-up and after-sales service.

The equipment which a business may need includes a wide range of items including telephones, computers and photocopiers, vehicles, and machinery used when producing a product or providing a service.

should the equipment be acquired now?

When a business starts up for the first time, it is easy to fall into the trap of making a 'shopping list' for resources, assuming that they all have to be acquired at once. This is not always the case, and great care should be taken in the planning process. A business will have to list all the items it wants to acquire, cost them, and compare them with the available financial resources. It can then decide which items have to be acquired immediately (telephones, delivery van) and which items can wait (the MD's new car).

should the items be bought or leased?

cars and computers – to buy or to lease?

Equipment can be bought outright or rented (leased). This choice exists for a wide range of items used in business, eg computers, photocopiers, machinery, cars and vans, for example. The term 'lease' is often used when a piece of equipment is rented: ownership remains with the firm 'leasing' it out.

How do you decide whether to buy or to lease? The main factor is the availability of money. If the finance is not available, the business cannot buy the item, and the decision to lease will be made. Another factor is how soon the equipment will get out of date. There is little point buying an expensive piece of new technology if next year the price will have fallen, or if the technology has gone out of date. For example, current thinking says that computer equipment used in business will only last for an average of two years before it needs upgrading.

Activity 10.5 – premises and equipment for ProntoPizza

If you are starting up a pizza home delivery business, you will need:

- premises in which to house the operation

- equipment for baking the pizzas

- a computer to run the accounts, to manage letter writing and price lists and to access the internet

- transport of some sort for pizza delivery

You are aware that there are various options for obtaining premises, equipment and transport.

1 What options are there open to your business for obtaining suitable premises? What would you advise, bearing in mind the fact that the business does not have much money to start with?

2 One of the partners suggests buying a computer as they are relatively cheap at the moment. What are the advantages and disadvantages of doing this?

3 Another partner has seen a very old van advertised for sale – he says he can get it very cheap. What are the advantages and disadvantages of doing this?

4 What forms of insurance would you suggest the business takes out to protect itself against normal risks?

Managing Materials and Stock

If the business you are planning is manufacturing a product or buying in goods which you are going to sell, you are going to need stock and materials. The price you pay and the terms you negotiate are critical for the profitability of the business. Purchasing has traditionally been defined as:

buying goods and services of the right quality, in the right quantity, at the right time, from the right supplier, at the right price

This may seem all very well in theory, but as most people in business will tell you, purchasing often gets a low priority in comparison with marketing and sales – although marketing and sales are, of course, very important.

getting the right price – efficient purchasing

> pay in 7 days and receive 2.5% discount
>
> 5% extra discount for orders over £5,000
>
> special terms – buy now and pay in three months

finding the right terms for your supplies

The price of materials and stock purchased is an important factor for a business which wants to make a profit. Achieving a price cut for raw materials and stock is a more efficient way of improving profitability than increasing sales. It can also be easier.

How are these lower prices to be found? Suppliers must be approached, and prices obtained from price lists, telephone enquiries and websites. If suppliers realise that a business is 'shopping around', they may be prepared to drop a price to gain a customer. Businesses must also be aware of discounts offered for early payment (cash discount) and large quantity orders. Businesses should also shop around for extended periods of credit: it will save them money to buy materials now and pay two months later – it would reduce the bank overdraft and interest charges.

A supplier must be able to keep to specified schedules. Any problems with supply could lose sales for the buyer: for example, a shop which is let down by a wholesaler and runs out of a popular item, or a manufacturer that is unable to obtain a vital component because the supplier has failed to deliver.

quality and purchasing

The quality of an item means, in very basic terms, 'How good is it for the job?' As far as a business is concerned, purchasing for quality means balancing cost and performance: the item must do the job well, but at the lowest obtainable cost. But there is no point compromising quality for price. A pizza that gives food poisoning loses the business a customer.

We will deal with the issue of quality management on the next two pages.

Activity 10.6 – managing stock and materials

ProntoPizza, a new home-delivery pizza business, is examining the ways in which it is going to obtain its supplies.

1 What stock and materials will a pizza business need on a daily basis?

2 What sort of deals from suppliers are likely to save ProntoPizza money?

3 How can ProntoPizza obtain these deals, both when it starts trading and also in the longer term?

Managing Quality

Quality is a concept that should be instilled in all processes and all people in the business – including the management of people, design, production, sales and customer service. Interestingly, the word is currently used in common speech to praise something – 'that's real quality'. In business, quality is used to gain a competitive advantage; it can also be used to justify a high price (eg Rolex, Ferrari, Gucchi).

The traditional term applied to the 'quality' concept is **Total Quality Management (TQM)** which encourages people working in business to take responsibility for the excellence of everything that they do. This term should not be confused with **quality control** which is an inspection process in the production function which attempts to reduce the risk of defective products in the first place.

TQM is appropriate for any size of business, from the large supermarket chain (quality service, quality products) to the sole trader who takes immense pride in the way he or she works. It applies equally to manufacturing businesses and service businesses.

As we saw in Chapter 2 (page 19), quality is an important business objective and so it must form an integral part of business planning and must feature in the formal business plan document.

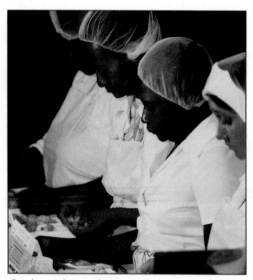
Quality in the production process

ways of achieving quality

Total Quality Management (TQM) involves the business being managed so that every individual has a responsibility to fellow employees for maintaining quality – it is particularly effective in **team working**.

Quality chains occur in the production process – either in a manufacturing business or a service business – in which a 'chain' of activities is set up between individuals who are encouraged to see each other as 'internal customers'.

Quality circles involve regular meetings of employees to discuss quality problems and to suggest solutions for problems in areas such as production, safety and design.

Quality control, as mentioned above, involves an inspection process in the production function which ensures that the next person in the chain receives a quality product or service.

monitoring quality

If quality is to be maintained, it is important that quality standards are monitored on a regular basis. This can take the form of **statistical monitoring** – ie recording on a regular basis the number of faults as a percentage of output. In a manufacturing business this could be the number of items rejected in the production process or the number returned as faulty by customers. In the case of a service business such as a holiday company this could be the number of complaints received.

Customer feedback from questionnaires or focus groups is another way of quantifying the level of satisfaction with product quality.

Businesses should set **targets** for quality – eg 95% of trains should arrive within five minutes of the scheduled time – and monitor those targets closely. This level of satisfaction may then be communicated back to the customers – for example, punctuality reports from train companies displayed in stations.

BSI kitemark

quality certification – ISO 9000

Many businesses see it as a competitive advantage to obtain certification through a set of internationally recognised quality standards – ISO 9000. These are rigorous procedures but a business which successfully achieves these standards can use the BSI kitemark (shown on left), which signifies that very high standards of quality have been implemented throughout the business. Visit www.bsi-global.com for details.

Activity 10.7 – quality management

If you were starting up a small business offering a home-delivery fast food service, such as ProntoPizza (featured in Activities earlier in this chapter), you should be looking carefully at the ways in which Total Quality Management can be implemented.

How would you ensure that quality is maintained:

1   in the production of the food?

2   in the customer service that the business provides?

CHAPTER SUMMARY

- Business planning is an ongoing process which affects all areas of the business. It involves the setting of objectives, the monitoring of the success of those objectives and the taking of appropriate action.

- Business planning operates on a number of levels, ranging from the general nature of the Mission Statement to the specific targets set in a 12 month operational plan.

- When a business starts up for the first time it will normally draw up a formal business plan which it presents to a potential lender or investor. This plan will also state the legal form taken by the business – sole trader, partnership or limited company.

- Sources of advice for businesses include the banks, professional advisers such as accountants and bodies such as the Department of Trade and Industry and Business Link.

- Successful businesses are generally the result of an enterprising entrepreneur promoting an innovative idea or an existing product in an innovative way.

- In formulating its objectives a business will need to take into account the needs of its stakeholders and take decisions about where its priorities lie.

- Effective marketing planning is essential if a business is to make a success of its products. This involves researching market demand, finding out who the customers will be, who the competitors are and what pricing policy should be.

- Human resources planning will also be needed to enable the business to recruit skilled staff and make the most of its existing human resources. It will also need to take account of the legal requirements placed on employers in respect of discrimination and insurance.

- Planning for business premises involves a series of decisions – whether to work from home or from other premises, whether to buy or to lease and how to deal with the many legal and insurance implications of operating a business.

- Planning for machinery and equipment also involves the buy or lease decision.

- Managing the resources of stock and materials involves obtaining the right terms from the right supplier and ensuring that quality is always maintained.

- Managing quality within the business is also a key to its success. The concept of Total Quality Management should permeate the whole business – its people, processes and products. Quality should always be monitored closely and action taken if standards fall. For many businesses Quality Certification through the ISO Standards provides a significant competitive edge.

KEY TERMS

business plan	a formal written document produced as a presentation to a potential investor or lender
business planning	an ongoing process affecting all areas of the business; it sets objectives and monitors the success of the business in meeting those targets
Mission Statement	a public statement by the business stating what the business does, what its values are and what it aims to achieve
corporate plan	the long-term (normally five-year) objectives of the business
operational plans	the short-term (normally one-year) targets for the various operational areas of the business
sole trader	a business owned by a single individual who takes on all the risks and debts of the business
partnership	a group of individuals who run a business together, aiming to make a profit
limited company	a business owned by shareholders and run by directors set up as a body separate from its owners
entrepreneur	a person who has the idea and energy for starting a business and who is willing to take the associated risks
stakeholder	a person or an organisation with an interest in a business
employer's liability insurance	insurance against the risk of an employee being injured at work
business interruption insurance	covers the business in the event of the business not operating because of a fire or other disaster
lease	an arrangement in which property or items such as cars and computers can be used by the business in return for regular payments
Total Quality Management	a concept which states that a business should be managed so that quality should be encouraged in all employees and processes within the business
ISO 9000	a set of internationally recognised quality standards which form the basis of quality management

11

Financing a new business

Starting point

One of the main hurdles when starting a new business is being able to raise the necessary finance. An entrepreneur starting a business venture will have to calculate as accurately as possible the costs of starting the business and the costs of running the business on a day-to-day basis.

Then the finance will have to be sorted. Where will the money come from to pay these set-up and running costs? How much capital has the entrepreneur got to invest? How much will have to be raised from outside sources and how will it be repaid? Should the entrepreneur form a company? Questions will need to be answered and careful thought given to the planning process before the entrepreneur takes the step of going in to see the bank's lending officer to ask for finance.

What you will learn from this chapter

- the costs of starting a business include start-up costs – which are 'one-off' costs such as buying premises and machinery, and running costs which are incurred on a regular basis, eg wages, insurance, stock and materials, phone bills

- the financing of start-up costs can come from the business owner (capital), from fixed bank loans and from grants

- the financing of running costs comes from the sales revenue of the business, from a bank overdraft (very short-term borrowing) and by relying on credit from suppliers (ie buying now and paying later)

- the finance that is available will depend on the type of business: a company is likely to be able to raise more funds than a sole trader

Start-up Costs

start-up costs and running costs – a choice

There are many different types of cost involved in running and managing a business. For the start-up business the owner (or owners) will need to distinguish between:

- **start-up costs**, which are 'one-off costs which have to be met before the business starts trading
- **running costs**, which are day-to-day costs incurred in running the business

The business owner(s) will need to plan carefully how all these costs are going to be financed. If there is a shortage of funds to start with, there is often the option to transform a start-up cost into a running cost, for example the owner can lease (rent) premises and equipment and make payments when the business is trading rather than buy the items outright.

what are the start-up costs?

The start-up costs of a business will depend very much on the nature of that business. A sole trader providing a service – a graphic designer, for example – may possibly operate from home and have little in the way of equipment to purchase, apart from a computer, a phone and possibly some furniture. An entrepreneur setting up a company to manufacture burglar alarms, on the other hand, will need premises, sophisticated manufacturing equipment and furniture and other equipment required for running a business. This will potentially involve a substantial investment.

Start-up costs therefore can include:

- premises
- equipment
- fixtures and fittings (the term used to describe all the furniture and other items used to operate a business)

We will now describe these costs in more detail in the form of a checklist. Remember that in many cases there is an alternative to tying up money in start-up costs – there is the **rental** alternative. Rental cost is a **running cost** which is payable over a period of time.

check-list for start-up costs

- **premises**   If premises are needed – and they may not be if the business can be operated from home – they can be **purchased**. Offices, shops and warehouses are available on the commercial property market and, like domestic

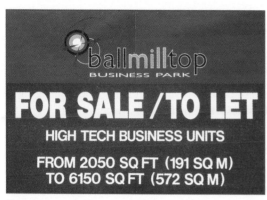

To buy or to rent?

property, have become very expensive, particularly as they are often used as 'to let' investments by large institutions such as insurance companies and pension funds looking for a steady return on their money.

Rental of commercial property by the new business is the common alternative. This completely avoids the major start-up cost of premises. Note that rent is not a set-up cost but a running cost. The normal arrangement is for the business to sign a lease of the property for a period of years.

■ **equipment**

The equipment used by a business will vary according to the nature of the enterprise. A manufacturing company, however small, will require specialised production equipment. Most businesses will also require a range of computer and other ITC equipment. Another type of 'equipment' used by most businesses is the vehicle such as the delivery van and the sales rep's car.

The alternatives, as with premises, are to buy or to lease. Buying the equipment is a start-up cost, leasing (renting) is a running cost. The shorter the life of the equipment (computers and cars are normally kept for only a couple of years), the more attractive the leasing option becomes as the business can then acquire brand-new and more up-to-date equipment and cars on a regular basis.

■ **fixtures & fittings**

Fixtures and fittings are all the extra items such as furniture, filing cabinets, carpets, lighting and fire extinguishers that a business needs in order to operate on a daily basis. These are normally a start-up cost. As the items are often low-value they are rarely available on a lease (rent) basis.

■ **marketing**

A new business will only stand a chance of survival if its potential customers need its products and know about them. It is therefore essential that effective market research and advertising are carried out before the launch of the new business. This spending will constitute a start-up cost. The marketing process will, of course, continue once the business is up and running – further market research and advertising will then become running costs and part of the marketing budget.

Running Costs

Remember the distinction:

Start-up costs are 'one-off' costs incurred in starting a business

Running costs are day-to-day costs incurred in running a business

We have already seen that some start-up costs can be transformed into running costs if the business does not have the funds – for example an office can be rented rather than purchased.

what are the running costs?

The **running costs** of a business relate to the various functional areas we explained in Chapter 4, including production ('operations' in a service business), marketing, human resources, and administration. These running costs are often also known as **expenses**. We will see in Chapter 15 that these expenses are important to the business planning and monitoring process as they form the basis for **budgets**, ie estimates of what the business should expect to spend and plans to spend. These budget figures are then monitored to see if there is any variance (difference) between the budget and the actual reported figures. Identification of all running costs is therefore an important process.

check-list for running costs

■ **production**   If a business is **manufacturing** a product it will have to estimate the cost of items such as:

- raw materials
- packaging
- wages of employees working in production

If a business is providing a **service** it will have to estimate the cost of providing each item, eg a holiday company will need to work out the cost of items such as:

- air fares
- hotel accommodation
- transfers to resorts

■ **marketing**   The costs of marketing include:

- market research
- promotion, eg advertising and sponsorship
- website design and operation
- selling – using reps, direct mail, telesales

- **human resources**   The cost of running the 'people function' in a business includes:
  - staff wages
  - recruitment
  - training
  - Health & Safety requirements

- **administration**   The day-to-day costs of running a business include items such as:
  - insurance, rent and rates
  - power and phone bills
  - postage and stationery
  - accountant's fees and bank charges

Activity 11.1 – start-up costs and running costs

A friend of yours, Sonal, is starting up a new translation bureau, LingoExpress. She provides you with a list of costs that she has researched. The figures are estimates. Where the costs are not 'one-off' costs the figure shows the expense for one year.

	£		£
Purchase of office	150,000	Purchase of computer system	25,000
Advertising for business launch	5,000	Advertising during the year	10,000
Wages	35,000	Business insurance	5,000
Office fittings	23,000	Electricity	800
Telephone bills	750	Postage	550
Travel	500	Business rates	1,250

1   Calculate the total start-up costs and annual running costs for the new business.

2   Sonal tells you that she is concerned about the high cost of buying premises and computers. She has looked into the possibility of renting and leasing and has been given the following estimated yearly costs:

Office rental   £15,000

Computer lease payments   £2,500

You are to calculate the total start-up costs and total running costs for the new business assuming Sonal is taking the leasing and rental options.

Financing Start-up Costs

The financing for a business start-up can come from three main sources:

- **capital** – money invested by the owner
- **commercial loans** – money loaned by the banks and others
- **Government assistance** – grants and incentives

FINANCING OF START-UP COSTS

We will deal with each of these sources of finance in turn.

capital

Capital is the money investment in the business made by the owner(s) of the business

A business starting up for the first time should always have a substantial investment made in it by the owner(s).

The legal form of the business will determine how much capital can be invested. In a sole trader and partnership business, the capital is the personal contribution of the sole owner or the partners. This means that the amount of capital raised will be limited to the personal wealth of the sole owner or partners. In some cases the capital can be very limited.

In the case of a limited company, however, the situation is quite different as the owners are the shareholders. Because there can be a large number of shareholders, many of whom do not necessarily take an active part in running the business, a limited company can potentially raise far more capital than a sole trader or partnership, as it will have more investors.

A public limited company, for example, can raise capital from a stock market issue of shares, when it 'floats' as a new company, and the public can buy shares. A limited company (public or private) can also raise capital through a specialist **venture capital company** which can purchase shares, but with conditions attached (please see next page).

Limited companies can also raise capital from **business angels**. This is the picturesque term used for wealthy individuals who invest in start-up and growth companies in return for shares and sometimes active participation in the company. Business angels will often have already made their fortune through other business ventures and are typically men aged between 45 and 65. Carry out an internet search on NBAN to find out more.

commercial loans

Businesses which need to fund their start-up costs often turn to commercial companies such as the banks for finance. The general rule of thumb is that the length of the loan should match the expected life of the item – the **asset** – financed. An 'asset' is an item owned by the business.

Common commercial loans include:

- **bank business loan**

  This is a fixed medium-term loan, typically for between 3 and 10 years, to cover the purchase of capital items such as machinery or equipment. Interest charged is linked to Base Rate (a centrally-set rate which determines interest rates for UK borrowers and savers), and repayments are by instalments.

- **commercial mortgage**

  If you are buying premises for your business you can arrange to borrow long-term by means of a commercial mortgage, typically up to 80% of the value of the property, repayable over a period of up to 25 years. Your premises will be taken as security for the loan: if the business fails, the premises will be sold to repay the lender.

- **venture capital loans**

  Venture capital companies, as well as providing share capital (see previous page), also invest money in the form of loans. In return, they may expect an element of control over the company and will possibly insist on having a director on the board of the company. A venture capital company considering investing will look for a business with a good sales and profit potential.

private loans

Another source of loan finance is a loan from a private individual such as a member of the family. This is not common and only occurs when the business is small – for example a shop run by a sole trader.

Government assistance

Another form of financing for business start-ups is promoted by the UK Government, through the Department of Trade and Industry (DTI), which

Assisted Areas

Article 87 (3)(a)
Article 87 (3)(c)

ENGLISH REGIONS
NW North West
NE North East
YH Yorkshire and the Humber
EM East Midlands
E East of England
WM West Midlands
SE South East
SW South West
L London

The Assisted Areas in England, Source: DTI

provides assistance to new and expanding businesses in the form of grants and loans. This assistance, known as **Selective Finance for Investment in England (SFI)**, is designed for businesses operating or planning to operate in the designated **Assisted Areas**. Similar schemes have been put into operation in Wales by authority of the Welsh Assembly and in Scotland through the Scottish Parliament.

Business Link offices will be the first point of contact for researching Government assistance.

Other schemes include the **Small Firms Loan Guarantee** which provides a Government guarantee of commercial borrowing which would not otherwise have been made available. Another and newer scheme, the **Enterprise Capital Funds** scheme provides share capital finance for small growth-orientated businesses.

Activity 11.2 – financing start-up costs

A local packaging company, Wrapitup Limited, has recently been sold and closed down. Five members of the management team of Wrapitup Limited, who were each given a £50,000 pay-off have decided to set up a new business specialising in film wrapping. The capital they have available for starting the business is the money received from Wrapitup Limited.

They are looking to buy a warehouse for £350,000 and manufacturing equipment for a further £100,000. They reckon the equipment should last them ten years. They prefer to buy rather than to rent or lease. This gives them a shortfall of £200,000.

They come to you for advice and ask a number of questions.

1   Should they set up as a partnership or as a private limited company? How would setting up as a limited company help them raise more capital?

2   If they decided to borrow, what form of financing would you recommend for the warehouse? Give reasons for your advice.

3   What form of financing would you recommend for the manufacturing equipment?

4   What support could the Government give them in setting up their new business?

Financing Running Costs

running costs are day-to-day costs incurred in running the business

Apart from when the business first starts up and requires money from the owner or the bank to 'kick start' it into operation, running costs are mainly financed from three main sources:

- **sales revenue** – money received from selling the products of the business
- **bank overdraft** – money borrowed from the bank on a day-to-day basis
- **trading on credit** – businesses can use money that is available because the business is buying on credit from its suppliers and has not yet paid the bills

FINANCING OF RUNNING COSTS

financing from sales revenue

The money received from selling the products of a business is known as **sales revenue** and is invariably paid into the bank to meet the running costs – **the expenses** – of the business. Note that the profit of a business is the surplus that is left after the expenses have been deducted from sales revenue:

profit = sales revenue minus running costs

We will explain more about profit in the next chapter.

overdraft financing

an overdraft is short-term borrowing on a bank account

There may be occasions when there is not enough money in the bank account to pay running costs. If this is likely to be the case, the business should request short-term borrowing – an **overdraft** – from the bank. As we will we see in Chapter 16, the requirement for financing by overdraft can be anticipated by a form of budget known as a **cash flow forecast**, which projects likely monthly inflows and outflows of money. The difference between inflows and outflows is related to what is in the bank account and shows up any shortfall which can be financed by a bank overdraft.

An overdraft is relatively cheap because the business only pays interest on what it actually borrows. A 'limit' up to which the business can borrow will be set by the bank, and reviewed from time-to-time, when it can be increased, decreased or renewed at the same level.

trading on credit

trading on credit is buying goods and services and being allowed to pay for them at an agreed later date

The whole business community is run on the basis that you can pay for goods and services at a later date. This can be advantageous if you are a supermarket – your sales revenue is all cash (same day) payment received over the checkouts and banked straightaway, but the goods sold will be paid for in, say a month's time. You then have the use of this sales revenue to pay running costs – wages for example – in the meantime. Not all businesses have the advantage of shops in receiving cash over the counter and being financed in this way, but many can use trading on credit to their advantage. This principle is explained in more detail in the next chapter.

Please note two commonly used terms which we have just introduced:

credit trading = buying now and paying <u>later</u>

cash trading = buying now and paying <u>now</u>

Activity 11.3 – financing running costs

Jason has just started a small printing business in the town and has completed his first week's trading. It is Friday and he is going to the bank, mainly to cash a cheque for wages so that he can pay his employees. He has a number of documents in front of him on his desk and he is looking concerned. The documents include:

■ the wages cheque for £3,500 which he has to cash at the bank so that he can pay his employees

■ cheques from sales totalling £20,000 to pay into the bank

■ a printout of the bank account balance (he has online access to his account) showing that there is £5,000 in the account

■ an invoice (bill) for £40,000 from a supplier for materials (paper, card, inks etc) which he is using in his business – no terms for credit trading have yet been agreed

1 Calculate the amount of running costs that need to be paid and the amount that is available to pay them. What is the shortfall?

2 Describe two ways in which Jason may be able to finance this shortfall.

CHAPTER SUMMARY

■ A new business will need to identify its start-up costs, including premises, equipment, fixtures and fittings and initial marketing costs.

■ A new business will also need to identify its running costs; these are likely to be incurred in the areas of production, marketing, human resources and administration.

■ Start-up costs can be financed from three main sources: capital introduced by the owner(s), commercial loans granted by bodies such as the banks and in some cases by means of Government assistance.

■ The amount of capital that can be raised will depend on the legal form of the business. A sole trader and partnership business will be limited to the personal contribution of the owner(s) whereas a limited company is able to widen its share ownership and raise extra capital through venture capital companies and business angels.

■ If a business borrows by taking a commercial loan, the length of the loan is normally matched to the expected life of the asset.

■ The banks offer a wide range of loan finance, ranging from the long-term commercial mortgage to the medium-term business loan. Venture capital companies also offer commercial loans.

■ The Government offers a variety of grant and loan schemes through the Department of Trade and Industry (DTI). Special schemes operate in the Assisted Areas and other products such as the Small Firms Loan Guarantee Scheme are widely available.

■ The running costs of businesses are mainly financed in the short term from three main sources:
- sales revenue (and eventually profit)
- bank overdraft
- relying on credit given by suppliers (ie buy now, pay later)

KEY TERMS

start-up costs	one-off costs which have to be met before the business starts trading
running costs	day-to-day costs incurred in running the business
sales revenue	money received from selling the products of a business
expenses	the running costs of a business (see above)
expense budgets	estimates of what the business should expect to spend
capital	money invested by the owner(s) of a business
commercial loan	a loan offered by a commercial organisation such as a bank
venture capital company	a commercial company which invests in the share capital of growing companies, requiring an element of control over the company and sometimes having a director appointed to the board
business angel	a wealthy individual, often a senior entrepreneur, who invests in the share capital of growing companies and normally requires an element of control over the company
business loan	a fixed medium-term loan (normally 3 to 10 years) granted by a bank to finance the purchase of items such as machinery and equipment
commercial mortgage	a long-term loan (typically 25 years) to finance the purchase of premises by a business
overdraft	short-term borrowing on a bank account to finance running costs
credit trading	buying goods and services and paying for them at an agreed later date
cash trading	buying goods and services now and paying for them now

Profitability and the profit & loss account

Sales		150000
Cost of sales (Purchases)		55000
Gross profit		95000
Less overheads:		
Wages	40000	
Rent	12000	
Rates	2500	
Insurance	3500	
Advertising	1500	
Other expenses	5000	
		64500
Net profit		30500

profit ≠ cash

Starting point

Managing business finance involves meeting business objectives. The prime objective of most businesses is to make a profit. This means having sales revenue that is greater than the running costs of the business.

A business should make sure that it will make a profit by keeping to planned levels of sales and expenditure. The techniques used here are budgeting and break-even. A business will also need to look back over a period of time to see if it has met its main objective and made a profit. It does this by means of a profit and loss account.

What you will learn from this chapter

- profit can be defined as sales revenue minus running costs

- future profit can be estimated in the master budget, part of which projects figures for sales revenue and running costs

- the point at which a business can start to make a profit can be estimated using a break-even analysis – this also projects levels of sales revenue and running costs

- making a profit is not the same as accumulating cash in a business; profit is used to re-invest in the business and to reward the owner(s)

- the profitability of a business can be measured by two indicators: gross profit (profit after the deduction of the cost of producing the product) and net profit (profit after the deduction of all the running expenses); these are calculated in a profit and loss account

- many stakeholders of a business – owners, employees, lenders and the tax authorities – will be interested in the level of its profits

What is Profit?

definitions

The profit motive is usually and understandably one of the main driving forces behind the entrepreneur who sets up a business. Profit is one of the main objectives of businesses in general and has the great advantage in that it benefits business owners – and most stakeholders.

Profit can be defined in financial terms as follows:

sales revenue minus running costs = profit (or loss)

The figure produced by this formula can either be a profit or, if sales revenue (ie sales income) does not cover running costs, a loss.

The products sold to produce the sales revenue can be manufactured goods or services. The profit calculation for a car manufacturer, a clothes shop or a health and beauty parlour is essentially the same – deducting running costs from sales revenue. You will see that the profit calculation does *not* include:

■ start-up costs such as the purchase of premises or equipment

■ financing items such as capital from the owner, or grants or loans

The profit calculation involves only:

■ income from day-to-day trading, for example sales of products and services

■ running costs – these include the purchase of materials and stock which a business can then sell, and overheads – day-to-day expenses such as wages, telephone bills, rates and insurance

profit budgeting and break-even

Business planning involves forecasting profit over a given period. This is carried out by the budgeting process (see Chapter 15) and also by break-even analysis (see Chapter 13).

Budgeting involves making a reasoned estimate of likely sales revenue and running costs over, say, a year, and from those figures producing a statement of profit (or loss) in the **master budget**. This gives the owners and management an idea of **how much** profit the business will generate.

Break-even uses the same projected figures, but involves analysing the running costs of the business to see at what point the business starts to make a profit. Break-even is useful in telling management **if** the business will make a profit and **when** it will make a profit.

the Profit and Loss Account

The **profit and loss account** – sometimes also known as a profit and loss statement – sets out the calculations involved in the profit (or loss) formula shown on the previous page:

sales revenue minus running costs = profit (or loss)

If the profit and loss account is forecast in the budgeting process, the figures will be taken from the various budgets of the business. The profit and loss account, however, is also commonly found as a calculation which looks back over a period of time such as a year. In this case the figures are taken from the accounting records of the business. The accounting system may either be maintained manually, or more likely, on computer, in which case the profit and loss account can be produced automatically at any time as a report printout.

The Case Study that follows shows how the profit of a small importing business is calculated in a profit and loss account.

Case Study – profit and loss account

Cuttingedge Limited imports and sells designer Italian kitchen knives.

At the end of the year, the company has extracted the following annual sales and running expenses figures from its accounting system:

Cuttingedge Limited

	£
Sales data	
Sales for the year	400,000
Running expenses	
Purchases of knives	220,000
Wages	95,000
Marketing	7,000
Rent and business rates	12,000
Electricity	750
Insurance	5,000
Office expenses	15,000

The figures are entered in the profit and loss account as follows:

PROFIT AND LOSS ACCOUNT
of Cuttingedge Limited for the year ended 31 December

	£	£
Sales		400,000
Less Cost of Sales (purchases)		220,000
Gross profit		180,000
Less Overheads		
Wages	95,000	
Marketing	7,000	
Rent and business rates	12,000	
Electricity	750	
Insurance	5,000	
Office expenses	15,000	
		134,750
Net Profit		45,250

FEATURES OF THE PROFIT AND LOSS ACCOUNT:

heading and format
The statement is headed up with the words 'Profit and Loss Account' followed by the name of the business and the financial period covered.

The statement is presented in two money columns: the expense items are shown on the left and their total is carried over to the right-hand column, as shown by the arrow.

cost of sales
The statement shown here is that of a business which sells a manufactured product. Cost of sales is the cost to the business of importing the knives that have actually been sold during the year. The cost of sales figure here equates to the total of the purchases of stock made by the business.

Whatever the type of business – manufacturer, retailer, service business – cost of sales is the total of the running expenses which directly contribute to the product itself, eg raw materials for a manufacturer, stock for a shop, flights and hotels for a holiday company.

gross profit

Calculating cost of sales – the cost of what has actually been sold – enables the business to calculate profit accurately.

Gross profit is the profit to the business before deduction of overheads (these are other running expenses which have to be paid anyway). The calculation is:

SALES – COST OF SALES = GROSS PROFIT

net profit

Net profit is the profit after the deduction of overheads such as wages, marketing, electricity and so on – the normal running expenses of a business. If the figure is negative, it will be a loss and it will be shown in brackets. The formula is:

GROSS PROFIT – OVERHEADS = NET PROFIT

Net profit is the most common and possibly the most useful indicator of business success; it is – literally – the 'bottom line'.

Distribution of Net Profit

profit ≠ cash

Net profit is the money that the business has earned for the owner (or owners) during the year. But it is important to appreciate that profit is not money in the bank; it is not the same as cash – which is why this paragraph is headed up **profit ≠ cash**, ie **profit does not equal cash**. Profit may have been earned during the year, but it may also have been spent. Profit is likely to be used:

■ to purchase business resources, eg more equipment, new computers

■ to pay the tax bill

■ to pay the owners

profit for the owners

If the owner is a sole trader or a partner, some of the net profit can be taken out during the course of the year in the form of payments known as **drawings**. If the business is a limited company some of the net profit will be paid out to the owners – the shareholders – in the form of payments known as **dividends**.

But business owners should not be greedy. It is good business planning to use some of the net profit to finance business expansion rather than buy the Managing Director a new Ferrari.

Price Setting: Mark-up and Margin

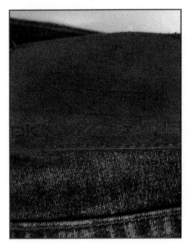

Another aspect of business planning which involves profit is the setting of the price of a product. Pricing policy is a fascinating area of business studies: how can designer brand companies charge £50 for a pair of jeans when leading supermarkets charge less than £5? It is, of course, all in the mind of the consumer. Given that the manufacturing cost will be very similar for both, the amount added to the manufacturing cost – the **markup** – will result in a far greater gross profit in relation to the selling price – **margin** – for the designer brand.

What is the difference between these two terms, mark-up and margin?

Mark-up is the amount added onto the cost of sales (ie what the product cost the business) to produce the selling price.

Margin is the amount of gross profit a business makes when it sells an item, expressed as a percentage of the selling price. The formula is:

$$\frac{\textbf{gross profit x 100}}{\textbf{selling price}} \quad = \quad \textbf{margin \%}$$

For example, if a clothes retailer buys a fleece at £10 and sells it for £15, it makes £5 gross profit on the sale. The margin % is:

$$\frac{\textbf{£5 x 100}}{\textbf{£15}} \quad = \quad \textbf{33.3\%}$$

The margin is an indicator of the amount of profit available to meet the running expenses of a business. The higher the percentage, the more 'cushion' there is to meet running expenses.

Note that large businesses such as supermarkets which can source their goods more cheaply and sell them rapidly in large volumes can afford to reduce their margins. Businesses which sell their goods more slowly, such as jewellers, need to mark-up their goods more to generate sufficient profit.

Stakeholders and Profit

Another consideration relating to profit for the management of a business is the significance of stakeholder pressure.

A stakeholder is a person or body who has an interest in what the business does

Internal stakeholders such as owners, managers and employees of the business, will benefit from payment schemes linked to profit. Owners and employees may also be shareholders and so will receive the benefits of dividends.

External stakeholders, such a customers and suppliers, will benefit from the financial well-being of the business – they will receive products and payments on time. The local community will benefit from local sponsorship and improvements to amenities. Lenders will be reassured that they will receive repayment of borrowing and interest, investors will receive healthy dividends. Because most tax is based on profit, high profits will bring more money into the purse of the tax authorities.

In short, the management of a business that makes a good profit can be sure of looking after the interests of most stakeholders and fulfiling its business objectives. The stakeholders that can be difficult to please are the pressure groups; this is because profit can sometimes be made at a social cost, eg from cheap overseas labour, or as a result of a manufacturing process which involves animal testing.

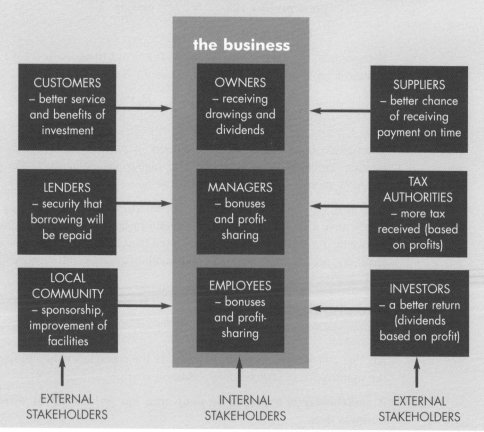

WAYS IN WHICH STAKEHOLDERS BENEFIT FROM PROFITS

Activity 12.1 – business profitability

Last year's figures for the receipts and costs of three different types of business are shown below. Study the figures and answer the questions that follow.

business	receipts		payments	
		£		£
Holiday company	Sales of holidays	245,000	Cost of holidays	165,000
	Loan from bank	5,000	Computer system purchase	5,000
			Running costs	40,000
Toy manufacturer	Sales of toys	350,000	Raw materials purchases	175,000
	Loans	250,000	Insurance	15,000
			Other running costs	80,000
			Premises purchase	300,000
			Machinery purchase	50,000
Clothes shop	Sales of clothes	250,000	Purchases of stock	180,000
	Capital	50,000	Wages	80,000
			Other running costs	34,500

1   Calculate both the gross profit and the net profit (or loss) made by the three businesses. If a loss has been made, show the figure in your answer in brackets.

   Note: before working out the profit (or loss) you will need to decide which items are start-up costs or financing items (loans, capital) because you will not be able to include these in your calculations.

2   The figures shown here look back over a year's trading. What planning calculations involving profit which look forward over a financial period might have been used by the businesses and how could they have helped the clothes shop in particular? Suggest practical actions relating to pricing and costs that could have been taken by the clothes shop to improve its financial performance.

3   The toy manufacturer is a limited company which is financed partly by the bank and partly by a business angel (private investor). Describe the way in which the stakeholders of the company might be interested in profit made by the business.

4   Explain to a new employee of one of the profitable businesses why the profit made during the year is not represented by a balance of cash in the bank account at the year-end.

Activity 12.2 – projected profit and loss accounts

You are working at a Business Link office and specialise in the giving of financial advice.

You have appointments with two individuals, Josh Henderson and Vicki Butler, both of whom are thinking of starting up new sole trader businesses operating designer clothes shops. You stress to both of them the importance of planning ahead carefully to make sure that each business will cover its running costs and make a profit to provide them with money for living expenses.

They work out figures for the year (shown below) for a projected profit and loss account as part of a master budget. They ask for your help in drawing up these profit and loss accounts.

	Josh Henderson £	Vicki Butler £
Sales	175,000	250,900
Purchases	95,000	102,984
Wages	45,600	67,800
Rent	5,000	5,690
Rates	3,450	4,010
Insurance	2,300	4,560
Advertising	2,000	13,450
Other expenses	200	2,057

1 Draw up a projected profit and loss account for both businesses, showing clearly:
   (a) cost of sales
   (b) gross profit
   (c) net profit
   Briefly explain what these terms mean.

2 Calculate the percentage gross and net profit margins in both cases (to the nearest percentage point) and compare the projected performance of the two shops. The formula to use is: (profit/sales) x 100

   Vicki says that she has heard that leading supermarkets have a gross profit margin of only 15% to 20% on clothes. Explain to her how they can survive on such a low margin.

Activity 12.3 – profit and loss on a spreadsheet

Draw up a spreadsheet for a profit and loss account and enter both sets of figures from Activity 12.2. Make sure that you use separate files or worksheets for each set of figures.

Use the format and formulas shown below if you wish. The shaded areas show where the figures should be entered.

Note that 'Profit and Loss Statement' is another term for 'Profit and Loss Account'.

Confirm the accuracy of your workings for Activity 12.2.

	A	B	C
1	PROFIT AND LOSS STATEMENT		
2			
3	name:		
4	period:		
5			
6		£	£
7			
8	Sales		
9	Cost of sales (purchases)		
10	**Gross profit**		=C8-C9
11			
12			
13	Less overheads:		
14	Wages		
15	Rent		
16	Rates		
17	Insurance		
18	Advertising		
19	Other expenses		
20			=SUM(B14:B19)
21	**Net Profit**		=C10-C20
22			

CHAPTER SUMMARY

■ Making a profit is one of the principal objectives in business. It benefits many stakeholders, including the business owner(s).

■ Profit is calculated by deducting running expenses from sales revenue in a profit and loss account.

■ Businesses can forecast profit, either as part of the budgeting process, which projects the amount of profit made over a certain period, or as part of a break-even calculation which is more simple and works out at what point the business starts to become profitable (see Chapter 13).

■ Profit is also calculated by looking back over a fixed period and working out levels of profit in a profit and loss account.

■ There are two main types of profit calculated in the profit and loss account. Gross profit is the profit after deduction from sales revenue of the cost of producing the product (whether goods or services). Net profit is gross profit minus all the other expenses of the business (overheads).

■ Net profit is the profit which is then available for the owner(s) of the business, for paying the tax bill and for investing back in the business, eg buying new equipment.

■ Making a profit does not mean the same as having money in the business bank account. The profit can be paid to the owner(s) and can be re-invested in the business to help it expand.

■ Businesses often look at profit in terms of mark-up (the difference between the direct cost of producing a product and its selling price) and margin (the gross profit as a percentage of the selling price).

■ Business stakeholders, both internal and external, are directly affected by the level of profit made by a business. Most stakeholders (eg employees, shareholders and lenders) benefit from business profits; some stakeholders may object (eg pressure groups with social concerns).

KEY TERMS

profit	The excess of revenue from sales over running costs of the business: PROFIT = SALES REVENUE − RUNNING COSTS
budgeting	an estimate of likely future income and expenditure over a given period
break-even	an analysis of the income and running costs of a business to calculate at what point the business starts to make a profit
profit & loss account	a financial statement covering a period of time setting out a profit calculation based on the formula: PROFIT = SALES REVENUE − RUNNING COSTS
master budget	the budget which contains a projected profit and loss account
cost of sales	the direct cost to the business over a period of time of the actual production of the products that have been sold
gross profit	the profit to the business after producing the goods and before deducting the other running costs (overheads): GROSS PROFIT = SALES REVENUE − COST OF SALES
overheads	the costs of running the business that do not normally vary with the level of production
net profit	the profit to the business after deduction of the cost of sales and the overheads: NET PROFIT = GROSS PROFIT − OVERHEADS
mark-up	the amount added to the cost of sales of a product to produce the selling price
margin	the gross profit a business makes when it sells an item, expressed as a percentage of the selling price: $\dfrac{\text{GROSS PROFIT} \times 100}{\text{SALES}} = \text{MARGIN \%}$
stakeholder	a person or an organisation that has an interest in the performance of a business

13

Financial forecasting – break-even

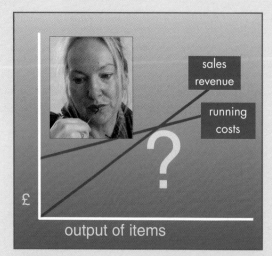

Starting point

In Chapter 12 we explained about costs and described how profit is calculated as the difference between sales revenue and running expenses. Profit is an important objective for businesses and so the ability of a business to make a profit is critical.

This ability can be tested by carrying out a break-even analysis, a form of financial forecasting.

This involves working out the point at which a business covers its running costs from its sales revenue and starts to make a profit.

But a business will want to know more than just when it starts to make a profit – it will want to know how much profit is likely to be made when sales hit certain levels and also how any variation in costs will affect the break-even point.

What you will learn from this chapter

- break-even is the point at which running costs are covered by sales revenue; after break-even has been reached, the business will start to make a profit

- running costs are made up of variable costs (costs that vary with the number of products sold – eg stock bought in to sell by a shop) and fixed costs (costs, such as insurance, that remain the same and have to be paid anyway)

- the break-even 'point' can be calculated by using a formula or by constructing a table of sales revenue and costs and then drawing a graph from this data

- a break-even graph is particularly useful in showing levels of profit (or loss) at different levels of output

the Break-even Point

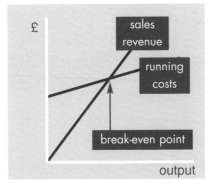

definition

Break-even is the point at which sales revenue is equal to running costs

In other words, after a business has reached break-even point it will start to make a profit.

Before break-even point the business is making a loss and at break-even point the profit is zero.

Note that the business costs involved in the break-even calculation are **running costs only**, eg wages, materials, and expenses such as insurance and rates. Start-up costs such as premises and equipment are not included in the break-even calculation – they will already have been financed by capital from the owner(s) or by outside finance.

running costs: fixed and variable costs

As we saw in Chapter 12, running costs are the day-to-day expenses of a business and include items such as:

■ purchase of materials which are turned into products (in a manufacturing business)

■ wages and insurance (in a service business)

■ stock which is sold as part of day-to-day trading (in a retail business)

Some costs are fixed and have to be paid anyway; others vary with the number of items a business produces or sells. When calculating break-even you need to distinguish between two types of running cost: **fixed costs** and **variable costs**.

fixed costs

Fixed costs are running costs which do not vary in line with the number of items produced

Fixed costs are running costs such as rent and insurance which have to be paid anyway, whatever the number of items produced or services sold by the business. Even if the business closes down over the Christmas break and nothing is produced or sold, the fixed costs still have to be paid.

Fixed costs can be shown in the form of a graph (see next page) which shows the cost (£) and the number of items produced, 'the output'. An 'item' can be a product made in a factory, an item sold in a shop, or a service provided.

COST £

at this point no items have been sold but fixed costs still have to be paid

FIXED COSTS

0

OUTPUT OF ITEMS

the number of items manufactured, items sold from a shop, or services provided

As you can see in this graph, the fixed costs of a business remain at the same level, however many items are produced – the line on the graph is a horizontal straight line.

variable costs

Variable costs are running costs which vary in line with the number of items produced

Variable costs relate to the production of the item itself – whether it is a manufactured item or a service. They include expenses such as purchases of materials and stock, and, in the case of a manufacturer, the wages paid to production line employees.

If the output is nil, variable costs will be zero, if the output increases, so does the total variable cost. As you can see from the straight line on the graph below, total variable costs rise as the number of items produced rises.

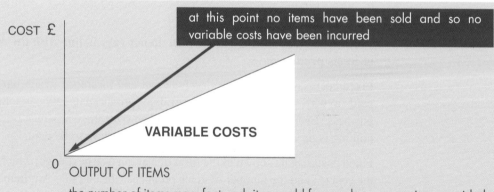

COST £

at this point no items have been sold and so no variable costs have been incurred

VARIABLE COSTS

0

OUTPUT OF ITEMS

the number of items manufactured, items sold from a shop, or services provided

total cost = fixed costs + variable costs

As a business will have to pay both fixed and variable costs, the two costs added together (the total cost) can also be shown in graph form:

Calculating Break-even

Break-even can be calculated in two different ways:

- by formula
- by drawing a graph

The formula method is the quickest, but the graph method provides more information to the managers of the business. We will describe each method in turn. First, however, we need to understand what is meant by 'contribution'.

contribution: paying off fixed costs and providing profit

Contribution is calculated as follows:

contribution = selling price of an item minus the variable cost of producing that item

In other words, each time an item is sold the money received will first pay off the variable costs of that item and then the money that remains – the **contribution** – will go towards paying off the fixed costs. When enough items have been sold to pay off all the fixed costs, two things occur:

- break-even point will have been reached because all costs – variable and fixed – have been paid off
- the contribution – which will still be received each time an extra item is sold – then becomes profit

Suppose a pizza business had revenue and costs as follows:

selling price of each pizza	£4
variable costs (eg pastry base, toppings, labour)	£2
fixed costs (eg rent, insurance)	£1,000 a month

The contribution of each pizza is:

£4 (selling price) minus £2 (variable costs) = £2 (contribution)

Each time a pizza is sold, £2 will go towards paying off the monthly fixed costs of £1,000. Therefore, when 500 pizzas have been sold (500 is £1,000 divided by £2), 500 contributions of £2 will have been made to cover the fixed costs and break-even point will have been reached because all costs will have been covered. If more pizzas are sold during the month, the subsequent contributions of £2 per pizza **will become profit** for the business.

contribution and the break-even formula

We can use contribution to produce a formula for working out the number of units a business needs to sell in order to cover its costs and to break-even:

break-even (units)   = $\dfrac{\textbf{fixed costs (£)}}{\textbf{contribution per unit (£)}}$

In the case of the pizza company

Break-even (units)   = $\dfrac{\textbf{£1,000}}{\textbf{£2}}$ =   **500 units**

Remember that the basis for this formula is:

$$\frac{\textbf{fixed costs (£)}}{\textbf{selling price per unit (£) minus variable cost per unit (£)}}$$

This formula provides the business with the basic information about the level of output needed in order to make the product viable and profitable.

Carry out the activity on the next page to see how this works in practice and how changes in costs and pricing can affect the break-even point.

Activity 13.1 – calculating break-even by formula

Luigi and Bella are starting up a 'fast' pasta outlet in the town. The monthly fixed costs of production are £1,200 and the variable costs of production of an average meal are £5 per unit. The average price of a similar meal in the town is £7.

Calculate the contribution and use the formula shown on the previous page to calculate the number of meals that will need to be produced and sold each month to break-even in the case of options 1, 2 and 3. Then answer the final question.

1 The average selling price favoured by Luigi is £6 per meal – he says that they need to sell at a low price to capture market share.

2 Bella thinks that the average selling price should be £10 – she thinks their cooking is especially good and that people will pay more for quality.

3 Just before they open up for business a competitor starts up a similar business, but selling at an average price of £5 a meal. Luigi wants to cut the average selling price of a meal to £5 as a special promotional offer.

4 State which of the three selling prices you would favour. Give reasons for your decision.

Constructing a Break-even Graph

Luigi and Bella in the above Activity will find the break-even calculation formula useful in setting a selling price, but will discover that it has its limitations. For example, the break-even point calculated by formula is always stated in terms of units. The management might ask questions relating to money amounts, such as profit and loss, for example:

'How much profit will we make if we sell 200 more meals per month than the break-even amount?'

'How much of a loss will we make if we set the selling price of a meal at £6 but then do not sell enough in order to break-even?'

The answer is to be found in the construction of a break-even table and graph which relate the number of units sold to money amounts. We have already seen a graph (page 211) showing fixed and variable costs. If a sales income line is then added to this, a break-even point can be plotted.

Examine the process in the Case Study that follows.

Case Study – break-even graph

Prontoys Limited is launching a new cuddly toy know as 'Wuffles'. It has decided to draw a break-even graph to check the feasibility of the scheme. Before a break-even graph can be constructed, a table will be drawn up setting out the income and costs for different numbers of units.

A table for Wuffles is shown below. The data used is: selling price per unit £20, variable cost per unit £10, fixed costs per month £5,000. Some of the figures from the table are then used to plot straight lines on the graph. These are:

■ the total cost line (Column C)

■ the sales income line (Column D)

units of production (Wuffles)	fixed costs A	variable costs B	total cost C	sales revenue D	profit/(loss) E
			A + B		D – C
	£	£	£	£	£
100	5,000	1,000	6,000	2,000	(4,000)
200	5,000	2,000	7,000	4,000	(3,000)
300	5,000	3,000	8,000	6,000	(2,000)
400	5,000	4,000	9,000	8,000	(1,000)
500	5,000	5,000	10,000	10,000	nil
600	5,000	6,000	11,000	12,000	1,000
700	5,000	7,000	12,000	14,000	2,000

notes on the break-even table

■ the units of production here are at intervals of 100

■ fixed costs (Column A) are fixed at £5,000 for every level of production

■ fixed costs (Column A) and variable costs (Column B) are added together to produce the total cost figure (Column C)

■ total cost (Column C) is deducted from the sales income figure (Column D) to produce either a positive figure (a profit) or a loss (a negative figure, in brackets) in Column E

As you can see, break-even occurs at 500 units.

construction of the break-even graph

The graph is constructed as follows:

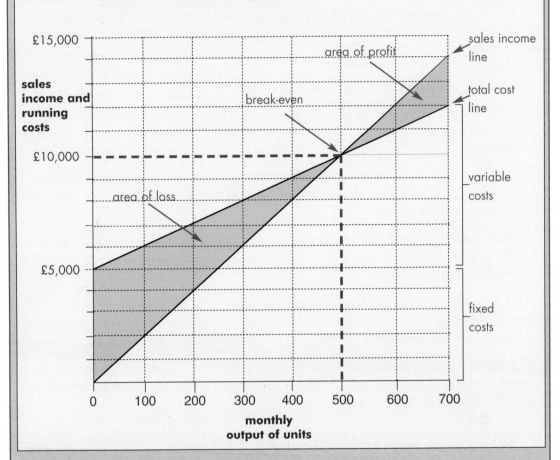

PRONTOYS LIMITED – break-even graph

notes on the break-even graph

- the vertical axis shows money amounts – the total cost and the sales income for different levels of production are plotted on this axis

- the horizontal axis shows units of output at intervals of 100

- the fixed costs of £5,000 are the same at all levels of output

- total cost is made up of fixed costs and variable costs

- the total costs line starts, not at zero, but at £5,000; this is because if the output is zero, the business still has to pay the £5,000 fixed costs

- the point at which the total costs and sales income lines cross is the break-even point

- from the graph you can read off the break-even point both in terms of units of output (500 units on the horizontal axis), and also in sales income value (£10,000 on the vertical axis)

working out profit and loss from the graph

If you look at the graph on the previous page you will see two shaded areas. On the left of the break-even point is an 'area of loss' and on the right of the break-even point is an 'area of profit'.

This means that for levels of output to the left of the break-even point (ie fewer than 500 units) the business will make a loss and for levels of output to the right of the break-even point, the business will make a profit.

If you read off the vertical distance (in £) between the sales income line and the total cost line (ie down the shaded area) you will find the exact amount of profit or loss for any level of output on the graph.

Note that each dotted 'box' on the graph represents £1,000 from top to bottom. For example, at an output level of zero you will make a loss of £5,000 (this is the fixed costs figure) and at an output level of 700 units you will make a profit of £2,000.

If you refer back to the table of figures from which the graph was plotted (page 214) you will be able to check these figures taken from the graph against the expected profit and loss totals in the far right-hand column.

how the graph helps Prontoys Limited

The type of questions which might be asked by the management of Prontoys Limited are:

'How much profit will we make if we sell 200 more Wuffles per month than the break-even amount?'

'How much loss will we make if production is short of the break-even point by 100 units.'

By reading the difference between the total cost line and the total income line, the answer to the first question is £2,000 and the answer to the second is a loss of £1,000.

These figures can be confirmed by looking at the table of data (page 214) or, if the figures are not on the table, by using the formula: PROFIT OR LOSS = SALES REVENUE MINUS TOTAL COSTS

Break-even Graph – Further Aspects

margin of safety

Another useful feature of the break-even graph is that it can show the margin of safety.

Margin of safety is the extent to which sales exceed the break-even point

Margin of safety is often looked at by management to see how far off the business is from a position where it starts to make a loss – just as a football team manager might look to see how far his/her team is away from the relegation zone in the league table.

The margin of safety can be expressed in units sold, sales revenue and as a percentage of the sales level at the time. The formula for the percentage is:

$$\frac{\text{current output minus break-even output}}{\text{current output}} \quad \text{x} \quad \frac{100}{1}$$

shortcomings of break-even graphs

The advantage of break-even is that it is a useful test of the viability of any new product and can provide management with the answers to a number of 'what-if' questions relating to costs, sales and profit. It is important to appreciate, however, that it does have some shortcomings which can be overlooked:

- it is based on a single product or type of product – a business which sells a diverse range of products would need separate analyses for each

- it assumes that all products produced will be sold – it does not allow for the situation where a product flops and does not sell

- it assumes that variable costs and fixed costs are constant – this would not be so if a product was very successful because variable costs might fall as volume increases and fixed costs would increase to allow for increased capacity

- following on from the last point, it is assumed that the lines on a break-even graph are always straight and it would then be tempting to extend the lines to obtain profit estimates for higher levels of production – as mentioned above, this would be a dangerous assumption as costs will vary at different levels of production

- break-even analysis tends to ignore external factors that might affect both costs and revenues, for example an interest rate rise which would increase fixed and total costs if the business was borrowing

Break-even on a Computer Spreadsheet

Break-even tables can easily be set up on a computer spreadsheet. They are particularly useful for showing the effects of 'what-if' scenarios, eg 'What if variable costs increased by £10? What if we put up the selling price by £10?' The two spreadsheets below show the data input and the formulas used.

spreadsheet for a break-even table - showing data input

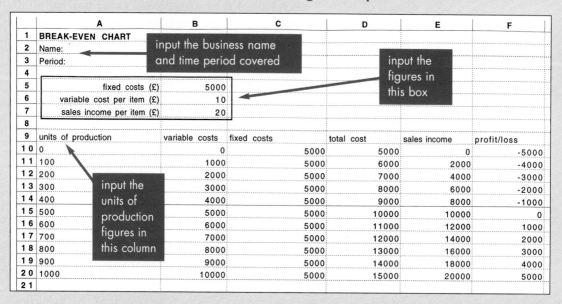

	A	B	C	D	E	F
1	BREAK-EVEN CHART					
2	Name:		input the business name			
3	Period:		and time period covered		input the	
4					figures in	
5	fixed costs (£)	5000			this box	
6	variable cost per item (£)	10				
7	sales income per item (£)	20				
8						
9	units of production	variable costs	fixed costs	total cost	sales income	profit/loss
10	0	0	5000	5000	0	-5000
11	100	1000	5000	6000	2000	-4000
12	200	2000	5000	7000	4000	-3000
13	300	3000	5000	8000	6000	-2000
14	400	4000	5000	9000	8000	-1000
15	500	5000	5000	10000	10000	0
16	600	6000	5000	11000	12000	1000
17	700	7000	5000	12000	14000	2000
18	800	8000	5000	13000	16000	3000
19	900	9000	5000	14000	18000	4000
20	1000	10000	5000	15000	20000	5000
21						

input the units of production figures in this column

spreadsheet for a break-even table - showing the formulas used

	A	B	C	D	E	F
1	BREAK-EVEN CHART					
2	Name:					
3	Period:					
4						
5	fixed costs (£)	5000				
6	variable cost per item (£)	10				
7	sales income per item (£)	20				
8						
9	units of production	variable costs	fixed costs	total cost	sales income	profit/loss
10	0	=B6*A10	=B5	=B10+C10	=B7*A10	=E10-D10
11	100	=B6*A11	=B5	=B11+C11	=B7*A11	=E11-D11
12	200	=B6*A12	=B5	=B12+C12	=B7*A12	=E12-D12
13	300	=B6*A13	=B5	=B13+C13	=B7*A13	=E13-D13
14	400	=B6*A14	=B5	=B14+C14	=B7*A14	=E14-D14
15	500	=B6*A15	=B5	=B15+C15	=B7*A15	=E15-D15
16	600	=B6*A16	=B5	=B16+C16	=B7*A16	=E16-D16
17	700	=B6*A17	=B5	=B17+C17	=B7*A17	=E17-D17
18	800	=B6*A18	=B5	=B18+C18	=B7*A18	=E18-D18
19	900	=B6*A19	=B5	=B19+C19	=B7*A19	=E19-D19
20	1000	=B6*A20	=B5	=B20+C20	=B7*A20	=E20-D20
21						

Activity 13.2 – reading a break-even graph

You have been given a break-even graph for Insight Limited. Study the graph and answer the questions at the bottom of the page.

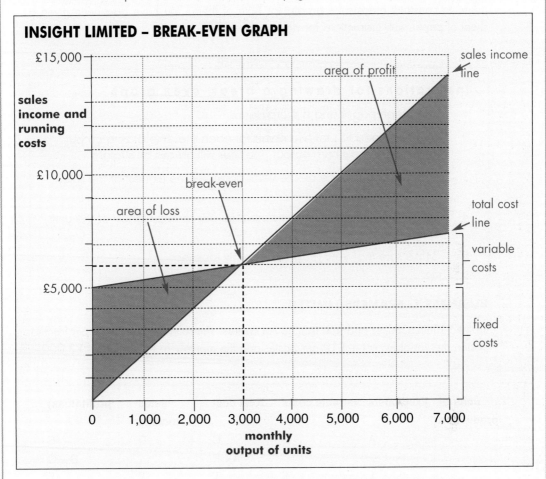

INSIGHT LIMITED – BREAK-EVEN GRAPH

1 How many units does Insight Limited have to produce to break even?

2 What are the fixed costs at the break-even point?

3 What are the variable costs at the break-even point?

4 What loss does Insight Limited make when output is zero units?

5 Why is a loss made when the output is zero units?

6 What profit is made by Insight Limited when the output is 6,000 units?

7 What is the margin of safety in terms of sales revenue and units and as a percentage when the monthly output of units reaches 6,000?

Activity 13.3 – constructing a break-even graph

You have been given the projected monthly figures for two businesses and have been asked to construct break-even graphs for both of them. You have also been given a sheet of paper with instructions for drawing break-even graphs.

instructions for drawing a break-even graph

1   Use graph paper and a sharp pencil.

2   You only need to plot two points for each line, one at zero output and one at maximum output. The lines will always be straight.

3   Allow enough space on the vertical axis for the highest of the sales income figures.

4   Allow enough space on the horizontal axis for the highest of the units of production figures.

5   Make sure that your graph is correctly labelled.

BUSINESS 1: FRAMERS LIMITED

Framers Limited makes and sells framed Art Posters. The selling price is £20 per framed poster, the variable cost is £10 per poster and the monthly fixed costs total £3,000.

units of production	fixed costs	variable costs	total cost	sales income	profit/(loss)
	A	B	C	D	E
			A + B		D – C
	£	£	£	£	£
0	3,000	0	3,000	0	(3,000)
100	3,000	1,000	4,000	2,000	(2,000)
200	3,000	2,000	5,000	4,000	(1,000)
300	3,000	3,000	6,000	6,000	nil
400	3,000	4,000	7,000	8,000	1,000
500	3,000	5,000	8,000	10,000	2,000
600	3,000	6,000	9,000	12,000	3,000
700	3,000	7,000	10,000	14,000	4,000
800	3,000	8,000	11,000	16,000	5,000

continued on next page . . .

tasks

1 Calculate the break-even point using the formula method to check the accuracy of the table on the previous page. The formula for the break-even quantity of output is:

$$\frac{\text{fixed costs (£)}}{\text{contribution per unit (£)}}$$

(remember: 'contribution' = selling price per unit minus variable cost per unit)

2 Draw up a break-even graph, using the instructions set out on the previous page.

3 Read off the graph the profit or loss if 100 posters are produced and sold each month.

4 Read off the graph the profit or loss if 600 posters are produced and sold each month.

5 Check the answers to 3 & 4 against the figures in the table on the previous page.

BUSINESS 2: WINTHROP FURNITURE

Winthrop Furniture makes and sells a wooden garden seat known as the 'Eden'. The figures for this business have not yet been set out in the form of a table. All you have been given are the following monthly figures:

Cost of timber and labour for making seat	£20 per seat
Selling price	£45 per seat
Monthly fixed costs	£15,000

tasks

1 Draw up a table showing fixed costs, variable costs, total costs, sales income, and profit or loss for production of seats in multiples of 100 from zero up to 1,000. You can alternatively use a computer spreadsheet (see page 218) to process your data.

2 Calculate the break-even point using the formula method to check your workings. (The formula is shown above in question 1 for Business 1, Framers Limited).

3 Draw up a break-even graph, using the instructions set out on the previous page.

4 Read off the graph the profit or loss if 200 seats are produced and sold each month.

5 Read off the graph the profit or loss if 1,000 seats are produced and sold each month.

6 Check the answers to 4 & 5 against the figures in the table produced in question 1.

7 The production manager of the company mentions that he has heard that interest rates are due to rise sharply over the next six months. He asks 'How does the graph allow for that? Would it change?' How would you answer him?

8 The marketing manager, who always looks on the bright side when it comes to sales performance, suggests that you extend the straight lines on the graph to project sales of the seat at 2,000 a month. What would be your reply?

CHAPTER SUMMARY

- A business which is starting up or launching a new product will need to carry out the processes of financial forecasting to see whether it is going to be profitable and, if so, at what point it is going to be profitable.

- Break-even is a form of financial forecasting which compares the projected sales revenue of a business with its running costs at different levels of production (for a manufacturer), sales of items (for a retailer) or services provided. This analysis will enable the business to forecast its profit (which is the difference between its sales revenue and its running costs).

- The break-even point is reached when the sales revenue equals the total running costs. At this point profit is zero. After break-even point (ie when further sales are made) the business makes a profit; before break-even point the business makes a loss.

- Running costs can be classified as either fixed costs or variable costs. Fixed costs are 'fixed' because they do not vary with the level of production, for example insurance costs. Variable costs 'vary' with the level of production, for example materials and stock purchased.

- Break-even can then be defined as the point at which sales revenue is equal to fixed costs plus variable costs.

- Contribution is the difference between the selling price per unit and the variable costs per unit. The contribution will be used to pay off the fixed costs and then when break-even is reached, it will provide profit for the business. The break-even point (in units) can therefore be calculated by using the formulas:

$$\frac{\text{FIXED COSTS } (£)}{\text{CONTRIBUTION } (£)} \quad \text{or} \quad \frac{\text{FIXED COSTS}}{\text{SELLING PRICE PER UNIT } (£) \text{ MINUS VARIABLE COST PER UNIT } (£)}$$

- Calculating break-even using formulas provides important but basic information. A break-even data table comparing costs and revenues and a graph drawn from that data give the business manager more information about potential profits and losses at varying levels of production. They can also illustrate the margin of safety at various levels of production.

- There are, however, shortcomings to break-even as a management tool for decision making. These include the fact that break-even deals with a single product or type of product and assumes a constant level of sales revenue and costs, which, in view of external factors, may well be an unrealistic assumption.

KEY TERMS

break-even
the point at which sales revenue is equal to running costs and profit is zero

fixed costs
running costs which do not vary with the number of items produced (items can be goods or services)

variable costs
running costs which do vary with the level of production

contribution
the money received from selling a product which goes towards paying off the fixed costs and then, after break-even has been reached, constitutes profit – it is calculated as the selling price of an item minus the variable cost of producing that item

break-even formula
an arithmetic method of working out the number of units which need to be produced in order to reach the break-even point:

$$\frac{\text{FIXED COSTS } (\pounds)}{\text{CONTRIBUTION } (\pounds)} \quad \text{or}$$

$$\frac{\text{FIXED COSTS}}{\text{SELLING PRICE PER UNIT } (\pounds) \text{ MINUS VARIABLE COST PER UNIT } (\pounds)}$$

margin of safety
the extent to which the level of sales exceeds the break-even point, expressed in units or sales revenue or as a percentage of the level of sales – a measure of how close the business is to making a loss

area of loss
the area on a break-even graph between the sales income line and the total cost line **below** the break-even point – used to measure how much loss is made at different levels of output

area of profit
the area on a break-even graph between the sales income line and the total cost line **above** the break-even point – used to measure how much profit is made at different levels of output

14

Liquidity and the balance sheet

no cash = insolvency

Starting point

Many businesses fail because they run out of cash and cannot then pay their bills. This can happen through bad luck and also through poor financial management.

Business owners and managers need to realise that the availability of cash and items that can easily be turned into cash – the liquidity of a business – is critical to its survival. A business can be profitable, but if it is not generating cash it can become insolvent – it can 'go bust'.

What you will learn from this chapter

- the liquidity of a business is its ability to pay off its debts as they fall due

- insolvency is owing more than you have got and being unable to pay off debts as they fall due; insolvency can involve court action and subsequent bankruptcy (individuals) or winding up (companies)

- the current assets of a business are items owned by a business or owed to it in the short term; current liabilities are items owed by a business in the short term

- liquidity and cash flow can be increased by items which can be turned into cash; these are included in what is known as 'working capital':

  working capital = current assets minus current liabilities

- the working capital of a business is a 'cushion' of resources – cash and 'near-cash' – which is available to meet its liabilities

- the working capital of a business is calculated and shown on a financial statement known as a 'balance sheet'

the Flow of Cash in a Business

the importance of cash

First a definition: the business term 'cash' does not always mean notes and coins but money that is available in any form, including bank accounts and notes and coins. 'Cash' often means 'money that is available now'.

We saw in the last chapter that making a profit is not necessarily the same as having cash to spare. When the supply of cash dries up, the business can fail and go 'bust'. In this section we look in detail at the way in which cash circulates in the business. As a first step, study the diagram below which shows the cash flowing in and out of a manufacturing business. Then read the notes that follow.

THE FLOW OF CASH IN A MANUFACTURING BUSINESS

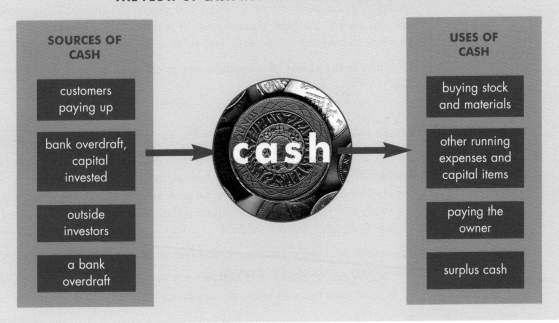

where the cash comes from

As you will see from the left hand side of the diagram, there are two main sources of cash:

■ cash from the sale of the products of the business – the more the business sells, the more cash it will receive

■ cash received from other sources, for example the bank overdraft, cash introduced by the owner(s) or other investors

where the cash goes

As you will see from the right-hand side of the diagram on the previous page, there are two main 'drains' on the supply of cash:

- paying for the product being sold – in the case of a manufacturing business this will be stocks of raw materials; if the business was a service business, the money would be spent on the costs of providing the service – this represents the 'cost of sales' in the profit and loss statement

- paying the other running expenses (the overheads), buying capital items (eg equipment), paying the owner

surplus cash and liquidity

You will also see from the diagram that another use of cash is a build-up of 'surplus cash'.

If a business is trading profitably, and the money from sales is being received promptly, the amount of cash received will exceed the amount being spent and will go into the bank account, until it is allocated for something else. This type of business can be described as being **liquid**.

Liquidity is the ability of a business to pay off its debts as they become due

where things can go wrong with the cash flow

As you will see from the diagram on the previous page, the flow of cash is vital to the running of a business. Just as the supply of electricity to a household can be cut off if the bill is not paid, with disastrous consequences, the owner of a business can face failure if the 'cash flow' is not maintained – either from sales or from the bank overdraft.

This cycle of money coming in and out of the business can be very precariously balanced. For example:

- What if sales fall well below the targets set?

- What if a big customer who owes money goes 'bust'?

- What if the premises catches fire?

- What if the bank will not lend any more money on overdraft?

In all these cases the supply of cash will be reduced and the business may not be able to pay important bills or pay its suppliers. Look at the danger points shown on the diagram on the next page.

Then read the Case Study which follows – it shows what can go wrong when the cash runs out.

DANGER POINTS IN THE FLOW OF CASH

| outside sources of cash | what if the bank asks for the overdraft to be repaid? | | what if there is no cash to pay the wages? | expenses which have to be met |

| customers who owe money | what if the customers fail to pay up? | cash | what if there is no cash to pay the suppliers? | purchases of stock and materials |

Case Study – cash flow problems

John Spender has started up in business making novelty clocks. He buys quartz clock mechanisms from a wholesaler whom he pays 30 days after he has received the goods and the invoice. He makes the casings from perspex in his workshop. He employs two production workers and does all the marketing, selling and administration himself.

He is very pleased that he has been able to secure contracts to supply a major department store chain and a catalogue mail order company with his clocks. They agree to pay him 60 days after he has supplied and invoiced the goods. He has a £5,000 overdraft with the Albion Bank to provide 'cash flow' for the period after he has paid for his materials, but before he receives payment from his two big customers.

this is what happens . . .

November
John and his production workers start to work flat out to supply the orders received – which are larger than expected. He has had to order more materials than expected, and his wages bill is bigger.

December
He has to pay for his first month's supplies. He has to borrow from the bank on overdraft to pay for them. The bank manager is reasonably happy about this, although he says the amount of £6,000 is larger than he was expecting from the budgeted figures that John had given him.

January

Disaster strikes. The department store's buyer telephones to say that some of the clocks have been returned by their customers complaining that they are faulty. The department store is returning the faulty ones, and will not pay for the remainder until they have been sold. The mail order company, on the other hand, have had no problems, and he receives his first cheque from them. John is so busy that he fails to tell the bank what is happening.

February

John issues a cheque to the supplier of the quartz mechanisms, but the bank refuse to pay it, saying that the overdraft is too high – he has borrowed too much already. The supplier refuses to send any more mechanisms. John only has three weeks' supply left in stock.

March

John finds that he has to lay off his production workers – he cannot make any more clocks, and he cannot supply orders received. He has no money to pay the workers.

April

The bank makes formal demand for the money owing on its overdraft, which now stands at £8,500. The bank has John's house as security, and can sell it if John cannot repay the borrowing.

May

John's business fails. He is insolvent – he owes more than he has got.

Activity 14.1 – cash flow problems

Read through the John Spender Case Study and answer the following questions, either in writing or through class discussion.

1 How much did John think he was going to need to borrow and why was he going to need this money?

2 Why did the amount of cash needed exceed John's initial forecasts (ie at the stage before he sent out any goods)?

3 Why did the supplier of quartz mechanisms refuse to supply any more, and why did John lay off his production workers?

4 What was the final 'death blow' to John's business. What could happen to him and his family?

5 What could John have done to avoid his business failing in this way?

Avoiding Insolvency

what is insolvency?

Insolvency is owing more than you own and being in a position where you are unable to pay debts when they become due

Insolvency is an unfortunate fact of business life. It is unfortunate for the business involved and also bad news for the people who are owed money by the business. If the people who are owed money – the creditors – consider they can get their money back through the courts they can do so by:

- making an individual (sole trader or partner) 'bankrupt' by court order

- 'winding up' a company – putting it into liquidation in the courts

The end-result of these legal processes is that most of the assets (belongings) of the individual or company will be sold under court supervision and the money used to pay off the creditors.

This does not mean that the creditors will get all their money back – the court costs will have to be met and it may be that lenders such as banks will have 'first cut' of the proceeds because they have security for their lending. In fact, trade creditors often get very little back at all.

**IN THE MATTER OF
THE INSOLVENCY ACT 1986**

DOJEE TRADING LIMITED

Notice is hereby given that John James Hillstone of 3 High Street, Mereford, MR1 2JF, was appointed liquidator to the company on 6 April 2006 by resolutions passed at meetings of the company's members and creditors.

Notice is also hereby given that creditors are required on or before June 30 2006 to send their names and addresses, together with particulars of their debts or claims, to John James Hillstone of 3 High Street, Mereford MR1 2JF, and if required by notice in writing

extract from a public notice of a company in liquidation

As you will have seen from the John Spender Case Study on the last two pages, business failure is often a result of cash flow failure. It is not always entirely the fault of the business owner(s) – bad luck can occur – but good financial management can help.

The lesson here for businesses that sell on credit is firstly to make sure that their customers pay up on time and secondly to take firm measures when customers delay payment – a tell-tale sign that the customer is experiencing cash flow problems.

how to avoid cash flow failure

Problems caused by cash flow drying up can normally be pinpointed to certain areas. Good management of these areas can help avoid this situation. This involves an understanding of **working capital**, which we will deal with next.

the Working Capital Cycle

current assets and current liabilities

It is important that the management of a business ensures not only that there is enough immediate cash to pay its debts as they fall due, but that there are enough short-term resources which can be turned into cash when the need arises. These non-cash resources include:

- money which is due from customers (debtors)
- stock which can be sold

Therefore a business will ideally have a 'cushion' of resources – cash and 'near cash' items – which will be available to meet its liabilities (items owed). The term for this source of funds for payment is **current assets**.

Current assets are items owned by a business or owed to the business in the short term

Current assets include, in order of liquidity (availability):

- cash held by the business
- money in the business bank account
- money owed by customers (debtors)
- stock which can be sold

Current assets are held in order to pay off the short-term liabilities (items owed) of the business. These are known as **current liabilities**.

Current liabilities are items owed by a business in the short term

Current liabilities include:

- money owed to suppliers (creditors)
- money owed to the bank in the form of an overdraft
- other items due in the short term such as tax bills

working capital – a definition

Working capital is the term given to the surplus of current assets over current liabilities. Working capital is the 'extra' amount of money or assets that can readily be turned into money that a business has at its disposal at any one time to meet its current liabilities. The formula is:

working capital = current assets minus current liabilities

Working capital is also sometimes referred to as 'net current assets'. Clearly the more working capital a business has in relation to its overall resources, the stronger that business is.

A business must make sure that working capital is well managed. This involves an understanding of what is known as the working capital cycle. We will now explain how this works.

the working capital cycle – keeping the business afloat

Working capital must keep circulating for a business to survive. The diagram below, which is based on a trading business, shows a series of stages which work in a circular manner – hence the term 'working capital cycle'. Note that the business sells its goods on credit. The stages of the cycle are:

1 suppliers (**creditors**) sell goods to the business on credit

2 stock is sold to customers (**debtors**) on credit

3 debtors make payment and the money is paid into the bank

4 the business pays the creditors from the bank account

Now follow these four stages on the diagram below, referring the numbers above to the numbers on the diagram.

The bank account will of course also see other payments received (eg cash sales, loans raised) and payments made (purchase of fixed assets such as computers) which will affect the bank balance. The important point here is that the business should control the **timing** of the payments which make up the working capital cycle.

THE WORKING CAPITAL CYCLE IN A TRADING BUSINESS

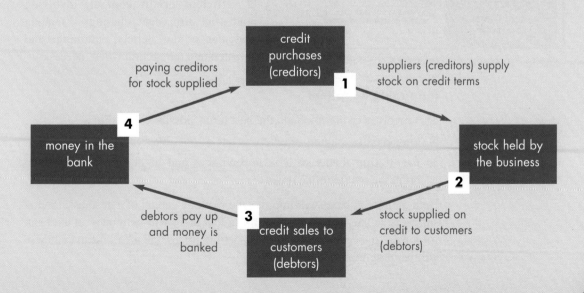

Working Capital Management

Good working capital management involves managing:

- **debtors** (customers who buy on credit terms)
- **creditors** (suppliers who sell on credit terms)
- **stock** (manufactured items and goods held by retailers)

These clearly apply to manufacturing or retailing businesses which hold stock. The same principles – apart from stock management – apply equally to service industries. We will now describe the principles of all three areas of working capital management.

managing debtors

Managing working capital efficiently means making sure that customers who buy on credit pay up on time. Money received on time means money in the bank and money available to pay current liabilities. The guiding principles of debtor management include:

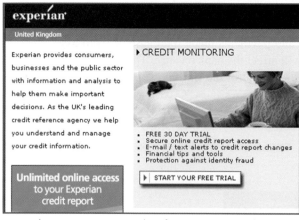

www.uk.experian.com – credit reference agency online

- **check out the customer** before granting credit – get trade references, a bank reference and a credit check, using a credit reference agency such as Experian
- **establish payment terms** which clearly set out when payment is to be received, eg at the end of the month following the invoice – and obviously the sooner the better
- **efficient credit control**, involving polite but firm debt chasing – sending statements and letters, phoning and threatening court action where necessary

managing suppliers

This involves trying to obtain the best terms possible, including:

- **long credit** – paying suppliers as late as possible
- **negotiating terms** such as lower prices and higher discounts to help bring the overall price down

Both of these policies will improve the working capital of a business. Paying suppliers as late as possible will mean that there will be money in the bank for longer to meet current liabilities, getting prices down will mean that there will be more money in the bank.

managing stock

Holding stock costs money and can be a drain on working capital. If a business has a high level of stock, cash will have been paid out to finance it – cash which could have been put to better use in the business.

If on the other hand too little stock is held, sales will be lost if an item is out of stock because the customer will go elsewhere. Some businesses, particularly those in the manufacturing sector, operate a just-in-time (JIT) method which, as the name suggests, replaces stock just before it will be needed.

A business therefore needs efficient stock control which will strike the balance between holding too much stock and too little stock.

Activity 14.2 – working capital management

Asaf was made redundant from Mellor Stationery Supplies for whom he had worked as Purchasing Manager for five years. With the redundancy money received he set up a stationery supply business Stationery4U six months ago, in January.

He negotiated a £10,000 overdraft from Anfield Bank and started trading at the beginning of the year. His suppliers were well known to him from his previous job, but as his business was a new one they required cash payment from him for the first six months of trading.

His main customers were a variety of businesses in the area. He was anxious to expand his customer base and started offering 60 days credit terms to new customers. He did not bother to take references because he was so busy. 'Sales is what I want!' he was often heard to say. 'Sell the goods and the profits will take care of themselves.'

Then things started to go wrong.

Asaf was given notice by the court that one of his largest customers, Preston Enterprises, was being taken through bankruptcy proceedings. Preston Enterprises owed him £7,500. Then he received a telephone call from the bank telling him that his overdraft had reached a balance of £12,000 overdrawn. He had also failed to pay the monthly invoice of one of his major suppliers. They were now asking for immediate payment. His stock supervisor emailed to say that because of slow sales, the stock levels were higher than he would like to see.

1   Explain to Asaf what exactly is going wrong – particularly in relation to the working capital cycle operating in his business.

2   Suggest how he could have managed his working capital better, relating your advice to the principles of good working capital management.

3   Warn Asaf about what could happen to his business if the present trend continues.

Measuring Working Capital: the Balance Sheet

A balance sheet is a financial statement which shows the assets, liabilities and capital of a business at a particular date

A balance sheet shows the state of the business at one moment in time – a balance sheet is often described as a 'snapshot' of a business. The money amounts of these assets, liabilities, and capital are taken from the accounting records of the business.

why a 'balance' sheet?

A balance sheet sets out a basic equation, both sides of which 'balance':

assets minus liabilities = capital

These terms mean:

assets	items owned by a business, either as current (short-term) assets or as fixed (long-term) assets
liabilities	amounts owed, either current (short-term) liabilities or long-term liabilities such as bank loans
capital	the investment of the owner(s) in the business

The formula **assets minus liabilities = capital** is therefore stating that:

assets (items owned) minus liabilities (items owed)

= capital (owner's investment)

The diagram below represents this equation in a simplified balance sheet.

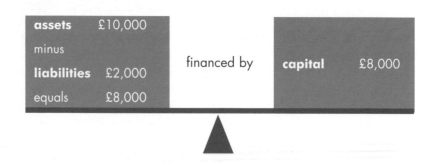

purpose of the balance sheet

The purpose of a balance sheet is to show the owner or owners (eg shareholders of a limited company) what is represented by their investment and what their investment is worth. The 'capital' section shows the value and the assets and liabilities section shows how that investment is made up. The balance sheet tells the owner(s) the value of assets owned and the extent to which the business is borrowing. The balance sheet could be compared to a form of financial 'health check'.

A balance sheet is normally set out in a vertical format as follows:

assets	£10,000
minus	
liabilities	£2,000
equals	£8,000

financed by

capital	£8,000

working capital on the balance sheet

We have seen in this chapter how vital it is that a business has sufficient working capital (working capital = current assets minus current liabilities) to keep it operating on a day-to-day basis.

The balance sheet shows working capital by separating out the current assets and current liabilities (in the dotted box) to produce a subtotal, which is then added to the fixed assets. Working capital is also referred to (as here) as **net current assets**. Study the diagram below and then read the Case Study that follows, which shows how a limited company balance sheet 'works'.

the working capital calculation on the balance sheet

fixed assets	£5,000
	plus
current assets	£5,000
minus	
current liabilities	£2,000
equals	
working capital (net current assets)	£3,000
equals	£8,000

financed by

capital	£8,000

Case Study – balance sheet

the business

Crafty Designs Limited is a craft product business run by its two directors, Julian and Sandy Horne, who each own fifty percent of the shares of the company.

start-up financing

The two directors have invested £150,000 of their own money as share capital, which is made up of 150,000 £1 shares.

The company has borrowed £75,000 from the bank in the form of long-term loans (long-term liabilities) to finance fixed assets (premises and equipment). it also has a £15,000 overdraft (current liability).

working capital

Current assets of £53,000 include stock, money owed by trade customers (debtors) and cash in the till.

Current liabilities of £33,000 include money owed to trade creditors, and the bank overdraft. **Working capital** is therefore £53,000 minus £33,000 = £20,000, which is a comfortable surplus to finance day-to-day needs.

net assets

The total of the top half of the balance sheet (the Net Assets) is: Fixed Assets + Working Capital – Long Term Liabilities, ie

£240,000 + £20,000 – £75,000 = £185,000

This £185,000 is Julian's and Sandy's stake in the business and equals their Capital (also known as Shareholders' Funds).

capital

The business is financed by the share capital and the profits made by the business up to the date of the balance sheet. This profit is shown as Profit and Loss Account and represents the total net profit shown on the bottom of the Profit and Loss Statement each year.

structure of the balance sheet

headings

The balance sheet shows the business on 31 December. The year would also be added.

fixed assets

These are the items owned by the business for the long-term.

current assets

These are the items owned by the business for the short term. 'Debtors' represents amounts owed by customers.

current liabilities

These are the items owed by the business in the short term. 'Creditors' represents money due to suppliers.

working capital

Current assets minus current liabilities, also known as 'net current assets'.

long-term liabilities

These are the items owed by the business in the long-term (over 12 months) – here bank loans.

net assets

This is the net total of all the assets minus all the liabilities.

financed by . . .

This shows how the business is financed and where the money has come from. In this case it is share capital (the owner's investment) and profits earned.

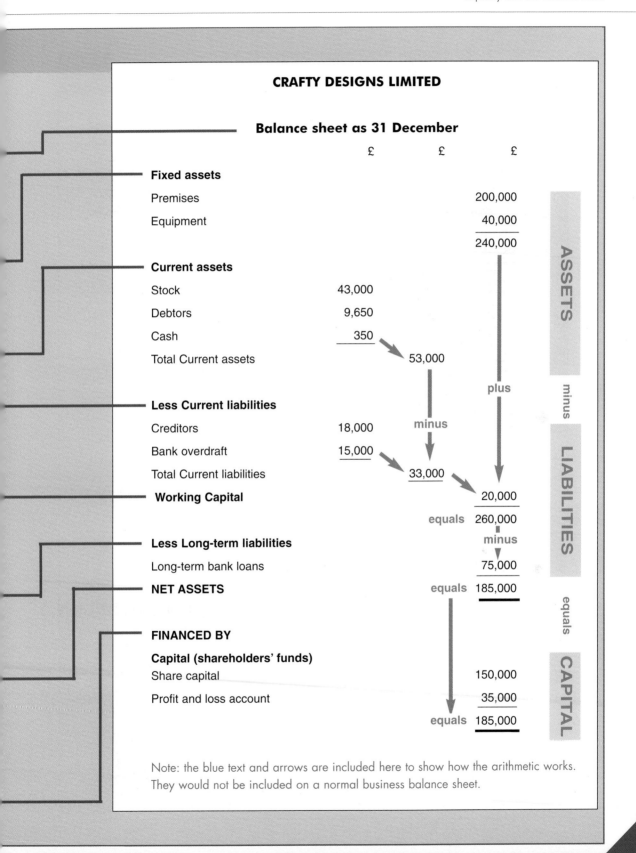

CRAFTY DESIGNS LIMITED

Balance sheet as 31 December

	£	£	£
Fixed assets			
Premises			200,000
Equipment			40,000
			240,000
Current assets			
Stock	43,000		
Debtors	9,650		
Cash	350		
Total Current assets		53,000	
			plus
Less Current liabilities		minus	
Creditors	18,000		
Bank overdraft	15,000		
Total Current liabilities		33,000	
Working Capital			20,000
		equals	260,000
			minus
Less Long-term liabilities			
Long-term bank loans			75,000
NET ASSETS		equals	185,000
FINANCED BY			
Capital (shareholders' funds)			
Share capital			150,000
Profit and loss account			35,000
		equals	185,000

ASSETS minus LIABILITIES equals CAPITAL

Note: the blue text and arrows are included here to show how the arithmetic works. They would not be included on a normal business balance sheet.

Activity 14.3 – understanding balance sheets

Optico Limited is a camera shop company owned by two sisters, Helen and Zoe, who are both directors and who both hold 100,000 £1 shares. They have recently completed their first year's trading and their accountant has drawn up their company balance sheet. This is shown on the opposite page.

The sisters have a number of questions to ask the accountant. These are set out below. How would you answer them?

1   How much profit have we made so far?

2   What is our total investment in the company on the date of the balance sheet, and what is it made up of?

3   What are our fixed assets and what are they worth, according to the balance sheet?

4   What are current assets and what does the term 'debtors' mean?

5   What are current liabilities and what does the term 'creditors' mean?

6   Why should current liabilities be deducted from current assets and what is the significance of working capital?

7   Why is the long-term bank loan a long-term liability and what is it financing?

8   **One year later . . .**
    The sisters have had a good year's trading in their shop and have extracted the following figures from their accounting records. You are to draw up their balance sheet as at 31 December of the second year.

	£		£
Premises	175,000	Shop fittings	60,000
Stock	135,000	Debtors	65,000
Cash	400	Creditors	74,600
Bank overdraft	15,000	Long-term bank loan	40,000
Share Capital	200,000	Profit and loss account	105,800

OPTICO LIMITED
BALANCE SHEET
as at 31 December

	£	£	£
Fixed assets			
Premises			175,000
Shop fittings			45,000
			220,000
Current assets			
Stock	127,000		
Debtors	55,100		
Cash	200		
		182,300	
Less Current liabilities			
Creditors	54,700		
Bank overdraft	41,000		
		95,700	
Working Capital (net current assets)			86,600
			306,600
Less Long-term liabilities			
Long-term bank loan			45,000
NET ASSETS			251,600
FINANCED BY			
Capital (shareholders funds)			
Share capital			200,000
Profit and loss account			51,600
			251,600

CHAPTER SUMMARY

■ The control of the flow of cash is an important aspect of the financial management of a business. If there is not enough cash to meet the day-to-day payment of business expenses, the business could be in danger of failing.

■ The sources of cash include the sale of products, short-term bank finance (overdraft), and money introduced by the owner(s) or investors.

■ Cash is used to pay for buying stock or materials (where the business is in manufacturing or retailing), running expenses, longer-term investments (eg machinery), paying the owner(s) and contributing to profit.

■ The danger points for the cash flow are if payments from customers dry up and the bank asks for repayment of its overdraft, or if vital payments cannot be made, eg wages or to suppliers.

■ Insolvency arises when business liabilities (items owed) exceed business assets (items owned) and the business is unable to pay debts when they become due.

■ Creditors can take an insolvent business to court. A sole trader can be made bankrupt and a company can be put into liquidation. In these cases the assets of the business are sold and distributed as far as possible among the creditors.

■ A business should ensure not only that there is enough cash to meet expenses but also that there are short-term resources available which can be turned into cash if the needs arises – eg money due from customers (debtors) and stock that can be sold. These are known as 'current assets'.

■ Working capital is the excess of current assets (short-term resources) over current liabilities (amounts owing in the short term). The more working capital a business has, the stronger that business is to withstand any cash flow problems.

■ The working capital cycle is the process involving buying goods on credit, selling them and then getting paid by customers, banking the money and finally paying suppliers.

■ Working capital has to be managed carefully so that no cash shortages occur. This involves making sure that debtors pay promptly, suppliers are paid as late as terms allow and that not too much stock is held at any one time.

■ Working capital is shown on the balance sheet of a business. A balance sheet is a financial statement which sets out the assets, liabilities and capital of a business at any one time. It tells the owner(s) the value of the assets owned, what the business is borrowing and what the value of the capital is.

KEY TERMS

cash	in business terms – immediate payment – ie notes and coins and money in the bank
liquid	having surplus cash
liquidity	the ability of a business to pay off its debts as they become due
insolvency	owing more than you own and being unable to pay debts when they become due
current assets	items owned by a business or owed to a business in the short term
current liabilities	items owed by a business in the short term
working capital	the surplus of current assets over current liabilities
	WORKING CAPITAL = CURRENT ASSETS – CURRENT LIABILITIES
net current assets	working capital (see above)
working capital cycle	a circular flow involving four stages:
	- suppliers selling goods on credit to a business
	- the business selling the goods to its customers
	- customers paying and the money being banked
	- the business paying the suppliers
debtors	customers to whom a business has sold on credit and who owe money
creditors	suppliers from whom a business has bought on credit and who are owed money
stock	manufactured items and goods sold by retailers
balance sheet	a financial statement which shows the assets, liabilities and capital of a business at a particular date
assets	items owned and amounts owing to a business
liabilities	amounts owed by a business
capital	the investment of the owner(s) in the business

15

Financial forecasting – budgeting

Capital items	195000		
Wages	7645	7645	7645
Rent/rates			290
Insurance	1500		
Services	200	200	200
Telephone			
VAT			
Vehicle expenses	200	200	200
Stationery	50	50	50
Postages	150	150	150
Bank charges			150
Interest			500
Loan repayments			
Advertising	1000	1000	1000
Packaging	500	500	500

Starting point

You will know on a personal level that budgeting is important – you have a certain amount of income and have to plan carefully how to spend it. Then when you run out of cash you have to change your plans.

Anyone starting up a new business – or running an existing business – also needs to plan ahead to achieve objectives and has to be flexible when those plans do not turn out as expected.

The creation of budgets is central to this planning process. Whereas a break-even calculation projects levels of future sales and spending in general terms, budgeting forecasts activity in different areas of the business, sets targets, monitors success rates and enables the business management to take action when performance targets are not met.

What you will learn from this chapter

- an important part of the business planning process is the setting of budgets which help management to measure performance and to make decisions

- budgets can be function or departmental budgets (which set targets for function areas and departments); they can also be income budgets (eg sales budget) or expenditure budgets (eg staffing budget)

- the individual budgets combine into the cash budget (which forecasts the flow of money in and out of the business bank account) and the master budget (which sets out a forecast profit and loss account and a forecast balance sheet)

- during the course of the year the actual figures will be compared with the budget projections and any difference ('variance') will be reported and acted upon

Budgets and their Benefits

definitions

A budget is a financial plan in the form of a table setting out revenues or costs (or both) for a given period of time

A budget may deal with **income** (eg from sales), or with **expenditure** (eg production, staffing and marketing).

A budget is commonly set in financial terms, eg a sales revenue budget, but it can also be expressed in terms of units, eg items produced, workers employed, items sold.

Most budgets are prepared for the financial year, and are usually broken down into shorter time periods, usually monthly. As time passes the actual figures achieved by the business can be compared with the budgeted figures and the differences between the two – the **variances** – can be entered on a **budget report** and investigated where necessary.

Budgets can therefore improve the way a business is run: they can help managers in assessing performance and in decision-making; they can also motivate employees to meet performance targets.

Types of Budget

There are a number of types of budget, and there are no fixed rules about which budgets have to be used. The budgets described here are likely to be used by a larger business. If the business is smaller, there will be fewer budgets because there will be fewer 'departments' – and maybe none at all. To help you appreciate this difference, the diagrams on pages 245 and 246 show typical budgets found in a large manufacturing business and a small business which provides a service.

function budgets

The function budget is a plan for a specific function within a business, eg:

- **sales budget** – which covers sales revenue to be received by the business

- **production budget** – which covers the number and cost of items produced; if the business is a service business, there will instead be an **operating budget** to cover the cost of producing the service

- **staffing budget** – which plans the workforce's wages and salaries costs

departmental budgets

The costs of running a business set out in its function budgets are also included in a number of different departmental budgets, eg marketing department budget, administration department budget. The object here is to make each department run efficiently: its managers – known as the **budget holders** – will be set specific targets for spending and staffing.

the cash budget (cash-flow forecast)

The end-result of the budgeting process is the production of:

- a **cash budget** which forecasts all the money received by a business and all the money spent by a business and relates those 'cash flows' to the balance of the bank account – its main function is to predict any need to borrow from the bank by means of an overdraft

- a **master budget** which takes the form of forecast financial statements – an estimated profit and loss account and balance sheet at the end of the budget period

The cash budget (also known as the 'cash-flow forecast') is covered in the next chapter.

the budget drafting process – limiting factors

A **limiting factor** is an aspect of a business which prevents it from expanding its operations any further – for example the volume of its products that it can sell. It is essential to identify these limiting factors. For most businesses the main limiting factor is sales – how much of its product range can a business sell? The starting point for the budgeting process is therefore normally the sales budget. The order in which the budgets are drafted will often be:

- **sales budget** – what can the business sell in the next twelve months?

- **production budget** – how can the business make all the items which it plans to sell? It will need to budget for materials, staffing and other production expenses (overheads)

- **departmental budgets** – what resources will be needed by individual departments?

- **capital budget** – what capital items (ie large expense items such as machinery and vehicles) need to be purchased over the next year?

- **cash budget (cash-flow forecast)** – what money will be flowing in and out of the bank account over the next year?

- **master budget** – a summary of all the budgets to provide projected financial statements, ie a profit and loss account and balance sheet

how are budgets set?

There are different approaches to the way in which the budget figures are arrived at, and they all depend on the type of organisation involved:

- **incremental budgeting** (also known as **historic budgeting**) is often found in a stable business and simply involves taking last year's budget figures as a basis and adding on percentage increases, either for inflation or where the circumstances demand it

- **zero-based budgeting** is often used in a new or less stable business – it means that each time the budgets are drawn up they are not based on previous years' figures but start from 'zero', ie they are based on entirely new costings and new projections of financial performance

THE BUDGETING PROCESS IN A LARGE MANUFACTURING COMPANY

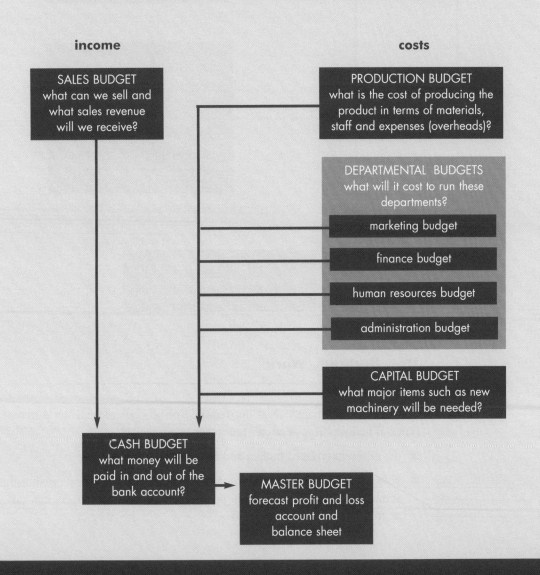

THE BUDGETING PROCESS IN A SMALL SERVICES BUSINESS

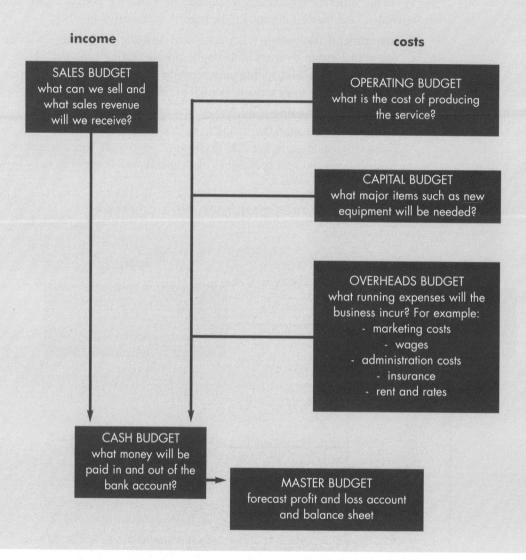

How Budgets 'Work'

Your course fortunately does not require you to construct all the different types of budget 'from scratch', but rather to appreciate:

■ the different types of budget and what they are for

■ how they work by forecasting levels of activity and then monitoring actual performance so that the business owners and managers can take appropriate decisions and actions

■ how they 'fit together' in the planning process – as in the diagrams on the previous two pages

The Case Study that follows sets out examples of some of the most common types of budget.

The cash budget (cash-flow forecast) is one of the most important types of budget, but will be dealt with separately in the next chapter.

Case Study – setting the budgets

Osborne Giftware Limited imports novelty goods and sells them in the UK through shops, agency sales and mail order. It also manufactures a limited number of games in its factory near Bolton.

sales budgets
Set out below are two of its sales budgets for the coming year.

sales budget by product (extract)	January	February	March	April	May	June	Total
	£	£	£	£	£	£	£
Product A	1,000	1,000	1,000	1,000	1,000	1,000	6,000
Product B	1,500	1,500	1,500	1,500	1,500	1,500	9,000
Product C	2,500	2,500	2,500	2,500	2,500	2,500	15,000
etc . . .							

sales budget by type of customer (extract)	January	February	March	April	May	June	Total
	£	£	£	£	£	£	£
Direct sales	10,000	10,000	10,000	12,000	12,000	12,000	66,000
Agency sales	5,000	5,000	5,000	5,000	5,000	5,000	30,000
Mail order	5,000	5,000	5,000	5,000	6,000	6,000	33,000
etc . . .							

Certain aspects of the structure of the sales budget (and any budget) will stay constant, whether they are income budgets or expenditure budgets. For example, the budget is subdivided into 'budget periods': either months or four-weekly periods (the 52 week year is conveniently divided into 13 four-weekly periods). The extracts from the sales budgets above show six of the usual twelve monthly periods.

production budget

When Osborne Giftware has established its sales budget ('How many of each product can we sell?') it is then in a position to work out its production budget for the items it manufactures ('How can we make those products on time?'). It must be stressed that a production budget applies to a manufacturing business; a business providing a service will carry out a similar process using an 'operating budget.'

The production budget will take into account when in the year the manufactured items (games) will be needed and when they are likely to be sold. The budget therefore shows:

■ the projected monthly sales figures

■ the finished products in stock at the beginning and end of each month

production budget

UNITS	Jan	Feb	Mar	Apr	May	Jun	Jul	Aug	Sep	Oct	Nov	Dec
Opening stock	100	275	450	600	550	500	450	300	175	325	475	125
add Units produced	325	325	350	350	350	350	350	175	350	350	350	400
minus Units sold	150	150	200	400	400	400	500	300	200	200	700	425
Closing stock	275	450	600	550	500	450	300	175	325	475	125	100

You will see from the production budget that it shows units of production. When the monthly production of units has been calculated, the budget can then be expressed in money terms – it will become a production cost budget. This will be made possible by applying a standard cost worked out by the business from the raw materials cost, the labour cost and the overheads (other expenses) which were needed to manufacture a single unit of production.

staffing budget

The staffing budget is a function budget which covers the staffing costs of all the departments within the business. It includes the pay before deductions, the employer's National Insurance and pension contributions. Six months' figures are shown here.

staffing budget (extract)

	January	February	March	April	May	June
	£	£	£	£	£	£
Gross pay	40,000	40,000	40,000	40,000	40,000	40,000
National Insurance	4,080	4,080	4,080	4,080	4,080	4,080
Pension payments	2,000	2,000	2,000	2,000	2,000	2,000

Budget Variances and Budget Reports

The budget, once it is set for the financial year, is monitored by comparing actual results with the budgeted figures. Any differences between the two are known as **variances**.

budgeted figures minus actual figures = variances

In a larger business, departmental managers will base their decisions on departmental budget reports, normally produced by the finance department. Less significant variances will be dealt with by the departmental manager and supervisors; significant variances will need to be referred to a higher management level. Many variances, if they are very small, will not need acting on at all.

In a smaller business the budgeting system will be less complex (see diagram on page 246) but the owner/manager will still operate on the same principles and take action whenever a variance becomes significant – for example if sales are 20% below target.

The illustration below sets out the format of a typical budget report for a sales department. The details shown are:

- the department and the budget holder responsible (the manager)
- budget, actual and variance figures for the current period (October here)
- year-to-date figures (these are optional)
- the variance trends: 'FAV' is short for 'favourable', ie better than budget, 'ADV' is short for 'adverse', ie worse than budget
- comments – the column here would be enough to record the reasons for smaller variances, but the manager would expect to receive a more detailed report for significant variances

BUDGET REPORT

Budget Centre Sales Department **Budget Holder** T Hussain

Period October **Date** 7 November

	current period				year-to-date				comments
	budget £000	actual £000	variance £000	trend	budget £000	actual £000	variance £000	trend	
Product A	200	250	+ 50	FAV	2,750	3,125	+ 375	FAV	
Product B	225	200	- 25	ADV	1,275	1,150	- 125	ADV	
Product C	425	450	+ 25	FAV	4,025	4,475	+ 450	FAV	

Factors that Cause Variances

It is important not only to be able to identify variances but also to assume the role of the manager and comment on their significance, ie 'What caused this labour budget variance? Was it overtime working? Does it matter?'

sales variance

sales variance = actual sales minus budgeted sales

A **favourable** (positive) variance will result when sales are better than budgeted. This might be the result of the price going up when demand for the product is strong, or special promotional offers for the product.

An **adverse** (negative) variance will result when sales are worse than budgeted. A fall in sales income from a particular product might be the result of overpricing or ineffective marketing.

If the variance is significant, management will need to take action. For example, if sales are down, management will want to know why. 'Is the price right? Can marketing be improved? Is the product going out of fashion? Should the business be switching to other products?'

Note that the sales variance relates to income. Materials, labour and overhead variances, on the other hand, relate to expenses.

materials variance

materials variance = standard (budgeted) cost of materials minus actual cost

Note here that the budgeted cost is referred to as the 'standard cost'. This is the cost of the quantity of materials a manufacturing business expects to use.

A **favourable** (positive) variance will result when costs are lower than budgeted: the cost of the materials may have gone down, or the quantity of materials used may have gone down.

An **adverse** (negative) variance will result when costs are higher than budgeted: the cost of the materials may have gone up, or the quantity of materials used may have increased.

labour variance

labour variance = standard (budgeted) cost of labour minus actual cost

A **favourable** (positive) variance will result when labour costs are lower than budgeted: the wage rate may have gone down (unlikely!), or the number of hours worked may be fewer – the business may have become more efficient.

An **adverse** (negative) variance will result when labour costs are higher than budgeted: there may have been an unexpected wage rise, or the number of hours worked may have increased more than was expected (the machinery or the computer systems may have broken down, leaving people idle).

overhead variance

The overheads are the running costs of the business.

overhead variance = standard (budgeted) cost of overheads minus actual cost

Here standard cost is the budgeted overhead cost, ie the expected cost of the running expenses of the business.

A **favourable** (positive) variance will result when running costs are lower than budgeted: the business may have switched to a cheaper power company or telephone provider; it may have moved to offices with lower rental.

An **adverse** (negative) variance will result when running costs are higher than budgeted: rates and office rental may have gone up unexpectedly, or the telephone bill may have risen after a telesales campaign.

Note that, as in break-even calculations, overheads costs are either **fixed** and do not vary with the number of items produced (eg office rental) – or **variable** (eg electricity bill) and vary with the volume of items produced. Sometimes a business may calculate separate variances for fixed overheads and variable overheads, as in the activity below.

Activity 15.1 – investigating variances

You have been presented with these cost figures for a manufacturing company. Note that the overheads (expenses) costs are divided into fixed and variable elements.

	standard (budgeted) cost £	actual cost £
materials	30,000	27,000
labour	60,000	75,000
overheads:		
fixed	30,000	27,500
variable	10,000	11,000
TOTAL COST	130,000	140,500

1 Calculate the variances for the four types of cost.

2 Identify whether they are adverse or favourable.

3 Suggest some factors which might have caused each of the variances.

4 If you were a manager of this business what would you want to investigate?

Activity 15.2 – commenting on a sales budget report

Premium Soft Drinks manufacturers a range of drinks which it distributes throughout the UK. You are given the following information about Premium's three main brands:

Sunzest is a healthy, additive free juice drink based on orange and lemon extracts aimed at the adult market.

Tingle is a brightly-coloured fizzy drink, aimed at the children's market.

Zing is a carbonated drink, sold in a fashionable can mainly to the teens market.

During the year the following events have occurred:

■ all brands have been heavily advertised

■ the summer was exceptionally hot

■ early in the year there was a health scare over food dyes in children's food and drink

■ in the summer a competitor launched a new competitively priced, additive free, children's drink which proved very popular

You are to

1 Write comments on the performance of the three brands shown in the budget report. Explain in each case the factors that have made the variance favourable or adverse, adding any further points which you think might be relevant.

2 State what course of action the manufacturer might take to reverse any adverse trend.

BUDGET REPORT: Premium Soft Drinks

Budget Centre Sales Department **Budget Holder** R Bolt
Period October **Date** 7 November

	current period			year-to-date			trend	comments
	budget £000	actual £000	variance £000	budget £000	actual £000	variance £000		
Sunzest	200	250	+ 50	2,750	3,125	+ 375	FAV	
Tingle	225	200	- 25	1,275	1,150	- 125	ADV	
Zing	425	450	+ 25	4,025	4,475	+ 450	FAV	

Activity 15.3 – completing a sales budget report

Paradise Travel is a holiday company which sells UK and foreign holidays largely by telephone, mail order and from its website. During the last few years it has seen considerable growth in foreign holidays, largely because of the poor UK weather and the strength of the pound sterling against other currencies.

The budget for the current year is as follows:

holiday type	budgeted sales	actual sales	variance	FAV or ADV
	£	£	£	
UK	540,000			
European Ski	450,000			
European Sun	670,000			
USA Florida Sun	375,000			
USA Ski	230,000			
TOTAL	2,265,000			

The sales figures for the present year are shown on the right.

You have been told that a number of factors have affected sales of holidays during the year. These include: a strong pound sterling, bad summer weather in the UK, scare reports about avalanches in the Alps, the popularity of TV 'holiday rep' programmes set in the

holiday type	actual sales
UK	496,000
European Ski	396,000
European Sun	801,000
USA Florida Sun	453,000
USA Ski	286,000

Mediterranean area, the popularity of Disney theme parks, good snow conditions in the US mountains, cheap US flights.

You are to

1 Draw up a budget report based on the format shown above, enter the actual sales figures and total, work out the variances and state whether they are 'FAV' or 'ADV'.

2 Take each of the types of holiday in turn and link them to the factors listed above.

3 Suggest ways in which any adverse trends, given the same conditions, could be reversed in the coming year.

4 State what could happen to sales in the coming year if the pound sterling fell in value against the US dollar and the Euro before the holiday prices had been fixed.

CHAPTER SUMMARY

■ A budget is a form of financial plan which sets out projections of income or expenditure (or both). It is normally drawn up for a year and broken down into monthly periods.

■ There are a number of different types of budget. The larger the business, the more budgets it is likely to have, because the organisation will be subdivided into different departments or functional areas, all requiring financial management.

■ Function budgets contain projections which relate to all areas of business operations – eg sales, production (or operations if a service is produced), staffing and overheads (expenses).

■ Where a business has separate departments – eg human resources and administration – there will be departmental budgets under the control of departmental heads, the budget holders.

■ The capital budget forecasts expenditure on major (capital) items such as new machinery.

■ The budgets are drawn up in an order which starts with the sales budget because the number of items the business can sell is the main limiting factor.

■ The budgeting process is brought together in the production of the cash budget (cash-flow forecast) and the master budget (projected profit and loss account and balance sheet). The cash budget is covered in the next chapter.

■ The basis for budget setting will vary according to the type of organisation involved. Stable businesses will tend to use incremental (historic) budgeting which takes last year's figures and adds a percentage increase. Less stable businesses may use zero-based ('start from scratch') budgeting.

■ A budget is a useful aid to management as it helps plan ahead and also enables performance to be monitored and decisions for corrective action to be taken where necessary.

■ Differences between budgeted and actual figures are known as variances and are normally presented in a budget report. They are known as 'favourable' and 'adverse' variances, depending on whether they are better or worse than budgeted.

KEY TERMS

budget	a financial plan setting out revenues or costs (or both) for a given period of time
incremental budgeting	a budget which uses the figures from the previous year's budget as a basis for its forecasts, often adding on a percentage increase (increment) – also known as historic budgeting
zero-based budgeting	a budget which makes no prior year assumptions for its forecasts but works 'from scratch' – from a 'zero' position
budget holder	the person responsible for a specific budget, eg a departmental manager
function budget	a budget covering a specific function within a business, eg staffing
departmental budget	a budget for a specific department within a business
limiting factor	an aspect of the business which prevents it from expanding its operations any further, eg sales
capital budget	a budget for large asset purchases, eg for machinery
cash budget	a budget which projects total monthly inflows and outflows through the business bank account, forecasting the bank balance at the end of each month – also known as a 'cash-flow forecast' (see next chapter)
master budget	a forecast profit and loss account for the year, together with a forecast year-end balance sheet
variance	the difference between budgeted and actual figures
favourable variance	the difference between the budgeted figure and the actual figure when the actual figure is better than the forecast figure – often written as 'FAV'
adverse variance	the difference between the budgeted figure and the actual figure when the actual figure is not as good as the forecast figure – often written as 'ADV'

16

Financial forecasting – cash-flow forecasts

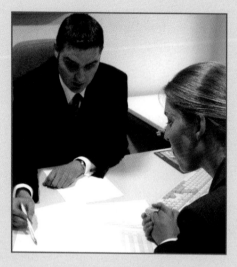

Starting point

We have seen in Chapter 12 that cash is the 'lifeblood' of any business. If the supply of cash dries up, suppliers cannot be paid and employees do not get their wages – the business may become insolvent.

Cash is part of the working capital – the liquidity – of a business, which is its 'cushion' of short-term resources, available to pay off debts such as suppliers' invoices and employee wages.

Another short-term resource is money borrowed from the bank by means of an overdraft. A business will clearly need to work out how much it is likely to have to borrow. The bank will undoubtedly ask the business to produce a cash budget – a cash-flow forecast – which is a projection showing how much money flows in and out of the business bank account each month and highlights the months in which the business may need to borrow from the bank.

What you will learn from this chapter

- a cash-flow forecast is a budget which estimates the need for bank overdraft finance over a period of time, normally six or twelve months

- a cash-flow forecast is set out in the form of table with monthly columns of figures showing (from the top) receipts into the bank account, payments out of the bank account and the projected month-end bank balance

- a computer spreadsheet is a useful method of setting out the figures of a cash-flow forecast and can be manipulated to show the effects of changes in receipts and payments on the month-end bank balance

- a cash-flow forecast is an invaluable financial management tool as it indicates any shortage of liquidity and the need for a bank overdraft

the Importance of the Cash Budget

We have seen in the last chapter that the budgeting process in a business involves:

■ estimating future income and costs

■ monitoring the figures over time to see if any variances occur (variances are differences between budgeted and actual figures)

■ taking action if the variance is significant

Income and costs all pass through the bank account which forms the basis of the **cash budget**. This in turn provides data for the **master budget** of the business – the forecast profit and loss account and balance sheet. These two budgets are particularly important when a business draws up a business plan to present to a potential lender or investor. They provide information about the profitability of the business and its liquidity – its ability to repay debts. As you can see from the diagram below, the cash budget is central to the whole budgeting process. Study the diagram and then read on.

THE PLACE OF THE CASH BUDGET IN THE BUDGETING PROCESS

income

SALES BUDGET
what can we sell and
what sales revenue
will we receive?

costs

BUDGETED COSTS
what will it cost to run the
business?

production budget

marketing budget

finance budget

human resources budget

administration budget

capital budget

CASH BUDGET
estimating receipts and payments and the
amount of money in the bank account

MASTER BUDGET
forecast profit and loss
account and
balance sheet

Format of a Cash Flow Forecast

A cash budget – also known as a **cash-flow forecast** – is a table which estimates the amounts of money coming into and going out of the bank account each month. Study the example on the opposite page.

A typical cash-flow forecast – which normally estimates figures for six or twelve months – sets out in a column for each month three distinct sets of figures:

- **receipts** – a totalled list of items paid into the bank account; these commonly include sales, capital paid in, grants and loans from the bank
- **payments** – a totalled list of payments made out of the bank account; these include items such as purchases of materials and stock, wages, marketing and other expenses
- the **cash flow** for the month and the **bank balance** at the beginning and the end of the month

working out the monthly bank balances

The bank account balances are worked out in the bottom section of the cash-flow forecast and are related to the **cash flow** for the month.

cash flow = total monthly receipts – total monthly payments

If the cash flow figure is positive it means that more money has come into the bank account than has gone out; if the cash flow figure is negative it indicates that payments out are greater than payments in. A negative cash flow is normally shown in brackets or with a minus sign.

The cash flow is added to the opening bank balance (the amount in the account at the beginning of the month) to produce the closing bank balance (the amount in the account at the end of the month). If the cash flow figure is negative it will be deducted from the opening bank balance. The calculation using a positive cash is:

cash flow for month + opening bank balance = closing bank balance

The closing bank balance is then entered in the next month's column as the next month's opening bank balance – it will obviously be the same figure because it represents the bank balance on the very last day of the month.

Note that if a bank balance is negative it is shown in brackets, or with a minus sign. This means that the business is borrowing from the bank by means of an overdraft.

Now study the example on the opposite page. To keep things simple, all balances shown here are positive.

FORMAT OF A CASH-FLOW FORECAST

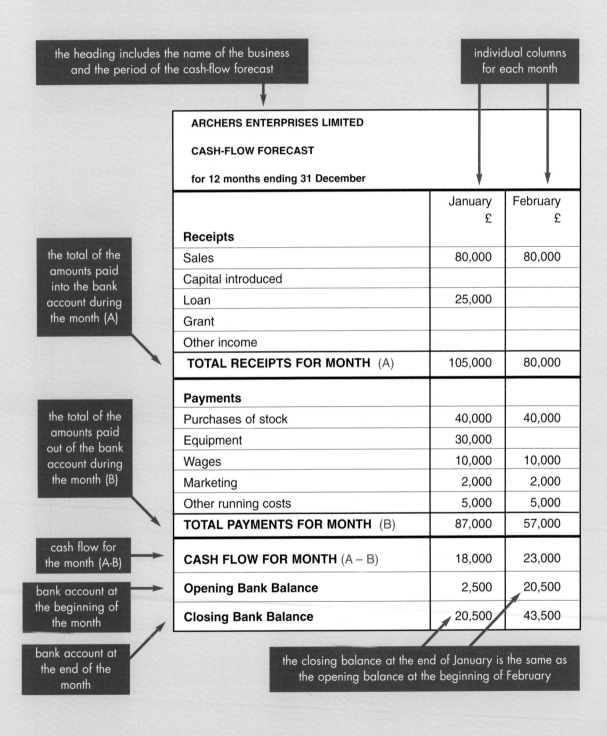

the heading includes the name of the business and the period of the cash-flow forecast

individual columns for each month

ARCHERS ENTERPRISES LIMITED

CASH-FLOW FORECAST

for 12 months ending 31 December

	January £	February £
Receipts		
Sales	80,000	80,000
Capital introduced		
Loan	25,000	
Grant		
Other income		
TOTAL RECEIPTS FOR MONTH (A)	105,000	80,000
Payments		
Purchases of stock	40,000	40,000
Equipment	30,000	
Wages	10,000	10,000
Marketing	2,000	2,000
Other running costs	5,000	5,000
TOTAL PAYMENTS FOR MONTH (B)	87,000	57,000
CASH FLOW FOR MONTH (A – B)	18,000	23,000
Opening Bank Balance	2,500	20,500
Closing Bank Balance	20,500	43,500

the total of the amounts paid into the bank account during the month (A)

the total of the amounts paid out of the bank account during the month (B)

cash flow for the month (A-B)

bank account at the beginning of the month

bank account at the end of the month

the closing balance at the end of January is the same as the opening balance at the beginning of February

Activity 16.1 – cash-flow forecast structure

You have been given figures for the estimated bank receipts and bank payments for three businesses for the months of January and February.

You have also been given the opening bank balances for January for each of the three businesses. Note that a bank balance in brackets is a minus figure; it shows that the business will be borrowing from the bank on an overdraft.

JANUARY FIGURES

	Apple Ltd £	Bruin Ltd £	Elstree Ltd £
Total Receipts	20,000	40,000	64,000
Total Payments	10,000	24,000	62,000
Opening Bank Balance	zero	6,000	(7,000)

FEBRUARY FIGURES

	Apple Ltd £	Bruin Ltd £	Elstree Ltd £
Total Receipts	20,000	40,000	70,000
Total Payments	16,000	25,000	80,000

1 Use the format shown below to calculate the bank balances at the end of January and February for all three businesses. Use brackets to indicate any negative figures.

	January £	February £
Total Receipts for Month		
Total Payments for Month		
Cash Flow for Month		
Opening Bank Balance		
Closing Bank Balance		

2 Explain what has happened to the bank balance of Elstree Ltd during January and February. What does this say about the liquidity of Elstree Ltd and what implications does it have for the future of the company?

Using the Cash Flow Forecast

A cash-flow forecast is a very useful tool for the financial manager:

- it helps to estimate how much a business may need to borrow by way of bank overdraft

- it highlights any future liquidity problems a business may have – in other words it shows if a business may run into trouble in paying its debts

- it is an important document in a business plan which will have to be prepared if a business wishes to borrow from the bank

A cash-flow forecast is also a very flexible tool. If it is set up on a computer spreadsheet it can be used to calculate liquidity situations in a variety of 'what if?' situations. For example:

> *'What will happen to the bank balance if monthly sales revenue falls by 10%?'*

> *'What will happen to the bank balance if the monthly wages bill rises by 10%?'*

The Case Study that follows illustrates these points by looking at a mail order business that sells cut-price DVDs.

Case Study – using the cash-flow forecast

a new business

Jo Dandini set up a mail order company in January selling cut-price DVDs. She called her enterprise DVD Express.

She works from part of a warehouse which she rents from a friend at a low rate.

She sells through her website which has an online shop; she also accepts telephoned orders. Her sales are mostly credit and debit card sales and she obtains her supplies from trade wholesalers.

Jo employees part-time telephone operators and packers; she also puts in a lot of time herself, adopting a very 'hands-on' approach to the business which enables her to assess the market and manage the business efficiently.

financing the business

Jo has invested £12,000 of her own money as capital in the business and has negotiated a bank loan of £8,000 to help her with her start-up requirements; these include computers and mailing equipment.

revenue and costs

Jo has budgeted for monthly sales of £10,000 and £5,000 for monthly purchases of DVDs. She has to pay for the DVDs in the month of purchase. She also has to pay various monthly overheads, the largest of which is the wages bill.

preparing the cash-flow forecast

Jo has been asked by her accountant to draw up projected figures for the first six months of trading. From these figures the accountant can prepare a cash-flow forecast which can be presented to the bank in case an overdraft is needed.

The accountant stresses that these figures, particularly the sales and running expenses will only be estimates.

Jo has opened up a business bank account but has not yet paid anything in. Her estimated figures are shown below.

ESTIMATED FIGURES FOR THE CASH FLOW FORECAST

Receipts	date	amount (£)
Capital provided by Jo	January	12,000
Bank loan	January	8,000
Sales of DVDs	Monthly	10,000

Payments	date	amount (£)
Purchases of DVDs	Monthly	5,000
Purchase of equipment	January	14,500
Purchase of equipment	February	15,250
Rent of warehouse	Monthly	575
Insurance	Monthly	50
Electricity	March, June	100
Telephone	Monthly	100
Wages	Monthly	1,000
Postage	Monthly	450
Marketing	Monthly	200

---

preparing the cash-flow forecast

Jo's accountant discusses these figures with her and then prepares a cash-flow forecast, using a computer spreadsheet. This cash-flow forecast is shown on the next page.

	A	B	C	D	E	F	G
1	DVD EXPRESS					cash-flow forecast 1	
2	CASH BUDGET for 6 months						
3		JANUARY	FEBRUARY	MARCH	APRIL	MAY	JUNE
4		£	£	£	£	£	£
5							
6							
7	RECEIPTS						
8	Sales	10,000	10,000	10,000	10,000	10,000	10,000
9	Bank Loan	8,000					
10	Capital	12,000					
11	TOTAL RECEIPTS	30,000	10,000	10,000	10,000	10,000	10,000
12	PAYMENTS						
13	Purchases	5,000	5,000	5,000	5,000	5,000	5,000
14	Equipment	14,500	15,250				
15	Rent	575	575	575	575	575	575
16	Insurance	50	50	50	50	50	50
17	Electricity			100			100
18	Telephone	100	100	100	100	100	100
19	Wages	1,000	1,000	1,000	1,000	1,000	1,000
20	Postage	450	450	450	450	450	450
21	Marketing	200	200	200	200	200	200
22							
23	TOTAL PAYMENTS	21,875	22,625	7,475	7,375	7,375	7,475
24	CASHFLOW FOR MONTH	8,125	- 12,625	2,525	2,625	2,625	2,525
25	Opening Bank Balance		8,125	- 4,500	- 1,975	650	3,275
26	Closing Bank Balance	8,125	- 4,500	- 1,975	650	3,275	5,800

The accountant explains the cash-flow forecast as follows:

- sales revenue is assumed to be £10,000 per month – this is only an estimate, the figure could be higher or lower

- the purchases figure in the Payments section is the cost of buying in the stock – the business has a mark-up of 100% (ie Jo doubles the cost price to get her selling price)

- the cash flow for January is £8,125 and as there is no money in the bank at the beginning of the month, this cash flow is also the balance at the end of the month (and the beginning of February)

- the cash flow for February is a negative figure (£12,625) because of the purchase of the equipment and there is not enough money in the bank to cover this – as a result the business ends the month of February with an overdraft of £4,500

- the cash flow for March is an improvement at £2,525, but the business still has an overdraft at the end of the month of £1,975

- from April the end-of-month balance is positive and the month-end balances continue to increase in May and June

The accountant explains that the bank should be happy to grant the overdraft shown on the cash-flow forecast because the projection shows that it will be repaid. But Jo is worried about the accuracy of her projections and asks what would happen if sales were only £7,500 a month, or looking on the brighter side, £15,000 a month.

Jo's accountant promises to draw up two more cash-flow forecasts incorporating these figures (and adjusted purchases figures too) – see the next page.

cash-flow forecast assuming sales rise from £10,000 to £15,000 a month

	A	B	C	D	E	F	G
1	DVD EXPRESS						
2	CASH BUDGET for 6 months					cash-flow forecast 2	
3		JANUARY	FEBRUARY	MARCH	APRIL	MAY	JUNE
4		£	£	£	£	£	£
5							
6							
7	RECEIPTS						
8	Sales	15,000	15,000	15,000	15,000	15,000	15,000
9	Bank Loan	8,000					
10	Capital	12,000					
11	TOTAL RECEIPTS	35,000	15,000	15,000	15,000	15,000	15,000
12	PAYMENTS						
13	Purchases	7,500	7,500	7,500	7,500	7,500	7,500
14	Equipment	14,500	15,250				
15	Rent	575	575	575	575	575	575
16	Insurance	50	50	50	50	50	50
17	Electricity			100			100
18	Telephone	100	100	100	100	100	100
19	Wages	1,000	1,000	1,000	1,000	1,000	1,000
20	Postage	450	450	450	450	450	450
21	Marketing	200	200	200	200	200	200
22							
23	TOTAL PAYMENTS	24,375	25,125	9,975	9,875	9,875	9,975
24	CASHFLOW FOR MONTH	10,625	- 10,125	5,025	5,125	5,125	5,025
25	Opening Bank Balance		10,625	500	5,525	10,650	15,775
26	Closing Bank Balance	10,625	500	5,525	10,650	15,775	20,800

cash-flow forecast assuming sales fall from £10,000 to £7,500 a month

	A	B	C	D	E	F	G
1	DVD EXPRESS						
2	CASH BUDGET for 6 months					cash-flow forecast 3	
3		JANUARY	FEBRUARY	MARCH	APRIL	MAY	JUNE
4		£	£	£	£	£	£
5							
6							
7	RECEIPTS						
8	Sales	7,500	7,500	7,500	7,500	7,500	7,500
9	Bank Loan	8,000					
10	Capital	12,000					
11	TOTAL RECEIPTS	27,500	7,500	7,500	7,500	7,500	7,500
12	PAYMENTS						
13	Purchases	3,750	3,750	3,750	3,750	3,750	3,750
14	Equipment	14,500	15,250				
15	Rent	575	575	575	575	575	575
16	Insurance	50	50	50	50	50	50
17	Electricity			100			100
18	Telephone	100	100	100	100	100	100
19	Wages	1,000	1,000	1,000	1,000	1,000	1,000
20	Postage	450	450	450	450	450	450
21	Marketing	200	200	200	200	200	200
22							
23	TOTAL PAYMENTS	20,625	21,375	6,225	6,125	6,125	6,225
24	CASHFLOW FOR MONTH	6,875	- 13,875	1,275	1,375	1,375	1,275
25	Opening Bank Balance		6,875	- 7,000	- 5,725	- 4,350	- 2,975
26	Closing Bank Balance	6,875	- 7,000	- 5,725	- 4,350	- 2,975	- 1,700

Activity 16.2 – cash-flow forecast analysis

Study the three cash-flow forecasts for DVD Express on the previous two pages and answer the questions below.

Bear in mind that a cash-flow forecast relates to other financial calculations and statements that you have studied. A cash-flow forecast, like a break-even calculation, is a forward-looking financial projection which deals with income from sales and various types of cost. Note also that many of the figures on a cash-flow forecast are to be found in a profit and loss account; they contribute to the projected profit and loss account which forms part of the master budget.

questions

1 Refer to cash-flow forecast 1 on page 263.

(a) What is the balance of the bank account at the end of June?

(b) In what month will the overdraft be repaid?

(c) What is the main reason for the month-end bank balance for January being positive and the month-end balance for February being an overdraft (negative)?

(d) What are the total sales and purchases of DVD Express for the first six months?

(e) What is the percentage mark-up of the business?

2 Refer to cash-flow forecast 2 on page 264.

(a) Why is no overdraft needed by Jo's business for the first six months of trading?

(b) What is Jo's gross profit for the first six months of trading?

(c) What is the percentage mark-up of the business?

3 Refer to cash-flow forecast 3 on page 264.

(a) What is the main effect on cash flow of sales revenue falling to £7,500 per month? What effect might this have on Jo's plans?

(b) Jo reckons that she should cut some of her costs if sales fall to this level. But why should the monthly cost of purchases fall to £3,750 and other costs such as rent and wages remain the same? What type of costs are these?

(c) Is there any other way in which Jo could cut her costs in her first six months of trading?

(d) If Jo approached the bank with a request for an overdraft with this cash-flow forecast, what is the reaction of the bank likely to be?

Cash-Flow Forecasts on a Computer Spreadsheet

This chapter has already illustrated how a computer spreadsheet can be used to set out a cash-flow forecast. There are a number of advantages of using a computer spreadsheet:

- complex calculations can be performed automatically
- the effect of 'what if' scenarios can easily be set up and illustrated (as in the Case Study)

The illustration below shows the structure and formulas that are needed to set up a suitable spreadsheet.

CASH-FLOW FORECAST SPREADSHEET WITH FORMULAS

	A	B	C	D	E	F	G
1	DVD EXPRESS						
2	CASH BUDGET for 6 months						
3		JANUARY	FEBRUARY	MARCH	APRIL	MAY	JUNE
4		£	£	£	£	£	£
5							
6							
7	RECEIPTS						
8	Sales	15000	15000	15000	15000	15000	15000
9	Bank Loan	8000					
10	Capital	12000					
11	TOTAL RECEIPTS	=SUM(B8:B10)	=SUM(C8:C10)	=SUM(D8:D10)	=SUM(E8:E10)	=SUM(F8:F10)	=SUM(G8:G10)
12	PAYMENTS						
13	Purchases	7500	7500	7500	7500	7500	7500
14	Equipment	14500	15250				
15	Rent	575	575	575	575	575	575
16	Insurance	50	50	50	50	50	50
17	Electricity			100			100
18	Telephone	100	100	100	100	100	100
19	Wages	1000	1000	1000	1000	1000	1000
20	Postage	450	450	450	450	450	450
21	Marketing	200	200	200	200	200	200
22							
23	TOTAL PAYMENTS	=SUM(B13:B22)	=SUM(C13:C22)	=SUM(D13:D22)	=SUM(E13:E22)	=SUM(F13:F22)	=SUM(G13:G22)
24	CASHFLOW FOR MONTH	=SUM(B11-B23)	=SUM(C11-C23)	=SUM(D11-D23)	=SUM(E11-E23)	=SUM(F11-F23)	=SUM(G11-G23)
25	Opening Bank Balance		=SUM(B26)	=SUM(C26)	=SUM(D26)	=SUM(E26)	=SUM(F26)
26	Closing Bank Balance	=SUM(B24:B25)	=SUM(C24:C25)	=SUM(D24:D25)	=SUM(E24:E25)	=SUM(F24:F25)	=SUM(G24:G25)

Cash-Flow Forecasts – Alternative Format

The format of cash-flow forecast shown in this chapter is widely used in business. Some spreadsheets adopt a slightly different approach to the way in which they deal with the bottom section. Instead of starting the section with cash flow for the month and then adding it to the bank balance at the beginning of the month, the alternative formula takes up four lines (rows of cells on a spreadsheet) and is set out as follows:

	Opening bank balance
+	Total Receipts
−	Total Payments
=	Closing Bank Balance

The end result of the calculation is exactly the same, the bottom line showing the bank balance at the end of each month.

Activity 16.3 – constructing cash-flow forecasts

You have been asked to draw up the cash-flow forecasts for two businesses for a six month period. The figures are shown below.

You are to:

1 Construct both cash-flow forecasts, using a computer spreadsheet if you wish (see opposite page for the formulas).

2 Comment on the cash flow of both businesses and explain the trends in the month-end bank balances.

ARBOR DESIGNS

	Jan £	Feb £	March £	April £	May £	June £
Receipts						
Capital	20,000					
Loan	15,000					
Receipts from clients	12,000	12,000	12,000	12,000	12,000	12,000
Payments						
Equipment	25,000					
Materials	5,000	5,000	5,000	5,000	5,000	5,000
Other expenses	2,000	2,000	2,000	2,000	2,000	2,000
Opening bank balance	zero					

GIGA CATERING

	Jan £	Feb £	March £	April £	May £	June £
Receipts						
Sales	30,000	30,000	30,000	30,000	30,000	30,000
Payments						
Stock and catering materials	15,000	15,000	15,000	15,000	15,000	15,000
Other expenses	5,000	5,000	5,000	5,000	5,000	5,000
Purchase of cooking equipment	15,000			30,000		
Opening bank balance	1,000					

CHAPTER SUMMARY

- The cash budget – also known as the cash-flow forecast – projects all income and payments which pass through the bank account, and so is central to the budgeting process in a business.

- The cash-flow forecast provides data for the master budget, which sets out a projected profit and loss account and balance sheet for the business.

- The cash-flow forecast is set out in three sections: receipts, payments and cash flow for the month.

- The cash flow for the month is calculated as follows:

CASH FLOW = TOTAL MONTHLY RECEIPTS – TOTAL MONTHLY PAYMENTS

- If the total of payments is higher than the total of receipts, the cash flow becomes negative and is shown with a minus sign or in brackets. This means that the liquidity of the business is under pressure and the business may not have the resources with which to repay its debts. If the total of receipts is higher than the total of payments, the cash flow is positive, which is good for liquidity.

- The cash flow section adds the monthly cash flow to the bank account balance at the beginning of the month to calculate the bank account balance at the end of the month, which is shown on the bottom line of the cash-flow forecast. If the cash flow is negative, it will be deducted from the opening bank balance. The formula is:

CASH FLOW FOR MONTH + OPENING BANK BALANCE = CLOSING BANK BALANCE

- If the figure for the closing bank balance is positive it indicates that the business has money in the bank; if the figure is negative it means that the business will be borrowing from the bank by means of an overdraft. An overdraft (negative balance) is shown either with a minus sign or in brackets.

- The closing bank balance for the month is entered on the cash-flow forecast as the opening balance for the next month, as it will always be the same figure.

- The cash-flow forecast is useful for a business because it shows how much the business will need to borrow and also if the business will have liquidity problems.

- The cash-flow forecast is an important part of a business plan which is presented to the bank when a business needs to request any form of borrowing.

- A computer spreadsheet is a useful way of setting up a cash-flow forecast and will allow the business to see the effect of changing income and costs using 'what if?' scenarios.

KEY TERMS

cash-flow forecast	a budget (also known as the cash budget) which presents the projected monthly flows of money in and out of the bank account and forecasts the month-end bank balance
master budget	projected profit and loss account and balance sheet which use data from the cash-flow forecast – normally included in the business plan to support an application for financing
cash flow	the difference between receipts into the bank account and payments out of the bank balance – shown on the cash-flow forecast either as a positive or a negative figure
opening bank balance	the bank balance at the beginning of the month – added to the cash flow for the month on the cash-flow forecast
closing bank balance	the bank balance at the end of the month, shown on the bottom line of the cash-flow forecast
overdraft	short-term borrowing from the bank on the business bank account, shown on the bottom line of the cash-flow forecast as a negative figure
liquidity	the ability of a business to pay off its debts as they become due
'what if' scenario	suggesting different situations when setting up budgets and other financial projections, eg increased sales figures or increased costs, a process which is made much simpler by the use of computer spreadsheets

17

Using ICT as a business resource

Starting point

Information and Communication Technology (ICT) has now become a fact of life in the business environment.

The advantages of the modern electronic office over the old paper-based office (shown on the left of the two pictures) can easily be taken for granted.

Rapid access to information, fast communication and the ability to process and analyse numerical data makes it easier for managers to make informed decisions.

The use of ICT in the office increases both efficiency and productivity.

What you will learn from this chapter

- ■ financial decision-making is greatly helped by the use of computer programs such as spreadsheets and accounting packages

- ■ other office computer applications such as word-processing, databases and presentation software have increased business efficiency

- ■ online applications of ICT such as email, the internet and e-commerce have extended the boundaries of communication and data interchange

- ■ the free flow of information has brought about the need for legal regulation to protect data and the privacy of individuals

NOTE TO READERS
There are no Student Activities included in this summary chapter. Activities involving computer spreadsheets are to be found in the chapters which deal with financial decision-making. The application of ICT methods are developed using study skills and in the presentation of this Unit Assessment.

Software for Financial Decision-making

using spreadsheets

A spreadsheet is a grid of boxes – 'cells' – set up on the computer, organised in rows and columns into which you can enter text and numbers. It enables you to make calculations with the figures. The computer program will work out the calculations automatically once you have entered an appropriate formula in the cell where the result of the calculations is required.

The major advantage of a spreadsheet is that if you change any of the figures the computer will automatically recalculate the total, saving you much time and effort.

Spreadsheets are used for a variety of functions in organisations:

- producing financial documents such as an invoice, which calculates the total due to a business on a sales transaction, including any VAT due

- working out budgets for future expenditure

- working out sales figures for different products or areas

A commonly used spreadsheet program is Microsoft Excel. The example below shows regional sales figures input into Excel.

	A	B	C	D	E
1	REGIONAL SALES				
2					
3		AREA A	AREA B	AREA C	
4		£	£	£	
5					
6	January – March	67987	32423	54342	
7	April –June	83792	38383	62627	
8	July–September	76352	29872	54664	
9	October–December	87383	30982	52420	
10	Total Sales by Area	315514	131660	224053	
11	Total Sales	671227			
12					

using charts

Figures in a spreadsheet can be used by management to monitor business performance. Sometimes figures can be analysed more easily if they can be displayed in the form of graphs or bar charts. A spreadsheet program such as Excel can produce these automatically. All that you need to do is to select the appropriate figures and the computer does the rest through its charting function. The seasonal sales shown on the previous page can be shown as a bar chart, as seen below. Note how the appropriate cells have been selected.

USING A SPREADSHEET TO EXTRACT A CHART

		AREA A £	AREA B £	AREA C £
January – March		67987	32423	54342
April –June		83792	38383	62627
July–September		76352	29872	54664
October–December		87383	30982	52420
Total Sales by Area		315514	131660	224053
Total Sales		671227		

Regional Sales

spreadsheets for financial forecasting

We have seen in earlier chapters that spreadsheets can be used to forecast financial performance and to make the budgeting process simpler and more flexible. For example, spreadsheets can be used for:

- projected profit and loss statement – which can be incorporated in the master budget
- break-even analysis – to find out if a planned product is financially feasible
- cash-flow forecast – to forecast the future liquidity of a business and identify any need for overdraft borrowing

We will set out all these spreadsheets on the next few pages, explaining how they help with business decision-making. We will show all the formulas used so that you can set up your own worksheets to help you with your studies.

profit and loss accounts

The profit and loss account (also known as the profit and loss 'statement'), as well as calculating the profit made by a business over a past period of time, can be used to forecast future profits as part of the budgeting process.

A projected profit and loss account forms part of the master budget. This is an important document in the business plan which is prepared by a business when it is applying for finance from an investor or from the bank.

The examples below show both the figures and the formulas that are required.

PROFIT AND LOSS ACCOUNT ON A SPREADSHEET

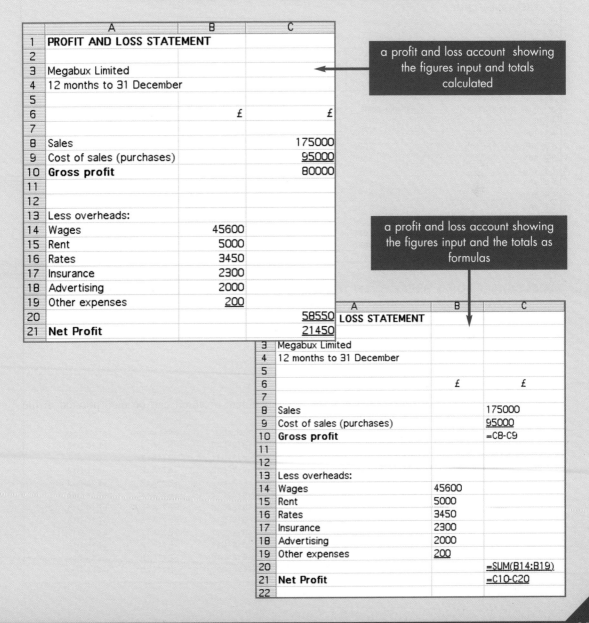

	A	B	C
1	PROFIT AND LOSS STATEMENT		
2			
3	Megabux Limited		
4	12 months to 31 December		
5			
6		£	£
7			
8	Sales		175000
9	Cost of sales (purchases)		95000
10	Gross profit		80000
11			
12			
13	Less overheads:		
14	Wages	45600	
15	Rent	5000	
16	Rates	3450	
17	Insurance	2300	
18	Advertising	2000	
19	Other expenses	200	
20			58550
21	Net Profit		21450

a profit and loss account showing the figures input and totals calculated

a profit and loss account showing the figures input and the totals as formulas

	A	B	C
1	PROFIT AND LOSS STATEMENT		
3	Megabux Limited		
4	12 months to 31 December		
5			
6		£	£
7			
8	Sales		175000
9	Cost of sales (purchases)		95000
10	Gross profit		=C8-C9
11			
12			
13	Less overheads:		
14	Wages	45600	
15	Rent	5000	
16	Rates	3450	
17	Insurance	2300	
18	Advertising	2000	
19	Other expenses	200	
20			=SUM(B14:B19)
21	Net Profit		=C10-C20
22			

break-even analysis

Break-even tables, which form the basis of break-even charts, can be set up on a computer spreadsheet. They are useful for showing the effect of changing costs (fixed and variable) and the setting of a variety of proposed selling prices. They enable the management of a company to see if a planned product is financially viable and to take decisions accordingly.

SPREADSHEET FOR A BREAK-EVEN TABLE - SHOWING THE FIGURES INPUT

	A	B	C	D	E	F
1	BREAK-EVEN CHART					
2	Name:					
3	Period:					
4						
5	fixed costs (£)	5000				
6	variable cost per item (£)	10				
7	sales income per item (£)	20				
8						
9	units of production	variable costs	fixed costs	total cost	sales income	profit/loss
10	0	0	5000	5000	0	-5000
11	100	1000	5000	6000	2000	-4000
12	200	2000	5000	7000	4000	-3000
13	300	3000	5000	8000	6000	-2000
14	400	4000	5000	9000	8000	-1000
15	500	5000	5000	10000	10000	0
16	600	6000	5000	11000	12000	1000
17	700	7000	5000	12000	14000	2000
18	800	8000	5000	13000	16000	3000
19	900	9000	5000	14000	18000	4000
20	1000	10000	5000	15000	20000	5000
21						

SPREADSHEET FOR A BREAK-EVEN TABLE - SHOWING THE FORMULAS USED

	A	B	C	D	E	F
1	BREAK-EVEN CHART					
2	Name:					
3	Period:					
4						
5	fixed costs (£)	5000				
6	variable cost per item (£)	10				
7	sales income per item (£)	20				
8						
9	units of production	variable costs	fixed costs	total cost	sales income	profit/loss
10	0	=B6*A10	=B5	=B10+C10	=B7*A10	=E10-D10
11	100	=B6*A11	=B5	=B11+C11	=B7*A11	=E11-D11
12	200	=B6*A12	=B5	=B12+C12	=B7*A12	=E12-D12
13	300	=B6*A13	=B5	=B13+C13	=B7*A13	=E13-D13
14	400	=B6*A14	=B5	=B14+C14	=B7*A14	=E14-D14
15	500	=B6*A15	=B5	=B15+C15	=B7*A15	=E15-D15
16	600	=B6*A16	=B5	=B16+C16	=B7*A16	=E16-D16
17	700	=B6*A17	=B5	=B17+C17	=B7*A17	=E17-D17
18	800	=B6*A18	=B5	=B18+C18	=B7*A18	=E18-D18
19	900	=B6*A19	=B5	=B19+C19	=B7*A19	=E19-D19
20	1000	=B6*A20	=B5	=B20+C20	=B7*A20	=E20-D20
21						

cash-flow forecasts

A cash flow forecast estimates monthly receipts and payments through the business bank account and calculates the month-end bank balance. It is a form of budget which is central to the budgeting system and is used extensively by management to assess liquidity and future overdraft borrowing requirements. It is also used to support requests for finance.

CASH-FLOW FORECAST SPREADSHEET (EXTRACT) SHOWING THE FIGURES PRODUCED

6							
7	RECEIPTS						
8	Sales	10,000	10,000	10,000	10,000	10,000	10,000
9	Bank Loan	8,000					
10	Capital	12,000					
11	TOTAL RECEIPTS	30,000	10,000	10,000	10,000	10,000	10,000
12	PAYMENTS						
13	Purchases	5,000	5,000	5,000	5,000	5,000	5,000
14	Equipment	14,500	15,250				
15	Rent	575	575	575	575	575	575
16	Insurance	50	50	50	50	50	50
17	Electricity			100			100
18	Telephone	100	100	100	100	100	100
19	Wages	1,000	1,000	1,000	1,000	1,000	1,000
20	Postage	450	450	450	450	450	450
21	Marketing	200	200	200	200	200	200
22							
23	TOTAL PAYMENTS	21,875	22,625	7,475	7,375	7,375	7,475
24	CASHFLOW FOR MONTH	8,125	- 12,625	2,525	2,625	2,625	2,525
25	Opening Bank Balance		8,125	- 4,500	- 1,975	650	3,275
26	Closing Bank Balance	8,125	- 4,500	- 1,975	650	3,275	5,800

CASH-FLOW FORECAST SPREADSHEET SHOWING THE FORMULAS

	A	B	C	D	E	F	G
1	DVD EXPRESS						
2	CASH BUDGET for 6 months						
3		JANUARY	FEBRUARY	MARCH	APRIL	MAY	JUNE
4		£	£	£	£	£	£
5							
6							
7	RECEIPTS						
8	Sales	10000	10000	10000	10000	10000	10000
9	Bank Loan	8000					
10	Capital	12000					
11	TOTAL RECEIPTS	=SUM(B6:B10)	=SUM(C6:C10)	=SUM(D6:D10)	=SUM(E6:E10)	=SUM(F6:F10)	=SUM(G6:G10)
12	PAYMENTS						
13	Purchases	5000	5000	5000	5000	5000	5000
14	Equipment	14500	15250				
15	Rent	575	575	575	575	575	575
16	Insurance	50	50	50	50	50	50
17	Electricity			100			100
18	Telephone	100	100	100	100	100	100
19	Wages	1000	1000	1000	1000	1000	1000
20	Postage	450	450	450	450	450	450
21	Marketing	200	200	200	200	200	200
22							
23	TOTAL PAYMENTS	=SUM(B13:B22)	=SUM(C13:C22)	=SUM(D13:D22)	=SUM(E13:E22)	=SUM(F13:F22)	=SUM(G13:G22)
24	CASHFLOW FOR MONTH	=SUM(B11-B23)	=SUM(C11-C23)	=SUM(D11-D23)	=SUM(E11-E23)	=SUM(F11-F23)	=SUM(G11-G23)
25	Opening Bank Balance		=SUM(B26)	=SUM(C26)	=SUM(D26)	=SUM(E26)	=SUM(F26)
26	Closing Bank Balance	=SUM(B24:B25)	=SUM(C24:C25)	=SUM(D24:D25)	=SUM(E24:E25)	=SUM(F24:F25)	=SUM(G24:G25)

Use of Accounting Software

the way forward

Although some organisations, particularly small businesses, may still use paper-based accounting systems, an increasing number are now operating **computer accounting systems**. Small and medium-sized businesses can buy 'off-the-shelf' accounting programs from suppliers such as Sage while larger businesses often have custom-designed programs. Computer accounting programs are easy to use and can automate operations such as invoicing which take so much time and effort in a manual system.

what a computer accounting package will provide

A typical computer accounting system will offer a number of facilities:

- on-screen input and printout of financial documents such as invoices
- recording of suppliers' invoices
- recording of money paid into the bank
- recording of payments to suppliers and for expenses
- payroll processing

management reports

A computer accounting program can provide instant reports for management, for example:

- an aged debtors' summary – a table showing amounts owed by customers and the time periods for which the amounts have been owing
- activity reports on customer and supplier accounts
- activity reports on expenses accounts

A customer report menu screen from a Sage program is shown below.

CUSTOMER REPORTS AVAILABLE FROM A SAGE ACCOUNTING PROGRAM

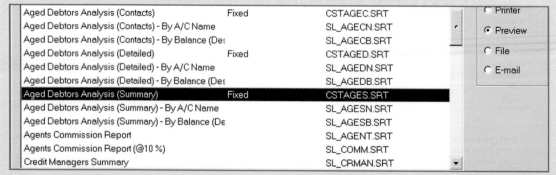

General Office Software

There are a number of computer programs available for general office use. They are normally designed so that they are integrated together and data can be moved across from one program to another. The main programs used are:

- word processing programs
- databases
- presentation software

word processing

Word processing programs – including Microsoft 'Word' – enable you to:

- enter and format text, eg set it out in columns and add bullet points
- change and edit text
- set up tables

Word processed text can be saved and printed out in the form of letters, memos, reports, and notices. Word processed text can also be sent electronically either on disk or as an attachment file on an email. Some of the text in Osborne Books publications is first input in Word and sent to Osborne Books on disk or by email. It is then imported into a page set-up program.

Word processing programs can be linked to other programs. For example the names and addresses from a computer accounting package or a database can be imported to 'mailmerge' into a set of letters sent out to customers.

A 'WORD' FILE WHICH HAS BEEN USED IN COMPILING THIS CHAPTER

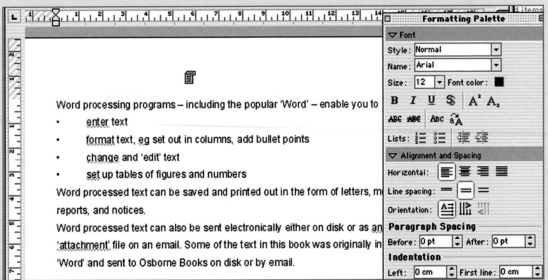

databases

A computer database enables you to input and store information in an organised way so that it can be readily accessed, sorted and exported. A database is essentially an electronic filing system which takes all the hard work out of sorting and retrieving information.

Databases are very useful to a business which needs to record and make use of data – for marketing purposes, for example.

A typical customer record is shown in the screen below.

A CUSTOMER RECORD FROM A COMPUTER DATABASE

Mode Select Format Script Window Help	
	Customers
Title	Mr
Initials	D
Surname	Foster
Address 1	12 High Street
Address 2	
Address 3	
Address 4	
Town/City	Mereford
Postcode	MR1 2GH
Telephone	01908 644234
Email	dfoster@solonex.co.uk
Organisation	Solonex Limited

If you assume that the 'Customers' record shown above is part of a list of the people and organisations to whom a business sells its products, the file could be expanded with further fields to record information such as:

■ the date on which the customer was last contacted and by whom

■ the customer status – eg current customers (those who have ordered) target customers (those who have not ordered), lost customers (those who have ordered in the past but have now stopped)

■ details of products sold

The 'Customers' file could then be accessed and searched to produce lists, for example, of customers not contacted within the last six months, target customers and customers who have bought a particular product.

The efficiencies available to the business of using a database and the value to the marketing function are self-evident. Imagine carrying out all the tasks mentioned here if the system was paper-based.

presentation software

Presentation software enables information to be set up as a series of slides which are professional in appearance. These can be used internally in business meetings or externally by, for example, the sales force. One of the most commonly used presentation programs is Microsoft 'Powerpoint' which can be displayed on a computer screen or using a digital projector. Slides are simple to construct and the software provides a variety of templates that can be used. The slide at the bottom of this page was produced in less than one minute by a complete beginner.

Note that your assessment for this Unit requires you to produce a presentation, using ICT, explaining the small business you have chosen to set up. The areas you have to cover are:

- a plan for the business, covering its legal form, objectives and stakeholders, and its market
- an explanation of the ways in which the business will manage its activities by using its human, physical and financial resources to provide a quality product
- financial management information, including costs, budgeting, cash flow and break-even analysis
- an explanation of how ICT can be used in the business and help it to operate efficiently

A PRESENTATION SLIDE PRODUCED IN 'POWERPOINT'

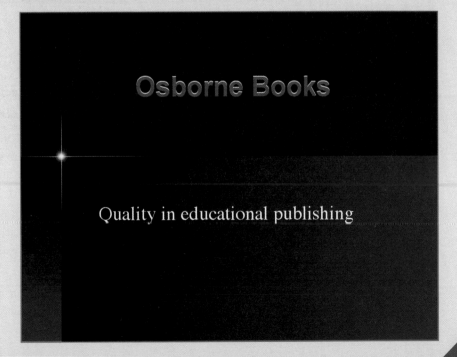

Online Resources for Business

Businesses are also making increasing use of online resources and communication methods. They are quick and cheap to use, and greatly improve business efficiency. They include:

- email
- electronic documents and EDI
- the internet
- e-commerce

email

Most businesses are now online and can send and receive external emails. Some businesses are also networked through an intranet and can send emails internally. Another important computer program is therefore the email management system. The screen below shows a typical outbox – which lists messages and enables you to access the texts sent. In this case a message has been sent to Osborne Books, the publishers of this book.

AN EMAIL OUTBOX

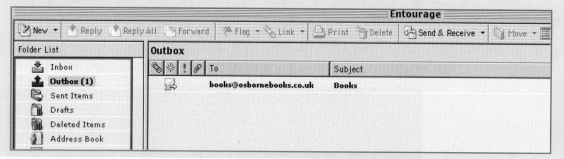

uses of email and attachments

Email is a very useful and inexpensive means of sending messages electronically not only within a business but also externally to customers and suppliers. Transmission is instantaneous. This can be an advantage, but can also be a disadvantage – it often demands a rapid reply.

Email acts as a link between many different types of computer program. Not only can a message be relayed in text form, email can also be used to transfer word processing, database and spreadsheet files from one computer to another in the form of an attachment file.

Documents – orders and invoices for example – can be generated on the computer and sent by email attachment to suppliers and customers.

electronic documents and EDI

Data and documents – eg financial documents such as orders and invoices – can also be sent electronically through Electronic Data Interchange (EDI) programs. This form of transfer employs software which is more specialised than the normal email management programs already mentioned. The process is reliable, fast and efficient and is used, for example, by supermarket chains in ordering and paying for goods.

the internet

The internet probably needs no introduction in a textbook such as this, as you will be accessing it on a daily basis. It is used widely in business as a resource and has reduced the reliance on paper-based data sources. As with email, it has brought about great efficiencies for businesses. Its uses include:

- internet banking
- shopping around for business supplies, eg computer stationery
- obtaining credit reports on new customers
- looking at the websites of competitors to see what new products they are introducing and looking at their pricing
- carrying out secondary market research, eg looking at statistics and trends to see what customers are buying and how much money they have to spend on products

The screen below is taken from www.statistics.gov.uk and illustrates computer usage by 11-18 year-olds. This data would be useful for the marketing department of any business selling computer-based products such as games and educational software to the 11-18 age group.

SOCIAL TRENDS FROM GOVERNMENT STATISTICS

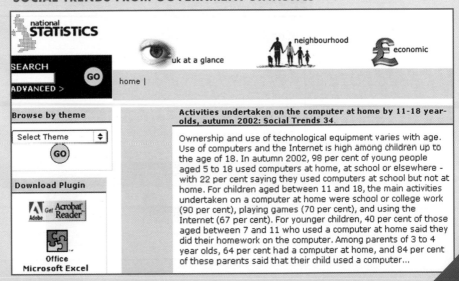

national **STATISTICS**

uk at a glance   neighbourhood   economic

SEARCH   GO   home |

ADVANCED >

Browse by theme

Select Theme

GO

Download Plugin

Get Acrobat Reader Adobe

Office Microsoft Excel

Activities undertaken on the computer at home by 11-18 year-olds, autumn 2002: Social Trends 34

Ownership and use of technological equipment varies with age. Use of computers and the Internet is high among children up to the age of 18. In autumn 2002, 98 per cent of young people aged 5 to 18 used computers at home, at school or elsewhere - with 22 per cent saying they used computers at school but not at home. For children aged between 11 and 18, the main activities undertaken on a computer at home were school or college work (90 per cent), playing games (70 per cent), and using the Internet (67 per cent). For younger children, 40 per cent of those aged between 7 and 11 who used a computer at home said they did their homework on the computer. Among parents of 3 to 4 year olds, 64 per cent had a computer at home, and 84 per cent of these parents said that their child used a computer...

e-commerce

Website shops have seen a phenomenal rate of growth at a time when 'high street' sales have levelled off and in some cases fallen. The reason for this is that it is relatively cheap for any business to set up an online shop which can be open 24 hours a day, seven days a week.

Popular products sold using this method include books, music, electronic goods, cars and holidays. If you have access to the internet try the on-line store www.amazon.co.uk or shopping sites available through web search engines such as Google. This form of selling by 'e-tailers' poses a serious threat to the traditional retailers who do not have an online presence. The two screens below show the Amazon site and the Osborne Books site.

If you are doing the Double Award, the topic of e-commerce is covered in full in the Optional Unit 'Investigating Electronic Business'.

OSBORNE BOOKS ON SALE ONLINE

Legal Issues of ICT in Business

Using ICT in the business environment involves complying with legal regulations in two main areas

■ data protection

■ Health & Safety at Work

data protection

The **Data Protection Act 1998** regulates the use of personal information held by organisations on computer file and on paper records. Every time a consumer fills in a form from a business and provides personal details, the information may be used for marketing purposes, unless the person withholds permission. The problem about this type of information is that:

■ it may be incorrect and misleading

■ it may be passed to other organisations without the consumer knowing

The Act requires that the information should be kept securely and confidentially and that the 'subject' can have access to it, for a fee. Visit www.informationcommissioner.gov.uk for further information.

Health & Safety at work

Using computers at work can involve a number of hazards which can be avoided if legal regulations are complied with.

computer work can harm your health

The **Health & Safety at Work Act 1974** requires that an employer must provide, among other things, safe equipment and machinery and systems of work. This means that trailing wires and overheating computer equipment should be avoided.

The **Display Screen Equipment Regulations 1992** set down rules for the use of computer workstations and VDU screens. A 'workstation' includes the computer equipment, furniture, space, light and atmosphere in which an employee works. Measures include:

■ employees must have regular breaks

■ employees must be offered eye tests

■ equipment and furniture must conform to strict standards of safety and comfort

CHAPTER SUMMARY

■ A computer spreadsheet is a powerful program for manipulating figures; it can be used in a variety of areas of financial forecasting:

- projected profit and loss statement
- break-even analysis
- cash-flow forecast

■ A computer spreadsheet can provide management with comprehensive and accurate data which helps with decision-making; it also brings efficiencies of time and cost saving to a business. It can also be used to produce charts of the data it has processed.

■ Computer accounting systems such as Sage software enable a business to run its accounting record-keeping systems efficiently, automating processes such as invoicing and the provision of management reports.

■ General office software such as word-processing programs and databases enable a business to manage its text processing and data handling functions efficiently. Presentation software can also be used internally and externally to improve communication.

■ Online resources can also improve the efficiency of a business by providing data rapidly, and, in many cases, free of charge. For example:

- email is rapid, informal and inexpensive
- EDI can be used to produce electronic documentation for trading businesses
- the internet is an immense source of data which can help businesses in obtaining information about purchasing, competitors and economic trends

■ E-commerce has brought about strong growth in internet shopping. It is relatively cheap to set up and has the advantage of providing 24 hour trading.

■ The growth of the use of ICT has brought about the need for legal regulation of two main areas:

- protection by the Data Protection Act of personal data held on computers
- protection of the employee against the health hazards of computer operation by the Health & Safety at Work Act and the Display Screen Equipment Regulations

KEY TERMS

spreadsheet	a grid table set up on a computer containing cells into which data (numbers and text) can be entered and used to process calculations automatically
profit & loss account	a financial statement covering a period of time setting out a profit calculation based on the formula: profit = sales revenue – running costs
break-even analysis	an analysis of the income and running costs of a business to calculate at what point the business starts to make a profit
cash-flow forecast	a budget (also known as the cash budget) which presents the projected monthly flows of money in and out of the bank account and forecasts the month-end bank balance
computer accounting	the use of a specialised computer program to record financial transactions and provide reports to business management
word-processing	the use of a specialised computer program to enter, format and edit text and to present data in a variety of formats
database	the use of a specialised computer program to input and store information so that it can easily be accessed and automatically sorted and exported as required
presentation software	a computer program which enables the user to produce a series of slides on templates for use in presentations
email	messages between computers linked by internal networks or by the internet
EDI	Electronic Data Interchange – the use of computer links between businesses to send electronic documents such as orders and invoices
e-commerce	on-line trading using website bookshops to buy and pay for goods and services
data protection	legal regulations protecting data held about individuals by businesses – including on computer file

Unit **3**

Investigating marketing

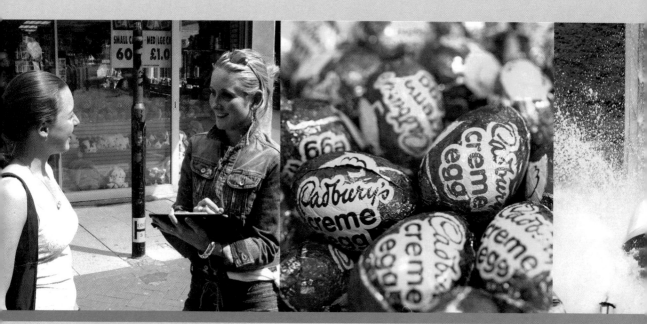

In this unit you will investigate the 'marketing mix' for a chosen product or service. This involves an examination of the whole marketing process which results in the successful sale of an item such as a cream egg or a flume ride. You will research:

■ the marketing aims and objectives of a business

■ the identification of market 'segments' – the 'types' of customer to whom a product or service is sold

■ the methods of market research used to identify a target market

■ a suitable 'marketing mix' – an action plan involving the defining of the product, the setting of a suitable price, promoting it in the marketplace and 'delivering' it in the right place

■ the constraints that you will have to face – for example the costs, legal constraints and environmental considerations

Unit 3

Chapters in this Unit...

18

Marketing objectives and customers

Starting point

When you get a job, whatever that might be, you will find that your business (or organisation) will carry out some form of marketing activity. It is therefore important to have an understanding of what marketing involves and the ways in which it affects the organisation's objectives and activities.

Businesses clearly need to make a profit, but they also have to allocate resources to attract new customers and ensure that existing customers keep coming back to provide that profit and safeguard jobs. Marketing is all about identifying and reaching the customer 'in the street' with the right product.

What you will learn from this chapter

- marketing is a complex and wide range of activities which involve fulfiling a series of objectives, satisfying the differing needs of a range of customers and being aware of what is going on in the marketplace

- specific marketing objectives include profitability, product development, promoting the brand, achieving market share and last, but not least, looking after the customers

- marketing is very much centred on the customer and successful marketing involves a business carefully identifying the market 'segment' or 'segments' – the types of customer – to which it will sell its products

- there are many ways of identifying customer types – by the area in which they live, age, income, social class and their lifestyle and sets of values

What is Marketing?

a definition?

Unlike business functions such as finance and human resources, marketing is difficult to define. It involves a very wide range of activities. If you ask the 'person' in the street what marketing is you are likely to get a variety of answers involving terms such as 'advertising', 'special offers', 'customer questionnaires', 'selling', 'launching a new product'. These are all part of marketing but are not in themselves a definition.

Taking all these key phrases quoted above you might describe marketing as:

getting the right product to the right people at the right price at the right time

Successful marketing is based on what are widely known as the 4 P's.

the 4 P's - the marketing mix

The four P's – **P**roduct, **P**rice, **P**romotion and **P**lace – are helpful because they provide a focus for an understanding of the marketing activities and the marketing planning carried out by a business. They are often known as the **marketing mix** because they provide a structure for a successful marketing campaign. As you will see they include many of the terms quoted by the person in the street at the top of this page. The ways in which the four P's are used in marketing planning are discussed fully in Chapters 20 and 21.

PRODUCT   **getting the product right for the customer**
Finding out what the customer wants using detailed market research and then designing and producing a suitable product, eg a drink or a holiday.

PRICE   **fixing the price at the right level**
Fixing a price at which the customer will buy the product. This will require research into what the competition are charging and what the customer is prepared to pay.

PROMOTION   **promoting the product to the right people**
Deciding how you are going to promote the product using a range of techniques including advertising, publicity and special offers.

PLACE   **getting the right product to the right people at the right time**
Deciding on where and how you are going to sell the product – whether locally, nationally, over the counter, by phone, over the internet – and how the product will be distributed.

your marketing assessment

It is worth at this point focusing on what you are required to carry out for your Unit 3 Assessment because your study of this textbook will help you at each stage. You are required to carry out a range of marketing activities (a 'marketing mix') for a new product or for a product that already exists. This will involve you in:

- identifying marketing objectives – ie what you want to achieve – for example developing a new product, improving market share, improving profitability, promoting the 'brand' image
- identifying and deciding what types of customer you are going to sell to
- carrying out market research
- deciding on a marketing mix – a strategy for achieving your objectives
- explaining and justifying your decisions

What you have to do is very practical. In this chapter we describe how you go about covering the first two points – identifying the types of objective you will be planning to achieve and distinguishing between the different types of customer you will be selling to.

'Corporate' Objectives and Marketing

objectives and strategies

Business objectives, as we have seen in Chapter 2, are a statement of where the organisation is heading over the long term; they are built into the planning process. These 'corporate' objectives are often summarised in a Mission Statement.

becoming a household name

Objectives, in simple terms, are where the business is heading for, and **strategies** are the means for getting there. All functions within the organisation – human resources, finance, production/operations, marketing – must be aware of these objectives and plan their strategies accordingly. In the case of the marketing function these strategies will often take the form of a marketing plan.

The following are examples of business objectives that will influence the activities of the marketing function:

- maximising sales and profits
- satisfying the stakeholders
- becoming a household name for its products
- being known for environmentally sound products and policies

Identifying Marketing Objectives

There are a number of marketing objectives a business might adopt. We will now describe these and then in the rest of the chapter provide an analysis of the different types of customer – the market segments – which a business can target for its products.

a note on conflicting objectives

When analysing these objectives you may notice that they do sometimes conflict, just as the main business objectives can conflict. For example, marketing may set targets for profitability which may result in customers not necessarily getting the best value for money.

understanding customer needs and wants

'One of our Values is to understand customers better than anyone. We go to great lengths to ask customers what they think, listen to their views, and then act on them. We look both at what customers say and what they do. This feedback guides the decisions we take.'

Tesco – putting the customer 'at the centre of things'

It is often said that successful marketing is a result of putting the customer at the centre of everything that the business is trying to achieve. The buzzword is to say that a business should be 'customer-centric' – at the centre of things. This objective is often quoted in Mission Statements. Look at the quote from the Tesco website shown on the left. Visit www.tesco.com

Understanding a customer **need** is providing a product which fulfils a basic customer requirement – food and clothing, for example. Good marketing can also persuade a customer to **want** a product – a designer label pair of jeans, for example.

Market research must establish whether the products and services provided by a business are satisfying customers' needs and wants. This involves analysing the image that customers and non-customers have of the business and its products. Are they getting value for money? Are they happy with factors such as quality, service and reliability? Do they themselves feel valued by the business?

developing new products

Nothing lasts forever, and this applies to the products and services that a business provides to the market. Market research will provide data about customer needs and wants and will help in the design of new products. The successful business is the innovative business which thinks of new ideas which become fashionable. It is difficult to believe, for example, that the first personal stereo, the Sony Walkman, was an entirely fresh idea and many people thought it would never catch on!

re-launching old products

Another way of bringing a new product to market is to revamp an existing product – it might be less expensive to do so and a technical update may make it possible. Old products may also become fashionable in their own right as the trend for the 'retro' look shows ('retro' means looking back).

diversification

Diversification means a move into a new product type as a result of market research identifying good opportunities elsewhere in the market. Some businesses grow rapidly through diversification. Look at the Case Study on page 7 which shows how the 'Easy' Group has expanded from cut price flights by diversifying into films, car hire, phones and cruise ships.

improving market share

Improving market share is another vital marketing objective which will help to increase profitability (see below). Market share is the percentage of sales made by a product or business within a specific market. The major supermarkets, for example, watch market share very closely on a regular basis. Market share can be improved by increasing brand awareness (see below) or brand quality. Introducing new products into an existing market or diversification into new markets will also improve market share.

brand identity

increasing brand awareness

Brand means giving a product or a business name a distinct identity. Brand image is very important in marketing, not only because consumers can recognise it worldwide (you are never far from a can of Coke) but because many brands can make the consumer 'look cool' because the brand names are widely recognised. Increasing brand awareness is therefore very important. It can be achieved in a variety of ways: imaginative product design, good advertising, good publicity.

improving profitability

Profitability is a major objective for any business and is often driven by the finance function in a business. Profit results from an increase in sales and cutting of costs. It is therefore an important marketing objective to maximise sales while at the same time keeping marketing costs within the budget targets. Your study of Finance will explain the important concept of 'margin' – the difference between price and cost.

Activity 18.1 – marketing objectives

Marketing is very much about setting objectives for the product itself. Carry out the activities below.

1 Identify a new product on the market that appeals to you. Describe how it is brought to the attention of consumers and explain how you have been persuaded to like it.

2 The American company IBM, which introduced the PC (personal computer) to the market in 1981, is rumoured to be stopping production of its own PCs in order to concentrate on more profitable areas. Explain the marketing strategy that IBM is using here. Visit www.IBM.com to find out more.

3 Choose three well-known brands of product that you particularly like (eg food, drinks, clothes). Describe where you can obtain these brands and how the brand name is promoted to the consumer. (These three brands should not include the product chosen for Activity 1 above.)

Now read the adapted article from 'Marketing' in the Case Study which follows. It shows what can happen if a business – or in this case a complete industry – forgets the basic marketing objective and ignores the customer.

Case Study – customer focus in marketing

FRENCH WINEMAKERS' ATTITUDE IS HARD TO SWALLOW

The French wine industry is in crisis. Less than two decades ago the French dominated the British wine market. Now France accounts for a paltry 20% of all wine sold in the UK. Australian wine is the UK market leader with US wine also selling strongly. Sales of French wine continue to decline yearly.

The problem is marketing – or rather the lack of it. French wine producers are providing a disastrous case study in product orientation; in other words, a focus on product and manufacturing at the expense of the customer. By contrast, Australian competitors are fully paid up members of the market-oriented club and the differences are telling.

French wine is classified by 'appellation', a system linked to the geographical location of the vine-yard (see bottle on right). For French producers this makes perfect sense, but for the British consumers the result is a confusing array of names and regions, which offers no clue as to the type or quality of wine.

Australian and other 'New World' wines focus on grape variety, and choose more accessible names and labels to create a strong and memorable brand image (see bottle on right).

The Australians have paid great attention to the changing tastes and growing numbers of wine drinkers through market research. This has enabled them to focus on producing fruitier and fresher wines just as the market began to demand them.

Until recently, the French have adopted the classic product-oriented approach of blaming customers for not appreciating their wines.

Finally, there are sales and promotions. Even the biggest French producers' marketing budgets and sales teams are dwarfed by the huge US and Australian producers and their economies of scale. According to a recent French government report, many of the single wine companies from Australia and the US outspend whole regions in France by a factor of 25.

So what can be done for the French producers? Their one last hope is a return to their customers and what the customers think is important.

Activity 18.2 – customer focus in marketing

Read through the Case Study above and answer the following questions:

1 What is the trend in market share for French wines in the UK and what is the current market share?

2 What is the main marketing objective that the French seem to have ignored?

3 What is 'confusing' to British consumers, and what are the Australians doing right?

4 What marketing objective are the Australians and Americans following in giving their wines memorable names?

5 How have the Australians managed to get their wines to appeal to the tastes of European wine drinkers?

6 What other marketing techniques have the Australians used to increase their sales and market share?

Defining the Marketplace

The Case Study on the last two pages shows clearly the importance of maintaining a customer focus in marketing. A concentration on 'product' is also vital in business and it is important to realise that product development should complement awareness of customer wants and needs.

The marketing function in a business needs to appreciate the different types of customer – the market segments – that exist in the marketplace and to identify the appropriate target market. The marketing plan can then set up to ensure that the right product gets to the right customers.

Market Segmentation – Social Classifications

Market segmentation is the process whereby the overall market is divided up into separate sets of customers (segments) who have separate identifiable product needs.

There are a number of different ways of identifying consumer market segments in terms of social groupings.

social stratification

A common way of segmenting the market is by social class. Each group will have its own product needs and pattern of income and expenditure. The UK social classes are divided into letter groupings (A to E) as shown below.

SOCIAL GROUP CLASSIFICATION IN THE UK

Social group	Social class	Occupation type
A	Upper/upper middle class	higher managerial, professional, eg director of a large company, partner in a firm of solicitors
B	Middle class	intermediate managerial, professional, eg commercial manager, salaried accountant
C1	Lower middle class	junior managerial and supervisory, eg insurance clerk, nurse, shop manager
C2	Skilled working class	skilled manual workers, eg electrician, fitter
D	Working class	semi-skilled and unskilled workers, eg warehouseman, driver, shop assistant
E	Subsistence level	the lowest paid and the unemployed

Market Segmentation – Demographic Classifications

Another form of market segmentation is **demographic segmentation**. Demography is the study of populations and their characteristics. A business needs to know how many consumers exist and in what proportions relative to age, gender and levels of income.

age groups

The age groupings chosen will depend on the research being undertaken. For example a 'whole population' survey would subdivide over the 0 to 100 range; a survey of the working population would span the 16 to 65 range. Common subdivisions include:

0-12	child
13-17	teenager
18-35	young working person
36-59	mature working person
60 plus	retired person

Segmentation by age group is clearly the objective of Club 18-30 (visit www.club18-30.co.uk).

gender

Products for 'him' and 'her' are clearly different market segments because there will always be differences between what men want and what women want, for example in the clothing and cosmetics industries. Businesses also exploit more subtle differences between the sexes when designing products such as drinks and cars.

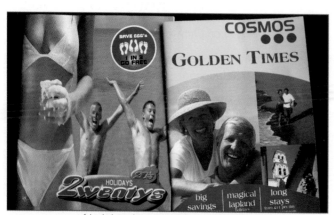

segmentation of holidays by age and also by income

income groups

Generally speaking, low income groups will look for a 'bargain' and higher income groups will look for quality and expensive products to advertise their wealth. Remember also that grouping by age will also determine how much spending power the consumer has. Younger people, for example, will look for cheaper clubbing holidays, and the mature population will tend to choose expensive cruises and luxury breaks.

geographic segmentation

Geographic segmentation means knowing where the consumer lives. This will affect the decision a business makes as to where to set up shops, agencies or factories. It will also influence the type of product offered. Try selling tripe or haggis in Surrey. Regional differences must be understood.

Activity 18.3 – market segmentation

Divide into small groups within the class. Discuss what different market segments should be considered by:

■ a clothes importer

■ a holiday company

■ a mobile phone manufacturer

Each group should make a list for each type of product and then compare and comment on the contents of the lists in full class session.

Psychographic Segmentation

In order to appreciate the needs of each market segment, planners must understand buyer behaviour, an area which involves an element of psychology. This leads to **psychographic segmentation** – an analysis of the differences in psychological motivation of the purchaser. The key point to appreciate is that consumers do not buy products and services: they buy the benefits that such products or services offer to them.

Factors that affect the buying decision are increasingly emotive rather than practical. Compare the two columns in the table below:

factors affecting purchase of a pair of jeans	
practical factors	**emotive factors**
price – are they good value for money?	are they designer label?
are they hard wearing?	will they look fashionable?
will they get a lot of use?	will they look expensive?
are they easy to clean?	does the colour suit me?
do they fit well?	will they make me look fit?

using consumer databases

Psychologists have commented at length on buyer behaviour as they analyse the basic needs and wants of individuals and groups.

Databases list and provide information about the people, or organisations, in any one market. Data can be purchased. One such database is 'Acorn', which stands for 'A Classification Of Residential Neighbourhoods' which uses postcodes to provide a picture of household size, age, shopping preferences, income and social classification.

lifestyle databases

Lifestyle databases include details of social class (income potential), cultural background, family data, reference groups, social interests and so on. They can be mixed with information on age, gender, location plus other

information on media usage (newspapers read, TV watched, radio heard) to build accurate market segment pictures. Lifestyles are often given catchy names such as SITKOM (Single Income, Two Kids, Oppressive Mortgage) and SOPPIE (Sensible Older Person with Pension and InsurancE).

values research

Values Research is a growth area of a similar type to lifestyle analysis, but it focuses on consumer beliefs and motivations more than on income levels and demography. It believes that

the 'values' appeal of a Lynx deodorant

fashions change even in the way we think, and that the values of say modesty, respect for authority and conformism are views of the past. Today is about excitement, escapism and sexuality. Such research has given us a new style of advertising for products such as cars, drinks and cosmetics.

Activity 18.4 – understanding buyer behaviour

1   Discuss in class current TV adverts for a single type of product, eg cars, drinks or cosmetics. Try if you can to record some examples to show to the class.

Analyse the methods the advertiser uses to appeal either to the lifestyle of the consumer or to the values of the consumer (eg excitement, escapism, sexuality).

2   Discuss in small groups in class and create ideas for a 'story line' for a TV advert for a widely purchased product such as a pair of jeans or trainers. What market segment would you aim for and what emotive factors could you use to persuade consumers to buy the product? Report back to the class with your ideas.

Market Strategies

There are different strategies for approaching different market segments. If you are launching a product, do you aim at one segment, or do you aim at all of them? The choice may depend on the breadth of the product's appeal, or the size of the business promoting the product(s).

A large concern can afford to promote a wide range of products to different segments; many small businesses, on the other hand, have successfully identified a gap in the market and undertaken **niche marketing** to a single market segment ('niche' means 'gap').

The traditional classification of strategies is:

mass marketing

This type of marketing is where a product is targeted at all sectors. This strategy can be expensive and wasteful, but can be successful where the product suits all markets, eg Coca Cola, the Mars Bar.

Interestingly, internet marketing can be seen as a form of mass marketing, enabling any size of business, including small businesses, to reach worldwide markets merely by having a website. This is how www.amazon.com, the online shop which claims to be 'Earth's most customer-centric company', started trading in 1994. The US division recently set a record of 2.8 million orders taken in one day.

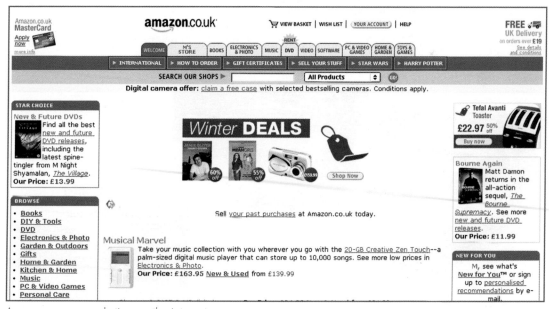

Amazon - mass marketing on the internet

niche marketing

This is highly defined marketing, whereby a product or series of products is launched at a specific market segment, for example 'singles' holidays, Saga products (for the over-50s) and even businesses that sell products for left-handed people.

Niche marketing is efficient for small businesses which may only have a limited marketing budget. It also works well for larger businesses which have developed a substantial market share in a specific niche.

Morgan Cars of Malvern, for example, are specialist hand-made cars for the motoring enthusiast (see picture on the left). They are in high demand and there is a waiting list for them.

Morgan Cars – handmade for the enthusiast

differentiated marketing

This form of market strategy promotes a range of different products, each designed specifically for a different market segment. It is costly in terms of promotion and production expenses, but it can be highly effective.

Examples include different types of financial services, and different types of car. The cars illustrated below are all manufactured by the Ford Motor Group, which owns 'differentiated' companies: Land Rover, Jaguar and Ford. Visit www.ford.com for a full listing of the different 'brands' of vehicle manufactured by the Ford Group worldwide.

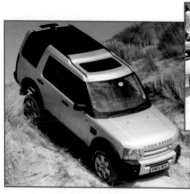

Land Rover Discovery – an upmarket 'sports utility' lifestyle vehicle

Jaguar XK8 – an upmarket lifestyle 'sports performance' vehicle

Ford Focus – a volume selling popular family car

Activity 18.5 – market strategies

1   The three website screens shown below are typical of mass, niche and differentiated marketing strategies.

Decide which screen is appropriate to which strategy and describe which market segment (or segments) is targeted in each case.

2   Write down examples of other businesses – well known or not so well-known – which have adopted mass, niche and differentiated marketing strategies.

CHAPTER SUMMARY

■ Marketing is difficult to define but may be summarised as activities which result in a business getting the right product to the right people at the right price at the right time.

■ The activities carried out by the marketing function in a business are very varied but generally make up what is known as the 'marketing mix'. These are summarised by the areas of Product, Price, Promotion and Place, the 4 P's.

■ Marketing objectives develop from the overall 'corporate' objectives of a business and state what the business wishes to achieve through its marketing activities. They include understanding the needs and wants of the customer (a prime objective) and product policy (including new products, revamps and diversification). Other objectives include improving market share, profitability and brand awareness.

■ Market segmentation is the process whereby the overall market is divided up into separate sets of customers (segments), who have separate identifiable product (goods or services) needs. These segments can be identified according to:
  – social groupings (from A to E)
  – age (child, teenager, young working person, mature working person, retired person)
  – gender (products for 'him' and 'her')
  – geographic areas

■ Market segmentation can also be carried out by exploring the psychological reasons behind buyer behaviour, ie what makes a person decide to buy. These include:
  – lifestyle (how the consumer sees himself/herself)
  – values (appealing to the values held by the consumer)

■ Market strategies choose between different approaches to the marketplace:
  – going for the mass market
  – identifying a niche sector
  – dividing the overall market into smaller differentiated segments

KEY TERMS

marketing mix	the range of marketing activities which may be used by a business to market its products
corporate objectives	statements of what a business wishes to achieve
marketing objectives	statements of what a business wishes to achieve through its mix of marketing activities
market strategy	the means by which a business achieves its marketing objectives
branding	giving a product or a business a distinct name and identity
customer focus	giving the wants and needs of customers a high priority
customer perception	what the customer thinks of the products and the business as a whole
market segmentation	the division of the total market into separate identifiable groups
demographic segmentation	segmentation of the population in relation to factors such as age, gender and levels of income
psychographic segmentation	segmentation which analyses the psychology of the buyer behaviour of different groups and asks the basic question 'what makes them buy that?'
lifestyle groups	segmentation by lifestyle – made up of factors including family situation, social interests, age and income
values research	a focus on consumer beliefs and motivation which can dictate purchasing decisions
mass marketing	marketing a product to a very wide range of market segments
niche marketing	marketing a product to a single market segment
differentiated marketing	marketing a range of products, each designed to appeal to a specific market segment

19

Market research and marketing planning

Starting point

If you were thinking of setting up in business, you would need to know as much as possible about the market you were entering. In fact, if you were also attempting to borrow money to start up, no lender would even consider you if you had not researched some basic facts, such as the nature of the market you were entering, its size and structure, and the competition you were going to encounter.

When you have done your market research you are then in a position to carry out marketing planning.

What you will learn from this chapter

- 'desk' research will provide background information about the market, using existing published data

- 'field' research is used to provide new and up-to-date information

- designing an effective questionnaire is important in obtaining the data needed for field research

- deciding on market segmentation is the key to choosing the right customers to research

- market research analyses customer attitude and behaviour towards new and existing products in the market place

- the construction of databases relies on both desk and field research; databases then make it possible to research further into lifestyles and buying habits

- the data obtained from market research is then used in marketing planning, using techniques such as SWOT and SLEPT analysis and the marketing mix

Introduction to Market Research

what is 'market research'?

Market research involves finding out, using a variety of techniques, about the market into which a business intends to sell (or is already selling) its products. More specifically market research:

- identifies target markets
- identifies the size and structure of the market and the way in which it works
- identifies competition
- searches for new product ideas
- tests new products before the decision to launch
- monitors the performance of the marketing activities on a regular basis

Market research provides the back-up data for decisions in all areas of the planning of marketing activities, known as the marketing mix – the four P's introduced in the last chapter.

Before we explain the terminology and workings of market research, we will examine the first three basic points from our list above.

target markets

When setting up a new business, it is important to identify which market and market segments are most likely to provide your business with a customer base. Your product or service idea must appeal to sufficient numbers or there is no point in starting up. Similarly, when existing organisations look to expand, new markets or new segments of the existing one must be identified.

the identified market

The size of the market must be investigated, as must its structure. Who else is already providing products or services for it? How is distribution organised ie through shops, agents, and e-commerce? Does the start-up need major investment? Is the market growing, static or in decline? These are the dynamics of your new venture.

the competition

Be careful when researching the competition. It is easy to see who sells the same product type, but ask yourself 'What am I really selling?', 'What needs and wants am I satisfying?' Suppose that you want to launch a new brand of crisps. You know that Walkers, Golden Wonder and others make and sell crisps, but that is only a part of the analysis you need to make. Every other maker of snack type products are your competition for the money consumers spend on snacking. So, are crisp sales in total rising or falling within the overall snack expenditure? Should you diversify into another form of snack food? Look at the different types of snacks produced by Golden Wonder:

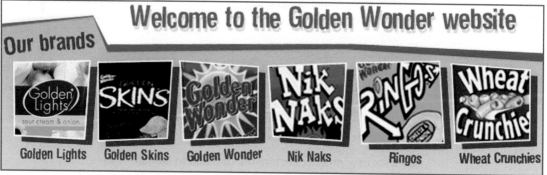

competing snacks produced by Golden Wonder

We will now explain the main terms that you will come across when dealing with market research.

the Language & Methods of Market Research

secondary research and primary research

Secondary (Desk) Research is the gathering and analysis of information. that is already available. This is a natural starting point because it is quick and cheap, and commercial organisations are always keen to save time and money. The problem is that information already available is already partly out of date. It may not be precisely what is required, either. Always check its collection date and relevance.

Primary (Field or **Original) Research** is the gathering of fresh information, specifically tailored to the business' own requirements. The problem here is the expense of the survey. Syndicated research is one answer: here the information seekers join together to conduct the research. Alternatively, established research agencies may undertake research and sell their findings to interested organisations.

Field and desk research are the most important classifications of market research, and the methods of carrying out the research will be covered in greater detail on the pages that follow.

quantitative and qualitative research

Quantitative Research collects numbers: the number of items bought, the price paid, the number of outlets stocking the product, and so on. Numeric data is easy to collect and analyse. Computers are often used in this analysis.

Qualitative Research examines opinions. Consumer opinions are sought by product and service providers, politicians, and virtually every organisation that exists. The key problem is that of obtaining useful data. Open ended questions, for example 'What do you think about . . .?' collect chatty responses but are not easy to analyse. Opinion research is usually quantified by presenting a range of choices, for example 'Do you think our customer service is: Poor? Fair? Good? Excellent?'. Look at the example Thomson Holiday questionnaire on pages 314 -317.

We will now describe the practicalities of desk research and field research.

Desk Research

Desk (secondary) research is an essential starting point for any research work: if information is available already, it saves time and money. What a new organisation must do, even before it is set up, is to evaluate all relevant data about the market, from whatever source. Desk research combines:

- an examination of the internal records of the business
- a study of external publications, compiled by experts in various fields

sources of internal data

Much data is available within an organisation which is already trading, for example:

- records of sales to customers: the number of items, frequency, how the goods were purchased (eg whether by mail order or through shops)
- accounts: the sales figures, costing and profit figures for individual items
- regional sales trends
- an analysis of the types of customer, eg using loyalty cards ('money back' or 'points' cards issued to customers for use at the checkouts)
- previous market research

From this data the organisation should be able to assess present trends, and have a starting point for predictions into the future.

external sources – Government publications

The Stationery Office and The Office for National Statistics, are important sources of national and regional data. These provide statistical data, including Social

Trends, Regional Trends and Economic Trends. Traditionally this data has been paper-based, but is now freely available online. Visit www.tso–online.co.uk or www.statistics.gov.uk and search for the relevant sector analysis.

SOCIAL TRENDS AND REGIONAL TRENDS AVAILABLE FREE ON www.statistics.gov.uk

Other sources of statistical data can be found on CD ROM such as SECOS (see www.statsed.co.uk) and educational websites such as www.bized.ac.uk

paper-based data

Much useful information can be gathered from organisations and societies which cater for the needs of businesses and particular trades and professions. These include the Confederation of British Industry (CBI), Chambers of Commerce – local and national, Business Clubs – local, the Chartered Institute of Marketing, and Trade Associations.

Resources – many of them to be found in libraries – include:

■ trade journals – the best up-to-date sources of information about each and every industry or trade.

■ directories – such as Kompass, Kelly's and Sell's, three excellent publications on products and organisations

■ Market Research organisations that undertake surveys of chosen industries on a regular basis – for example Mintel (Market Intelligence), Keynote or Market Research Great Britain.

Activity 19.1 – market research

Your Unit 3 Assessment requires you to plan out the marketing activities for a new or existing product. This will involve you in carrying out market research. For this Activity you can either use the product you have chosen for your Assessment, or another product of your choice. You are to:

1 Explain the difference between primary and secondary market research.

2 Explain the difference between qualitative and quantitative data.

3 List the published data that you think would prove useful in obtaining information about the market for your chosen product. Provide examples if you can.

Field Research

As we saw at the beginning of the chapter, the most valuable method of market research is the collection of primary or original data out in the marketplace, ie field research. It is this area of investigation that the 'person in the street' normally identifies with market research.

Field research consists of several stages:

1   clarify the objectives of the research – What do you need to find out?

2   choose a suitable data collection (market research) method

3   construct a questionnaire, if required

4   decide on the sampling techniques (Whom are you going to question?)

5   carry out a sample survey to test the questionnaire

6   brief the interviewers for the main survey

7   collect the data in the field

8   bring together, analyse and interpret the data

9   present your findings – normally in a written report

We will now explain some of these stages in more detail.

clarify the objectives of the research

Ensure that you establish exactly what the research needs to find out. If you are carrying out school or college project work, this means discussing it with your teacher or lecturer.

data collection – surveys and sampling

Surveys are the core of fieldwork. Using a variety of techniques, questions are put to a selected sample from the target group (the 'population') using a carefully planned questionnaire.

A **sample** is a selection taken, randomly or otherwise, from the market being investigated. Sampling must be carefully planned. It could be **systematic** (eg interviewing every tenth person, giving an element of randomness), or it could be based on a **quota** (eg selecting 10 males, 10 females).

The **respondent** is the user or potential user of the product or service who answers the questions in a survey.

The **population** is the total market, or market segment, under review. This may involve people or businesses.

data collection – observation

Observation records numbers and events, for example counting cars passing a certain location, or noting the 'walk past rate' when assessing the potential of a retail site. Much of this recording is done automatically by CCTV. The information recording system and the categories used must be carefully planned beforehand.

telephone research

Telephoning the respondent is one of the fastest methods of collecting data. It is very useful for industrial research, with firms well scattered; it is intrusive and effective, but the number of questions asked must be kept short. It has become increasingly popular in consumer research, with specialist agencies offering this service to clients. The research tends to be in the evenings/at weekends to catch the respondents at home, and to make use of the cheaper telephone rates.

postal research

Questionnaires are sent to respondents, fairly cheaply, and a large geographical area can be covered. Costs increase when reply paid envelopes have to be included, or when reminders and gifts are used to persuade people to respond. It has become very popular to offer 'entry into a competition' as the incentive to respond. One drawback of postal research is that the sample gained may be unrepresentative – it may be comprised only of people interested in the subject, or those with a complaint to register.

street interviews – the personal touch

face-to-face interviews

The personal interview is usually the best research method. Interviews can be:

Street interviews, which are fast and the results quickly analysed, but the questions must be simple (no time for thought) and their number limited. Street interviews have the advantage that queries about questions can be dealt with straightaway.

Home or office interviews, which can take more time to achieve but will provide more data. Detailed questions can be set, and the number of questions increased. The drawbacks include the added cost of making the visits, and the time spent finding the chosen target group.

Focus groups/group research, are invaluable in obtaining qualitative information (opinions). Groups are chosen from people who fit the required categorisations eg age, gender, social background, and the interview is 'focused' on a particular product area. The interview may be structured, with specific questions asked, or unstructured, with the group allowed to talk generally around the topic. Discussions are usually recorded for analysis.

field trials and test marketing

This involves research into the acceptability of new products, or product variations, usually in small geographical areas of the market. Such pilot projects enable any aspect of the product to be tested, but the key factors usually are product acceptability and price. More than one location or area will be used.

using telecommunications and technology

Telecommunications and technological developments in market research have been made possible by advances in computer technology. This has led to the creation of flexible databases of customers which can select market segments in categories such as age, income and lifestyle. This makes selecting the right groups for sampling (ie interviewing) much more accurate. Also, it has enabled a greater quantity of information to be handled, leading to an improvement in the quality of marketing decisions.

The information itself is often gathered electronically.

Electronic interviewing involves asking questions of respondents who subscribe to telephone and television networks. This technique offers high speed 'real-time' responses.

loyalty cards record EPOS purchasing

Electronic gathering and transmission of data is becoming commonplace with the use of lap top computers at interviews. Answers are recorded by the interviewer on the computer and the information downloaded at the end of the day to a central computer for instant analysis.

Electronic point of sale (EPOS) data enables trends in sales within an outlet to be noted and acted upon. Most shops use these for stock control, but also for instant research information for forecasting purposes. Your 'loyalty' card links your purchases to your personal data, collected when you applied for the card.

These and other techniques create databases, which if compiled correctly and kept up to date, lead to a much better understanding of an organisation's customer base.

Activity 19.2 – field research

Suggest a suitable method of data collection for the situations listed below. In each case explain why your choice best suits the need of the business.

1 Maria is thinking of setting up a designer clothes shop. She has found a shop in the town with a reasonably cheap lease but is worried about its location. Will she get enough customers?

2 Luigi is thinking of starting up a home delivery pizza and pasta business in his area but realises that he will have to assess local demand very carefully as he thinks that he is not fully in touch with what local people want.

3 A car manufacturer is designing a new 'lifestyle' vehicle aimed specifically at young earners with a high level of income who are looking for a practical family vehicle which is also 'fun' to live with and to drive.

4 A car garage has had one or two isolated complaints about its standards of car servicing. The managing director says to the marketing manager 'I need to find out if there is a problem here – and quickly!'

5 A national food supermarket chain has recently diversified into electrical and entertainment retailing using a new brand name. It needs to find out what type of customers it is attracting and what they are buying in its 25 new stores.

Constructing a Questionnaire

We will now describe the construction of a questionnaire that can be used in market research. A questionnaire comprises a list of questions which can provide data including:

- factual information

- opinions

The length of the questionnaire will depend on the type of interview used, whether it is postal, face-to-face, or telephoned. The principles of questionnaire construction will, however, remain the same.

face-to-face or telephone interview questionnaire

When you are carrying out an interview, either face-to-face or over the telephone, tell the respondent who you are and ask for his or her co-operation. Explain the purpose of the survey. Keep the questioning as short as possible, especially when interviewing in the street or on the telephone. There is always the danger that the respondent will walk away (or put the telephone down). When you have finished, thank the respondent for his or her time.

construction of the questionnaire

- include 'Instructions to the interviewer or respondent', eg 'tick the relevant boxes' so that answers are recorded accurately and consistently – this is particularly important if the questionnaire is to be sent through the post.

- plan a logical sequence so that easy, confidence building questions come first, and the respondent can begin to take an interest

- record only as many personal details as are essential for your analysis. If details like 'salary' or 'age' are required, try leaving this until last and give 'ranges' for their answers. Common age classes are: under 16, 16-24, 25-40, 41-60, over 60, but you must decide which are relevant.

designing questions

- keep the language simple

- avoid biased or 'loaded' questions

- questions should not be leading, ambiguous, too personal or misleading

- use closed questions, to which the answer is a clear 'yes' or 'no'

- open ended questions – asking for opinions and comments – should be limited, as they are difficult to record; they are, however, a useful source of qualitative data

- create questions of a multi-choice nature - these can be factual multiple choice, for example 'How do you travel to work?' giving the options of bicycle, car, public transport, or 'other'

- create questions of a multi-choice nature to obtain qualitative data (opinions) by requiring the respondent to choose between a defined range of 'excellent, good, fair, poor' and ticking the relevant box (the technique used in the Thomson questionnaire shown below). An alternative to this is to make a statement, for example 'The teaching here is of an excellent standard' and then offer a range of responses 'agree strongly, agree, neither agree nor disagree, disagree, disagree strongly'. This second range of responses is known as the Likert Scale.

Now read the Case Study that follows. See how the principles explained on the last few pages apply to the Thomson Holiday questionnaire. Then carry out the activities that follow.

Case Study – Thomson Holidays questionnaire

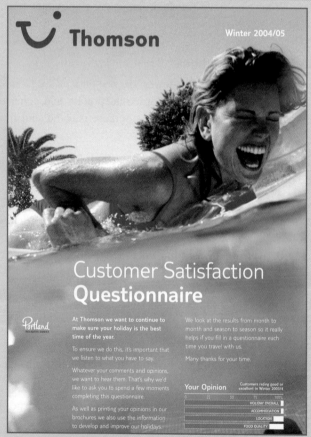

The Customer Service function at Thomson Holidays takes great care to ensure that the comments and opinions of its customers are collected and used to develop and improve its holidays.

The Customer Satisfaction Questionnaire illustrated on the next three pages is analysed by Thomson and the results printed in the following year's brochure.

Thomson Holidays offers people who complete the questionnaire the chance to win £2,000 of holiday vouchers, a valuable incentive reflecting the value of the data collected.

Osborne Books is grateful to Thomson Holidays for giving permission for the reproduction of this questionnaire.

1. Your Details

Title _____ Initial(s) _____

Surname _____

Partner's Title _____ Initial(s) _____

Surname _____

Address _____

_____

_____

_____

Postcode _____

Home tel. no _____

Today's date _____

2. Your Holiday Details

A Which holiday company are you with?

Thomson .... ☐   Portland Direct......... ☐

budgetholidays.com ...... ☐   Just.................. ☐

Other *(please write in)* .... ☐ _____

B If you booked an airfare/flight only, what type of accommodation did you stay in?

Own Property .... ☐   Own Timeshare .... ☐

Hotel .... ☐   Rented: Apartment/Villa . ☐

With friends/relatives ..... ☐   Other .... ☐

C Was this a Thomson Young at Heart or Portland Direct Magic Moments holiday?

Yes ☐   No ☐

D The name of your hotel/villa/apartments: (name all accommodation stayed in)

_____

E The name of your resort(s) or name of your tour/safari/cruise:

_____

F Accommodation and food arrangements:

Self Catering .... ☐   Bed & Breakfast .... ☐

Half board .... ☐   All Inclusive .... ☐
                                (all meals, drinks etc included)

Full Board .... ☐   Room only .... ☐

Flexible Dining .... ☐

G If accommodation not specified/included until you arrived in resort, was this a:

Late Deal .... ☐   Pricebreaker........... ☐

Flydrive (flight & car rental only) .... ☐

H Number of nights abroad:

6 or less	7	8-13	14	15-20	21 or more
☐	☐	☐	☐	☐	☐

I Adults I am travelling with (please tick the one that best applies):

No other adult .... ☐   In a couple .... ☐

With other adult(s) ...... ☐   With other adult(s) ..... ☐
of mixed sex   of the same sex

With an organised group of six adults or more. ☐

J Ages of children travelling with you (if applicable):

☐ yrs   ☐ yrs   ☐ yrs   ☐ yrs

2. Your Holiday Details (cont.)

K Did you use a brochure to select your holiday?

Yes ☐   No ☐

L If yes, how accurate was the brochure description of your accommodation/resort:

Excellent	Good	Fair	Poor
☐	☐	☐	☐

M How did you book this holiday?

In a Travel Agency .... ☐   Phoned Tour Operator/ ..... ☐
                                    Travel Agency Direct

On the internet .... ☐   Other .... ☐

3. Flights

How would you rate:

		Excellent	Good	Fair	Poor
A	UK airport check-in	☐	☐	☐	☐
B	Overseas airport check-in .	☐	☐	☐	☐
C	In-flight comfort	☐	☐	☐	☐
D	Cabin cleanliness to resort .	☐	☐	☐	☐
E	Cabin cleanliness to UK ...	☐	☐	☐	☐
F	In-flight food	☐	☐	☐	☐
G	Cabin crew friendliness ...	☐	☐	☐	☐
H	Cabin crew professionalism	☐	☐	☐	☐
I	Cabin crew service ...... and assistance	☐	☐	☐	☐
J	Flights overall	☐	☐	☐	☐
K	If applicable, ticket ...... collection before check-in	☐	☐	☐	☐

4. Your Accommodation

How would you rate:

		Excellent	Good	Fair	Poor
A	Rep's service	☐	☐	☐	☐
B	Rep's friendliness	☐	☐	☐	☐
C	Location	☐	☐	☐	☐
D	Reception desk service ...	☐	☐	☐	☐
E	Bar service	☐	☐	☐	☐
F	Cleanliness	☐	☐	☐	☐
G	Public areas: .... furnishings and decor	☐	☐	☐	☐
H	Bedroom comfort	☐	☐	☐	☐
I	Food quality	☐	☐	☐	☐
J	Waiter service / .... buffet efficiency	☐	☐	☐	☐
K	Villa / apartment ...... kitchen equipment	☐	☐	☐	☐
L	Organised daytime activities	☐	☐	☐	☐
M	Leisure facilities	☐	☐	☐	☐
N	Evening entertainment ...	☐	☐	☐	☐
O	Children's club: facilities ...	☐	☐	☐	☐
P	Children's club: activities ..	☐	☐	☐	☐
Q	Children's reps	☐	☐	☐	☐
R	Accommodation overall ...	☐	☐	☐	☐

5. In-resort Service

How would you rate:

	Excellent	Good	Fair	Poor
A Rep greeting on arrival at overseas airport	☐	☐	☐	☐
B Transfer journey to and from your accommodation	☐	☐	☐	☐

Did you:

	Yes	No
C Ask your Rep for any help or advice?	☐	☐
D Go to the What's On Welcome?	☐	☐
E Go on any Thomson company excursions?	☐	☐
F Buy any excursions from another company?	☐	☐
G Use the resort 24 hour holiday line?	☐	☐

How would you rate:

	Excellent	Good	Fair	Poor
H The information given by Rep; regarding your journey home	☐	☐	☐	☐
I The What's On Welcome: presentation and content ..	☐	☐	☐	☐
J Thomson Excursion: choice	☐	☐	☐	☐
K Thomson Excursion: value for money	☐	☐	☐	☐
L Thomson Excursion: commentary and knowledge of guide	☐	☐	☐	☐
M The 24 hour holiday line service.	☐	☐	☐	☐

6. Overall

Taking everything into account, how would you rate:

	Excellent	Good	Fair	Poor
A Resort	☐	☐	☐	☐
B Weather	☐	☐	☐	☐
C Reps	☐	☐	☐	☐
D Holiday overall	☐	☐	☐	☐
E Value for money	☐	☐	☐	☐
F Holiday company overall ..	☐	☐	☐	☐
G Holiday company's ability to treat you as an individual ..	☐	☐	☐	☐

H What classification rating would you give your accommodation:

1 star	2 star	3 star	4 star	5 star
☐	☐	☐	☐	☐

7. Holiday Experience

A Not counting this one, how many holidays abroad have you taken in the last 12 months?

None	1	2	3	4+
☐	☐	☐	☐	☐

B Have you been on a package holiday to this resort in the last two years?

Yes ☐ No ☐

C Have you been on a package holiday to this accommodation in the last two years?

Yes ☐ No ☐

D With which company did you take your last package holiday abroad?

☐

7. Holiday Experience cont.

E How likely are you to recommend this holiday company to a friend or relative?

Definitely	Probably	Possibly	Not likely
☐	☐	☐	☐

8. Car rental

A Did you rent a car on your holiday?

Yes ☐ No ☐

If applicable please rate:

	Excellent	Good	Fair	Poor
B Car rental: value for money	☐	☐	☐	☐
C Car rental: service	☐	☐	☐	☐
D Car rental: overall	☐	☐	☐	☐

E Which car rental company did you use?

Europcar	☐	Hertz	☐
Dollar	☐	Other	☐

F Was the car:

Pre-booked in UK via agent/holiday company ...	☐	Booked overseas via your Rep...........	☐
Pre-booked in the UK direct with car rental company ..	☐	Booked overseas direct with car rental company .	☐

9. About you

A What is:

Your date of birth? ☐

Your partners? ☐

B Are you:

Male .... ☐ Female .... ☐

C Are you:

In full/part time employment or self employed	☐
A full time housewife/househusband ☐ A student............. ☐	
Retired .... ☐ Otherwise not employed. ☐	

D If you are in employment, which best describes the type of job you do, or if retired, the last job you did?

Skilled trade/craft	☐
Plant and machine operator/driver etc.	☐
Foreman/supervisor	☐
Manual worker/factory worker	☐
Service worker (eg. shop assistant/cleaner/catering/ caretaker/goods delivery)	☐
Clerical/secretarial/other office work	☐
Technical (eg. programmer/technician/nurse/representative) .	☐
Junior management/junior professions/executive	☐
Senior and middle management/professions	☐

Other (write in) ☐

E If unwell during your holiday, please specify:

Sunstroke/sunburn	☐	Infection..............	☐
Stomach upset (lasting more than 24 hours) ..	☐	Other	☐

9. About you cont.

F Whilst on holiday did you park your car at the airport?

Yes ☐   No ☐

G In which month is your motor insurance renewed? ☐

H Where do you live?

Own home (with mortgage) ☐   Own home (no mortgage) . ☐

With parents .... ☐   Renting privately .... ☐

Renting from Council ..... ☐

I In which month is your contents insurance renewed? ☐

J Which newspapers do you read? (Please name)

a) Daily ☐

b) Sunday ☐

K In total, how much money do you estimate you and your party spent while on holiday? (Exclude flights & accommodation)

Up to £250 .... ☐   £251-£500 .... ☐

£501-£750 .... ☐   £751-£1000 .... ☐

£1001-£1250 .... ☐   Over £1250 .... ☐

L Which group in £000's best describes your COMBINED household income?

0-10 ☐   11-15 ☐   16-20 ☐   21-25 ☐   26-30 ☐

31-35 ☐   36-40 ☐   41-50 ☐   51-60 ☐   60+ ☐

M Which of the following do you use regularly?

Cheque Guarantee/Debit Cards .. ☐   Amex .... ☐

Mastercard .... ☐   Visa .... ☐

9. About you cont.

N What are your interests and hobbies?

Golf .... ☐   Wildlife/Environment .... ☐

Gourmet foods/wine ..... ☐   Books/Reading......... ☐

Winter sports .... ☐   Football .... ☐

Exercise/Sport .... ☐   Gardening............ ☐

Theatre/Arts .... ☐   Fashion Wear .... ☐

O What type of charity do you tend to support?

Cancer Research .... ☐   Third world........... ☐

Pets .... ☐   Wildlife .... ☐

Local Charities .... ☐   Childrens .... ☐

	Yes	No
P Do you have internet access at home?	☐	☐
Q If yes, with broadband?	☐	☐

R Preferred e-mail address*

☐ @

☐

S Do you buy goods and services via:

Internet ☐   Mail Order/Telephone ☐

T Return flight number: ☐   Seat row: ☐ Letter: ☐

U UK Airport: ☐   Resort Airport: ☐

Activity 19.3 – Thomson questionnaire

Study the Thomson questionnaire and answer the following questions. In each case give reasons for your answers.

1 How does Thomson achieve the 'sample' – ie how does it get people to complete the questionnaire? Do you think this will result in a representative cross section of people?

2 What type of segmentation is identified in Section 9, questions A,B,C,D, and L?

3 In questions G,H and I of Section 9 there are a number of enquiries relating to insurance. Why do you think these questions are asked, and what use do you think will be made of the information?

4 In question N of Section 9 the questionnaire asks about hobbies. What type of segmentation will be identified here and how could the information be used?

Market Research Data and Product Development

It is important to analyse all the data collected from both field and desk market research to provide the 'complete picture' which will enable new product development to take place. If sufficient market research does not take place there is a danger that a new product which may seem a 'good idea' will not find a market and so will not be successful.

The Case Study that follows has kindly been provided by Cadbury and shows the focused market research that takes place in launching a new confectionery product, aimed particularly at younger female chocoholics!

Case Study – the Cadbury 'Dream'

NEW PRODUCT DEVELOPMENT (NPD)
A company cannot afford to stand still. It must change to survive. Developing a successful new product, in a market where the vast majority of ideas come to nothing, is full of problems. It may take years for an idea to grow into a product achieving national distribution, and dropping the whole project can occur at any stage. New product Development (NPD) requires teamwork from Research and Development (R&D), Marketing, Market Research, Engineering, Legal and Finance.

The development of the Cadbury 'Dream' bar is one such case.

MARKET RESEARCH CARRIED OUT
The first stage was to try to spot a gap in the market. This was done by qualitative research, using small (focus) groups of consumers to examine the market's needs and wants. When ideas were a little more advanced, quantitative research, the potential size of the market, was examined. This was further broken down into regional analysis, to help choose a launch area, and other categories ie age and sex, to help choose the right brand name and promotional approach. Ongoing research would provide launch data (retailer uptake and early sales levels) and sales growth statistics.

The public's reactions to the new 'Dream' concept was monitored at every stage. Researchers had identified a gap in the market for white chocolate in the adult sector; in particular women aged between 16 and 34, but generally all white chocolate devotees.

The final recipe and shape (a moulded block) was developed by R&D following weeks of consumer testing of different product versions. A new packaging style (flow wrap) was tested at the same time. A number of different brand names and pack designs were researched before the 'Dream' pack with blue and white packaging was selected. Focus groups of 16 to 34 year old females were seen as particularly important. An ideal test area was needed and this had to have the demographics and confectionery purchasing habits that were representative of the whole population. Desk research provided the data for this decision.

The early product range comprised different sizes, a multipack, a filled egg for Easter and 'Dream Snowbites' for Christmas. Other versions followed, each analysed for volume and consumer opinion.

The key to a successful launch is to generate consumer excitement and retailer enthusiasm through a genuinely innovative product offering, ie attention grabbing promotions and retailer incentives to stock the product.

Brand awareness research and trade audits would report on the success of these. In-depth briefing sessions were held by the market researchers to assess every element of the launch and to decide whether the appeal of the product was strong enough for it to continue. Research never ends!

Activity 19.4 – researching the 'Dream' product

Read the Case Study on the last two pages and answer the questions that follow.

1 What functions within the business are involved in new product development? What role in relation to the new product do you think is played by each of them in the process?

2 What qualitative research was used to spot a gap in the market?

3 What market segment was identified as the target 'gap' in the market?

4 Describe the further desk and field research that was carried out to complete the product design?

5 Identify the areas of ongoing market research that are needed to monitor the ongoing success of the Cadbury 'Dream'.

Analysing Market Research Information

Market research also monitors changes in the market. Businesses need up-to-date information about sales trends and the performance of individual products. Typical 'monitoring' questions include:

- Are sales rising or falling?
- How do sales compare with the competition?
- Is market share being gained or lost?
- Is profitability being maintained?
- How do prices compare with the competition?
- Do the product prices fit the product's image in the customers' minds?

This final point is very important. If the image of the product is portrayed as 'up market', yet the price appears too low to justify that image, consumers are less likely to buy. 'It can't be any good at that price' is a comment heard.

Research carried out on a regular basis is therefore very important. For example, **trade audits** examine sales out from the shops (as opposed to sales from the manufacturer into the shops). A number of market research agencies specialise in supplying market share information to their clients on a month by month, or even week by week basis. Examples include A C Nielsen and Mintel. Visit www.acnielsen.co.uk and examine some of the recent articles available for download.

Marketing Planning – Using the Data

For any organisation to function efficiently and effectively the marketing 'team' must analyse past performance and present trends, and attempt to predict the future in some form of a Marketing Plan. The 'marketing team' in the case of a larger business is likely to be the Marketing Department; in the case of a smaller business it might be just the the sole trader owner or the partner who deals with selling. The Marketing Plan should be the result of careful research, consultation and discussion.

There are a number of planning techniques and processes which have been successfully tried and tested over the years. These include:

- SWOT analysis
- Marketing Mix
- assessing external factors – SLEPT analysis

We will explain each of these in turn. It must be stressed that these are techniques which can be used singly, or, more commonly, in combination.

SWOT Analysis

SWOT stands for **S**trengths **W**eaknesses **O**pportunities **T**hreats

SWOT analysis is a technique much used in many general management as well as marketing scenarios. SWOT consists of examining the current activities of the organisation – its Strengths and Weaknesses – and then using this and external research data to set out the Opportunities and Threats that exist. The process can be illustrated by the practical Activity which follows.

Activity 19.5 – SWOT analysis for marketing

Take as an example the school or college where you are studying, and make suggestions for each of the four SWOT categories as they relate to marketing. Some points are already listed to get you started. Your lecturer/teacher/trainer could lead the discussion and add to the list. Make recommendations as to what needs to be done as a result of your findings

strengths	a large catchment area
weaknesses	old buildings, overcrowding
opportunities	offering new subjects and courses
threats	falling numbers of 16 year-olds

the Marketing Mix – an Introduction

This is the traditional approach to marketing planning which is based on the four P's:

Product – getting the product right for the customer

Price – fixing the price at the right level

Promotion – using advertising, branding, packaging and publicity

Place – selling the product and getting it to the consumer

We will now describe in more detail each of the four P's. They will also be discussed in the next two chapters.

product policy

'Product' is the range of products (goods or services) that the organisation offers to the marketplace. Decisions have to be made about quantities, timing, product variations, associated services, quality, style, packaging and branding. Some organisations produce a range of products of differing quality for the different market segments.

A 'brand name' establishes the product in the consumer's mind, eg Vodafone, Coke, Adidas. Branding is an integral part of product policy and we will examine it in detail in Chapter 20 as a promotional activity.

price policy

'Price' is a vitally important decision area because although it is a 'promotional' tool in many respects, it is the main source of income to the business. If prices are lowered for promotional purposes, the cash flow within the business, and its long-term profitability, could be seriously affected.

As with products, there is normally a range of prices. These can vary according to the quantities bought, the importance of the customer, and the market segment. Pricing can be long-term (set at a level for sustained profit-making) and short-term (cut prices for tactical reasons, such as trying to get extra sales and increase market share). Pricing can involve discounts, special offers, allowances, credit, and 'trade-ins'. It is vitally important to get pricing decisions right.

promotion policy

'Promotion' consists of a number of techniques which create awareness of the products and persuade the potential customer to make the buying decision.

Promotion involves all communication with actual and potential consumers. The techniques include:

- advertising – using different media

- branding – promoting the brand image of the product

- packaging – also promoting the brand image of the product

- publicity/public relations – making sure the business features in areas such as media coverage and sponsorship

- sales promotions – special offers and benefits such as air miles

- merchandising – ensuring the product is accessible to the buyer

Each technique differs from the others but all, or all of them thought relevant to a given situation, will be used to create a unified product image and an image for the organisation, the 'corporate identity'.

Note that selling is also part of 'promotion'. Selling is a personal activity carried out by a salesperson with some form of direct contact between buyer and seller. Most promotional activity, on the other hand, is impersonal, aimed generally at a market segment and with no personal contact. Businesses need to decide what emphasis needs to be placed on selling and what resources devoted to other forms of promotion. Selling chocolate, for example, is 80% promotion while selling computer systems involves 80% pure selling.

place policy

A business, when planning its marketing, will ask a number of questions relating to place, for example 'Through which outlets should we sell the product? How do we physically move the product to these chosen outlets? How far afield do we wish to operate (locally, nationally, or internationally)?' Place, or distribution policy, is a complex decision area that incorporates these three problems, and potentially more. These matters are discussed more fully in Chapter 21.

the marketing mix – conclusion

The marketing mix provides a plan by which to operate to influence and satisfy the buyer/consumer. The four P's approach is not perfect, and does not cover, for example, Market Research. Research, of course, is the provider of information for the decisions in all of the four P areas.

the marketing mix and the small business

A small business may have limited resources, and so will have to plan its marketing mix with care. It may have a limited range of products and a limited market. Price may be determined by larger competitors. Some promotional activities may be too expensive and place may be limited to a single outlet.

Activity 19.6 – the marketing mix

Work in small groups within the class:

1 Think up an idea for a new product which you think consumers will need (use a 'brainstorming' session for this).

2 Work out how you are going to implement the marketing mix (the 4 P's) for the new product.

3 Give a five minute presentation to the rest of the class explaining and justifying your ideas.

Now read the Land Rover Case Study which follows. It shows how the marketing mix (the 4 Ps) is used by a car manufacturer.

Case Study – Land Rover and the 4 P's

INTRODUCTION

LAND ROVER: FROM 'FARMERS' FRIEND' TO '4X4 FASHION'

In 1948 the car manufacturer 'Rover' designed a 'go anywhere' vehicle for the construction, farming and military markets. In 1970 a second market was targeted successfully, that of 'tough luxury', for Land Rover users who wanted something more suitable to their lifestyle outside the work environment. This proved to be the start of the 4x4 (4 wheel drive) market that we recognise today, but which although growing, represented in 2003 only 7% of total UK car sales – so remaining a 'niche' market.

PRODUCT POLICY

Land Rover Defender

As the car market expanded in the 1960s, the company felt the need to take its image up market, away from its agricultural roots, but retaining the goodwill built up by the original brand. It was decided to rename the original model the 'Defender', so that Land Rover could be used as the company name, to be associated with individual model brand names as they were introduced.

1970 saw the introduction of the Range Rover, a premium priced brand designed for the top ranks of country society. The model's appeal spread to the affluent in urban areas, and

Range Rover

the brand has remained the company's pinnacle product ever since. By the mid-1980s market research had identified growing interest from the family, leisure and commercial markets for a multi use, load bearing, 4x4 car with larger capacity.

The 7 seater 'Discovery' was launched in 1989 to challenge the growing number of imports from Japan. In 1997 the latest addition to the 'family', the Freelander, was launched and within the year had become Europe's best selling 4x4. This was a 'volume product' aimed at the sports utility vehicle (SUV) market which needed a 4x4 lifestyle but at a lower price. Land Rover entered and really developed this market.

UPDATING THE RANGE

New models take years to bring to market, and at great financial cost (and risk). Updating an already successful brand to extend its life cycle often proves a better investment. New design, technological development and/or approaching a new market sector can be a successful way ahead, in the short term.

Land Rover relaunched the Range Rover in 2002 boasting 'leading edge technology', a new Freelander with design changes based on the Range Rover in 2003, and in 2004 a new Discovery – a premium sports utility vehicle aimed at the young and affluent.

Freelander

In addition to this, the Range Rover Sport was revealed in November 2004. This latter 'product diversification' targeted a newly identified market segment ie the wealthy professional, at the top end of the market. All of these changes followed detailed quantitative and qualitative research.

Competition for the Range Rover is light, but the Discovery and the Freelander are under constant pressure from imported 4x4s. The Defender remains a 'workhorse' throughout the world.

the new Discovery

PRICE POLICY

long-term

The Range Rover maintains a premium pricing strategy. There are high costs involved in offering personalised products to customers, but the brand's image can command a top price. Its customers expect to pay more for 'the best'. The price could be described as 'aspirational'. At the lower end of the range, where competition is high, the company will respond to competitor actions. Comparisons with other manufacturers are made on a regular basis. Supply and demand data is monitored, as is the price elasticity (the sensitivity of consumers' buying decisions to changes in price). Land Rover describe this as routine.

short-term

Opening offers for new models do not happen. Quite the reverse! The launch of a new model appeals to the 'early adopters' and 'opinion formers'; consumers who 'must have' the latest and are prepared to pay top price. Discounting will occur as models are about to be replaced, or as registration plates are about to change, to sell off existing stock. Such reductions in 'profitability per unit' are shared between Land Rover and its retailers.

PROMOTION POLICY

Land Rover use a number of specialist agencies to cover public relations, advertising, research into policy effectiveness etc, but the overall coordination of this is the responsibility of the Marketing Director and his team at Head Office.

advertising

The key medium for new models is the Press, and within this category the Trade press. Space is bought, well in advance of a launch, in the top motoring journals. Key journalists in the trade will have been informed, and will have expressed their opinions in articles to appear in the same journals. This publicity is hopefully favourable to the brand being advertised. Suitable premium lifestyle magazines like 'Esquire' and 'Tatler' are used for advertisements stressing the desirability of the new model. An in-house magazine 'One Life' keeps existing customers informed of latest events.

National newspapers are covered, and regional press advertising is key to supporting the company's retailers in their area.

Television has been used since the launch of the Discovery and the Freelander, to appeal to a larger ABC market and create awareness and excitement around the products. Local Radio tends to be the medium of the car retailers, who target motorists at key 'drive times'.

Poster campaigns coincide with a launch for two weeks, on as many as 2,000 sites nationwide, to catch the travelling public.

Good Publicity and PR are vital. Press releases are used to give out company information, and articles in the media are monitored.

Direct marketing involves posting catalogues and leaflets to potential customers who have shown interest when in showrooms and when online. The internet website www.landrover.com displays product, price and place details, and is a key promotional device that leads to enquiries, test drives and orders. Banner ads are placed on other selected sites, and emails sent to people who have requested information.

Land Rover has stands at all major national and international exhibitions relating to the car industry, like the British Motor Show, and at lifestyle shows such as 'The Game Fair'. The former are considered prestige events for a prestige company, gaining much publicity. New models may be unveiled at the shows.

Merchandising takes place in the showrooms of franchised agents, with regular checks by Land Rover on all aspects of product presentation.

Sponsorship is important. Well known individuals like the Beckhams, teams such as England rugby (co-sponsors with O2), and events like the Burleigh Horse Trials, gain valuable publicity for the models.

Other promotional activity includes having 10 'adventure zones' nationally near retail parks, which provide fun drives in a themed environment, and free off road driving lessons for new customers.

The Corporate Image of 'The Land Rover Experience' brings cohesion to the brand whilst offering variety with a choice of products.

PLACE (DISTRIBUTION) POLICY

In the UK, retail sales are made through franchised agents (dealers) not owned by Land Rover. They are chosen by reputation, the facilities on site, the local level of demand and by post code (not too near to each other). Large company 'fleet' orders come directly to Land Rover, but those for under 100 vehicles are serviced by the local agent.

Export sales, to 140 countries, are serviced according to volume, ie a small market would receive from the UK direct, larger numbers via an agent in the area, larger still via a regional office and ultimately a depot or an assembly plant may be set up in the country. The decisions would be affected by the economics and politics of the country.

MARKET RESEARCH

Every aspect of the business is examined, either in house or by outside agencies.

New product research starts with focus groups of potential buyers discussing a loose theme- 'what we might like to see developed'. This becomes a concept product idea with sketches, then a foam or clay model and finally a fibre glass model. Each stage is discussed by groups from the target market over a two year period. The price range is examined.

Promotional research looks at 'How can we sell it?', using focus groups for psychometric testing – 'What motivates them to buy?'

Post launch sees quantitative analysis of sales, in total and by region, awareness in the target market of the product, and the promotional activity – how many enquiries were received and what percentage of these turned into sales. Qualitative research would seek opinions of the product, its image and its promotion. With company reputation and profitability at stake, nothing goes uninvestigated.

Osborne Books is grateful to Land Rover for the contribution of this Case Study.

Activity 19.7 – Land Rover and the marketing mix

1 What is the evidence of Land Rover being in a niche market?

2 For which market segments are the following vehicles targeted: Defender, Range Rover, Discovery, Freelander?

3 What is the evidence of recycling existing products rather than launching new ones? Why would Land Rover adopt this approach to product policy?

4 What new market segment has Land Rover identified?.

5 What is the price policy maintained by Land Rover?

6 What range of advertising is used by Land Rover?

7 How does Land Rover distribute its vehicles in the UK?

8 Describe the way in which focus groups are used by Land Rover to help with its marketing.

Planning for External Factors – SLEPT Analysis

All businesses are influenced by what is happening in the world around them. There are **S**ocial, **L**egal, **E**conomic, **P**olitical and **T**echnical demands upon them, all in some way affecting the costs and organisation of a business. These initial letters spell out SLEPT, which is a good way of remembering the categories when you do the research into the influences on your chosen product or service.

All of these factors involve **change**. When carrying out marketing planning it is important to bear all these influences in mind.

social factors

'Social' means the ways in which we deal with our fellow human beings. In the case of businesses this means the effect that they have on issues such as:

■ providing employment in the local community and not using overseas call centres

■ ensuring that products such as food are healthy and beneficial to consumers and do not cause obesity

■ discouraging over-consumption of alcohol and subsequent drink-driving

■ encouraging 'Fair Trade' (selling products from third world countries)

These issues may be embodied in the Corporate Responsibility policies of many large companies which have been explained in Chapter 2 (page 20). It is important that people in marketing understand the value placed by society on these policies. Visit www.kraftfoods.co.uk to find out how it is reducing the salt content of its products:

KRAFT FOODS CONTINUES SALT REDUCTION INITIATIVES

Kraft Foods has reduced still further the salt content of some of its popular brands in the UK and Ireland and plans new labelling initiatives as part of its continuing global health and wellness strategy.

Kraft has already reduced the salt content of its products which are most popular among children:

■ Salt content has been reduced by an average of 30 per cent across the entire Dairylea range of cheese and snacks over the past two years.

■ There is now 33 per cent less salt in Dairylea Cheese Spreads (tubs and portions), Cheese Slices, Strip Cheese and Dairylea Dunkers, compared with pre-reduction levels.

■ Last year, Kraft reduced the salt in Dairylea Lunchables by one third, with the salt content of the average pack falling from 3.1g to 2.1g.

legal factors

Legal factors include not just statute law relating to dealings between buyers and sellers, but also the codes of practice by which businesses in a particular industry regulate their own conduct.

buying goods and services

The main law protecting consumers who buy **goods** is the **Sale of Goods Act 1979**. This states that goods should be sold: 'as described' and that they should be 'of satisfactory quality' and be 'fit for the purpose for which they are intended'.

The **Supply of Goods and Services Act 1982** protects the consumer when a service is provided by a business. This Act states that anyone who supplies a service – a train journey, a holiday – must carry out the work with 'reasonable' care and skill, within a 'reasonable' time and at a 'reasonable' price. The question of what is reasonable is established by standards laid down by various bodies: Trade Associations, professional bodies, or one of the official 'Watchdog' bodies which keep an eye on public services.

setting standards

The **Trade Descriptions Act 1968** makes it a criminal offence to make false statements about goods offered for sale and to make misleading statements about services. This Act affects false or misleading adverts, packaging and labels.

The Weights and Measures Act 1986 requires that the weights and quantities of goods for sale should be clearly and accurately indicated. The Act makes it a criminal offence to label goods so that consumers do not receive the weight and quantity of goods that the labelling indicates.

There are many other statutes which regulate the ways in which marketing can be carried out, but the laws listed above are particularly important.

voluntary codes of conduct

These are agreements within a trade or industry designed to regulate what is and what is not acceptable trading practice. An important controlling body which regulates 'promotion' in marketing is the **Advertising Standards Authority** (ASA).

The ASA receives complaints about dubious advertising and then decides whether the Codes of Advertising Practice set up within individual industries have been broken. Its rulings are published weekly on the ASA website, www.asa.org.uk . The codes cover areas such as misleading advertising, offensive advertising, adverts aimed at children and adverts for alcohol, health products, beauty products, financial services, employment and business opportunities, and gambling. The ASA supervises adverts in all of the advertising media, both broadcast and non-broadcast, and adverts from direct marketing organisations and on the Internet. The following example shows how the ASA helps to protect the consumer.

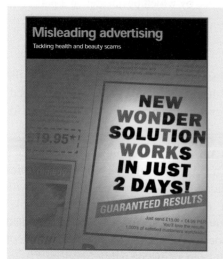

Misleading advertising
Tackling health and beauty scams

NEW
WONDER
SOLUTION
WORKS
IN JUST
2 DAYS!
GUARANTEED RESULTS

Just send £15.00 + £4.99 P&P
You'll love the results!
1,000's of satisfied customers worldwide

ASA SUPPORTS 'SCAMS' AWARENESS DRIVE

As part of an initiative to spread awareness and increase consumer protection the Advertising Standards Authority (ASA) is supporting the ongoing drive by the Office of Fair Trading (OFT) to highlight the problems of 'misleading' and 'scam' advertising. Whether it is a prize draw mailing offering money for nothing (but doing exactly the opposite) or a bogus slimming product which promises miracle results, the ASA wants to alert consumers to the way unscrupulous advertisers operate and how they can avoid falling victim to scams. The poster on the left has been produced to draw the public's attention to such scams.

economic factors

There are a number of economic factors that have to be taken into account when planning the marketing mix – ie where and when and at what price to promote a product. These factors include:

- **the economic cycle**

  Over a period of years most economies move from boom to recession and back again, in a continuous cycle. In the good years, consumers have money to spend, most businesses are profitable and there is demand for marketing of new products. When economic activity slows, demand and profitability fall off and marketing departments have to look more critically at their budgets and product planning.

- **change within an industry**

  As you know, 'nothing lasts for ever'. This applies not just to product types but to whole industries. It is important to know whether your industry is growing or in decline. This will affect the decisions about the product range and the need to diversify.

- **regional prosperity**

  Market research will reveal trends in regional prosperity. Consumers in some regions have less money to spend than consumers in other regions. Local service businesses in particular will need to investigate demand for the product and the prices that can be charged.

political factors

Political factors can also affect decisions when planning the marketing mix. The major arguing point is the level of government control that should be applied to business activities. All political parties are keen to be seen as 'business friendly', and there are a variety of grants and tax incentives available, as well as a number of economic controls that will affect businesses and their marketing planning. Listed below are some of the issues that may affect the level of demand for products and the ways in which businesses operate.

- a high rate of Income Tax will reduce the level of consumer demand

- Value Added Tax (VAT) affects the price to the final consumer

- a guaranteed minimum wage will give employees more buying power, but may reduce employment levels because of the cost to the employer

- the rate of interest will affect levels of consumer demand and business investment in new products – a high rate will depress demand

- investment grants encourage Research and Development into new products, and the creation of new businesses

- Regional Aid encourages businesses to set up in certain areas to stimulate employment and generate demand

technological factors

call centres have revolutionised telesales

Technology has become one of the main driving forces for change in business and in marketing planning. Worldwide call centres have revolutionised telesales and customer services and the potential resources of the internet have affected all of the four Ps.

■ product and market policy

Apart from the obvious increase in technologically advanced items such as computers, mobile phones and digital cameras, the demand for many traditional products – such as paperback books – remains as strong as ever. The main changes relate to market policy, where the use of websites and online selling enables even small companiesto reach a worldwide market at low cost. Look at the Osborne Books website shown on the next page and appreciate how market penetration, market development, promotion and distribution are made so much easier using internet technology.

■ pricing policy

The web has generally brought prices down because dealing on-line cuts the cost of dealing with middlemen (for goods), and the need for large numbers of staff for services like banking (which also benefit from call centres).

■ promotion policy

The impact of technology on promotion is immense. By setting up low-cost web pages, a business can display its entire range of products. Specific market segments can also be reached by placing banners or pop-up ads on the pages of other carefully selected web sites.

■ place policy

Technology in the form of computerised ordering, despatch and tracking systems has made distribution more efficient, with in some cases the problems of 'site' disappearing altogether. A small manufacturer can set up an online 'shop', doing away with the need for a High Street presence.

THE USE OF WEBSITE TECHNOLOGY IN MARKETING BY A PUBLISHER

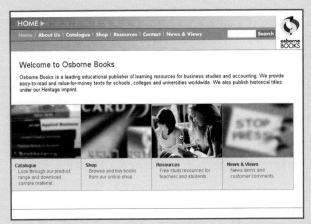

Osborne Books makes extensive use of its website www.osbornebooks.co.uk for marketing purposes:

■ The **Catalogue** is divided into subject areas, providing product details such as prices and enabling visitors to the site to download sample chapters.

■ The online **Shop** provides a secure shopping and payment facility for Osborne Books products. Books ordered online are delivered to the customer in a matter of days.

■ The **Resources** section provides a wealth of downloadable material: extra questions, documents and revision materials.

■ The **News and Views** section provides details of publicity and public relations events which all promote the image of the publisher and its products

Activity 19.8 – the influence of external factors

You are taking part in a business marketing planning meeting. Your company produces 'instant meals' for the retail market and you are discussing a new range of pasta-based meals to be introduced. These meals have a fairly high fat content. How would you answer the following questions?

1 'What should we do to answer the concerns of the pressure groups that say that the contents of instant meals cause obesity?'

2 'Could we state on the packaging that the new meals are good for slimmers?'

3 'What about having an advert which shows a lot of very slim girls and claims that the meals are more slimming than instant meals from our competitors?'

4 'What about the effect of high interest rates and inflation on our pricing and product image? Consumers do not have much money to spend at the moment.'

5 ''How could we use a website to help market our products?'

CHAPTER SUMMARY

■ Marketing research identifies target markets, investigates their size and structure and identifies the competition.

■ Marketing research may identify a need or opportunity for a new product, suggest changes to an existing one, or even advise on its eventual replacement. Research is a continuous business activity.

■ Desk research is the usual starting point for an information search, using paper-based information and internet resources, both available at reasonable cost.

■ Field research provides any necessary new information on the market, using an established format of setting objectives, choosing from a variety of data collection methods, surveying samples from the total population and then collecting, collating and analysing the data to enable reliable business decisions to be made.

■ Field research by questionnaire is a common form of data collection and effective questionnaire design is therefore essential.

■ Some questionnaire research is quantitative in that it gathers facts in number form eg, 'How many did you buy?'; 'How often did you go?'; 'How much did you pay?'.

■ Some questionnaire research is qualitative in that it examines opinions, eg 'did you enjoy the holiday?'; 'what do you think of the local bus service?'. Answers are usually graded.

■ Sampling involves choosing the right group of people to interview to provide data for the questionnaire.

■ Markets are segmented so that the behavioural patterns of the various segments can be examined and their needs identified by the product and service producers. External research agencies can be used to obtain the data.

■ Market research provides the essential information for marketing planning involving the marketing mix of product, price, promotion and place.

■ The results from market research can also lead to planning using a variety of analytical techniques known by their mnemonics (initial letters). SWOT examines the current activities of an organisation in the light of marketing research while SLEPT concentrates on the influences of external change on business activities.

KEY TERMS

market research	research into the market segment(s) targeted by the business for its products
secondary research	gathering and analysis of published information (also known as 'desk' research)
primary research	gathering and analysis of fresh data (also known as 'field' research)
quantitative research	gathering numerical values (ie numbers)
qualitative research	gathering opinions
sample	a selection of respondents from the chosen market sector
population	the total market, or market segment, under review
respondent	the user of the product or service who provides answers to the questions in a survey
focus group	a group of people belonging to the targeted market segment(s) who discuss a new product area and provide qualitative data
marketing mix	an approach to marketing planning which is based on the four P's: **P**roduct – getting the product right for the customer **P**rice – fixing the price at the right level **P**romotion – using a mix of promotional techniques **P**lace – selling and getting the product to the customer
SWOT analysis	examining the current activities of a business (**S**trengths and **W**eaknesses) and using external research data to assess the **O**pportunities and **T**hreats which will affect the planning process
SLEPT analysis	analysis of the influences of change on the marketing process and used in marketing planning: **S**ocial, **L**egal, **E**conomic, **P**olitical and **T**echnological

20

Marketing mix: product and price

Starting point

When your research has identified a market opportunity, you will need to plan a coordinated approach that fulfils the needs of the chosen market segment – the teens market, for example. The product or service you have in mind must be tailored precisely to those consumers, priced at a level that they will see as representing 'value', promoted to fit their image and lifestyle, and made available where they would expect to buy it.

Normally the four P's of the marketing mix are considered together in the planning process. This chapter covers the first two P's – product and price. Promotion and place will be covered in the next chapter.

What you will learn from this chapter

- the marketing mix must be an integrated whole, covering policies relating to product, price, promotion and place

- product policy controls the type and range of goods and services that an organisation offers to its markets, and is influenced by the product life cycle

- marketing planning decides on the segment(s) to be targeted, eg mass or niche; by demography, geography and/or psychography

- pricing is influenced by a mixture of short-term and long-term factors

- price can influence a customer's perception of the product

- small businesses can compete with larger businesses, but not always on price

Product Policy

'**Product**' is the first of the four P's and is central to the marketing planning of a business. The product can be a tangible item such as a can of Coke or it can be a service such as a taxi ride.

Product policy decides what the product or range of products should be. This is sometimes the hardest part of setting up a business as you will know if you have carried out an Enterprise project.

The product or product range itself will change over a period of time, because markets for products and services are dynamic (constantly changing). The marketing function should always be researching ideas for tomorrow's products.

There are a number of factors to consider when formulating a product policy:

the American Adventure theme

product positioning

Where does your product stand in the market? When a market is highly competitive it is vital that the target market segments – your customers – have a clear idea of the benefits of your product in comparison with competitor products – eg the looks, safety features and reliability of a car.

product themes

A successful way of combining a product mix is the development of product themes. This has become increasingly popular in the leisure industry, where theme parks such as 'The American Adventure' present all of their entertainment under a single coordinated style.

complementary or competitive products

The product planners also have other factors to consider: some products are complementary to one another; others are competitive.

Complementary products sell together. Retailers selling sports equipment also sell trainers and sports clothes. Customers for one product might be persuaded to buy some of the other items. In fact, the customer would expect this range of products and may use only the manufacturer or shop that provides it.

Competitive products, as the name suggests, compete with each other for the buyers' attention. Competitive products may be produced by the same manufacturer. Why? There are several reasons: consumers have different requirements. The wide range of breakfast cereals from Kellogg's, for example, is an attempt by one business to attract as many buyers as possible.

Apple iPod – new and fashionable

new product development

Innovation and creativity are important factors in identifying strategies for changing market position and for introducing new products. There must be new ideas, and time should be allocated to brainstorming and R&D (Research & Development). New product development requires substantial investment in market research, technical research and the study of current product development and their markets.

The Apple iPod, for example, has been an outstanding success story in making downloadable music accessible in a fashionable and technically advanced way.

Activity 20.1 – product policy

Some businesses provide good examples of the use of a particular type of product policy, eg the use of product positioning, product themes, complementary products, competitive products, innovative products.

Match the type of product policy listed above that best describes the strategies adopted by the businesses listed below. In each case give examples of the products which illustrate the product policy. Visit the websites if you need information.

1 Disneyland (www.disney.co.uk)

2 Rolex (www.rolex.com)

3 Cadburys (www.cadbury.co.uk)

4 Sony (www.sony.co.uk)

5 JJB Sports (www.jjb.co.uk)

Product Life Cycle

In the commercial marketplace products and services are created, launched and withdrawn, in a process known as the **product life cycle**.

The graph on the next page shows the product life cycle as a series of five stages. It plots the money value of sales (the upper line) and the profit on those sales (the lower line) against the five stages, which we will explain in turn.

Stage 1: development

No product or service is dreamed up on the Monday and produced and sold on the Tuesday. Each new product idea has to be researched, designed and tested. This may take a few weeks or, in the case of hi-tech products, many months or years. The process is the same for a large company and a small business. It will all require financing, so it is important to calculate the costs when making the decision to develop a product. Costs include: market research, technical research, test marketing (a limited trial run) and management time to decide whether to 'go ahead' or 'discontinue'. Note that the 'development' stage shows on the graph as a loss on the 'profits' line; this stresses the importance of a successful launch to recover the development expenses.

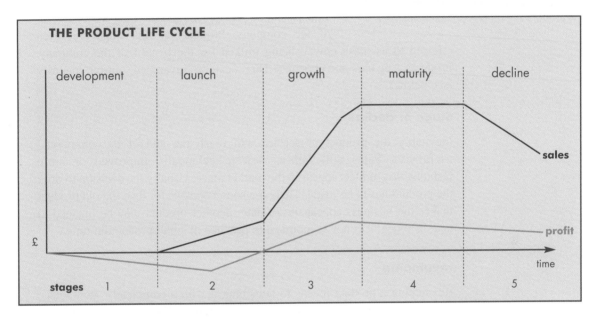

THE PRODUCT LIFE CYCLE

development | launch | growth | maturity | decline

sales

profit

£ | time

stages 1 | 2 | 3 | 4 | 5

Stage 2: the launch

The go-ahead has been given and the new product is introduced to the market place. This is a nerve-testing time in business. The real test for the new product is 'Will the customers buy it again, and again, and again?' The diagram shows a slow sales uptake and an even deeper trough in the 'profits' curve – Why? This is because a product launch entails the costs of extensive promotion (advertising and publicity) and distributing the product to the market.

Stage 3: growth

If the launch is successful, consumers take to the product and sales take off. Depending upon the uniqueness and originality of the new product, profitability should be strong. Vigorous promotion will take the product into all the required outlets and sales to the final consumer will be influenced by the 'newness' factor. Inevitably, the fast rising sales curve will begin to level off as the new product excitement is lost and the competition reacts to your success. Sales continue to rise but new customers are harder to find. The profits curve reaches its peak.

Mars Bar – a long and profitable maturity

Stage 4: maturity

This stage is more of a plateau than a curve, and its length can vary from months to years. When a product reaches this stage it is in the interests of the business to keep it there as long as profitably possible. Certain products seem to go on for ever – eg Cornflakes and the Mars Bar – and these are very valuable to the business because they produce the revenue needed for new product development and the long-term survival of the company. Products at this stage are often referred to as 'cash cows', being milked for the benefit of the company. Products – eg cars and chocolate bars – can be 'revamped' during maturity (see below).

Stage 5: decline

Inevitably the product or service will reach the end of its commercial usefulness. Sales will fall as newer, technically improved or more fashionable products appear in the market place. Usually the decision to drop the product has to be made. There are sound reasons for this: the old product makes the business appear out of date; another product may be planned to take its place; it is not economical to produce in small production runs.

revamping

Revamping a product means re-launching it with a completely 'new look'. The revamping of a product during the product life cycle is a common marketing strategy, particularly when the existing product is losing ground to the competition or going into decline. Changes to the product might involve complete redesign and or just involve new packaging.

the Product Portfolio

The product life cycle explained on the last few pages shows the lifespan of a single product. It is important to appreciate that any business with a range of products will have at any one time a range of product life cycles at different stages of development. Some products will be new, some will be growing in market share, some will be mature and producing healthy revenue and profits, some will be in decline and may soon lose money.

It is sound marketing policy to have a range of products at different stages in their product life cycle. This is so that existing products can help to finance new products. This range of products and product life cycles is known as the **product portfolio**, shown on the next page.

You will see from the diagram how the product life cycles for individual products overlap in terms of time scale, providing the business with a steady source of income and profit.

THE PRODUCT PORTFOLIO

Activity 20.2 – marketing objectives – customer focus

1 Look at the product portfolio diagram above and identify the position that each product has reached in its life cycle at point (a) and at point (b).

2 What should the business be doing at point (b) as part of its product policy?

Product Portfolio Analysis – the Boston Matrix

A business that promotes a range of products will need to look critically at each product in relation to:

■ its market share in comparison with competing products

■ the rate of growth of the market for that product

Common sense tells you that a business has a 'winner' on its hands if the product has a high market share and that market is growing quickly – in fact it has a 'star' in its portfolio. One analytic matrix is known as the **Boston Matrix**. Look at the diagram on the next page. Products are positioned on the diagram according to their share of the relevant market (shown on the horizontal axis). The markets themselves are also analysed for growth rates (shown on the vertical axis). Study the matrix and then read the notes below which explain the meaning of the four types of product. As you will see, some products are more valuable than others; some the business will want to keep and develop (stars and cash cows), some it may eventually want to get rid of (question marks and dogs).

question marks

A 'question mark' has a low market share in a growing market – it is a question mark because it could either be a promising new product in an expanding market, or alternatively a less promising and struggling product.

stars

A 'star' is often associated with the growth stage of the product life cycle. Sales are increasing, and the star could become a product leader in an expanding market. Stars are sometimes referred to as 'rising stars'.

cash cows

These products sell well and have a good market share, but in a mature market that has low growth. They provide profit and cash for the development of new products.

dogs

Dogs are associated with the decline stage of the product life cycle, and may be discarded if they become unprofitable.

All products in the portfolio must be monitored on a regular basis using up-to-date sales data. Do 'question marks' fail to make it? Do 'rising stars' fail to mature into long-term money makers ('cash cows')? Should 'dogs' be put down?

Services as Products

Sunshine is not included in the guarantee

If your choice for your portfolio is a service rather than a product, the marketing activities remain the same but there are additional issues and some disadvantages to bear in mind:

intangibility

Intangibility means something that cannot be touched. A service cannot be picked up, examined or tried out before it is purchased. Therefore the reputation of the business providing the service is very important. Service providers therefore often quote customer feedback to reassure potential buyers – this is one of the main purposes of the Thomson Travel questionnaire on pages 314 - 317.

uniformity of the product

It is clearly difficult for a business to make one service provided exactly the same as the previous. Whereas one Mars Bar you buy will be identical to the last one you bought, Thomson Holidays cannot guarantee that all holidays in the Caribbean will the same – you may even end up with a hurricane. Quality control and customer feedback therefore become very important in monitoring performance and customer perception of the product.

Activity 20.3 – types of product

1   Identify examples in the current marketplace of cash cows and stars. Try and find out how long the cash cows have been in the marketplace.

2   Why are cash cows important to a business? Does it matter that they sell in a low growth market?

3   If you were starting a small service business with limited resources

(a) would you go into a low growth or high growth market?

(b) how would you make sure that your customers could rely on your product?

Give reasons for your answers.

Pricing Policy

importance of pricing

Price – one of the 4 P's – is an important element of the marketing mix. The price charged for a product can determine whether a consumer will buy it, and the level of sales achieved may decide whether or not the business will make a profit. Pricing is decided through **pricing policy**.

different views on pricing

The question is – what price to charge?

what price for bottled water?

The business accountant's view of pricing is **cost plus**, ie the cost of the product plus a profit margin. Price is also affected by factors such as what competitors are charging, the stage reached in the product's life cycle, and above all else, what price customers are prepared to pay. From the marketing point of view, the customer is what matters.

importance of market research

Price will vary according to the circumstances. Think about what you pay for bottled water in a shop and the amount you are charged at a club for the same quantity. If you are starting a new business you will have to research the market very carefully, examining competitors' pricing very carefully. You will need to find out if the target market is **price sensitive**. Will customers buy on price, ie buy the cheapest? Or will they buy regardless of price, eg touted tickets for the sold-out football cup match or for the fashion item which is in short supply?

Pricing Strategies

There are a number of **pricing strategies** which can be used. The choice of pricing strategies will depend to some extent on the **long-term objectives** of the business – how it wishes to position itself in the marketplace, or how important its financial needs are. Here are some examples of long-term objectives:

- making a profit
- pricing to keep the competitors out of the market
- pricing which positions the company at the luxury end of the market
- pricing to maximise sales and make the business a market leader

There are a number of shorter-term pricing strategies which can be used. As you will see, some require high prices, some require low prices.

pricing strategies – pushing the prices up

setting a high price that people are prepared to pay

■ **skimming**

Charging high prices for new products that at first have no competition, eg today's new technology – this helps to recover development costs.

■ **psychological pricing**

This involves a study of what motivates a consumer. Is it possible to price too high? Of course it is. Is it possible to price too low? Surprisingly, yes. Consumers have a perception of value. Have you ever heard someone say 'it can't be any good at that price'. So, put up the price and sell more!

pricing strategies – pushing the prices down

■ **penetration pricing**

This is setting a low price to penetrate an existing market, and is used by new businesses to establish themselves in the market. It has been very successful when used by the low cost airlines.

5p off a litre of fuel!

two for the price of one!

setting a low price to attract buyers

■ **destruction pricing**

This knocks out the competitors by cutting prices aggressively, a process commonly known as 'price wars'. This can only work for a business which has other products which will provide the cash flow and profit to support the loss of revenue. Supermarkets have sometimes cut their fuel prices to such an extent that some independent garages have gone out of business.

■ **promotion pricing**

Special offers or 'sale' pricing can attract buyers to buy products they have not bought before, or to buy more than they normally would. An example of this is the 'two for the price of one' promotion technique.

■ **loss leaders**

This involves very aggressive price cutting which means that the product is actually sold at less than cost price, but it attracts buyers to other products or repeat purchases which will provide the necessary revenue and profit. Selected airline flights sold at prices such as 99p are a striking example.

Activity 20.4 – pricing strategies

1   The finance manager and the marketing manager of a clothing shop are having a heated discussion about the pricing of a new range of shirts. The marketing manager wants to set the price at £15 each but the finance manager wants to set a higher price of £30. What points about pricing policy are the two managers likely to make in their discussion? Who do you think should win, and why?

2   Two friends run their own separate businesses, one runs a filling station and the other a jewellery shop. How is petrol and jewellery different in terms of pricing and what is the attitude of consumers to the pricing of the two types of product?

3   Identify and explain a current example of each of the following types of pricing strategy:

   (a)   loss leaders

   (b)   destruction pricing

   (c)   promotion pricing

price setting decisions

A business will have to consider its options very carefully when setting prices. Detailed market research will be needed into the competitors' pricing and into the price sensitivity of the market – Will a higher price put customers off? – Will it in fact attract customers if they think they are getting a high quality product?

If the business decides to go for a lower price it must consider the advantages and disadvantages. It will sell more products if customers are attracted by lower prices and it should take sales from the competition. On the downside, a lower price may cheapen the image of the product and cut into the profits needed for new product research. It may even start a price war.

Pricing for the Small Business

So far in this chapter we have concentrated on marketing carried out by large 'household name' businesses. It is important to appreciate that effective marketing is essential for the survival of smaller businesses. The difference here is that the resources available to smaller businesses are strictly limited.

Smaller businesses which enter into the same market as their larger competitors will obviously have little or no effect on their competitors' price level. They are unlikely to be able to undercut their competitors because this will reduce or remove their profitability. Their pricing is therefore very much 'market driven'. They may therefore use 'non price' alternatives to appeal to the market, adapting their marketing mix to offer attractions such as specialist expertise, the personal touch, local availability and home delivery.

Product and Price Policy in Action

In the following Case Study that concludes this chapter we turn again to the larger business and illustrate how the Alton Towers theme park uses product and price policy in its marketing.

Case Study – Alton Towers: Magic Moments

INTRODUCTION

Alton Towers, based in the Staffordshire countryside, is Britain's best known theme park. It is part of the Tussaud Group's portfolio of leisure attractions, which include other theme parks, Warwick Castle, the London Planetarium, and the original waxworks exhibition in London, now with offshoots around the world. So, Alton Towers is itself a part of another organisation's product policy, and its own decisions will be influenced by this.

PRODUCT POLICY

The Alton Towers Product range consists of all of the elements that go to make a complete family day out, with something for everyone.

The rides vary from the gentle, for youngsters with mother, to the 'white knuckle' for teenagers and young adults. The latter type of ride is key to gaining the necessary publicity that draws attention to the park, and as such investment in new attractions is crucial. Like all good companies however, financial limits need to be set, and so market research into new product ideas is vital. As we have learnt, all products have a life expectancy, and with technology constantly changing, it is important to make the right choices. For example, the 'Corkscrew' was introduced in the 1980s and still runs, whereas the 'Haunted House', introduced in 1992 with leading edge technology, had to be revamped recently after research classed it 'dull'. It is the task of the top management 'Blue Sky' team to investigate new technology and take note of customer suggestions that come from the questionnaires filled in by guests after their visit. The key requirement of major rides is that they bring customers back for a second visit, as well as attracting first time visitors.

Services are all important in ensuring a pleasant day out. Food and drink of good quality is provided to cater for visitors 'on the move'. No one wants to spend time in a restaurant waiting to be served. In the early days, AT provided its own refreshment, but customer power saw the introduction of known brand names to the park. The visitor reasoning was that 'captive' pricing might mean higher prices, and so known providers like McDonald's and KFC were invited in as well, so long as their prices stayed the same as in their High Street outlets.

Entertainment provision has changed, again customer led. Visitors are on the move, not prepared to sit down to watch a show, and, that peculiar British trait, not much interested in joining in, so the switch is being made to street theatre, with entertainers going to the crowd as they stand in a queue, or move from one ride to another.

Customer service provision covers information kiosks, especially as people come through the gates, and well trained staff easily recognisable in uniform. Even the mundane facilities of toilets and rubbish collection are vital services in ensuring visitor enjoyment. Facilities for moving people around are part of the enjoyment, with a ride from car park to entrance on a monorail, and an overhead cable car to take visitors round the park. For the tired and weary, a deliberate change of mood is offered by a superb sunken garden, a leftover from the original stately home.

Accommodation. Alton Towers cannot go to the customer, and travelling time eats into the family day out, so overnight accommodation (hotels on site) became part of the park's product range. This facility is supplemented by sending visitors a leaflet detailing local B&B establishments, should they require an off-park base.

Seasonality led to product range extensions with the hotels being developed to offer conference facilities, to create revenue in the closed season (the theme park closes from October 31st through to Easter). Special events such as bonfire night displays and music concerts occur only within the season.

MARKET RESEARCH

Market research is vital to any business. Several methods have been mentioned, but also the company employs specialist agencies to ask focus groups about image, value, pricing, advertising, and even why they do not visit the park. Databases containing customer information are used to study market segmentation. Internet website visits also offer useful facts about the enquirer. Finally, AT staff make visits to other similar attractions to see what the competition is doing. Clearly, the product 'package' has to be right, to provide good value and 'keep the customers coming back'.

PRICING POLICY

Alton Towers' pricing policy has never changed: visitors pay an entrance fee and get the rides free. The reasoning is that budgeting is easier, security is tighter with less cash collection points, and the visitor knows what it will cost for this part of the experience. There are of course other price decisions. Food and drink is sold at commercial High Street levels, and fairground games to win prizes need to generate a profit.

The actual entrance fee for a family (2 + 2) remains fixed throughout a season, but beyond that there are many price variations. Categories include individuals, groups, seasonality, age, disability and many special offers. A 'trade sales' team visits societies, companies, coach firms, hotel chains etc. to negotiate special rates.

Enquirers on the internet can often obtain discount vouchers. Even a 'bad weather' forecast may stimulate a special offer to local residents if a poor attendance is feared. Refunds are rare and only occur if thunder and lightning force the closure of rides.

Osborne Books is grateful to Alton Towers for the contribution of this Case Study.

Activity 20.5 – types of product

1   Alton Towers can be seen as one of the products in the Tussauds Group product portfolio. What are the other products in the range? Are they complementary or competitive? Visit www.tussauds.com for up-to-date information.

2   What is the product range offered by Alton Towers? Are the products complementary or competitive?

3   How does Alton Towers use its product range to cope with seasonality?

4   What evidence is there of the management of the product life cycle in the Alton Towers range of rides?

5   How does Alton Towers carry out its market research activities and what form do they take? What is the key requirement of rides that has to be monitored?

6   Why were 'High Street' fast food names invited to sell their products in the theme park? Would Alton Towers not make more profit if they provided the catering?

7   What is the pricing policy for entry to Alton Towers and what is the reasoning behind it?

8   What special offers are available for entry to Alton Towers, and what is their purpose?

CHAPTER SUMMARY

■ The product policy of a business decides which product(s) to provide and sell to defined market segment(s).

■ Products marketed by a business in a product range can be complementary or competitive, ie they can sell together or in competition with each other.

■ New product development – being innovative and creative – is important if the business is to capture new markets and expand its product range.

■ The product life cycle is important in marketing planning because it takes into account the potential time and resources needed for development, launch, growth, maturity and decline of a product.

■ The product portfolio contains the complete range of products of a business. The product life cycles are likely to be at different stages of development, which is advantageous because products bringing in revenue can help to support new products needing revenue.

■ The Boston Matrix is a useful way of looking at products at different stages of their life cycle. It shows the market share of individual products and the rate of growth of the relevant market. It identifies high market share products that should be retained (cash cows and stars) and low market share products that should or could be discarded (dogs and question marks).

■ The marketing of services needs special consideration because services are intangible and the quality of service can vary. Regular customer feedback and monitoring for quality are therefore very important.

■ A number of product pricing strategies may be used. The choice of pricing strategy will depend on the long-term objectives of the business: profitability, beating the competition, becoming a luxury brand name, becoming a market leader.

■ The finance function in a business will want a cost plus pricing policy, ie revenue will have to cover the cost of the product and also include a margin of profit.

■ Pricing strategies that push the prices up include skimming (high prices for new products with no competition as yet) and psychological pricing (products known to be luxury and quality items).

■ Pricing strategies that push the prices down include penetration pricing, destruction pricing, promotion pricing and loss leaders (see key terms for definitions).

■ Pricing policy for the smaller business will be largely market driven as smaller businesses are unlikely to be able to affect the price levels of their competitors.

KEY TERMS

market policy	deciding to which markets to sell
product policy	the type and range of products to be supplied to the chosen market segments
complementary products	products that sell together and do not compete with each other, eg sports equipment and sports clothes
competitive products	products that compete with each other – but can be marketed by the same business, eg breakfast cereals
product life cycle	the stages that a product goes through in its lifespan, ranging through development, launch and growth to maturity and decline – and the time that this takes
revamping	revision and relaunch of an existing product in order to extend its lifespan
product portfolio	the range of products promoted by a business, all with varying product life cycles
Boston Matrix	a matrix (table) showing products in a product range in relation to market growth and market share – useful for identifying products that can supply revenue for the development of new products
pricing policy	the overall use of pricing strategies to achieve business objectives such as profitability
cost plus	pricing a product by adding a profit margin to its cost
skimming	high prices for new products which have little or no competition
psychological pricing	setting a price which the consumer sees to be the value of the product – it is all in the consumer's mind
penetration pricing	setting a low price to penetrate an existing market
destruction pricing	setting a low price to knock out the competitors' sales
promotion pricing	using special offer pricing to attract buyers
loss leaders	cutting prices of products to attract buyers to the product range, but making a loss on the cut price items

Marketing mix: promotion and place

Starting point

However good the product or service is, it is useless until the target consumers get to hear about it and know where to find it (as with the Tesco pop-up advert for Tesco on-line shopping on the left).

Marketing communication solves these problems by promoting the product to the consumers, getting the product to where they can inspect it (or getting them to where they can access the service), and then persuading them to buy it.

In the last chapter we covered the first two P's – product and price. This chapter covers the last two P's – promotion and place.

What you will learn from this chapter

- 'promotion' creates awareness of a product and tries to persuade the consumer to buy it, using the techniques of:
    - advertising – using a wide variety of media and messages
    - branding to encourage consumer loyalty
    - packaging to protect and promote a product
    - publicity (being newsworthy) and public relations (building the right 'corporate image')
    - sponsorship – helping promote a product as part of a CRM (Cause Related Marketing) campaign
    - sales promotions (special offers) and merchandising (the appearance and location of the product in a sales outlet)

- direct marketing uses adverts to encourage immediate ordering

- effective customer service is essential in persuading a customer to buy again

- 'place' policy decides how to get the product to the customer, either through direct sales or through indirect sales

what is Promotion?

'Promotion' consists of a number of techniques which create awareness of the product and persuade the potential customer to make the buying decision

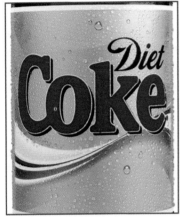

promoting the brand

Promotion is all about communication – it involves a number of techniques:

■ **advertising** – using different media such as TV, newspapers and magazines, posters, the internet, sponsorship

■ **branding** – promoting a specific brand image of the product or the business which implants itself in the mind of the consumer

■ **packaging** – promoting the brand image of the product in the way it is presented to the consumer

■ **publicity/public relations** – making sure the business features in areas such as media coverage and sponsorship

■ **merchandising** – ensuring the product is accessible to the buyer, eg new books in the front of a bookshop

■ **sales policy** – the organisation of the actual selling process

Clearly large businesses have the advantage of resources in promoting products to a mass market. Small businesses, however, can make use of a variety of promotional techniques in a local area or niche market and achieve good communication with the target market. One of the best promotional tools of a small business is a well-designed website.

In your assessment for this Unit you will need to deal with promotion as one of the four P's in the marketing mix for your chosen product. We will deal with all these aspects of promotion in turn.

Advertising

Effective advertising can be defined as:

the most persuasive selling message to the right people at the lowest cost and at the right time

Advertising has its critics and its supporters. Its critics would say that it is expensive and pushes up the price of the product, it can offend people and persuade consumers to buy products which they cannot afford. Its supporters on the other hand claim that it increases demand for the product, stimulates competition and causes prices to fall. Both points of view can be true.

We will now explain the various stages which combine to create a successful advertising campaign.

plan the advertising campaign

An advertising campaign in a business will be managed by its marketing function and may employ an independent advertising agency. A smaller business is likely to have a more limited budget, but it will still be able to make effective use of the advertising media (methods of advertising).

identify the right markets

The advertiser must be aware which markets, or market segments, are being targeted. This is a straight-forward market segmentation exercise. With consumer goods, the choice might be age, gender, social grouping, occupation, region or lifestyle.

identify the right media

How would you attract and influence the chosen target group(s) with your product or service? The choice of media is large, with the internet becoming increasingly popular. The diagram below shows the wide variety of advertising that is available.

Vision & sound
TV
radio
cinema
video

Paper-based text
national papers
local papers
magazines
trade directories

Leaflets & Catalogues
mailed
door-to-door
inserts

Electronic
internet
teletext
mobile phones

advertising methods

Sponsorship
individuals
teams
events

Transport related
vans
buses, trains
roadside posters

Exhibitions
national shows
local shows
in-store
on the street

Giveaways
caps
T shirts
bags
pens

When planning an advertising campaign and selecting advertising media (methods of advertising), the questions that should be asked include:

- Is the cover to be local, regional or national?
- What forms of advertising will the advertising budget cover?
- How many people can be reached?
- Which market segments should the advertising reach?
- How often can the message be put over – hourly, daily, weekly?
- How important are aspects such as sound, movement, colour and size?
- Will the results be measurable, eg replies to a single advertisement?

These are the key questions to be asked when selecting suitable media. As noted on the previous page, the choice will be limited both by the size of the business and the market that is being targeted.

Activity 21.1 – choosing the advertising media

Discuss or write a list of the media you would choose to advertise . . .

- a revamped chocolate bar
- 18/30 holidays
- a new compact computer
- a local coffee shop
- a range of cosmetics
- a local drain clearance service

creating the 'right' message – stressing the benefits!

It is the job of advertising to create the 'right' message – one that appeals to the market segment identified, and suits the type of media chosen. Advertisers are always searching for a USP – a Unique Selling Point or Proposition. What makes a successful message? Messages generally fall into one of two types, both of which set out the benefits to be gained by purchasing the product. These two types are:

- factual messages
- emotive messages

For example, a manufacturer has a new car to advertise. What possible features could be stressed? What benefits does it have?

REASONS FOR BUYING A NEW CAR

factual	emotive
price and value	status – must be rich or important to own one
acceleration	pulling power – attracting a partner
economy of performance	family comfort and safety – the caring parent
3 year guarantees	personality – sports car performance
safety record	comfort – arrived relaxed
reliability	health – of others – low emissions

identify the right timing

Timing of the advertising is crucial. Too soon before the event, and the customers forget; too late and they have bought something else. Seasonal markets need careful timing. A media expenditure plan should be drawn up, detailing at what stages of the campaign the money should be spent, and which media need to be informed first so that stocks of the new product will be available when consumers get to hear about it. Clearly an initial burst of advertising would accompany the launch of a new product. After that it will be a matter of choice when follow-up advertising takes place.

A media expenditure plan is a table that lists months across the top and the chosen media down the left-hand side. Expenditure is then listed in this spreadsheet as required.

calculate the cost of the campaign

This area is one where marketing personnel and accountants sometimes disagree. It is obviously desirable that costs are covered by sales, but marketing personnel may want a boost to the advertising budget if sales are unsatisfactory, whereas the accountant may argue for a reduction. Costs can be found in BRAD (British Rate and Data). Your tutor may be able to get a slightly out-of-date copy from a local advertising agency (they are expensive). Alternatively ask your local newspaper or radio station head office for a 'rate card'.

Now read the Case Study which sets out the scope of a national advertising campaign for coach travel cards. Then carry out the activity which follows.

Case Study – National Express and student travel

www.nationalexpress.com

Coach operator National Express has launched a discount card aimed at 16 to 26 year-olds as a challenge to the Young Person's Railcard.

The NX2 card was introduced in time for the new academic year when students often sign up for railcards. National Express hopes to cash in on students' freedom to travel.

A spokeswoman said that the £10 card, which offers a 30% discount on travel for one year, would suit 16 to 18 year-olds who may find low-cost airline fares are beyond their means.

The cards are available in six designs which appeared in a teaser campaign on postcards, washroom panels, small ads and beer mats to drive people to the website. Consumers can then select their favourite design online when they order their card.

The design features a '2' icon, which is used throughout the campaign with catchy messages such as 'P@'#* off 2 anywhere for £5'.

A radio and press campaign ran for two months in the autumn, promoting the launch offer of £5 for a single ticket to travel anywhere in the UK.

Source: adapted from an article in 'Marketing'

Activity 21.2 – the advertising campaign

Read the National Express Case Study above and answer the questions below.

1 What is the product? Briefly describe its benefits.

2 What market segment has been identified, and what is the competition?

3 What advertising media have been chosen and how are they appropriate to the target market?

4 What is the USP (Unique Selling Point) of the product?

5 What was the timing of the product launch and why was it chosen?

6 What pricing strategies have been used by National Express?

Branding

Branding is a method of identifying a product by creating a name, term, design or logo which is unique to that product. Branding creates an image which fixes the product in the consumer's mind and makes it different to the products of competitors.

advantages of branding

The establishment of a brand name will save on future advertising costs. The product has become 'known'. To the consumer a brand name represents a known quality of product, the next one bought being of the same quality as the last. To the manufacturer branding allows a range of products to be offered, to different market segments. It also allows brand loyalty to be established, ie some consumers always specify and buy the same 'name'. They know that the product will provide them with what they want.

types of brand

There are a number of different ways in which brand names can be used:

- **individual brands** are those which stand alone, with no reference to the maker's name, eg Persil (made by Unilever)

the Heinz 'means beans' story

- **family brands** often carry the name of the company or group, eg Heinz, Boots, as a guarantee of quality – visit www.heinz.co.uk for a history of the famous brand. A 'family' brand allows new products to be established more easily but should one product gain a bad reputation it may drag down all the rest

- **multibrand strategy** – this involves the use of more than one brand in the same market segment to increase the chances of a company product being selected – for example, the Ford Motor Company (www.ford.com) manufactures a range of car brands – Ford, Mazda, Volvo and Jaguar, for example, which all compete for sales

- **house branding** – 'own' brands, eg Marks & Spencer, Tesco, Morrison all have their own version of consumer goods made specially for them and they sell under the retailer's own name or a chosen alternative – once a house brand name has been established, it is customary to maintain the chosen quality or 'good value' image

changing a brand

Sometimes a brand – or its image – has to be changed. This can happen because it needs revamping: it may have become old-fashioned, as any 'product' image will.

A change in the presentation of a brand can also occur when the original brand image has become 'tarnished' in the eyes of consumers. An example of this is the way in which the McDonald's brand has been moved away from the 'Big Mac' eat-as-much-as you-can image and re-aligned with the concept of healthy eating promoted by a variety of pressure groups, including the anti-obesity lobby.

Activity 21.3 – branding of products

1 Write lists of as many brand names as you can think of in the following categories:

(a) famous individual product brand names

(b) family brands – where the product sells on the basis of the name of the company

(c) multibrands – where one company promotes competing product brands

(d) house branding – find examples where the 'own brands' are used to identify with customer perception of factors such as quality or value-for-money

When the lists have been compiled, hold a class session where a member of the class (or the tutor) writes the names of the brands on the board in the four categories. Discuss the findings in class and come to some group decisions about branding.

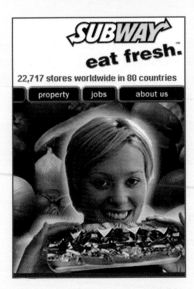

2 Investigate the Subway brand (www.subway.co.uk) and explain:

(a) what form of business Subway is

(b) how the business has become a worldwide success and appeals to consumer preferences

(c) how the Subway brand differs from many other fast food brands

Packaging

The packaging of a product is a major aid to promotion and product presentation. Note the difference between 'packing' and 'packaging':

- ■ **packing** is the wrapping for the product – it protects it from damage
- ■ **packaging** is the total appeal to the customer and is part of Promotion – it attracts the shopper's attention, especially at the point of sale

Packing protects against breakage, bacteria, chemical change (such as shrinkage, discolouration, rust), all of which can create the marketing problems of lost reputation, lost orders and customer complaints.

packaging can help to sell a product

Packaging enhances appearance using colour, shape and size. It carries the brand name, product photographs and information about product use. It may allow the product to be seen whilst keeping it clean (eg in meat packaging), offer 'ease of use' advantages and continue to have marketing value even after the product has been used – biscuit tins and coffee jars are sometimes kept for general storage purposes – and will continue to bear the brand name. A change in the appearance of a product's packing (colour and shape) can even increase sales and product life cycle.

Packaging can also apply to services – you can buy a packaged holiday (which includes transport, accommodation, tour guide, insurance); the financial institutions often package financial products (mortgages, insurance and pensions).

legal issues of packaging

Note that producers are legally bound to include detailed information about each product on its packing. This is monitored carefully by consumer groups and their legal advisers. Manufactured food products, for example, should be labelled with details of additives and fat content.

Activity 21.4 – packaging

1 Describe the ways in which packaging can attract attention.

2 Give examples of the ways in which packaging may lose sales.

3 Explain why packaging is criticised by environmentalists.

4 Explain the reasons why consumer groups and lawyers study and inspect packing materials.

Publicity

Publicity is obtained by a product being 'newsworthy' and being quoted in the media. Very often it is a case of good luck, as in the case of the lady climber who was rescued from a snowdrift in the Scottish Highlands and emerged saying 'I could just do with a glass of Guinness'. Publicity is therefore never quite under the control of the marketing team. It depends upon what others say about the product or organisation.

Publicity can also be bad – eg scares about the harmful content of food products – although it has been said 'there is no such thing as bad publicity' because any publicity will draw attention to the product!

Also, publicity is free, and can greatly help a small business with a limited advertising budget.

The significant differences between advertising and publicity are therefore:

- advertising is a known cost for an agreed amount of contact with the market – publicity tends to be non-controllable, often unplanned

- publicity has far greater impact in that it appears to come from a third person, and is thus more believable; if the press favourably review this book, it will sell more than any advert could achieve

- publicity catches readers off guard, whereas when they read an advert they know they are being sold to and tend to 'switch off'

- advertising allows the repetition of the message several times, whereas publicity has the limited life of a news story

Public Relations (PR)

'If I had one last marketing dollar, I'd spend it on PR' Bill Gates, Microsoft.

Public Relations (PR) aims to safeguard and promote the image of the whole organisation, as well as its individual products. In the political world is has become known as 'spin'.

PR is an extension of the publicity approach in that it tries to coordinate the effort. It may consist of press releases about the organisation's achievements, whether they be new product concepts, technological breakthroughs or environmental concerns. Other approaches may involve appearances on radio and TV in relevant programmes or in the news; open days for the public at the factory or showroom and the distribution of leaflets. Sponsorship is another important area for publicity and for PR.

Sponsorship and Cause-Related Marketing

Worcester Warriors – rugby team sponsorship by a local employer

Although **sponsorship** is technically an advertising medium, recent changes in approach have linked it very firmly with PR. Originally used in advertising by supporting an individual athlete, football team, or event, it has developed into other areas such as TV programme sponsorship.

Sponsorship can be local as well as national. Businesses wishing to be seen as caring members of the community in which they are based carry out community relations exercises linking their name with local schools and projects for environmental care. Sponsorship of local sports teams has also become a useful promotional tool.

Cause Related Marketing (CRM) involves businesses sponsoring good causes and often appears on company websites included in the section headed **Corporate Responsibility**. (Note that CRM confusingly also stands for Customer Relationship Management, another important focus area for the marketing function in a business.) For further information, visit www.bitc.org.uk (BITC stands for 'Business in the Community').

Examples of Cause Related Marketing (Corporate Responsibility) include the Tesco 'Computers for Schools' and 'Race for Life' (Cancer Research UK) campaign and the BT originated 'Childline' campaign which provides a lifeline for child victims and is now supported by a wide range of companies (visit www.childline.org.uk).

Activity 21.5 – publicity, PR and sponsorship

1 Look through your local newspaper for examples of publicity gained for businesses, eg sponsorship of events or news of business expansion. Some papers have a special 'Business' section or page with news of local firms. What benefits do the businesses in question gain from this publicity?

2 A major supermarket found that one of its own brand of foods had become contaminated with a poisonous chemical. What function within the business will need to deal with this problem? Describe how it might deal with the problem.

3 Investigate and describe the CRM (Cause Related Marketing) policy carried out by a large company (visit www.tesco.com, for example). How can the marketing department use this policy to promote the company to its external stakeholders?

Sales Promotions

A **sales promotion** is an important aspect of the overall 'Promotion' policy for a business. It is essentially a 'one-off' limited period promotion which aims to stimulate sales of a product (including a service). There are two types of sales promotion:

■ trade promotions – manufacturers promoting to retailers and wholesalers

■ consumer promotions – manufacturers and/or retailers promoting to the final consumer

trade promotions

The object of a trade promotion is to get the retailer to stock a product, or more of a product, or to stay loyal to the manufacturer. Types of trade promotion include:

■ quantity discounts – if more than a stated number of items per period are ordered by the buyer, an extra discount or a prize will be given

■ tailor-made promotions linked to one store, ie the manufacturer puts on a special display free of charge in the shop (if there is room in the store)

Trade promotions are easily targeted as the manufacturer knows which outlets do, or might, stock the product.

consumer promotions

Consumer promotions involve some form of special offer or incentive offered to the consumer in order to raise the level of sales. Examples include:

■ money off this or the next purchase, or two for the price of one

■ competitions

■ free gifts

■ loyalty incentives (eg points cards) that reward regular customers

Activity 21.6 – sales promotions

Visit retailers or read the press to find evidence of consumer promotions.

■ Note the type of promotion and the product involved.

■ Gather evidence for discussion in class.

■ How successful do you think these promotions are?

■ Is there a particular type that is popular at the moment?

Note: any visits to shops could also be used to collect evidence for the next Activity.

Merchandising at the Point of Sale

Merchandising is displaying a product at the point of sale, or the outlet itself, in an attractive manner to encourage consumers to buy. Merchandising is an integral part of **product presentation** which combines the skills of packaging, display, and choice of outlet or site, all designed to make the consumer visit the outlet and buy the product.

spot the promotions in this store

Merchandising leans heavily on the psychology of advertising in its research into what motivates the consumer. Factual and/or emotive messages, package design, brand names, publicity, short-term promotions all influence the consumer. Factors such as shop layout, lighting, outer and inner appearance – and smells – will also affect the buying decision. Food supermarkets which bake on the premises, for example, will often duct the 'yummy' smell of fresh bread and cakes into the entrance of the store in order to make the customers want to buy. This is clever merchandising because the customer is unaware of it.

Most people can remember making an 'impulse' purchase. Why? Was it previously seen advertising? The known brand name? The appearance of the package? Or was it the general 'feel' of the shop that inspired the additional buy, or the change from the usual brand? If it was the latter, the people in charge of merchandising have been successful.

Activity 21.7 – successful merchandising

Arrange to visit local stores in small groups. You may need the permission of the appropriate store manager to do this. You should study 'in store appeal', ie:

- product positioning and the use of space
- special promotions (see previous Activity)
- colour schemes and the use of music
- lighting and ventilation and any smells intentionally introduced
- customer facilities such as lifts, rest areas and 'coffee shops'

You should write a short informal report presenting your findings. If your tutor is in contact with the store manager (or other official) your findings could be useful to that person and could be discussed with him or her.

Direct Marketing

Direct Marketing combines the art of advertising with the need to get the person who sees it (or hears it) to take immediate action. Direct Marketing takes a number of forms:

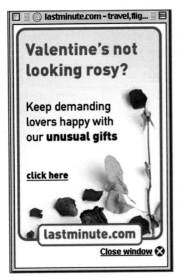

online 'pop-up' advert

websites

Obtaining sales direct from websites has been a major growth area in recent years. Online adverts with direct links to the appropriate website appear on many regularly-used sites, with 'pop-up' adverts becoming very popular.

direct mail

Direct mail uses the postal service to contact prospects (prospective customers) directly with advertising material linked to 'fill in response forms'. These should be targeted with great accuracy, using up-to-date databases. The phrase 'junk mail' is often used by recipients, but if material is targeted correctly, it should be relevant, not junk!

off-screen selling

Selling off-screen uses an advert on a TV screen which gives a telephone number to ring or a website address to contact to place an immediate order. It combines this technology with the credit card facility to make the payment instantly. Teletext is another effective form of selling from the TV screen. Many holidays are booked in this way, especially at short notice.

selling off-page

The technique of selling off-page has traditionally used an advert that contains a cut out response box for easy ordering, but today it may carry a direct call telephone number. Both techniques rely on a well designed advert that will convince consumers to act straight away.

telemarketing

The growth of direct marketing has come about partly because of the revolution in telemarketing capacities. Telemarketing is the provision of a telephone number in an advert to stimulate an immediate enquiry or order. Telephone bureaux are needed to receive the rush of calls that follow a convincing advertisement.

Sales Policy

Sales policy is a further aspect of 'Promotion': it brings the product to the attention of the customers and persuades them to buy.

the sales campaign

A sales campaign may be defined as:

a range of selling activities taking place within a specified time period (a year, or a short period) to achieve a specific level of sales

The campaign should be a coordinated part of the overall marketing plan. The campaign will need the organised involvement of all sales personnel, and efficient communication with everyone who is involved in the campaign: agents and dealers, wholesalers and retailers.

sales organisation

the sales force 'on the road'

The sales force for a larger business will involve a variety of people working **within the business**. Communication would be via internal email and regular sales meetings, often in the time before the store opens for the day. Much communication will be face-to-face. Training days will ensure that staff are updated on procedures.

The sales force **'on the road'** working for a manufacturer, wholesaler or service provider could be organised in a variety of ways: regionally, by 'territory' – by far the most common method, or by type of product, or type of customer.

Many salespersons work from home, ie they are not office based. Head office communication with the team – using phone, fax and email – must therefore be efficient in time and cost.

the selling process

Selling – whether over the telephone or face-to-face – involves specific skills, and a sales force trained in the right skills is essential for a successful sales campaign. Selling involves a number of stages:

1 researching for and making contact with the customer
2 establishing the customer's needs
3 presenting the product, explaining features, but most of all, stressing the benefits that will accrue to the customer
4 answering questions and overcoming doubts
5 assessing whether the customer is ready to make a decision
6 closing the sale – asking for and getting the order

Effective Customer Service

the needs of organisations

The achievement of customer satisfaction must be a major objective of a business, or the other objectives such as profitability will not be achieved. A customer-orientated organisation with the right products in the right place at the right prices at the right time should soon achieve an increase in market share.

needs of customers – customer care

Most people entering a shop, or contacting a business by letter or telephone, are showing that they have a need. Some customers are only looking for information. They may be uncertain as to their precise requirements, or wish to be made aware of the options, or need to examine items that advertising has told them are available. It is the sales and customer services staff's responsibility to try to turn that initial contact into a sale or to provide the information that they need accurately and courteously.

providing information – customer service at Tesco

point of sale service – staff training

Training should enable the sales or customer services staff to find out what the customer wants. Time may be a crucial factor, in which case there must be quick and easy purchasing systems or a prominently located customer services desk, whichever is required by the customer. Clear and accurate information must be evident in the form of signs, product brochures and helpful, well-informed staff. If a refund is needed, or goods need exchanging, help must be available with the minimum of fuss. Occasionally, customer complaints may arise: this too must be part of the customer service policy. Whatever the need, the employee's attitude is a key factor. He or she must be genuinely helpful rather than just 'go through the motions'.

point of sales service – clinching the sale

Point of sale service is often the key to finalising a deal. Everything must ensure that a decision to buy does not get reversed at the last moment. A careless last word from a salesperson, the lack of a till free from queues, the positioning of a till, the poor attitude of a tired till operator – all may lose the sale. The organisation must be such that the sale is completed quickly and efficiently – enough tills, plenty of carrier bags, help in packing the bags, many ways of making the payment – cash or card.

after-sales service

After-sales service is an essential element of customer service in any type of organisation. In the retail situation it may involve an insurance contract for a TV. After-sales policy may cover faulty goods, refunds, exchange of goods, complaints about goods, service and hygiene. It is likely to require the employee to be aware of aspects of the relevant laws on sale of goods and services.

Activity 21.8 – sales and customer service

Visit a well-known retail store in your area and investigate the way in which the sales and customer services functions are carried out. Use the following checklist as a guide:

1 How many tills are in operation? Are they all manned? How long are the queues?

2 What seems to be the general attitude of the staff on the tills?

3 Is there a Customer Services desk in operation?

4 What seems to be the general attitude of the staff on the Customer Services desk?

5 Does the store have a defined refunds policy? What does it say?

6 Does the store have a Customer Charter? What does it contain?

7 Does the store have any form of questionnaire or feedback form asking for customer opinions on customer service? What sort of questions does it ask?

Evaluation of a Promotional Policy

It is important to monitor the success of a promotional campaign: money has been spent on it and sales should result from it. How is success measured?

Advertising campaigns can be monitored very easily in terms of sales made, by measuring the changes in sales volume. Direct mailing and advert successes can be counted precisely.

Other areas are less distinct, but many market research firms provide data, either for a firm or by reports on an industry, on matters such as brand awareness and advert recall. 'Marketing' publishes tables ranking brand recall, each week covering a different medium. Researchers also can offer views on which message was best received and where and when the advert was seen. Other data which can be collected includes:

■ sales promotions – judged on the level of sales before, during and after the event

- numbers of customers visiting retail stores – 'footfall' – can be recorded by camera
- numbers visiting an exhibition stand or company owned outlet can be counted, as can the resulting orders
- visits to a website, brochures requested and orders received can all be counted
- a company's sales force visiting retail and other customers will record attitudes to and effectiveness of campaigns and any increased sales, into and out of the shops, can be counted.
- a scoring system for publicity gained (used by the phone company O_2)

Promotional Policy and the Small Business

The promotional policy of a small business may be limited by the lack of funds, so this makes it even more important to get the decisions right. Studying what larger businesses do is useful, to see what might be achieved on a smaller scale, or to help select one or two methods on which to concentrate.

With advertising, selecting the right media is crucial, and concentrating on one or two is usually best. A local shop or leisure outlet may use the local press and local radio. Then, as a buyer of advertising, it might look to gain free publicity in the form of an article or interview in the paper. Leaflets, either door-to-door or as inserts in the press, could be another alternative.

Small manufacturers may use trade journals for national coverage of their products.

For all businesses the setting up of a website is becoming the most favoured technique of reaching a wider audience. For as little as £5,000 it is possible to create web pages to describe your business and its products, set up an email facility, and open a 'shop' for orders with a direct payment facility.

Whatever the media choices made, the business must think very carefully about the message being given and the timing of the campaign.

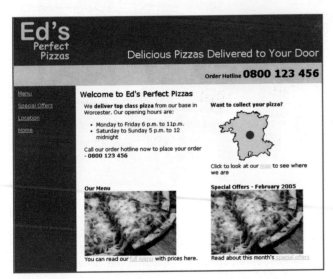

using a website for promoting a small local business

Now read the Case Study below on the promotional methods used by World Cancer Research Fund (WCRF) UK, a not-for-profit organisation.

Case Study – WCRF UK and Promotion

INTRODUCTION – WORLD CANCER RESEARCH FUND (WCRF) UK

World Cancer Research Fund (WCRF) UK is a not-for-profit organisation. It is a registered national charity committed to increasing awareness and knowledge of the relationship between food, lifestyle and cancer, and of cancer as a preventable disease.

WCRF UK's primary objective is to prevent cancer in the UK, but it is also part of an international network, which has a more global mission - 'to prevent cancer worldwide'. To do this it needs to maximise the funds raised through promotional activity whilst minimising the cost of doing so.

IDENTIFYING THE MARKET

This is a complex activity. Firstly, the market for donations must be identified, together with finding the volunteers to help raise these donations. There is also the need to identify those people who will influence the public, ie the health professionals they turn to for advice, such as dietitians, doctors, health visitors and practice nurses. The latter need to be supplied with materials to assist them in their work.

The **market sectors targeted** for donations are many, but in particular they are older charity donors with a particular interest in health. The profile of supporters is currently predominantly female, over 55 years of age. Distribution of fundraising efforts is however nationwide and diverse. The HQ in London coordinates fundraising activities across the UK, including special events, legacies, committed giving and house to house collections, and is helped by a nationwide team of volunteers. Database lists of helpers are compiled, for the circulation of newsletters and volunteer packs.

targeting the young – a healthy eating campaign

The market sector for the message is 'all ages', but there is also emphasis being put on the young. 'The Great Grub Club' is for 4 to 7 year-olds, who receive a tri-annual newsletter, and it is here that the objective of teaching children about healthy eating and being physically active is implemented.

IDENTIFYING THE RIGHT PROMOTIONAL MEDIA

The use of high profile media such as television advertising is extremely limited due to high costs, but individual print adverts are used to cover special events, such as the London Marathon. Some specialist publications, such as 'Charity Choice' are used to target people to encourage legacy donations. The Supporter Services team run programmes designed to develop WCRF UK's relationship with those who have pledged their support. These use both postal and telephone contact and the level of contact with donors differs depending upon the programme.

Newsletters are sent out to the organisation's supporters, to the public on request, and medical health and lifestyle conferences. All WCRF UK education material is available free. **Booklets and leaflets** are circulated to help people help themselves. They are also available in schools, doctors' waiting rooms and some hospital receptions, where people may be more receptive to the message.

Direct mail and direct marketing target particular types of donor with specifically themed campaigns, such as legacy giving, memorial donations, Christmas appeals, general funding, and research and education programmes. There are many others. WCRF UK rents lists from other charities and organisations, it also rents its own lists of donors who are happy for this to happen. Many of the campaigns incorporate several methods of direct marketing, such as traditional mail, email marketing, web activity and telemarketing, to try to increase the potential for recipients to interact with and donate to the charity.

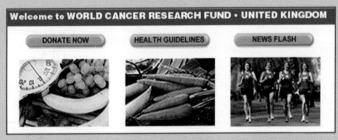

The internet is used to provide information about WCRF UK's work and its current fundraising activities. It also brings the public up to date with recent and relevant health legislation such as the new Childrens' Food Bill. Log on to www.wcrf-uk.org.uk. WCRF UK also advertises on specialist websites, for example, www.realrunner.com and www.timeoutdoors.com.

CREATING THE RIGHT MESSAGE

WCRF UK's strapline is 'Stopping cancer before it starts'. WCRF UK promotes positive messages about the long-term benefits of 'healthy eating and living' to the public. One of several objectives is to promote the message that 'eating healthily plus staying physically active and maintaining a healthy weight can cut cancer risk by 30-

40%, and that this is increased further by not smoking.' A wide range of programmes carry this and other messages, including the news of how the funds raised are being used. One example of the latter is the WCRF UK's Science Department which supports the scientific community with funds and grants for researchers in UK medical schools, universities and other research centres.

. . . at the right cost

This will always be a difficult decision for a charitable organisation. Promotional expenditure must come out of donations received, and yet without marketing spend the money collected will fall.

Television advertising is considered to be too expensive for this small organisation, despite the high profile and low cost per prospect reached. Advertising in all the Yellow Pages publications costs about £20,000, but this will last a full year. WCRF UK's website is seen as excellent value for money, with the ability to change the message throughout the year. Exhibitions are high profile, reach the target market of health specialists, and are relatively cheap to attend. Direct mail is very cost effective providing that mailing lists are always up-to-date. Spending on education packs serves to advertise the charity and represent the whole purpose of WCRF UK, which is to educate the public at an early age.

PROMOTIONAL METHODS

Branding consists of the use of the organisation's name in full and the use of the logo design. The latter is of most value when dealing with the medical profession, as it is a symbol based loosely on the caduceus - an insignia modelled on Hermes' (messenger of the gods) staff and used as the symbol of the medical profession.

Packaging in this instance is represented by the creation of advertising and information packs that will appeal to the relevant parts of the target markets. The education packs are of particular significance.

Public Relations and **publicity** are extremely important. WRCF UK works with consumer publications such as health and fitness magazines,

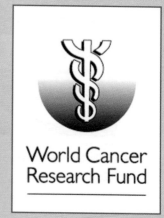

the WRFC logo

men's and women's lifestyle magazines and regional and national newspapers to create public interest stories on the benefits of healthy eating and living in the promotion of good health and the prevention of chronic diseases. Market research findings about eating habits are released as news items, mainly to journalists associated with health issues. Lottery funding was granted for a research grant into cancer prevention. This received good publicity.

Cause Related Marketing (the use of sponsorship) is looked at with care. WCRF UK is anxious not to be seen to be endorsing directly related manufacturers' products in return for funds. However, funding from for example the Department of Health sponsoring WCRF UK's Cancer Prevention Week and the 'Fruity Friday' campaign are considered acceptable.

Sales promotion activity is organised by the fundraising department, whose brief is to obtain the fundraising support of volunteers, community fundraisers, events participants, schools, trusts, corporates, supporters and the general public.

Selling depends upon the Supporter Services Department at HQ, who support fundraising campaigns by making outbound calls to donors, to build a relationship between the charity and the individual groups. The latter distribute educational material to raise awareness of WCRF UK's work.

CONCLUSION

The growth of the organisation depends on fundraising activities, good public relations and sound marketing in the increasingly competitive charity sector. Although direct mail remains an essential source of income for WCRF UK, both fundraising and charitable trust funding of major projects have seen growth. The development of more modern fundraising initiatives, such as Telemarketing campaigns, ensures that the fundraising mix – and subsequent income – remains diverse and not reliant on only one source.

Osborne Books is very grateful to WCRF UK for their help in contributing this Case Study.

Activity 21.9 – promoting a charitable organisation

1   What is the 'message' of the World Cancer Research Fund (WCRF)?

2   Which market segments make up WCRF's target market? Why is there such a difference in the target age groups?

3   What promotional media are used to get the WCRF message across?

4   Why is budgeting for a promotional campaign 'a difficult decision' for a charitable organisation?

5   How does WCRF use public relations and publicity to further its cause?

6   Visit the WCRF website (www.wcrf-uk.org.uk) and identify the ways in which it promotes the charity's cause.

Place Policy

'Place' is the fourth 'P' of the marketing mix. It refers to the need to get the product – whether goods (actual items) or a service – to the customer. This is part of the function of **distribution**, also referred to as **logistics**.

Goods have to be physically delivered to the customer's address or to shops where they can be bought. The provider of a service usually requires the customer to come to him, eg the retailer, the leisure centre or cinema or hotel. A 'Place' (choice of site) policy is therefore required.

The producer of a manufactured item or a service can sell to the customer in two very different ways:

direct sales

Sales can be made direct from the producer to the customer – helped by direct marketing methods (selling through direct response advertising) or using direct personal contact (eg telesales, door-to-door selling, sales force activity or setting up an internet website).

indirect sales

Selling by indirect methods means using an intermediary (middle-person), such as a retailer or agent. In other words, the goods are sent through national (and even international) distribution channels before they reach the consumer. The most common example of this is selling through a shop.

The diagram below illustrates these two methods. The indirect methods are shown in red and the direct method in blue.

DISTRIBUTION OF GOODS FROM A MANUFACTURER

goods passed through intermediaries to final consumers

manufacturer → wholesaler / agent / distributor → retailer → consumer

goods purchased direct by consumers – cutting out the intermediaries

We will look first at direct sales methods.

Direct Sales Methods

Direct sales involve the producer of the goods or service selling direct to the consumer, using 'direct marketing' techniques of direct response to advertising. Direct selling is a major growth area. It benefits both producer and consumer because there are no intermediaries involved who take some of the profit 'margin'. It often makes use of new technology, using a website with a website 'shop' to sell its products to internet shoppers. Visit the shop at www.osbornebooks.co.uk.

Other examples of direct selling are described below.

direct mail – catalogue selling

Here the manufacturer sends a catalogue to the chosen market segments with details of the product and price, and details of how to order. Sports equipment manufacturers and many others use this method.

door-to-door sales

You may have received a home visit from a Betterware rep (www.betterware.co.uk). This company uses commission-only salespersons, each working their area on a regular and reliable time pattern. Catalogues are hand delivered at the first call, orders being taken at the return visit.

Usborne Books at Home

Usborne Books at Home is the direct-selling division of Usborne Publishing in the UK and Europe.

With Usborne Books at Home you can build a profitable home-based business selling books to families, schools, playgroups and workplaces - and earn at least 24% commission on everything you sell.

direct selling from the home – www.usbornebooksathome.co.uk
Note that this company has no connection with Osborne Books.

party selling

Party selling is a very effective way of using amateur sales persons, supervised by a few full time area organisers. Selling parties are held in private homes, with friends of the home owner invited. Product demonstration is followed by order taking, with the 'guests' often feeling obliged to buy. Many products are sold in this way – clothing, jewellery, art products, perfume, children's books and even sex aids.

network selling

Network selling involves an individual making an agreement to sell the product, whilst taking the opportunity to recruit new salespersons into the organisation, who then also recruit new members. Commission and rewards (such as holidays) are paid both on direct sales and also on the sales of the people recruited, and the sales of the people recruited by the people recruited! You can soon see that the person who starts the business will become very well off at the expense of the new recruits.

telesales

Selling by telephoning the prospective customer direct – telesales – has become big business, particularly as databases have become available which pinpoint the type of customer who might be interested in the product concerned. Telephone calls can either be made to existing customers or to new customers ('cold calling').

Businesses have to take care when cold calling because it is illegal to cold call people who have indicated that they do not want to receive calls by registering with the Telephone Preference Service.

direct selling – the 'pros' and 'cons'

Consumers gain the feeling of security by dealing directly with the producer and often a known representative; they also enjoy the benefits of armchair shopping. However, the profusion of junk mail, sales calls by phone or at the door, and friends exerting sales pressure could eventually prove bad for business. Manufacturers gain by cutting out all intermediaries, thus keeping control over pricing, products and after sales service. Using representatives means that they can provide personal customer service.

Indirect Sales Methods

Selling by indirect methods means using an intermediary (middle-person), such as a retailer or agent. Look at the diagram on page 374. You will see that the red arrows represent the traditional selling route where the goods pass through a number of people organisations, each making a profit on the transaction. The chains of supply include:

- **manufacturer – wholesaler – retailer – consumer**

  The local corner shop is an example of this traditional route. The intermediaries all have to share the profit margin and the consumer gets a local service, but often at a higher price.

- **manufacturer – retailer – consumer**

  The growth of retail chains such as Tesco led to direct distribution to retailers. Mail order companies such as Kays, the catalogue company, are also retailers that buy direct from the manufacturer.

■ **manufacturer – agent/distributor – retail store – consumer**

Sometimes a manufacturer will use a nominated agent or distributor to distribute goods to the retail stores or to the final consumer. This can happen

- on a national scale if the manufacturer does not have the resources (or the inclination) to warehouse and distribute its goods

- on an international scale – an exporter of goods will use an agent in another country to organise the distribution of the exported goods

Activity 21.10 – direct and indirect sales methods

1 Identify products which are sold direct to the consumer by the producer, each using a different method of direct sales. In each case describe the method used and the advantages of adopting that method.

2 Identify products which are sold indirectly to the consumer by the producer, each method using different types of intermediary. In each case describe the chain of supply used and the advantages of employing intermediaries.

Remember that a 'product' can include goods or services.

'Place' Policy for Services

Note that consumers use services provided by businesses such as travel firms, theatres, plumbers and insurance companies. People often deal directly with these businesses, many of which have made themselves more available through high street agencies or service collectives, as you will see when you look through the Yellow Pages.

To the service provider who deals with the customer face-to-face, the siting of the place where the service is provided can be critical. Once the leisure facility or hotel has been built it is not going to be moved. Here are some considerations for the choice of site:

■ Accessibility. Can it be reached, by customers and suppliers? Is there good parking in the area? Do many people walk past?

■ Image. The 'right' part of town. Is it suitable and fashionable? Are the neighbouring businesses suitable? Is the area safe for customers?

■ The competition. Should the business be close to them or well away? There are advantages in either – a shopping mall might group together its food outlets, but a department store might wish to be the only one in town.

Evaluating 'Place' policy

As in any business operation, it is important to monitor and evaluate the success of the siting of the business and the distribution methods. If there are problems, action must be taken. It is obviously easier to change distribution methods than it is to move the site of a shop or hotel. This makes it critical to make the right decisions in the first place. Methods of evaluation used include:

- counting sales volumes through the various outlets – and by region if appropriate
- counting 'footfall' – the daily number of people visiting each outlet
- measuring the service levels and efficiency, the cost of intermediaries such as agents and wholesalers, the cost of transport and distribution

Sales trends by region may show the need for more or fewer outlets in an area. Ineffective outlets can be closed and intermediaries can be changed.

Now read the following Case Study of Tesco PLC which in its study of 'Accessibility' highlights many of the issues of 'Place' explained in this chapter. Then carry out the Activities that follow.

Case Study – Tesco, Accessibility and 'Place'

INTRODUCTION

Tesco is the most successful supermarket chain in the UK, and has become so by strong management supported by clear and consistent marketing activity.

Tesco is a huge organisation, but one from which every small retailer

can learn. Retailers have always understood that location is paramount, but at Tesco 'there is a desire to understand all locational aspects of store performance, site potential and consumer behaviour to the benefit of the company as a whole'. Its marketing mix is well coordinated, and although, in this case, we look only at 'Place', this fits solidly into the overall plan.

As with all service industries the choice of 'Place' is critical, because once chosen and acted upon, it cannot be changed without considerable cost to the company and inconvenience to the customer.

DEVELOPMENT STRATEGY

Tesco rate 'Place' decisions so highly that it has a permanent 'Site Research Unit' as part of its Marketing Department, looking at new store development as well as extensions to and refurbishment of existing ones. Tesco covers all of the UK, but still reviews the market for new opportunities to serve customers. These may occur in parts of a city, a whole town, or a group of villages. Where a suitable opportunity

a Tesco Express supermarket

is found through research, then the decision is made as to the type of outlet to be opened, such as Tesco Express (a small convenience store), a standard supermarket, or Tesco Extra (a large store).

RESEARCH

Research is a fundamental part of the decision making process, and the increased accuracy of sales forecasting techniques has become an essential part of any site acquisition decision. Locational expertise has been developed in databases, and by spatial modelling and statistical analysis. The company now has an intimate knowledge of the retail geography of the UK, including both grocery and non-grocery based opportunities.

Some key information comes from outside research agencies. The national Census is a starting point, but this occurs only every ten years and so becomes rapidly out of date. However, the census spawned many other valuable 'continuous research' projects which were undertaken by established market research firms, to whose work Tesco subscribes.

'Mosaic' is a geodemographic classification system resulting from a statistical clustering exercise of various demographic variables. Each household is categorised as one of 11 key 'lifestyles', such as 'leafy suburbs', inter-war semis', 'depressed council housing' etc. These give a profile of any existing or planned store's catchment area, and combined with in-house 'digitised road network' information, Tesco is able to determine market potential for a wide range of products, for any given location.

One key in-house database details competitor information relating to size, grid reference and address for every foodstore in Great Britain of over 5,000 square feet in area. In addition, most of the larger (over 10,000 sq.ft) stores have been visited, and detailed knowledge has been collected on issues such as number of checkouts, car park type and amount of selling space devoted to non-food.

Decisions to move a store do have to be made occasionally, where market circumstances have changed, or where space for expansion is not available.

National and local planning regulations are a further factor in the above. The current trend is for 'in town' rejuvenation and away from green field development. Government policies to 'get people out of car dependency' also affects the above. These are taken into account.

ACCESSIBILITY AND COMPETITION

For a store to be placed in a new area, demand factors are researched. These relate to the area's potential in terms of affluence (spending power) and mobility (car ownership and public transport). Clearly the amount of direct competition in the area is a factor, but Tesco know their offer is popular with customers. 'Brand appeal' is researched. This means that although consumer research states that Tesco is the most popular brand, just how far will consumers travel to action this preference? – if Sainsbury or Kwiksave were the nearest store, how near would Tesco need to be for consumers to forego the convenience of the nearer store? Distance lessens the attraction. Because of this, Tesco have computerised models to predict customer behaviour and locational decision making – these models help them to understand how a new store will trade.

the right part of town

Customer safety is built into the planning, with adequate lighting in the car parks and security staff on hand. Tesco have successfully developed a network of Regeneration Partnerships, demonstrating how new markets can be created, even in the most deprived communities.

the right neighbours

There are two points here. For the out-of-town stores, retail parks often present attractive opportunities, where other buying experiences will attract shoppers. Quality stores such as Marks and Spencer are considered good neighbours. For the 'in-town' site the High Street is preferred, with its prominence and high 'walk past' rate; alternatively, nearness to public transport facilities and/or car parks is seen as important. For the smaller Express stores, local shopping centres are normally chosen.

a traditional 'red brick' Tesco Store

the building

High quality architecture is the norm and standardisation is the key, so that regular customers visiting other towns recognise a Tesco Store and are reassured by the continuity. Change does occur over time however, as fashions and consumer views change. Those of you used to the 'red brick' style with the pitched roof might be surprised to visit another area and see the more modern stores with large glass frontages, allowing natural light to permeate the building. Signage and window displays are consistent across the UK. Once again, local planning regulations may affect style.

Accessibility is again a major factor. Entrance to, and exit from, the car park could cause frustration and prevent a return visit. This is considered in the planning, as is the car park spacing and the general look of the site. Trees, shrubs, litter bins and good signage all influence the customer, and are arranged to this end. The entrance to a store must not create congestion, or difficulties in manoeuvring trolleys and pushchairs. With this in mind, Tesco endeavour to ensure entrances are spacious and uncluttered.

Inside the store the key is ambience – the feeling of well being for the customer which leads to increased spending and return visits. This will come from a mixture of suitable lighting, heating, eye pleasing layouts, smell, and noise levels, but a modern key factor is the additional facilities built into the stores. Pharmacies, baby changing rooms and coffee shops are all part of the customer experience. Lengths of queues at checkouts are monitored at local level, to support Tesco's policy of 'One in Front' – aiming to ensure there is never more than one customer queuing in front of another.

'One in Front' at the checkout

Cost is a factor in all business decisions, and affects 'where to build' in terms of land prices. The latter however are often symptomatic of the wealth and spending power of the area, and so this is taken into consideration. Budgets are set for building costs, but again will be influenced by area.

The decision to erect a new store is only taken after painstaking research that leaves little to chance.

Osborne Books is very grateful to Tesco PLC for their help in contributing this Case Study.

Activity 21.11 – Tesco and 'Place'

1 Identify the three main types of Tesco store. Why do they vary so much in size?

2 Describe the 'Mosaic' geodemographic classification system. Explain why it is so important to the planning of Tesco stores and the products that they stock.

3 How does Tesco monitor the 'Place' policy of its main competitors?

4 Identify the 'Accessibility' factors that Tesco considers when planning the location of a new store.

5 Describe the 'in-store' factors that Tesco sees as being important to its customers.

CHAPTER SUMMARY

- This chapter has examined the last two of the four P's of the marketing mix: promotion and place. These must be linked to product and price to form an integrated strategy.

- 'Promotion' policy requires that organisations must communicate with their target consumers using a range of promotional techniques that tie in with the corporate image or 'brand'.

- These techniques include advertising, branding, packaging, publicity, public relations, merchandising, sponsorship and direct marketing.

- Organisations must approach the right audience, with a co-ordinated message, at the right time, and within agreed budget limits.

- The message must stress the benefits of the product or service.

- Sponsorship helps promote a product as part of a Cause Related Marketing (CRM) campaign.

- Sales promotions (special offers) and merchandising (the location and appearance of the product in a sales outlet) both attract the customer in a sales outlet.

- Direct marketing asks the customer to respond immediately to an advert (eg by phone, post or internet).

- The one-to-one sales approach and the need for fixed outlets are declining in the face of selling by email and internet, but businesses still need to choose between direct and indirect (the use of intermediaries) routes to the consumer.

- The internet allows the small firm to reach large geographical areas without needing fixed site outlets or agents, but it still requires a distribution method to move the goods to the customer.

- Effective customer service cannot be achieved without an efficient back-up internal and external administration system.

- 'Place' policy involves getting the product to the customer, a process known as distribution or logistics.

- 'Place' policy either uses direct sales (where the sale is made direct to the customer) or uses indirect sales where intermediaries such as agents or wholesalers are employed.

- 'Place' policy requires service providers to make sure that the site of premises is accessible, has the right 'image' and takes account of the competition.

KEY TERMS

promotion	techniques which create awareness of a product and persuade the consumer to make a buying decision
advertising	the most persuasive selling message to the right people at the lowest possible cost and at the right time
branding	a name or logo that distinguishes a product or organisation from others
corporate image	the overall image of an organisation to the public
packaging	the physical wrapping around a product that attracts attention at the point of sale, or the 'bundling' of services
publicity	news coverage for a product, not paid for by the seller
public relations	safeguarding and promoting the image of a product or company
sponsorship	associating a product or company with a team or event
sales promotion	a technique for creating interest in a product using a special offer over a limited time period
merchandising	displaying a product at the point of sale, or the outlet itself, in an attractive manner to encourage consumers to buy
product presentation	combining the skills of packaging, display, merchandising and choice of outlet or site
direct marketing	persuading the consumer to respond to an advert by placing an order immediately by phone, post or email
direct selling	supplying directly to the customer without using intermediaries such as retailers, agents or wholesalers
indirect selling	supplying the customer using intermediaries
sales campaign	an organised sales effort to achieve a specific objective over a specific time period
customer service	looking after the needs of customers – giving information, after sales service and providing solutions for problems in a courteous way
place	the methods of getting the product (whether goods or a service) to the customer – using distribution and either direct or indirect sales methods

Unit 4

Investigating electronic business

Welcome to the World's Worst Website!

...signed to graphically demonstrate the most common mistakes made by new ...

Where am I and where are the links to other pages?

An easy to use navigation structure is essential to any well designed website! Important information should never be more than 2 clicks away.

As you can see, this text is difficult to read. There needs to more contrast between the background color and the text color. Here's another example of a poor choice of a background text color and size

Keep your backgrounds simple. White or light colors usually work best. Your background should not compete with the content of the page for the users attention. If you would like to use a background picture, select a picture that uses muted colors or format your picture as a watermark. Select text colors which will contrast well with the background picture.

Constantly running animations can be distracting when used excessively. There should be no more than one animated object in your view at any time. Also in this category are...

TV BOXSETS
SAVE UPTO 70%

THE HITCHHIKERS GUIDE TO THE GALAXY
SAVE UP TO 40%

Ed's Perfect Pizzas

Menu
Special Offers
Location
Home

Welcome t...

We **deliver to** Worcester. Ou...

- Monday t...
- Saturday midnight

Call our order
- 0800 123 4...

Our Menu

In this unit you will investigate a variety of websites which have been set up by organisations to promote their products and services. You are likely to see examples of good design and poor design. You will learn how to assess these sites and also how to plan and build your own site. You will research:

- the purposes of a website and the ways in which a website can help an organisation achieve its aims and objectives

- the impact that a website has on the organisation, its customers, suppliers, competitors and employees

- the features that make a website a 'good' website

- the factors an organisation will need to consider when setting up a website

- the practicalities of planning and building a simple website

Chapters in this Unit...

Pizzas Delivered to

Order Hotline **080**

izzas

base in

Want to collect your

.m.
2

your order

Click to look at our m.
we are

Special Offers

22

The purpose and impact of a website

Starting point

It is said that a website is increasingly becoming a 'must have' for an organisation, and particularly for a business which has to compete for its survival.

But why should a website be so important? It could be argued that while some businesses such as Amazon 'are' their websites, other businesses do not need them to such an extent.

What is it that a website achieves for a business? What makes a good website and a bad website?

What you will learn from this chapter

■ an effective website should fulfil a number of different purposes for the business – these involve helping it to achieve its aims and objectives, particularly sales and profit maximisation, and providing a high level of customer service

■ the areas in which a website can be effective in this way include:
- providing detailed and accessible product information globally on a 24 hour, 7 day a week basis
- allowing customers to purchase goods and services and to provide feedback

■ a website will have substantial impact, not only on its customers, but also on its other stakeholders: employees, suppliers and competitors

■ it is useful to establish 'benchmark' checklists of what makes a 'good' website and also what constitute the characteristics of a 'bad' website

Requirements of your Assessment

the internet jungle

Unit 4 'Investigating electronic business' is a very practical Unit, requiring you to spend a considerable time online navigating your way through and analysing a wide variety of websites, and then planning your own website.

One aspect of the internet is that it lacks any form of discrimination: excellent sites and bad sites jostle for your attention and, apart from your own judgement, there is no way of telling them apart. It is as if a bookshop decided to stock every single book on the planet on any particular subject leaving you decide which is the best book on, say, sushi or salmon farming. The internet can be a real jungle in which only effective websites succeed.

This Unit is designed to enable you to appreciate the way in which an effectively designed website can help promote the products or services of a business and enable it to fulfil its aims and objectives.

your assessment

The Unit assessment requires you to provide evidence in four areas:

(a) **Compare the websites of two organisations to assess to what extent they fulfil the purpose of an online presence.**

This will involve learning about the purposes of a website, eg promoting a business and its products or services and helping it to meet its sales and profit targets. It will also require you to investigate a wide variety of websites and choose two for comparison to see how successful they are in promoting the business. The two chosen websites should ideally be an effective one and a less than perfect one.

(b) **Evaluate one of the two chosen websites and make recommendations for improving it.**

To produce this evidence it is suggested that you look critically at the less successful of the two websites and make practical recommendations for improving it.

Areas (a) and (b) are covered in this chapter. The remaining two areas (c) and (d) are covered in the next chapter, which deals with the issues of setting up a website by a new business and explains how you can plan and set up your own working website.

These further assessment requirements are explained in detail on page 411.

the Purpose of an Online Presence

the growth of the internet

It is easy to take websites for granted and to assume that every organisation must have one, but it is important to have a sense of historical perspective. The use of the **internet** by a wide range of organisations is a comparatively recent development, and until this development took place, organisations relied very effectively on 'bricks and mortar' premises, face-to-face meetings, written and telephoned communications and printed information for functions such as:

- providing product and service information
- providing advice
- shopping
- providing after-sales support

This all worked very well, but as you will appreciate, the introduction of websites changed the way businesses operated. The internet, which in effect enables an organisation to set up a virtual electronic 'reality' which appears on computer screens worldwide, altered consumers' perception of organisations. It introduced the expectation that any organisation should have a website, just as it has a postal address.

Who needs to access a website? There is a wide range of website connections which you will need to investigate. These are listed below and shown in the diagram. Note the 'text' style abbreviations in brackets:

- government departments which advise and regulate businesses (g2b)
- government departments which advise consumers (g2c)
- businesses which buy from and sell to other businesses (b2b)
- businesses which provide information and sell to consumers (b2c)

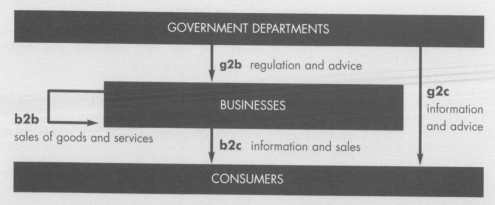

WEBSITE USAGE

GOVERNMENT DEPARTMENTS

g2b regulation and advice

BUSINESSES

g2c information and advice

b2b sales of goods and services

b2c information and sales

CONSUMERS

Activity 22.1 – types of website

Access the internet and use search engines to find examples of all the types of website listed below. In each case explain briefly the purpose of the organisation concerned.

1 Government websites which either advise or regulate businesses.

2 Government websites which provide information and advice to consumers.

3 Business websites which provide goods and services to other businesses.

4 Business websites which provide goods and services to consumers.

is a website really necessary to a business?

There is a danger in assuming that all businesses need a website. Some do – Amazon and eBay, for example – because without a website this type of **e-commerce** business will be unable to operate. E-commerce simply means conducting business online. Other smaller and more local businesses such as the laundrette around the corner are unlikely to benefit from an internet presence – they rely on local custom and operate solely from their physical premises in the locality. A laundrette customer would not expect to have a duvet dry-cleaned online.

There is a middle ground, however, occupied by retail and services businesses – selling, for example, CDs and holidays – which stand to benefit from the opportunities offered by a website. These opportunities help to promote many of the business aims and objectives you will already have studied in Chapter 2. The question to be asked when assessing these websites is 'How successful are they in supporting business aims and objectives?'

website support of business aims and objectives

The table below lists a number of the commonly recognised business aims and objectives and shows how a website can help to promote them.

OBJECTIVE	ways in which a website can promote objectives
increasing sales globally	■ providing full details of products and services, 24 hours a day, 7 days a week worldwide, and increasing the customer base ■ providing an online shopping facility so that the goods can be supplied direct and on a worldwide basis
maximising profit	■ reduction in costs by selling direct rather than using intermediaries such as wholesalers – the end result being higher margins for the business

attracting new staff	■ a 'vacancies' or 'recruitment' section on a website is often used by businesses, some of whom also provide the facility for online job applications
improving customer service	■ most websites have a 'Contact Us' page for customer feedback; some have online questionnaires to refine the information; online shops sometimes have a 'Where is my order?' facility
cost cutting	■ direct selling from a website can reduce the cost of employing sales staff
	■ the use of a website can avoid costly premises – offices can be set up in out-of-town locations and warehousing costs can be reduced
	■ the cost of promotion can be reduced as there is less reliance on expensive printed brochures which have to be distributed
increasing efficiency	■ stockholding by retail websites can be reduced to a minimum because reordering from suppliers can be carried out automatically and electronically
	■ online payment systems mean that payments can be received more rapidly, which will improve the cash-flow position of the business

the purpose of a website

An analysis of the objectives listed in the table above shows that a website can fulfil a number of purposes which will help to make a business more effective in a competitive market:

■ communication is improved

A website can provide a business presence which is immediately and very visibly available 24 hours a day, 7 days a week ('24/7') throughout the world. A combination of easily-read text and images can promote the corporate image. Websites can be set up in a number of different languages (eg an airline such as www.easyjet.com – see below). Communication can be made to the business by email or by telephone.

How would you like your easyJet.com?

Comment aimerez vous votre easyJet.com?

¿Cómo desea su easyJet.com?

www.easyjet.com

■ flexibility of location

A website effectively brings a business into the home, enabling the consumer to obtain information and buy products such as a book, DVD or holiday. An online presence also provides flexibility of location to the business. A retail business, for example, does not have to rely so heavily on prime 'High Street' locations. Some retail organisations, such as www.amazon.co.uk, sell exclusively online and have flexibility of choice in siting their administration and warehousing. This can result in great efficiencies of cost.

Fulfilment Centre: Marston Gate, Milton Keynes
Marston Gate is 20 minutes from Luton Airport and a short walk from the Thames Link rail service. Located at Junction 13 on the M1, our impressive fulfilment centre is easily accessible to most motorways.

www.amazon.co.uk

■ being user-friendly and responsive

An important area of customer service is the need for business employees to be welcoming, informative and helpful. As there is no direct human contact online, the website should be easy to use and provide plenty of opportunity for feedback, on a 'Contact Us' page, for example. An online sales website should ideally contain features such as FAQ (Frequently Asked Questions) pages and 'Where is my stuff?' order tracking and account access facilities.

Thank you for your order.
We will send you an e-mail confirmation shortly.

Note: If you ordered several items to be delivered to the same address, we may send them to you in separate packages to give you the fastest service. This will not affect your delivery charges.

Manage Your Order
- Track the status of this order
- Remove items from this order
- Edit Delivery Method
- Apply a gift certificate to your account
- Add giftwrap and write a free message
- See the status of all your orders

www.amazon.co.uk

■ giving information about the organisation

One marketing advantage of a website is that a comparatively small business with a well-constructed website providing plenty of information can appear 'larger' than it actually is, a factor which can help persuade customers to make the buying decision.

Readily accessible, up-to-date information is essential on a website. If you are buying a camera, for example, a good retail website will provide you with prices, illustrations, technical specifications and links to reviews.

People browsing the internet may want to know about the business which operates from a website. An 'About Us' (or equivalent) button can be found on many sites, leading to pages which provide information about the type of business, its customers, markets served, and, even in some cases, its financial results. Visit the 'Corporate Information' link at www.johnlewis.com

Activity 22.2 – the functions of a website

The website page extracts shown on this and the next page illustrate the various functions carried out by a website.

Analyse and discuss the pages shown here and describe the ways in which they:

(a) support the aims and objectives of a business (eg making a profit, maximising sales, cost cutting etc)

(b) are user-friendly and effective in communicating to the prospective customer

(c) overcome the barriers of location

(d) offer high standards of customer service

(e) provide information about the business

Not all of the pages shown carry out all of these functions. You should, where possible, select individual pages to illustrate individual points.

John Lewis Partnership

Home Page · Contact Us

About Us · Careers · Corporate Social Responsibility · Customers · Education · Financial · Media Centre · Suppliers ·

The John Lewis Partnership is one of the UK's top ten retail businesses with 26 John Lewis department stores and more than 166 Waitrose supermarkets. It is also the country's largest example of worker co-ownership. All 63,000 permanent staff are Partners in the business. We believe that the commitment of Partners to the business is a unique source of competitive advantage which has fuelled 75 years of profitable growth and a reputation amongst customers and suppliers unparalleled in the UK retail industry.

www.johnlewis.com

CONTACT ▶

Home | About Us | Catalogue | Shop | Resources | Contact | News & Views   Search

How To Find Us

osborne BOOKS

Contact Osborne Books

Tel: **01905 748071**

We welcome your queries, suggestions and comments about this site, our products and our service.

If you would like to contact Osborne Books you can do so through this form. Alternatively you can use the email link at the bottom of the page.

If you would like to receive updates on our site, products and special offers, please click here.

www.osbornebooks.co.uk

play.com

Corporate Social Responsibility

Trust, honesty, participation, ethical values and a written constitution that requires good environmental practice are the unique elements that make the John Lewis Partnership Britain's most successful employee-owned business.

'The Partnership was ahead of its time in recognising that commercial success depended on showing the highest level of good citizenship in its behaviour within the community. Today we are best known for the fact that our business is owned for the benefit of our employees, but we know that to cut our way through tough competitive conditions, we have to continue to prize sound relationships with our customers and suppliers, and sustain a keen sense of civic responsibility.'

Sir Stuart Hampson, Chairman of the John Lewis Partnership

A different sort of job

www.johnlewis.com

Welcome to the John Lewis Partnership (JLP) recruitment portal, your resource for discovering the wealth of jobs and careers available within John Lewis department stores, Waitrose food shops, and John Lewis Partnership headquarters and Management Services (our IT division).

The John Lewis Partnership is Britain's biggest and longest-surviving example of industrial democracy and worker co-ownership. All permanent employees are Partners in the business, enjoying a share in its success.

Please click on one of the images below to explore the opportunities.

Job Opportunities

For vacancies ranging from shop floor assistant to specialist roles.

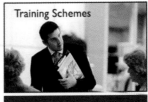

Training Schemes

For graduates to school leavers, retail development and vocational training.

the Impact made by a Website

your assessment requirements

The first part of your Unit assessment requires you to:

- investigate a wide variety of websites
- compare two websites – ideally an effective one and one which has some room for improvement
- make recommendations for the improvement of one of the websites – by implication this means the less successful of the two

We have already looked at the way in which a website helps a business achieve its aims and objectives. We will now take a more critical view of the 'pros and cons' – the advantages and disadvantages – of a website presence as it affects the business and its stakeholders – customers, suppliers and competitors.

A useful assessment technique which can be applied to a website presence is a **SWOT analysis** which weighs up:

- **S**trengths – the resources and benefits provided by an online presence
- **W**eaknesses – the skills and resources shortfall for having a website
- **O**pportunities – the way in which a website opens up new possibilities for products and promotion
- **T**hreats – from competitors or from hackers

the impact of an online presence on a business

Strengths and **opportunities** include:

- **increased enquiries** – a growing number of 'hits' received by prospective customers visiting the site and requesting brochures and quotations – all of which can be measured electronically by the web server, leading to:
- **increased customer base** – from a wider geographic coverage available 24 hours a day, attracted by search engines and by online shopping facilities, leading to:
- **increased sales** – from competitive pricing and rapid delivery
- **increased profit** – made possible by selling direct to the customer and increasing margins by avoiding intermediaries
- **reduction in costs** – made possible by moving administration and warehousing to the less expensive areas where rental and wages levels are lower

Weaknesses and threats of operating a website include:

- **technical requirements** – the need for costly technical expertise to set up and operate the site

- **training needs** – the requirements for training staff who have to deal with the demands of electronic trading

- **security** – the dangers of outsiders 'hacking' into the website, damaging it with viruses, putting it out of action or stealing sensitive information by breaking through a firewall into the company intranet

- **credit card fraud** – the dangers of customers refusing to use an online shop because they are worried about their credit card details being stolen

- **being impersonal** – the removal of the 'personal touch' achieved by selling a product or service on a face-to-face basis

- **losing direct customer feedback** – providing information and trading online can reduce the customer feedback about product and service that is so valuable to the marketing team

All these SWOT factors will have to be weighed up in assessing the impact on a business of establishing a website.

Generally speaking, an online presence will be more advantageous to a larger business – with or without a 'High Street' presence – which deals with commonly used products and services. A business that relies on the personal touch, where the product is individual to the customer, will find a website to be a useful reference point (like Yellow Pages) but will receive fewer of the benefits listed on the previous page. Hairdressing and landscape gardening are examples of this type of business.

Activity 22.3 – customer perception of websites

Devise a survey to assess what the public think about businesses that have an online presence.

Questions could be asked to find out how many people have access to the internet, how many use it for information and how many for making purchases. Issues raised could include the fear of using a debit or credit card online, the lack of personal contact and the worry that if an item such as a DVD is purchased, there will be limited after-sales service. Remember that purchases will normally be limited to people who are aged 18 or over.

Discuss your findings in class and use the points raised to help you in your assessment of websites.

longer-term problems of a website

One of the main problems of a website is that, unlike a printed catalogue which is binned when it is out of date, it sits on the server and has to be updated regularly. There is nothing more off-putting for a visitor to a website to find that product information and prices are out of date and that there are news items dating from 1999 looking forward to the Millennium.

An out-of-date website can:

- lose a business its customers – they will lose confidence in it
- reduce the number of visits from other businesses – they too will lose confidence in it and will not want to deal with it
- demotivate its staff who will see better sites run by competitors

For a website to be effective and attractive to visitors, it must be monitored and updated regularly. This can be a time-consuming and costly operation, but it is essential.

the impact of an online presence on stakeholders

The impact of an online presence on the **stakeholders** of a business – its customers, suppliers and competitors – is also significant to the SWOT analysis, as the activity above will have shown.

The **customers** of a business, for example, see websites as a convenient method of doing their banking, making a purchase or obtaining information and a quote. Because of the normally rapid response to an order and delivery of an item purchased on the internet, customers now expect a 'next day' service. They also expect detailed product information, guidance and recommendations: 'If you bought this CD, you will also like this one . . .' Some websites have been established to compare the location and prices of retailers to help the consumer. Enter the description 'digital cameras' in a search engine or in www.kelkoo.co.uk, for example.

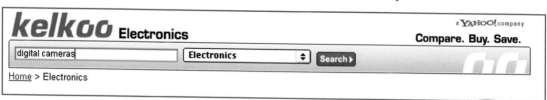

Competitors of a business will also benefit from examining its website. Competitors can monitor prices – 'We will equal that price'. One of the effects of price monitoring is to drive prices down – as in the low-cost airline market – and this will put pressure on existing providers.

Competitors can also copy products – 'They have got a great idea there, we can copy it'. The number of competitors will therefore increase when entrepreneurs realise that a certain website is very successful. This will also help to drive prices down.

Suppliers of a business can also benefit from it having an online presence. On a practical basis, the ordering and payment systems can be linked up through EDI (Electronic Data Interchange) which leads to efficiencies and cost cutting. Suppliers may even become competitors of the businesses they supply and sell direct online themselves.

Website Essentials

Part of your Unit assessment requires you to compare two websites and then analyse one of them. In order for you to surf the internet and identify suitable sites for comparison, you need to appreciate exactly what features are needed for an effective website. We will approach this in two stages, providing checklists at each stage.

The stages are:

1   Providing **a guide to website essentials** so that you can make an informed comparison between two sites and assess to what extent they fulfil the purpose of an online presence – this basically comprises lists of the pages a site *should* have and pages that it *could* have.

2   Providing a **critical checklist** so that you can identify the shortcomings of one of the chosen sites and make recommendations for its improvement – this is more technical in nature and also includes a list of website 'do nots'.

a guide to website essentials

The basic structure of a website should always include a home page, an 'About Us' page, a 'Contact Us' page and details of the product or service provided by the business.

BASIC STRUCTURE: PAGES A WEBSITE SHOULD HAVE

HOME PAGE

↕ link   ↕ link   ↕ link

| ABOUT US a description of the business | CONTACT US direct email and telephone details | PRODUCTS/SERVICES full descriptions, prices and appropriate details of the products or services provided |

website feature pages

The structure and content of a website will depend on the nature of the organisation presented on the site. The website of a local pizza home delivery business will be very different from that of a major insurance company or supermarket chain. When you are assessing and comparing sites you need to bear this very much in mind.

The diagram below shows some of the possible pages featured on a site, grouped in boxes related to the functions which they fulfil.

FEATURES: PAGES A WEBSITE COULD HAVE

ABOUT US
- map and directions — to direct visitors to the business
- FAQ (Frequently Asked Questions) — to provide customer service information
- jobs available — to help recruitment
- environmental policies — to promote the business aim of sustainability
- community involvement — to promote the business aim of social responsibility

SALES
- online shop
- special offers

both of these will promote direct sales and so increase profit

MARKETING
- news items — to provide publicity and promote PR
- customer feedback — for both customer service and market research

NAVIGATION
- site map
- site search

both of these will make the site user-friendly

ADDED VALUE FEATURES
- tips and guides
- quizzes
- competitions
- free pictures
- links to sites for software downloads

all these features are designed to attract new customers to the site

LEGAL SECTION
- privacy statement — how personal data will be kept confidential
- accessibility statement — how the site can be used by disabled people
- terms and conditions — disclaimer against errors on the site, copyright

Activity 22.4 – assessing two websites

As part of your Unit assessment you have to identify two sites for comparison. You can do this by taking guidance and suggestions from your business studies teacher or by entering topics that interest you in search engines.

It is important that you choose a website that is effective in illustrating the purposes of an online presence and also one that needs work doing to it because it is lacking in certain areas. You will need to discuss your choices with your teacher. The diagrams on pages 397 and 398 will give you an idea of the features of a standard website.

You will need – either on your own, or in a group – to devise a list of criteria against which to make your judgement about the chosen sites.

As a reminder, the aspects of the websites that you have to consider in your comparison are shown below. These aspects have already been covered in this chapter.

■ Do the websites support the achievement of business aims and objectives, for example sales maximisation and profit maximisation?

■ Do the websites provide effective communication, geographically, 24/7 and visually?

■ Are the sites user-friendly and ready to provide information?

■ Do the sites give adequate information about the business?

Improving a Website

a benchmark

When you have chosen the website for which you are to suggest improvements you will need some form of benchmark against which to measure the site.

We have already on the last two pages given a general overview of the features required on a website. In the remainder of the chapter we provide further guidance in the form of:

■ a **good website guide** – features of good structure and design

■ a **website danger list** – a list of some of the less successful features of websites, which will be useful in enabling you to suggest improvements to the less successful sites

This guide and danger list will also help you when you come to plan and design your own website in the other part of your Unit assessment.

THE GOOD WEBSITE GUIDE

A site should have a registered business domain name

Q Does the business website use a registered domain name, www.domainname.co.uk for example, rather than a name issued by an internet service provider, for example www.companyname.demon.co.uk?

A site should be easy to locate on the internet

Q Is the website easy to find using the major search engines?

Q Have other techniques been used to draw visitors to the site, eg using a links page to build reciprocal links to other sites?

A site should be quick to load

Q Is the web-hosting service reliable, able to serve pages to viewers without delays and is it continually available?

Q Does the first page of the website take less than 10 seconds to load over a dial-up modem?

Q Are the following features slow to download:
 - video?
 - animation?
 - sound?

A website should be consistent with corporate identity

Q Is the company or organisation's logo in the same prominent place on each page of the website?

Q Is the general design of the website in keeping with all other promotional material such as brochures and adverts (if available)?

Q Do the colours used in the website reflect those used in the logo and other marketing materials

Q Has an identifying Mission Statement or strapline been used?

The play.com website (see next page) always has the company's logo in the top left-hand corner of the screen together with its strapline 'Movies Music Games'. The orange and blue colours used in the logo are also used in the navigation menu bar and for highlighted areas of text.

Is the site accessible to all users?

Q Does the site work using the web browsers on all types of computer, eg PCs and Macs?

Q Does the site work for people using older web-browser software?

Q Is there any information available on the website telling viewers of the steps taken to make sure that the website is accessible to all users, and that the site complies with the Disability Discrimination Act?

The Lloyds Bank website www.lloydstsb.com has a useful section on accessibility. The page shown below describes the steps taken to make sure everyone can use the site.

Are there contact details?

Q Are contact details readily available on every page of the site?

Q Are the different ways of contacting a company clear and easy to understand?

The 'Contact Us' link is available in the same place on every page of the play.com website. In addition to complete contact details, including phone numbers, email addresses and opening hours, the contact page shows the most frequently asked questions that may be able to help viewers immediately.

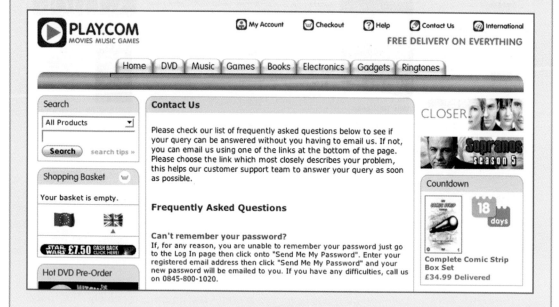

Are photos and illustrations used effectively?

Q Are the graphics used in a site sharp enough and large enough to show their subject properly?

Q Is there an opportunity to make pictures larger using a pop-up magnifying window, eg for illustrations of products?

Q Is the text used within an illustration large enough to read?

Is animation used appropriately?

Q If there is animation, is it necessary?

Q If animation is used, is it too distracting to ignore?

Q Does animation improve the viewer's focus on one important area?

Q Is animation slowing down the website because it takes a long time to download?

The play.com home page (see page 401) uses animation sparingly, which makes concentrating on the offers they are providing easier for viewers. The quality of the graphics is excellent.

Is the text of good quality?

Q Has the text been written so that it is in plain English and is easy to understand?

Q Is the text in a clear font (typeface) and a reasonable size so that it can be read easily?

Q Does the text colour contrast with the background colour to make it easy to read?

Q Are there any spelling mistakes?

Q Are bullet points used to present important information?

Q Can long blocks of text be printed out or downloaded for reading off-screen?

Q Where technical terms are used, has a glossary or other explanatory feature been used?

Is the home page simple and effective?

Q Is the home page used to highlight the most important areas of the site?

Q Is there too much information on the home page making it busy and difficult to use?

Navigation and structure – is it easy to move around the site?

for all sites:

Q Is the main menu bar consistent and in the same position on every page?

Q Can viewers use links within a section to go to other pages within that section without having to return to the home page?

Q Are links clear and easy to identify?

Q Do links say where they link to?

Q Are the names of links to different sections of the website easy to understand, eg 'Contact' leads to a page that contains contact details?

Q Is any information more than 2 or 3 clicks away from the home page of a website?

Q Do all the links to other pages in the site work?

and for larger sites:

Q Is there a site map showing viewers all the pages in the website?

Q If there is a search facility, does it work effectively, ie can you find what you are looking for?

Q Is there a breadcrumb trail showing where you are in the web site with links back up to the home page? A 'breadcrumb trail' is an onscreen tracking of the route through the various menus from the home page to the current page (see below):

This example of a breadcrumb trail shows how the details of a battery charger (and other pages) are reached from the Home Page.

Is the website content fresh?

Q Is the information on the website up-to-date, eg products and prices?

Q Are there recent news articles and has old information been removed?

Is helper software made available?

Q Is additional software that may be needed to read information – eg Adobe Acrobat – provided on the website, or a link provided so that it can be downloaded?

Is the website secure?

Q Does a padlock appear in web-browser software when secure information such as credit card details is being asked for?

Q Are viewers told that their information is secure?

Q If a padlock in the web browser is double clicked, does a security certificate from a reputable company, eg Thawte or VeriSign appear?

The play.com server shown on the next page is secure. There is a padlock icon at the bottom of the web browser. play.com also uses part of the page to display the VeriSign logo and state that shopping is secure.

VeriSign security logo   padlock security icon

Does the website comply with all relevant legal requirements?

Q Does the website provide access to a privacy policy where data is collected, eg via a contact form (Data Protection Act)?

Q Is there an opt-out opportunity if the user does not want to receive marketing emails?

If the website has an online shop, does it comply with the UK Distance Selling Regulations, a selection of which are referred to below?

Q Is the consumer given clear information about the goods or services offered?

Q Is the seller's name and postal address available?

Q Is the consumer sent confirmation after making a purchase?

Q Is the consumer aware of a cooling-off period of 7 working days?

Q Is the consumer aware of the right to return the goods within that period?

Q Are prices and delivery costs shown, including all taxes?

Q Are the arrangements for payment available?

Q What are the arrangements and date(s) for delivery?

the Website Danger List

As part of your analysis of websites you will need to be able to recognise bad practice as well as good practice. The 'danger list' on the next two pages highlights some of the world's worst website practices.

There are a number of websites which can explain features of poor design and provide links to some of the best examples of the 'world's worst' websites. Visit the following:

■ www.webpagesthatsuck.com

■ http://www.angelfire.com/super/badwebs/main.htm

A screen from the angelfire site is shown on the next page. The limitations of a book page unfortunately (or fortunately!) do not allow you to appreciate the irritation factor provided by really bad animations.

THE WEBSITE DANGER LIST

Q Is the website stored with a free web-hosting service that may not provide a good quality of service and may result in the website being unavailable for periods of time?

A free hosting service usually results in a website address that bears no relation to the name of the company whose website is being looked at.

Q Is a splash page (a page in front of a home page) used which may cause viewers to become frustrated with a site and leave?

Q If a splash page has to be used, is there a way of bypassing it?

Q If animation is used, is there a means to switch it off?

Q Has provision been made for viewers with older web-browser software on a site where cutting edge technology has been used in a website?

Q Is there too much information on each page of the website?

Q Is all of the content in the site strictly necessary? Examples of possibly superfluous information include:

■ world news

■ current weather and pollen count in Arizona

■ third-party advertising

Q Are there banners encouraging viewers to leave the site for another site?

Q Is there background music – which cannot be turned off?

Q Is there a patterned, animated background? In order to see the orange screen below and other design horrors, visit http://www.angelfire.com/super/badwebs/main.htm

Activity 22.5 – analysing strengths and weaknesses

Your assessment requires you to analyse one of the websites you have chosen and to identify strengths and weaknesses.

It is suggested you use both the checklists presented in the text to provide you with criteria which you can build into your own checklist.

To achieve higher marks you should concentrate on the detail provided in your analysis and recommendations rather than just providing a long list.

CHAPTER SUMMARY

■ The dramatic growth in the number of websites has led to the common perception that all organisations should have an online presence.

■ Websites are operated by a wide variety of organisations: government departments that advise businesses and consumers, businesses that sell to other businesses and businesses that sell to consumers.

■ Websites can be used to help fulfil the aims and objectives of businesses, including sales maximisation, profit maximisation, improving customer service, effective recruitment.

■ The aims and objectives of businesses can be fulfilled through a website because an online presence helps to improve communication, provides flexibility for the location of business resources, and can provide up-to-date information in a user-friendly way.

■ The need for a website can usefully be analysed using a SWOT analysis (Strengths, Weaknesses, Opportunities, Threats).

■ The strengths and opportunities of a website include the possibilities for increased enquiries, sales, customer base, profit and reduction in costs.

■ The weaknesses and threats of an online presence, on the other hand, include all the technical requirements of setting up and running a website, the problems of security and the lack of personal, face-to-face contact with the customer. Keeping a website up to date is also a major ongoing task.

■ A website also has a major impact on the stakeholders of a business for a variety of reasons – its customers appreciate its immediacy and convenience, competitors find it a useful source of market information, and suppliers use it to increase efficiency in ordering and payment.

■ It is difficult to state precisely what features a 'good' website should have, but the structure should include a home page, an 'About Us' page, a 'Contact Us' function and full details of products or services. Other features could include a shop, navigation aids, and added value aspects such as free downloads, quizzes and guides.

■ Because of all the technical possibilities of website construction it is all too possible for a website to fail in its objectives of increasing sales and profit. Common failings include information overload, distracting use of animations, over-complex design, poor text layout, inefficient navigation and slow download times. These problems are likely to cause visitors to leave the site.

KEY TERMS

internet	the collection of inter-connected networks linking millions of independent networks into a global network
website	the online presence of an organisation on the internet
e-commerce	conducting business online, including consumer buying and selling, and businesses ordering and making payments through Electronic Data Interchange (EDI)
web browser	a software program on the surfer's computer that is used to look at various kinds of internet resources
home page	the web page that a browser is set to use when it selects the website, also the main web page for a website, referred to as the index page or the default page
splash page	an optional web page which is accessed on connection to the site before the home page appears
'about us'	the pages on a website which contain all the details of the organisation and its employees
'contact us'	the section of a website which enables the visitor to email the organisation; it may also include a postal address and telephone numbers
hit	a single request from a web browser for a single item from a web server, eg a web page, a picture
domain name	the unique name that identifies the address of the internet site; to prevent repetition of domain names, all domain names must be registered
privacy statement	a statement which explains that a UK organisation will use personal data placed on the website in accordance with the Data Protection Act
accessibility statement	a statement which explains how a site is made accessible to people with disabilities
terms and conditions	the terms and conditions of use of the site by the user – a statement which limits the liability of the organisation for errors and states the copyright of the site

23

Setting up a new website

Starting point

A business must ask whether or not it is worth setting up a website and, if it is a feasible option, what sort of website would be suitable.

A business in this position might be a start-up enterprise, such as a specialist retailer planning to sell jazz CDs, or it might be an existing business such as a local landscape gardener who already has a flourishing business.

Both businesses will need to carry out an analysis of the 'pros and cons' of establishing an online presence. If they decide to proceed, their websites are likely to be very different.

What you will learn from this chapter

- a business considering setting up a website should carry out a detailed analysis – for example, a SWOT analysis – considering the advantages and disadvantages of setting up an online presence

- the factors to be considered by the business setting up a website include not only the issues raised in the last chapter – for example, the fulfilment of business objectives – but also the very practical factors of costs and the constraints set down by legislation

- the best way to appreciate the factors to be considered when setting up a new website is to do it yourself; this chapter will provide practical guidance on

  – drawing up a plan for a website

  – using web-authoring software to set up a site

Requirements of your Assessment

In the last chapter we covered the first two parts of your assessment: a comparison of two websites and an analysis of one of them. In this chapter we develop your analysis skills further and also your practical IT skills.

The last two parts of the Unit assessment require you to provide evidence in two areas:

(c)   **Carry out an analysis of the factors influencing the use of the internet by a new business.**

For this we will provide further information about the practical implications of setting up a website, including the costs and the legal requirements. We will also provide two Case Studies showing how two very different businesses carry out an analysis of the factors affecting the decision to establish an online presence – resulting in the establishment of two very different sites.

(d)   **Plan and create a simple website.**

We will provide practical guidelines for planning a website and creating suitable web pages. For highest marks you will need to create a website and make it go 'live'.

the SWOT Analysis

As we saw in the last chapter (pages 394-395), **SWOT analysis** is a useful technique. It enables a business to look critically in two directions:

- **internally**
  - at the **STRENGTHS** in terms of increased sales and profits that can be given to the business by an online presence
  - at the **WEAKNESSES** in the potential lack of skills and resources available to meet the challenge
- **externally**
  - at the marketing **OPPORTUNITIES** that can be given to the business by having a website
  - at the **THREATS** posed by competitors and also by more malicious hackers and criminals who access the site

SWOT analysis can usefully be focused both on the business itself and also on the external stakeholders: customers, suppliers and competitors.

A potential internal weakness, therefore, is the lack of resources available for setting up a website. A business must carefully **cost** the exercise by drawing up a budget. It must also ensure that it has acquired the necessary **legal expertise** to comply with the increasingly complex demands of UK legislation. We will cover these two areas in turn.

the cost of setting up a website

If a business has IT experts in-house who have the technical expertise to plan, build and launch a website, this will count as a significant strength in the SWOT analysis. If this expertise is missing, most businesses will take the usual step of employing website consultancy. This could involve an individual or a company that will deal with all the necessary design, building, registering and maintenance of the website. This business is also likely to host the website, in other words it will store the site on its servers (computers) which will be its direct link to the internet. Visit www.hughesmedia.co.uk to appreciate the range of services that are available and also some websites that the company has built.

A typical budget for a small website is shown below. The list is not exhaustive, but it does show the main items to be considered. Prices are not standard but will vary from supplier to supplier and from area to area.

WEBSITE BUDGET

Activity	Cost	Frequency
Registering a domain name	from £10	per year
Design and construction fee	£1,000 to £10,000	'one off' cost
Broadband/Dial up connection to the internet	from £25	per month
Getting a good search engine listing	from £100	per month
Online shop and arranging a secure payment system	from £3,000	'one off' cost
Hosting fee (site storage)	from £200	annual
Accessibility testing (ref disabled users)	from £1,000	'one off' cost
Usability testing – eg how easy is it to find information?	from £1,000	'one off' cost
Website promotion – adverts on the internet	from £100	per month
Providing regular web site statistics on usage	from £10	per month
Email virus scanning and spam checking	from £10	per month
Staff training in the management of the website	from £350	'one off' cost
Website updates: design, information, functionality	from £40 per hour	per month

dealing with the legal requirements

If the legal expertise is not available within the business – which is quite likely – the necessary advice can be provided either by a solicitor or by the website consultant. The latter will probably cost less. The main legal regulations are explained below.

Disability Discrimination Act

Visit www.disability.gov.uk

The **Disability Discrimination Act** makes it unlawful for a service provider to discriminate against a disabled person by refusing to provide any service which it provides to other members of the public.

Professor Tim Berners-Lee, who invented the World Wide Web, expected what became the internet to provide a level playing field for disabled and non-disabled people alike. He stated:

> *'The power of the Web is in its universality. Access by everyone, regardless of disability, should be an essential aspect.'*

The Disability Rights Commission (www.drc-gb.org) is working (at the time of writing) with the British Standards Institute to issue guidelines to ensure that this will be the case.

Distance Selling Regulations

Visit http://www.dti.gov.uk/ccp/topics1/guide/distsell.htm

The **Consumer Protection (Distance Selling) Regulations** state that a seller of goods on the internet or digital television, by mail order, including catalogue shopping, by phone or by fax, must provide clear and comprehensible information to enable the consumer to decide whether to buy. Key features of the regulations are:

- the consumer must be given clear information about the goods or services offered
- after making a purchase the consumer must be sent confirmation
- the consumer has a cooling-off period of 7 working days

These regulations will affect the way a business operates any online shop.

Sale and Supply of Goods Act and Trade Descriptions Act

Visit http://www.dti.gov.uk/ccp/topics1/saleandsupply.htm

Internet traders are bound by the standard legislation which applies to any trader. The **Sale and Supply of Goods Act** protects against defective goods; the **Trade Descriptions Act** makes it an offence for a trader to make false or misleading statements about goods for sale or services offered.

Copyright

Visit www.intellectual-property.gov.uk

Copyright gives the creators of a wide range of material, such as literature, art, music, sound recordings, films and broadcasts, economic rights enabling them to control use of their material in a number of ways, such as by making copies, issuing copies to the public, performing in public, broadcasting and use online. Businesses that operate websites must therefore take great care when selling products such as music downloads, digital pictures and e-books (books in digital form) to make sure that they are not infringing copyright.

Data Protection Act

Visit www.informationcommissioner.gov.uk

The purpose of the Data Protection Act is to regulate the holding and processing of information relating to individuals, eg names, addresses and information gleaned from market research. Organisations are not allowed to release this information to third parties without authority from the person involved. Businesses that operate websites must therefore abide by this Act when capturing names and addresses input by visitors when making enquiries on websites. Businesses should make the position clear in a Privacy Statement on the website.

Privacy and Electronic Communications (EC Directive) Regulations

Visit http://www.informationcommissioner.gov.uk/eventual.aspx?id=35

These regulations, introduced in 2003, restrict the sending of marketing emails. They state, for example, that businesses cannot send a message to an email address provided to a website by a visitor – unless the visitor has given permission for emails to be sent by declining an 'opt-out' clause.

Activity 23.1 – website costs and legal red tape

You have been approached by Saskia, who is setting up a business selling fine perfumes; she is considering commissioning a website which will have an online shop.

She is investigating both the advantages and the disadvantages of establishing an online presence.

She asks you your views on the costs involved and all the legal 'red tape' that she will get involved in. How would you advise her?

What sort of costs will she incur? Could they be a problem and affect her profitability?

What legal obligations will she incur? Will they be any different from those that affect a trading business without a website?

Website Strengths and Opportunities

In this section we look at the positive side of a SWOT analysis and explain how a website can:

- be a source of strength to a business
- provide opportunities to a business

There are a number of opportunities created by the existence of e-commerce (electronic business) which can in turn be turned into strengths:

- the ability to promote a consistent corporate image
- personalised marketing, through direct 'dialogue' with customers
- increased efficiency of an on-line ordering system
- the use of a secure payment site
- a global audience

company image

Company image can be promoted by a web presence: a small company can look like a big company on the web and large companies can promote an impressive corporate image. Some companies are known only by the image their site gives, eg eBay, Amazon and other 'web only' businesses.

personalised marketing

Personalised marketing includes an email message or newsletter addressed personally and 'buy' recommendations shown onscreen. These will be based on details logged by the website of the customer's past purchases, items looked at, or added to a shopping basket and then not bought. Information can be personalised by viewer choice – for example, the ability to view a site in different colours to help people with reading disabilities.

Customer response can be received through user response forms, surveys or monitored through a study of website statistics provided by the web host. Statistics will show the most and least popular pages (viewers voting with their mice!). Customer feedback helps the business to develop new products and services, to improve the existing range and to phase out less popular items from the catalogue.

opportunities offered by online ordering

Online orders can be channelled via a payment system into a company's internal order system. This can lead to huge efficiencies as fewer people are likely to be needed to process an order. The speed with which an order is processed can be increased, and the accuracy of an order improved as the customer enters and selects products, proceeds to the order verification process and presses the button – 'please review and confirm your order'.

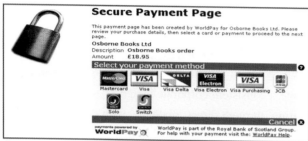

Secure payment through Worldpay

a secure payment site

Customers are understandably nervous about using debit and credit cards on an online payment system: they do not 'trust it' and are concerned about the level of fraud. Many businesses now pass the processing of payments to a third party such as Worldpay which offers a separate and very secure payment environment.

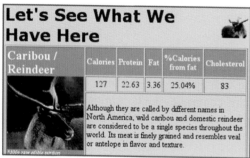

Reindeer meat online

a global audience

A global audience is most useful to a business not selling commodities or other easily sourced items. For example, you do not need to look globally to source a supplier for apples, but you may need to for reindeer meat, frogs legs or rattlesnake fillets. Visit www.exoticmeats.com (see left). A global audience also offers, of course, a potentially enormous customer base.

other internal business efficiencies

A website can affect all aspects of a business, usually helping to improve efficiency or automate manual processes:

- stock levels can be controlled and viewed by suppliers and customers
- product/service specifications can be provided and online demonstrations made available through the use of images and video
- electronic payments can be made to suppliers
- instant customised brochures can be produced using databases as opposed to the mailing of paper-based catalogues
- logistics may be improved via parcel tracking numbers, eg UPS tracking codes which tell the sender – online – where a parcel is at any time
- businesses can make the website their internal computer system and use it as a central repository for all financial and marketing data that can be accessed by employees
- profits can be increased by selling direct to end users.

Website Weaknesses and Threats

In this section we look at the negative side of a SWOT analysis and explain how a website can:

■ show up the internal weaknesses of a business

■ make the business become vulnerable to external threats

skills shortages

A website makes demands for specific skills, not only in its construction and updating, but also on the business itself and the employees who have to look after it. Orders received online have to be turned into goods for despatch or services supplied; web statistics have to be downloaded, interpreted and communicated.

A global audience also places demands: languages might be needed, export regulations and customs regulations understood. The company's products may be on a restricted list, eg exotic plants sent to the USA. Have the employees of the business got the necessary skills?

Employee motivation might also be a weakness: will redundancies have been made if there is more reliance on direct online sales? These are all issues which will have to be considered in a SWOT analysis.

ugly sites

If a website is the only point of contact between a viewer and a company, a poor site can lose customers. Bad sites mean that people cannot find the information they are looking for and so will go elsewhere. Customers will not trust a company to fulfil its marketing promises and they will not trust the security system when payments are taken. Potential employees may be put off applying for jobs if a site looks poorly constructed. Bad sites are slow, ugly and hard to use. That is the picture of the business a viewer will build up – slow, ugly and difficult to deal with. The viewer will simply go way.

external threats

Security is a very important factor on the internet. It can be easy to steal information from a website. Any information that can be viewed on the web can, in theory, be taken and used elsewhere. This includes photographs which may have been commissioned at great expense or databases of information compiled at great cost. Hackers can also cause mayhem. A business that relies on computers and/or a website can be crippled by a virus in the same way as a company is brought to a halt when its premises burns down.

instant information and instant response

Making prices public can help competitors and lead to price wars and downward spirals in the market. Promotional ideas and methods can be taken; unique products or services can be copied. Detailed 'how to' information can be 'borrowed' by competitors.

Customer pressure may increase. The internet is instant in many people's minds: they expect delivery the next day and a business has to react quickly – too quickly and mistakes can be made. More stringent checking systems may need to be put in place.

In the Case Studies that follow we look at two contrasting businesses and describe the issues they will have to analyse when setting up a website. One is an existing business – a landscape gardener; the other is a new enterprise, a jazz enthusiast wanting to set up a jazz CD store online. Read the Case Studies and answer the questions that follow.

Case Studies – Laura's Landscapes and Blue Shelf

LAURA'S LANDSCAPES

Laura Stone has an established landscape gardening business, 'Laura's Landscapes'. She operates from home in a small town and employs a team of three full-time labourers. She contracts out specialised building and construction work.

Laura likes to oversee the work herself and always provides a personal service to her clients, visiting them and discussing progress, taking a pride in the quality of her work.

She makes a comfortable living, relying very much on 'word of mouth' recommendations, listings in the Yellow Pages and adverts in the local press. She has also received useful publicity by having an article about her work published in a national 'glossy' magazine, *Landscape World*.

Laura is never out of work and often says, 'I don't want to expand. I have enough to manage as it is and I enjoy what I am doing. What I would like to do is to make a better level of profit. But I cannot complain. I live comfortably off what I make.'

A friend of hers, who is an IT expert, has recently suggested that Laura should set up a website to attract more work. He knows a consultant who can do it for her. He says, 'If you have a website you can get more contracts. You will get people calling you from all over the country and maybe from overseas. With your talent and track record you will be making more money in no time.'

Jack Daniels is a jazz fanatic who has recently been made redundant. He has enough capital to start up a business dealing with what he really enjoys – jazz CDs. He will call it 'Blue Shelf'.

He has the idea of renting a small retail unit in the city in which he lives. The lease is quite expensive but Jack thinks that there will be plenty of potential customers who will call into the shop. He has got the product knowledge which will enable him to attract customers and provide good customer service. He has got as far as drawing up a business plan with the help of a business adviser. This shows that he can afford to set up the business with the capital that he has got, plus an overdraft from the bank to help with day-to-day trading requirements. The adviser has, however, warned Jack that his projected income from sales is not supported by any form of market research. How does he know that he will take £5,000 a week in the shop?

Jack's mate, Nat, is a website consultant and tells Jack that setting up an online presence with a shop would be the best thing to do. He says, 'You would reach far more customers by trading online than you ever would in a poky little shop. You could supply jazz fanatics all over the world. You could even work from home and keep your stuff in the garage if you wanted to save on costs.'

Jack is interested in the idea – it will give him wider sales and potentially more profit, but he is worried that he does not have the knowledge and skills to set up or to operate a website.

Activity 23.2 – suitability for a website

Read the two Case Studies above and answer the following questions.

1 To what extent will an online presence help the two businesses achieve their aims and objectives?

2 How has Laura promoted her business and how successful has she been? What additional marketing opportunities would a website offer to Laura's Landscapes?

3 Describe the weaknesses of Laura's business that she would have to take into account when considering whether or not to set up a website.

4 How would a website help Jack to promote his business? Should he be worried by online competitors?

5 Identify a major weakness of Jack's plans for a website. How could he solve the problem?

6 If Laura and Jack were friends of yours, what would you advise them to do, and why?

Setting up a Website – the Practical Issues

In the last chapter we explained the ways in which you can assess business websites by examining factors such as ease of use and standards of design. In this chapter we look at many of the same concepts, but from a different angle – we examine the way in which websites are constructed.

Your assessment requires that you plan and, if possible, build your own website. In this section we look at many of the practicalities you will need to consider. We will then present a Case Study of a small business setting up a very simple four-page website – very much along the lines of the requirements of your assessment.

What we will *not* do is to go through all the technicalities of actually putting web pages together. There are a number of reasons for this:

- there are many different programs available for website construction and we might use a program you do not have
- the construction process is very 'hands on' and would require another book to explain it in full
- your teacher/tutor/IT specialist should be available to give you on-the-spot instruction

Instead, we will explain the practical issues.

web authoring - HTML

If you are software-savvy, you can set up web pages using **HTML** code. This stands for **h**ypertext **m**arkup **l**anguage which is a coding system which is applied to text using 'tags' which format and describe page and text elements to form hypertext pages for use on the internet. Basically it is a system which tells the computer how to display the finished web pages.

The standards for HTML are set by the World Wide Web Consortium (W3C) – visit www.w3.org The aim of this organisation is to develop specifications, guidelines and software to 'lead the Web to its full potential'.

The main problem with HTML is that it is *not* WYSIWYG (pronounced 'wizzywig'), ie **w**hat **y**ou **s**ee **i**s **w**hat **y**ou **g**et. In other words, what you see on the screen with HTML bears no resemblance to the finished web page – it is just a series of words, letters and symbols. If, however, you wish to master HTML, there are free tutorials on the site www.htmlgoodies.com

web authoring - software packages

If you prefer to work with web-authoring software which does show you on screen what you are going to get (WYSIWYG), there are a number of dedicated packages available, including:

■ **Dreamweaver** – used by the professionals, flexible, complex and comparatively expensive and not recommended for the beginner

■ **Frontpage** – used by keen amateurs, less flexible, less expensive and easier to use and a better recommendation for the beginner

Microsoft Office includes a web page facility, but it is fairly basic.

creating and registering a web address

You will need to create a **domain name** – a web address – for a business website. The address should obviously be recognisable as belonging to the business. The address for the publisher of this book, for example, is www.osbornebooks.co.uk The 'co.uk' means that the site belongs to a commercial organisation ('company') and is based in the UK.

Other letters included in domain names are:

■ com – a organisation trading internationally or in the USA

■ ac – an academic institution such as a college

■ gov – a government department or agency

■ org – a not-for-profit organisation

■ net – an organisation whose function is related to the internet

Domain names, like car registration plates, are unique and have to be **registered**. You cannot choose to set up a website and call it www.tesco.com because that name is already likely to be in use. Domain names in the UK can be checked at www.nominet.org.uk, registered and protected for a small fee. Note that Nominet is an 'org'. Worldwide registrations can be checked at www.nic.com

Some of the web links quoted here contain more than the domain name: http://www.dti.gov.uk/ccp/topics1/guide/distsell.htm, for example, takes you to the Distance Selling Regulations. All the text after http://www.dti.gov.uk leads to the location of the appropriate file on the web pages. This long reference is known as an **URL** (**u**niversal **r**esource **l**ocator).

www.nominet.org.uk

choosing a host

The website host is the organisation that stores website pages and makes them available on servers by fast connection to the internet. Businesses are well advised to chose a reputable organisation for this service. Visit URL http://www.webperf.net/

Planning the Website

structure

It is critically important that a structure plan is drawn up for a website and that there are not too many levels of pages. In other words, you should ideally be able to get to any web page with a maximum of 3 mouse clicks.

The structure plan will, of course, depend on the nature of the business. The website www.johnlewis.com serves a very large retail organisation, but despite its size, is a model of clarity. A smaller business, as noted in the last chapter, needs only a very simple site (see below). This is possibly the type of site you should be planning for your assessment.

It must be stressed that this plan is only a suggestion. As we will see in the Case Study on page 425, the pages may vary, but the basic functions will remain the same.

design principles - text, images and sound

The appropriate use of design – colour, images and text layout – has been covered in some detail in the last chapter. The guidelines set out below should be followed when planning and building a site.

- **Visual criteria** – the appearance of the website – should be **branded** in line with all the promotions of the business. It should include a company's logo, corporate colours and corporate fonts (typefaces) where applicable.

- **Information** should be laid out in a clear format; text should be large enough to read and contrast with the background colour. Large chunks of information should be broken up to make them easier to read onscreen by using techniques like bullet points, narrow width columns (as in newspapers) to retain the reader's concentration. **Pictures** should load efficiently and visual information delivered using formats that are widely accessible such as the widely-used Flash.

- **Information should be well organised** in different sections. A site should not be deep, ie a viewer should not have to drop several levels down into a site to find information. A consistent navigation bar in the same place should ideally be present on every page.

- The **home page** of a web site should (ideally) download in approximately 10 seconds on a dial-up connection. Where possible, graphics should be created that are common to all pages that do not have to be reloaded several times. All information should be a maximum of 3 clicks from the home page.

   Do not make a website hard work for the user. If you have a large information-rich website, provide a site search facility. Make links recognisable and make sure buttons work and look like buttons.

- Using **sound** is not always a good idea. The internet is private and many people have no sound capabilities, especially in a business environment.

- **Video** takes a long time to download. It should be used carefully with the target market in mind, eg a rock band might make use of video on its site; an equipment manufacturer may want to show videos demonstrating equipment. The user should always be given the choice of whether or not to download the video.

design for the target market

Remember that the website design should always be focused on the **target market**, which could be defined by age, geography or lifestyle.

The design should also reflect the purpose of the site – does it aim to sell a product or is it an entertainment site, an educational site or a site which provides advice? For your assessment you are most likely to be planning a business site which aims to sell a product or service.

When setting up a business website it is a good idea to carry out an internet search to look at sites offering similar products or services and get a 'feel' of what customers will expect in terms of both design and content. The design should ideally reflect other promotional material – such as printed brochures and leaflets – related to that market segment. You may be able to download material such as catalogues or advice leaflets which you can study in printed form.

promotion on other websites

Larger businesses are likely to promote themselves on other websites as well. For example, **adverts** can be taken on Google search pages where the advertiser pays 'by click' (ie when the viewer clicks on the adverts on the relevant page. Visit http://www.google.co.uk/ads/ for further information. Businesses can also liaise with **stakeholders** – even competitors – to promote their products. For example, a number of major airlines have combined to run www.opodo.co.uk which offers a number of travel-related services, including holidays and car hire.

registering with search engines

It is critical that a business registers its website with the main recognised **Search Engines**, eg www.google.co.uk

This will ensure that anyone carrying out a search on the internet using key words or phrases relating to that website (eg 'pizzas' or 'Spanish holidays') will find the address on a search engine listing. It is helpful if the important words and phrases relating to the activities of the business are included on the home page, because that is where the search engine will look first.

the need for security

It is important to appreciate the issues of security. Computer users should install anti-virus software and firewalls. If a website includes an online shop, it should provide a secure payment system.

Anti-virus software should be installed on any computer with access to the internet. Popular brands are Norton and McAffee. Virus definitions (a list of known viruses) should be updated as regularly as possible, and ideally daily. All email should be scanned, especially attachments, as should all disks inserted into a machine, eg floppies, CD-ROMs and USB memory sticks.

Firewalls are software or hardware barriers that prevent external people accessing your computer. Popular brands are Zone Alarm and Norton as well as the free firewall built into versions of Windows software. Firewalls should be set to prevent external access to a computer and should be installed on all computers with access to the internet.

Any credit card information on **online payment systems** should be given and received via a secure link (SSL). A padlock symbol should appear in a viewer's web browser. Secure links are used together with a 'certificate' to establish security. Popular certificate providers are Thawte and VeriSign (see page 405).

rationale for a website and design issues

The Case Study which concludes this chapter examines a pizza restaurant and home delivery service. It explains the reasoning behind the setting up of a website and shows how a simple and effective site can be constructed using only four web pages. Visit www.edsperfectpizzas.co.uk to see for yourself.

Case Study – Ed's Perfect Pizzas

the background

Ed runs a popular pizza restaurant, 'Ed's Perfect Pizzas'. It is always busy. His recipe for success is the use of very fresh and low-fat ingredients which appeal to weight watchers and health-conscious customers. The pizzas are also very tasty. Ed varies the menu regularly and runs special promotions which attract further sales.

the new idea

The city of Worcester, where Ed operates, has a fast-growing population and he sees that a further market for his pizzas has developed out in the suburbs. Many people who work in these outlying areas find it too much of an effort to get into the city centre for a quick pizza.

Ed thinks of two possible solutions. One is to open another outlet on the east side of the city where the greatest expansion has taken place. The other is to employ motorbike riders to deliver the pizzas to the homes of customers throughout the city.

The first solution has its attractions, but Ed realises that it will involve a large capital investment which he cannot afford from his own resources. The extra outlet can be achieved if he franchises the operation, but Ed is worried that with someone else managing the other restaurant he will lose the control and personal touch which contribute to his present success.

The motorbike delivery system, which Ed knows works well in other urban areas, seems the better alternative. Customers could phone in their orders and delivery could be made rapidly, payment taken and the personal touch retained.

The problem for Ed is that of promotion. An extra restaurant would be its own advertisement, but a delivery system will need publicising. Ed asks the advice of his friend, Nikki, who works in a local advertising agency.

Nikki makes some suggestions: 'Why don't you use local media: adverts in the local press, leaflets delivered with the local free newspaper and slots on local radio?'

Ed agrees that most of these would be suitable, but he wants some system of permanent promotion which will bring in the extra customers.

'Why don't you set up a website?' asks Nikki.

Ed thinks that a website will cost a fortune, and an online ordering system will not really work in practice. He reckons that the telephone is so much better for communication and customer service.

the solution

Nikki says that she knows a website consultant who could set up a very simple site relatively cheaply. It would not involve a shop, just four pages showing products, prices, special offers and how to get the pizzas – either by phone or by visiting the restaurant. Ed's business would become known as www.edsperfectpizzas.co.uk, an address he would have to register.

Ed agrees to go ahead with this idea. The website consultant takes digital pictures of pizzas at Ed's restaurant, finds a map, gathers the necessary product information and produces a four-page website shown in this Case Study.

the website

The structure of the website is shown in the diagram below. It contains:

- a **home page** which has links to all the other pages and sets out all the contact details that customers will want – it fulfils the 'Contact Us' function
- a **location** page – a map for visitors to the city centre restaurant and its opening hours – this fulfils the function of an 'About Us' page
- a **menu** page – the product and price page
- **special offers** – a further promotional page to attract orders

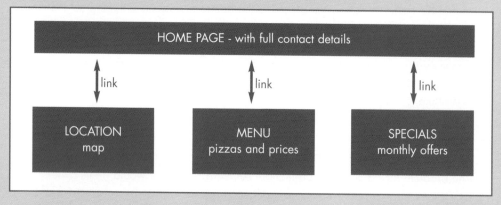

These web pages are illustrated and explained in the remainder of this Case Study.
Note also that Ed will need to:

- find a hosting service for his website
- register the domain name www.edsperfectpizzas.co.uk with Nominet
- register with the major search engines
- ensure that the information on the website complies with all necessary legislation
- make sure that the website name is displayed prominently on all his other promotional material, including pizza boxes, leaflets, menus, adverts and the motorbikes
- update the site regularly, introducing new features such as free recipes

home page

All the major design features and essential page elements are indicated here. Note the clarity of the text and the message conveyed, the use of images and colour (mouthwatering cheese and tomato), the repetition of contact details and the ease of navigation to other pages by single clicks on links and also on images (the pizzas and the map).

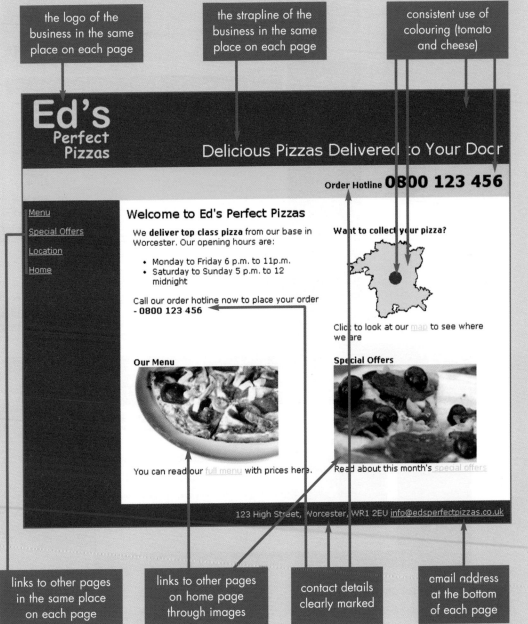

the logo of the business in the same place on each page

the strapline of the business in the same place on each page

consistent use of colouring (tomato and cheese)

Ed's Perfect Pizzas

Delicious Pizzas Delivered to Your Door

Order Hotline **0800 123 456**

Menu
Special Offers
Location
Home

Welcome to Ed's Perfect Pizzas

We **deliver top class pizza** from our base in Worcester. Our opening hours are:

- Monday to Friday 6 p.m. to 11p.m.
- Saturday to Sunday 5 p.m. to 12 midnight

Call our order hotline now to place your order - **0800 123 456**

Want to collect your pizza?

Click to look at our map to see where we are

Our Menu

You can read our full menu with prices here.

Special Offers

Read about this month's special offers

123 High Street, Worcester, WR1 2EU info@edsperfectpizzas.co.uk

links to other pages in the same place on each page

links to other pages on home page through images

contact details clearly marked

email address at the bottom of each page

menu page

This is the 'products' section of the website – a simple page with all the information required. Note all the elements (navigation, colour, contacts) are consistently repeated from the home page.

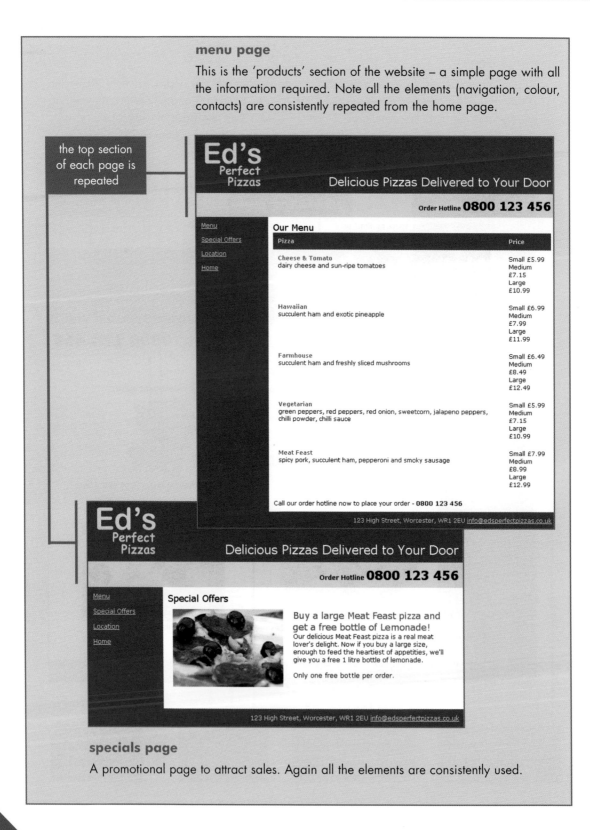

the top section of each page is repeated

Ed's
Perfect
Pizzas

Delicious Pizzas Delivered to Your Door

Order Hotline **0800 123 456**

Menu
Special Offers
Location
Home

Our Menu

Pizza	Price
Cheese & Tomato dairy cheese and sun-ripe tomatoes	Small £5.99 Medium £7.15 Large £10.99
Hawaiian succulent ham and exotic pineapple	Small £6.99 Medium £7.99 Large £11.99
Farmhouse succulent ham and freshly sliced mushrooms	Small £6.49 Medium £8.49 Large £12.49
Vegetarian green peppers, red peppers, red onion, sweetcorn, jalapeno peppers, chilli powder, chilli sauce	Small £5.99 Medium £7.15 Large £10.99
Meat Feast spicy pork, succulent ham, pepperoni and smoky sausage	Small £7.99 Medium £8.99 Large £12.99

Call our order hotline now to place your order - 0800 123 456

123 High Street, Worcester, WR1 2EU info@edsperfectpizzas.co.uk

Ed's
Perfect
Pizzas

Delicious Pizzas Delivered to Your Door

Order Hotline **0800 123 456**

Menu
Special Offers
Location
Home

Special Offers

Buy a large Meat Feast pizza and get a free bottle of Lemonade!
Our delicious Meat Feast pizza is a real meat lover's delight. Now if you buy a large size, enough to feed the heartiest of appetites, we'll give you a free 1 litre bottle of lemonade.

Only one free bottle per order.

123 High Street, Worcester, WR1 2EU info@edsperfectpizzas.co.uk

specials page

A promotional page to attract sales. Again all the elements are consistently used.

location page

This is the 'About Us' section of the website – showing the customer where the restaurant is and when it is open. Note again the repetition of the logo, strapline, colours, page links and contact details, all consistently placed.

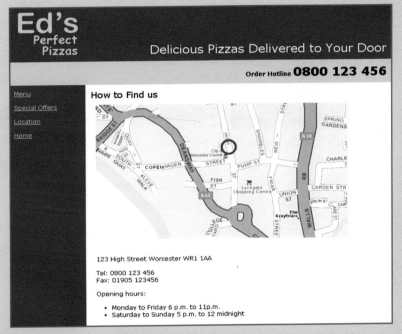

important note

The website in this Case Study can be accessed at www.edsperfectpizzas.co.uk The pages may also be downloaded from the Student Resources pages at www.osbornebooks.co.uk and used as templates for your own designs.

Activity 23.3 – Ed's Perfect Pizzas

Read through the Case Study and answer the questions set out below.

1   What are the two options for Ed's expansion plans?

2   Explain the reasons for Ed's decision.

3   Suggest any problems that could be caused by customers and competitors as a result of Ed's decision.

4   Explain why Ed's website design could be considered successful.

5   Suggest features which Ed might be able to add to the website in the future.

6   Ed is criticised by the local anti-obesity pressure group. How might he answer the criticism on his website?

CHAPTER SUMMARY

■ A SWOT analysis is a useful technique for a business assessing the viability of an online presence. It looks at internal factors (strengths and weaknesses) and also external factors (opportunities and threats).

■ A business should carefully cost the setting up and running of a website. It should also be aware of and cover the various legal requirements. If the website has a shop, the Distance Selling Regulations are particularly important.

■ The advantages offered by setting up a website and e-commerce include:
- the ability to promote the corporate image
- personalised marketing – emails, newsletters, 'buy' recommendations
- the efficiencies and security of an online ordering system
- the opportunities of accessing a global audience

■ The potential problems and disadvantages of setting up a website include:
- the lack of the necessary technical skills within the business
- possible loss of customers through having a poor ('ugly') site
- external threats from hackers, viruses and theft of information
- threats from competitors who have instant access to product information
- customers who expect very high standards of service, eg next day delivery

■ A person setting up a website can choose from a variety of web-authoring programs such as Dreamweaver and Frontpage, or can use HTML coding.

■ A web address (domain name) must identify the business and should be registered to prevent anyone else using it.

■ A website will be located on the servers of a web 'host' and linked to the internet.

■ When building a website, you should draw up a structure plan, making sure that the site is logical and does not contain too many levels. The nature of the structure plan will depend on the type of business.

■ Common design guidelines should be followed when setting up the individual pages. Colour, images and text layout should be used consistently and simply.

■ A website should be designed for the target market and reflect other promotional material used by the business in its marketing.

■ A website should be registered with the main search engines.

■ Site security should be considered carefully. Anti-virus software and firewalls should be installed and payment systems made secure.

KEY TERMS

SWOT analysis	analysis of an organisation which involves assessing its Strengths, Weaknesses, Opportunities and Threats
Distance Selling Regulations	regulations governing remote selling (eg from a website or by telephone, allowing the purchaser rights, including a 7 day cooling off period and a right to return)
HTML	hypertext markup language – the code used for creating web pages by the insertion of 'tags'
W3C	the World Wide Web Consortium which develops specifications and guidelines to develop the web to its full potential
domain name	a web address – which identifies a website
domain registration	registration of a website address with an organisation to ensure that no other organisation can use the same address
URL	a universal resource locator – an extended 'address' which leads the viewer to the appropriate page on a website
website host	the organisation that stores the web pages on a server and connects them to the internet
home page	the main page of a website (also known as the index page or default page)
Flash	software which enables the use of animation on a web page
search engine	a database system that searches the internet for key words and phrases requested by a visitor and displays the addresses of sites where the information is stored
pay by click adverts	adverts (with website addresses) on the search result screens of search engines which are charged to the advertiser each time the advert is 'clicked on' by a mouse
anti-virus	software which protects a computer from viruses by regularly scanning its hard disk and other storage media
firewall	a software or hardware barrier which prevents people accessing a computer from outside

Investigating customer service

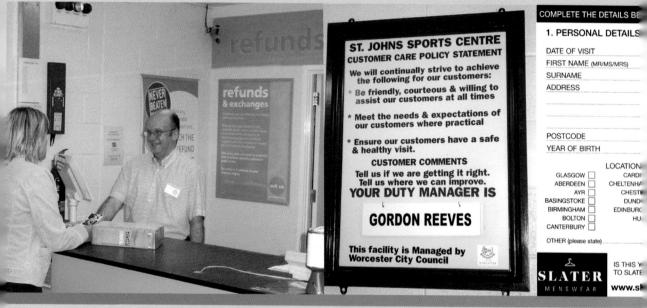

Keeping a high standard of customer service is essential if an organisation is to retain its customers and build on its reputation. In this unit you will research:

- the different types of customer an organisation will deal with

- the needs of the different types of customer and the levels of service that those customers can expect

- the ways in which customer service can be provided by an organisation – using its staff and its premises, for example

- the importance of communication in customer service

- the ways in which standards of customer service are set

- the methods of monitoring and then improving customer service

- the legal background to customer service

(NO STAMP REQUIRED) & YOU C[

2. QUESTIONNAIRE (Please

WAS THE SERVICE

WAS THE SELECTION

WERE THE PRICES

STAFF APPEARANCE

ALTERATIONS

COLLECTIONS

PLEASE RATE THE SERVICE Y
OUR STAFF (The names are on you

ENTER YOUR RECEIPT NO. HE

                              NAME

SALES ASS'T

SALES ASS'T

SALES ASS'T

CASHIER

Chapters in this Unit...

24

Customers and customer service

Starting point

Businesses rely on customers for their survival. The pressures of competition dictate that customers must be at the centre of everything that a business does. For example, the core purpose of Tesco is 'to create value for customers to earn their lifetime loyalty'.

Value is relatively easy to achieve, but lifetime loyalty can only be achieved when a customer is given good service and wants to come back again.

What you will learn from this chapter

- customers are important to an organisation such as a business: external customers can include a wide range of 'types' identified by market research in categories of age, culture and lifestyle; internal customers include immediate colleagues, people in other departments and other supporting organisations

- customers all have different needs which must be looked after by a business – these relate to factors such as age and disability

- customers have come to expect certain levels of customer service that they will receive before, during and after the sale of a product or a service; the extent of these expectations will vary with the nature of the product or service

- customer service relates to issues such as staff attitude, the premises and the products (or services)

- good customer service relates very much to the use of communication skills – an employee of a business must be able to tell the customer about the product or service and be able to deal with complaints

Requirements of your Assessment

stage 1 - contrast two organisations

The **first stage** of your assessment for Unit 5 requires you to investigate customer service in two contrasting organisations. You will need to appreciate in both cases who the external and internal customers are, and how the customer service meets the expectations of customers.

The need to choose two 'contrasting' organisations opens up a wide range of possibilities. You could choose:

- a small business and a large business offering a similar product or service
- a business selling a product and a business selling a service
- a private sector business and a public sector organisation

You could theoretically choose your own school or college, although you would have to be guided by your teacher/lecturer.

stage 2 - analyse one of the organisations in more detail

The **second stage** of your assessment for Unit 5 requires you to be more analytical. You will need to choose one of the organisations which features in the first stage and carry out the following in relation to that organisation:

- evaluate the strengths and weaknesses of its customer service activities and make suggestions for improvements
- research and analyse the ways in which the chosen organisation maintains, monitors and then improves the quality of its customer service
- investigate the way in which current legislation affects the way in which customer service operates

In this chapter we will illustrate the elements of customer service with a Case Study of a large retail business (private sector). The next chapter uses a local authority Sports Centre (public sector) to illustrate quality standards.

stage 3 - present your findings

The **evidence** for your investigation should take the form of a presentation with speaker notes. You could use Powerpoint to present your evidence.

The notes that you have compiled when investigating customer service should support your submission and be accompanied by a detailed witness statement from your teacher/lecturer.

You will be allowed to work in pairs if you wish, but there should be evidence of your individual contributions.

Customers

what is a customer?

The traditional definition of a customer is:

someone who buys goods or services

a patient customer

A customer is someone who buys something, whether it is a magazine from WH Smith or a train journey from Virgin Trains. This person is a customer of a **private sector** business where a product or service is sold for profit. If a private sector enterprise loses its customers, it lose its sales, profit and in some circumstances its future.

Widening the definition further, the 'customer' culture is also applied to the **public sector** where you are a 'customer' if you borrow a library book or end up in hospital. Interestingly, business principles also apply here: if local doctors do not refer enough cases of, say, chest problems, to a certain hospital's chest division, either because of its location or reputation, that department may have to close and future patients – 'customers' – will be referred to another hospital.

The definition of a customer may therefore be modified to:

someone who obtains goods or services

another type of customer

When you are investigating organisations for your assessment, note that the term 'customer' may include any of the following examples:

- a student at a school or college
- a patient at a hospital
- a member of a gym
- a shopper at a supermarket
- a passenger on a bus
- someone booking a holiday

new and old customers

Some customers can be classed as **new customers** – the prospects that the marketing department of a business want to persuade to make a purchase. These are the people who will provide future income and profit and become part of a customer base which the marketing department will want to retain and develop.

An organisation such as a business must also look after its **existing customers**. It must make sure that these customers will come back and buy again, and buy more. This will lead to increased sales and profit.

Look at the statistics:

---

why do businesses lose customers?

1%   die

3%   leave the area

4%   naturally float between businesses – they have no loyalty to any business

5%   change because a friend tells them about other businesses which they say are better

9%   find the products or services are cheaper somewhere else

10% just like complaining – they actually enjoy it!

but the most important figure is:

68% go elsewhere because they are unhappy with the service that they were given

---

We will discuss the ways in which an organisation retains its customers later in this chapter, and also in the next chapter. The basic principles are to:

- keep in touch with them on a regular basis
- reward them for their loyalty

internal and external customers

The term 'customer' is commonly used to mean someone who buys goods or services. That person is clearly an **external customer**. What is less commonly appreciated is that when you work in an organisation there are people, departments and suppliers who are in effect your 'customers' whom you have to look after. These are **internal customers**.

Consider the following examples:

- the finance department of a business provides sales figures for the marketing department – which is then an internal customer
- a school reprographics department photocopies handouts for a teacher – who becomes an internal customer within the school
- a chef in a restaurant is an external customer of the supplier who provides him with food; the waitress who sends in orders from the restaurant to the kitchen is his internal customer; and the people eating in the restaurant are her external customers – there is clearly a long chain of customers here, all of whom must be kept happy and provided with good service

The concept of **external customers**, is more easily understood. In your assessment you will be investigating different types of organisation and different types of external customer. The ways in which they are looked after by the organisation will vary considerably. External customers can be classified in various ways:

■ by age, eg children, adults, senior citizens

■ by disability – eg customers with mobility problems

■ by nationality – differing languages and culture

We will look at the needs of these customers in the next section.

Activity 24.1 – internal and external customers

As part of your assessment you will need to identify two contrasting organisations and identify the customers – both internal and external – of those two organisations.

In preparation for this you should:

1 Draw up a shortlist of two contrasting organisations on which you could base your investigations. State whether they are in the private or public sector and in what other respects they are different from each other.

2 Draw up a list of the different types of internal customers of the two organisations.

3 Draw up a list of the different types of external customers of the two organisations.

Suggestion: draw up all this data in the form of a table.

Customer Needs

Each different type of external customer will have specific needs which have to be looked after. As noted above, the requirements relate to issues such as age, disability and nationality.

customer age groups

Most age groups need no special attention as most people are fortunate in being able-bodied and mobile. Extra attention is needed where the customer is either very young or very old.

Employees need special skills and the right kind of personality when dealing with **children**. Children pose certain problems for businesses such as shops including:

■ being a nuisance – they can be noisy and, if allowed to run riot, may damage goods on display

special care for the young

- they can unintentionally 'steal' items by picking them up
- they can get lost

For very young children a good investment for a business – especially in larger shops – is a crèche. It keeps children amused and safe while parents get on with the serious job of shopping.

At the other end of the age spectrum, very old people also require special care. They may need:

- seats to rest on
- patience on the part of checkout staff as they may be slow in paying and dealing with the shopping
- help with carrying purchases out to the car park

groups with particular needs

Other groups which impose specific requirements include heavily pregnant females and disruptive and anti-social individuals. The former may need a seat and help with shopping while the latter may need some physical assistance from security staff to help them to leave the premises.

customers with disabilities

a wheelchair lift in a store

Dealing with customers with disabilities (special needs customers) calls for a special level of care.

Customers with **physical disabilities** will need special facilities and staff will have to be very helpful to them. They may need lifts, ramps and special toilets if they are in wheelchairs.

Remember that if they cannot get to parts of the business because there are no lifts (or the lift entrances are too narrow) this may be an offence under the Disability Discrimination Act 1998, which came into full force in 2004.

Customers with **learning difficulties** are people who may have problems with carrying out routine transactions or instructions. They need a lot of help and support.

Another group of disabled people are the **hearing-impaired** and the **visually-impaired**. Some customers will be completely or partially deaf, so employees should speak clearly and face to face (so that the customer can read their lips).

Blind people and their guide dogs will often need help. Employees may be asked to accompany a blind person round a large store because he or she will not know the layout.

customers, languages and cultures

There are a number of situations where businesses will deal with people whose command of the English language is limited or non-existent. Examples include:

■ tourist hot spots, eg hotels and ticket agencies in Central London

■ urban areas in the UK where English may be a second language

■ internet sites where the customer base is potentially global

In these situations, employees may well be taken on who have the appropriate language skills. In the case of websites used internationally, it is becoming common practice to be able to choose the language in which the information will be presented. The illustration below shows the British Airways website in both French and German. Visit www.ba.com

ba.com - A MULTILINGUAL SITE

Businesses also need to be sensitive to different **cultures** and their customs. An example of this is the choice of food offered. Pork scratchings would definitely be off the menu in some areas.

Activity 24.2 – assessing customer needs

Visit two organisations. They could be the two organisations you have selected for your assessment or if you have not yet made a choice, they could be large shops in your area.

In both cases investigate whether they allow for the needs of their customers in terms of providing facilities:

1 for children aged up to 5

2 for an old person with a walking stick

3 for someone in a wheelchair

4 for a person who comes in with white stick and a guide dog

If the organisations do not provide facilities for these customer types, suggest what action they could take to remedy the situation.

Customer Expectations

Organisations need to anticipate the needs of customers in a variety of different situations.

If the organisation is in the **private sector** selling goods or services, this means persuading the customer towards the buying decision, completing the sale so that the customer thinks that the right decision has been made, and then making sure the customer is satisfied with the purchase afterwards. This will help towards increasing sales and profit for the organisation.

If the organisation is in the **public sector** – a doctor's general practice, for example – customers need to be 'treated' well so that government-set targets can be met, the customer is satisfied with the outcome and the medical practice awarded with points and rewarded accordingly.

One very simple (if cheesy) definition of effective customer service is:

effective customer service = having happy customers

There are three main stages in the creation of a 'happy' customer, all with a specific set of customer expectations. Central to all this is the 'transaction', which could be the sale of goods or services, having a filling at the dentist, or taking an exam or driving test.

stage 1: before the transaction takes place

This stage could include browsing around a shop, surfing through internet sites, booking an appointment and sitting in a dentist's waiting room, or attending a driving test centre.

Take the case of a shop. The ways in which a customer can be put in a 'buying' frame of mind have been studied by psychologists and include:

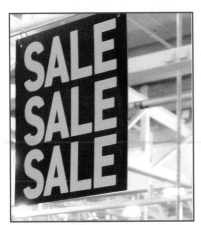

special Sale offer – buy now!

- providing a relaxing, spacious environment, possibly with suitable 'chill out' music (although this can be a difficult choice to make)
- the 'right' smell (again psychologists have shown this to be very persuasive) – examples include the smell of fresh cooking ducted into a supermarket entrance, and coffee served in a bookshop which encourages shoppers to sit down, read and then to buy
- attractive and informative displays
- special offers – especially near the entrance where customers buy on impulse
- staff circulating on the shop floor ready to provide advice
- a customer service desk providing information and advice

Of course, not all organisations are shops, but the same principles apply to put the 'customer' in the right frame of mind. A website, for example, should be easy on the eye, informative and easy to navigate so that the customer will want to buy the product or service. A dentist's waiting room should be a comforting and relaxing place with plenty to look at and read, and preferably out of earshot of the sound of the dentist's drill.

stage 2: the transaction

In the case of an organisation such as a shop, an online retailer or a sports centre the transaction will be the purchase of goods or services: a tin of paint, a DVD or a game of badminton. This should ideally be a trouble-free experience. Again, take the example of a shop. A successful purchase – in terms of customer service – should ideally involve:

friendly service at the checkout

- a minimum of queuing
- friendly service from the checkout operator or sales assistant
- a variety of payment methods available
- secure payment arrangements (no-one apart from the customer should be able to see a PIN number being entered)
- the use of a loyalty card (eg Tesco Clubcard, Homebase Spend & Save) which will give the customer the satisfaction of knowing that points – and value – have been gained from the transaction
- giving out vouchers to set against future purchases
- help with the packing at the checkout if needed or 'gift wrapping' if it is a special purchase
- an unobstructed route out of the shop

The objective – whatever the organisation or type of transaction – should be a contented customer who will want to come back again.

stage 3: after the transaction

This stage is traditionally known as 'after-sales service'. It is important that the customer knows two things:

- if anything goes wrong it will be put right
- the organisation has not forgotten about the transaction and will keep in touch with the customer to provide future benefits – eg special offers and store events (in the case of shops)– and that a **relationship** now exists between the customer and the organisation

This second point relates to the concept of **customer relationship management (CRM)** which is now considered to form the basis of good customer service.

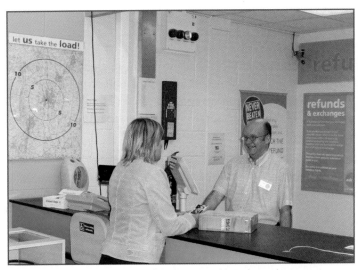

a Homebase customer service desk - providing after-sales service

The place where complaints are heard and problems are 'put right' in a large retail organisation is the **customer service desk**.

If you examine the situation and the posters and equipment shown in the picture on the left, you will see that this desk provides in addition a wide range of 'after-sales' facilities including:

- provision of advice

- refunds for faulty goods

- exchange of goods

- a delivery service

The customer services desk is also where customer complaints are received and dealt with. Note that the customer services assistant here is friendly and welcoming. Disabled customers are also catered for – on the front of the desk to the left of the customer is a disabled customer writing surface which folds down through 90 degrees to wheelchair height.

Other types of organisation will all have their own version of 'after-sales' customer service. An online retailer, for example, is likely to have features on the website such as 'Frequently Asked Questions' (FAQ), order tracking ('Where's my stuff?') and the opportunity to email or telephone with queries ('Contact Us').

As noted on the last page, the purchase (the 'transaction), is only the start of a customer relationship which an organisation will work hard to maintain and develop through loyalty schemes and mailings – all part of its marketing drive. These issues will be explained more fully in the next chapter.

Activity 24.3 – customer expectations

Visit two organisations. As in the Activity on page 440 they could be the two you have selected for your assessment or they could be a couple of large shops in your area.

1 Describe how they provide customer service before a transaction takes place (eg before a purchase is made).

2 Observe and describe the customer service provided as the transactions take place.

3 Describe in each case the ways in which customer service is provided after the transaction has taken place.

How Much Customer Service?

In the examples of customer service given so far in this chapter we have described fairly large and complex businesses operating in a very competitive environment. In some cases competition for customers can be so fierce that the level of customer service can help decide whether that business remains profitable, or stays in business at all.

But it must be appreciated that the levels of customer service – and customer expectations of customer service – will vary enormously from business to business, and this must be borne in mind when you are carrying out your assessment.

For example, if someone is buying a new TV he/she will need a great deal of information and expert advice in answer to questions like 'What type of screen should I have? What channels can I get? Do I need separate speakers to create a home cinema effect?' and so on. On the other hand, buying a litre of milk should not prove to be so much of a challenge.

Activity 24.4 – degrees of customer service

Describe the features of customer service you would expect in the following circumstances:

1 You buy a newspaper from a stall in the street.

2 You buy a wedding dress (male students should use some imagination here).

3 You buy a ticket from a bus driver.

4 You book a holiday with a local 'high street' travel agent.

What features of customer service would you expect to be common to all four situations?

Effective Customer Service?

the importance of customer satisfaction

The main objective of customer service is **customer satisfaction**. Customer satisfaction, as we will see in the next chapter, can be measured through questionnaires completed by customers. A 'satisfied' customer does not mean someone who has no complaints: a satisfied customer is someone who is genuinely happy with the service, the product and the whole experience of dealing with the organisation. As noted earlier, there is then a 'feel good' relationship which has been established with this customer. It is then up to the organisation to develop the relationship into profit, using the techniques of **customer relationship management**.

The advantages of this relationship are:

■ happy customers are less likely to go over to a competitor

■ they will recommend the organisation to other people – 'You ought to shop there, the products are good value for money'

■ they will not complain about the organisation to others – the statement 'I'll never go there again; they are rubbish' is very bad news to marketing teams

■ happy customers are likely to deal with the organisation regularly and contribute to profitability

■ happy customers result in happy staff who in turn attract more customers

what makes effective customer service?

In the next stage of your assessment you will chose one of the two organisations you have decided to investigate. You will need to evaluate the strengths and weaknesses – the overall effectiveness – of its customer service activities and make suggestions for improvements.

What will you need to evaluate? The main areas you need to look at are:

■ the staff

■ the premises

■ the quality and value of products or services

In the text that now follows we suggest aspects of customer service that you could assess in your investigations.

staff contribution to customer service

The contribution made to customer service by the staff can make or break an organisation. Many of these aspects may seem obvious, but it is when they are not present that the problems start:

■ **general appearance** – tidiness and personal cleanliness and hygiene are important; a uniform can help to give a good impression but a strong dose of garlic or unwashed socks can do a lot of harm to customer relations

■ **mood and expression** – a smile can make such a difference

■ **attitude** – helpfulness can give a customer confidence

■ **product knowledge** – staff ignorance and uncertainty put the customer off; if a staff member does not know the answer to a question, he/she should be able to find someone who does

a smile and a uniform at Tesco

Here are five great reasons for having teams.

Nobody can do it all

No single person has all the specialist skills and knowledge needed to run the store, so you have the team. Everyone in the store is part of the team – whatever they specialise in, wherever they work and whatever their job title.

Whether it's someone in the warehouse or a manager in the office, they all play a part – like a sports team where different players are expert in their own bit of the game.
On their own they can't win, but when they work together it creates an extra dimension.

teamwork at Boots

Teamwork is an essential element of the effective functioning of any workforce. It relates to all functions of an organisation – not just customer service. Teamwork is currently a popular method of management. It encourages a democratic approach – 'let's talk about how to do this' rather than 'I want you to do it this way'. Through this, individual team members learn to take responsibility for what is going on and are motivated by success. Organisations encourage this approach to customer service, grouping its sales staff into 'customer service teams' and holding team meetings to discuss customer problems – complaints procedures and shoplifting, for example – and new product campaigns.

Customers can soon sense when teamwork is breaking down – for example, when staff members do not take responsibility for errors or problems and blame others. The statement 'I am sorry it is not in stock, I will put one aside for you when it next comes in' is more impressive than 'I know – they are so slow in getting them here.'

Effective **staff training** is another essential element in providing a high level of customer service. In the Case Study on pages 449 to 450 we show how Homebase trains its staff to deal with customers.

the need for communication – face to face

Effective customer service relies on effective communication.

In this chapter we have used shopping to illustrate customer service because the retail environment is where most people come into contact with the main principles of customer service. Retail staff are trained to communicate with customers in order to present the required image of the business. For example:

how would you deal with this customer?

- speaking clearly and using polite phrases
  - 'Can I help you?'
  - 'How would you like to pay?'
- dealing with complaints and learning how to calm a customer down
- dealing with difficult customers who cannot be calmed down
- reading and using body language, knowing what it means when
  - a customer makes eye contact and smiles (you are making good progress)
  - a customer repeatedly looks at his watch and then at the exit door (he wants to get out – and quickly)

a call centre – specialised telephone skills

the need for communication – the telephone

Some organisations, eg holiday companies, carry out a substantial amount of business using the **telephone**, in which case training is given in telephone technique.

Some businesses specialise in telephone contact – **call centres**, for example – and you may find yourself making a telephone enquiry to your local bank which is answered and dealt with in India. This is a problem if you are calling to say that you have left your glasses in the bank branch.

Staff working in this environment will have to be well trained in telephone skills, although there is a tendency to rely on set 'scripts'.

Contact Us

Please check our list of frequently asked questions below to see if your query can be answered without you having to email us. If not, you can email us using one of the links at the bottom of the page. Please choose the link which most closely describes your problem, this helps our customer support team to answer your query as soon as possible.

Frequently Asked Questions

Can't remember your password?
If, for any reason, you are unable to remember your password just go to the Log In page then click onto "Send Me My Password". Enter your registered email address then click "Send Me My Password" and your new password will be emailed to you. If you have any difficulties, call us on 0845-800-1020.

www.play.com – customer service by email and telephone

using email

Businesses which operate online are likely to communicate with customers by **email**, which is generally less formal than the traditional **letter** which is still widely used in customer service communications and requires very specific skills.

The problem with email communication is that although it is informal, it can also be impersonal. Sometimes email responses are automated – for example, a notification when goods have been despatched from an online shop. The information is useful but the personal touch has been lost.

effective use of premises

The layout and organisation of premises are important factors in welcoming customers and putting them at ease. Issues to consider when assessing the premises of, say, a supermarket include:

- is the layout logical and are the product areas well signed?
- is it tidy – or are there boxes lying around, blocking customer access?
- are the aisles wide enough?
- are special offers prominently placed – at the end of the display stands?
- are the display stands well stocked?
- if the customer needs a trolley, are they readily available and is the car park easily accessible?

assessing virtual premises

If you are assessing a non-retail organisation you will need to rethink these questions, but applying the same principles of layout, tidiness, accessibility and availability of the product.

For example, if you are analysing an online shop such as Amazon, you will need to assess features such as site navigation, clarity of page design, up-to-date content and ease of use of the online checkout.

the right product

An easily overlooked feature of customer service is the product itself. Returning to shopping again – is the product of high quality or does it provide value for money?

It all depends on what the customer expects. Some retailers pride themselves on high levels of **quality** – customers will expect to pay more for a Rolex watch or a Rolls Royce car. The objective of other businesses is to provide **value for money**, and, although claiming to provide a quality product, the quality of their goods may not always match those of their more expensive competitors. The 'cheaper' shops may also fall short on the quality of product information and after-sales service. As the common saying goes, 'You gets what you pays for.' That is what the customer will expect and the shopping environment will reflect it.

customer needs and organisational needs

It must be remembered that the customer is only one of a number of **stakeholders** of an organisation. Stakeholders are people who have an interest in the business, eg shareholders, employees and suppliers. The objectives of customer service must tie in with the demands of these other stakeholders and not see them out of pocket. For example, a business in its drive to produce a high-quality product must not incur costs that will significantly reduce its profits and the dividend payments to its owner shareholders. On the other hand, a business that aims to provide good value to its customers must not drop its prices to attract customers and then expect its suppliers (who are also stakeholders) to foot the bill by dropping their prices as well. You may be able to think of examples of this practice.

a note on identifying customer service problems

In your assessment you will need to be able to identify customer service shortcomings. Activity 24.6 on page 451 helps you to do this. First, however, read the Case Study on the next two pages which illustrates good practice in customer service. Osborne Books is very grateful to Homebase for their help in compiling this study.

Case Study – customer service at Homebase

the background

Homebase is the second largest DIY brand in the UK. It has a clear strategy for growth, building on its strong position in the DIY market and expanding into home furnishings to meet the rising demands of increasingly sophisticated customers.

a Homebase store

Homebase offers approximately 40,000 DIY, home and gardening lifestyle products with a growing emphasis on design and décor, including an own-brand range as well as branded and designer-led labels.

Homebase has nearly 300 stores in the UK and the Republic of Ireland, employing over 17,000 staff in the UK who are trained to a high level, ensuring they have a thorough product knowledge, including how to use items, and a good understanding of features and benefits. Homebase serves over 1.5 million customers a week.

customer service – premises & products

The Homebase brand is characterised by a fresh green and yellow colour scheme which predominates in its premises, which are light and airy with wide aisles, providing a relaxing and welcoming shopping environment.

The service desk is a focus of customer service provision. Customers can obtain information, home deliveries, refunds and exchanges from the staff here. Disabled customers are well looked after with a wheelchair height writing surface and an amplification device for people with hearing problems.

Homebase also provides value-for-money products and runs numerous promotions, prominently placed at strategic places on the shop floor.

This is a writing surface only

a Homebase service desk with facilities for the disabled

customer service – staff and staff training

The Homebase staff offer friendly and informed customer service. The training programme they undergo encourages an active approach to helping customers, the objective being that the customer will leave the store happy and come back again.

> This customer looks confused I better help

Dealing with customers is based on a four-stage approach, illustrated by four cute fishy posters pinned up in the Homebase staff room.

1 **'be ready'** – look out for customers needing help and anticipate their needs (see above)

2 **'be there'** – be available to help when help is needed

3 **'be helpful'** – use communication skills to find out what the customer needs and then fulfil that need, or pass the customer to someone who is able to help

4 **'be remembered'** (illustrated below left) – this is an important objective – to get the customer to remember the good service given so that he/she can tell others and also come back to shop again. This then establishes the highly valued customer 'relationship'.

> Would you like me to help you to your car?!

> What a great service

Staff are asked to 'commit' to these four stages by writing a commitment statement and their name on a form and pinning it up on the staff room wall below the posters. An extract from this form is shown below.

I commit to _making every customer I serve leave the store happier than when they came in_

Activity 24.5 – customer service at Homebase

Read through the Homebase Case Study and answer the questions that follow. Visit a local Homebase store if you are able to, and make notes on what you see to reinforce your answers.

1 How does Homebase plan its premises to provide a customer-friendly environment?

2 What is Homebase's policy on product promotion to customers, and why does this appeal to customers? How is this seen in the Homebase stores? Are there any other ways (not mentioned in the Case Study) in which Homebase carries out this policy?

3 How does Homebase train its staff in customer service skills? Why is it so important to Homebase that it is remembered by customers?

Activity 24.6 – how effective is the customer service?

Part of your assessment requires you to evaluate the strengths and weaknesses of the customer service activities of one of the organisations you have investigated and to suggest improvements that could be made.

This will involve a thorough investigation of the organisation concerned. The evidence you should gather to obtain highest marks will:

■ present a **wide range** of customer service activities rather than just a few

■ link the customer service activities where possible to the **aims and objectives** of the organisation (see the Mission Statement, if there is one)

■ focus on the **strengths** and **weaknesses** of the customer service provided so that you can come to a reasoned judgement when you suggest improvements (you can use a SWOT analysis)

■ state which activities you think are the **most important** and give weight to these in your argument

The object of this Activity is to prepare you for this investigation and evaluation. You will then be able to make an informed judgement about possible improvements.

The following list of tasks is a suggestion only:

1 Identify the areas of the organisation where the customer service 'message' is put over. These will obviously vary from organisation to organisation but could include:

    - **premises** – design and layout and facilities for all types of customer (the term 'premises' can include shop, office or website)

    - the **products** or **services** provided – whether they fulfil the aims of being high quality or value products/services

    - the **staff** themselves – the means of communication used, the skills needed and the staff training provided.

2 Make a checklist of these areas for investigation, related to the organisation being investigated.

3 Find examples of evidence of these customer service features, making the range as wide as possible.

4 Against each item note down any significant strengths or weaknesses. For example, a strength would include the provision of facilities for the disabled in a shop; a weakness would be staff who were not prepared to approach customers to offer help.

5 Against each item which has a weakness, note down any improvements you can think of, eg extra staff training in communication skills.

The **organisation** of this data will be an important factor. Based on the checklist (see 2 above) you could set up a table in Word or a spreadsheet with separate columns headed 'Examples of customer service', 'Strengths', 'Weaknesses', 'Improvements'.

CHAPTER SUMMARY

- A 'customer' is someone who is provided with goods and services by the private sector or the public sector – by a supermarket or a dentist.

- Customers can be classified in a variety of ways.

- New customers are valuable to an organisation as they bring extra sales or activity; existing customers must be looked after to ensure that they stay.

- External customers are people outside the organisation which provides the goods or services; internal customers are employees or departments within the organisation who depend on other employees or departments.

- Customers have very specific needs which have to be looked after: for example, customers in dependent age groups (children, old people), people with disabilities, people with language difficulties and different cultural backgrounds.

- Effective customer service will result in happy customers.

- Effective customer service means fulfilling customer expectations in three distinct stages: before the transaction (eg encouraging the customer to buy), during the transaction (eg during the payment process), and after the transaction (eg the after-sales service).

- The aim of providing good customer service is to establish an ongoing customer relationship in which the satisfied customer will come back again and recommend others to do the same.

- In order to achieve customer loyalty, the organisation will need to keep in touch with the customer and reward his or her loyalty. This is the basis of customer relationship management (CRM).

- The level of customer service offered will vary according to the nature of the transaction, eg buying a newspaper, having hair styled.

- Effective customer service relies on the customer service 'message' being put over through the premises, products and staff of the organisation.

- Effective customer service relies on the staff of the organisation being well trained, working as a team and using a wide range of communication skills.

- Customer service within an organisation must tie in with its aims and objectives. The focus on customers should not adversely affect other stakeholders such as shareholders and suppliers.

KEY TERMS

customer	a person or organisation that obtains goods or services
internal customer	a person or department within an organisation that is dependent on another employee or department
external customer	a person or organisation outside the organisation that obtains goods or services
customer service	turning a customer into a satisfied customer
customer care	providing customer service
customer satisfaction	a 'feel good' factor which affects both customer and staff and which encourages the customer to come back again
customer service desk	the counter in a shop or other organisation open to the public which offers all features of customer service: advice, refunds, exchanges, lodging of complaints
customer relationship management (CRM)	the process of establishing a relationship with an existing customer and then developing that relationship and customer loyalty through regular contact and the provision of customer benefits
teamwork	organising the staff so that they work as members of a coherent team, each member taking responsibility for what the team does and sharing in the rewards for achievement
stakeholder	a person or organisation which has an interest in a business

25

Customer service – keeping the quality

CUSTOMER SUGGESTION BOX

PLEASE POST HERE

Starting point

In order to retain customer loyalty, organisations must maintain the quality of their customer service.

Quality means keeping to a set of established standards. Organisations must carry out a constant process of monitoring standards and aim to improve on them. They do this by keeping in touch with their customers and by asking staff for feedback.

In this way organisations aim to build up a loyal customer base and, in the case of businesses, ensure future profitability.

What you will learn from this chapter

- Standards for customer service should be maintained by all organisations who deal with customers. These standards may be internally set, or they may be established by external industry bodies. They are often published in the form of customer charters or codes of practice.

- The levels of customer service should be monitored closely by analysing feedback from customers through suggestion schemes, questionnaires and customer complaints. This will enable problems to be identified and standards of service improved.

- The organisation itself will also monitor customer service levels through staff feedback and 'mystery customers' – outsiders employed to pose as customers.

- Organisations must be aware of, and comply with, all the legislation and regulations which affect the way customer service operates.

Requirements of your Assessment

In the last chapter we concentrated on:

- a comparison of customer service in two contrasting organisations
- an evaluation of the strengths and weaknesses of the customer service activities of one organisation and suggestions for improvements

In this chapter we provide guidance for your continued evaluation of one chosen organisation. You will need to:

- research and analyse the ways in which the chosen organisation maintains, monitors and then improves the quality of its customer service
- investigate the way in which current legislation affects the way in which customer service operates

All this investigative work will lead up to your **presentation** of your findings.

Remember that the notes that you have compiled when investigating customer service should support your submission and be accompanied by a detailed witness statement from your teacher or lecturer.

Maintaining the Quality

We have seen in the last chapter that organisations need to keep their customers and keep them happy. An unhappy customer is a lost customer: one bad meal or a complaint ignored is enough to send a loyal customer away, never to return.

setting the standards

It is essential, therefore, that the high standards of customer service outlined in the last chapter are maintained at all times. This is easier said than done. How are standards set for an organisation? How is the management of the organisation going to ensure that they are maintained? The answer to this lies to a large extent in the **size** of the organisation.

In the case of a **small organisation** such as a small business, there are unlikely to be any written standards. It will be up to the owner(s) to monitor how well staff are dealing with customers. This may be no bad thing: it is often the small businesses which offer the best customer service because the customers get to know the staff personally and receive individual attention. The relationship in psychological terms becomes social in nature. Customers return because they 'feel at home' with the staff of a small organisation.

codes of practice and customer charters

In the case of **large organisations** such as local authorities, NHS trusts and public limited companies – eg Boots, Homebase and utility companies – standards of customer care are often set down formally. They can take a number of forms:

- **codes of practice**, established by an industry, eg the standards of service of the Association of Energy Suppliers (AES) which represents energy companies, or the Banking Code issued by the Banking Code Standards Board and adopted by the UK financial services industry (banks and building societies)

- **customer service charters** established by individual companies, either adopting the guidelines from codes of practice, or if these do not exist, establishing independent 'rules' for dealing with customers

Study the examples of these codes and charters shown on the next page.

customer service standards

Whatever the size of the organisation, the same principles are likely to govern customer care:

- attention to the customer
- response times
- dealing with complaints

The manager of a small business, for example, might issue guidelines to staff as shown below. They are simple, but will help to maintain customer loyalty and staff motivation.

CUSTOMER SERVICE

Staff are expected to:

1 Greet customers politely

2 Know the products

3 Respond to communications promptly:

- answer the telephone after three rings
- answer emails the same day
- answer/acknowledge letters the same day

4 Deal with complaints using the standards complaints form, resolving the complaint within seven days

These standards of service will be monitored closely by the management.

Examples of excellence in customer service will be rewarded with a £20 wage bonus.

Remember! A happy customer is a customer who comes back again.

Charter Marks

Note also that public sector organisations may apply for a **Charter Mark**, which indicates compliance with a high standard of customer service.

CHARTER MARK
Putting the customer first
Promoting choice, flexibility and innovation in public service

CHARTER MARK

Charter Mark is the government's national standard for excellence in customer service in the public sector.

www.chartermark.gov.uk

CODE OF PRACTICE

The Banking Code and You

Setting standards for banks, building societies and other banking service providers

We subscribe to the Banking Code. Not all financial institutions do. Doing your banking with someone who subscribes to the Banking Code gives you extra confidence. You should check that any other financial institution you deal with for banking services (such as savings accounts, current accounts, loans and credit cards) also subscribes.

The Banking Code sets minimum standards of good service that you can expect from banks, building societies and other providers of banking services. This leaflet tells you about our key commitments and responsibilities to you under the Banking Code.

COMPANY CHARTER: GUARANTEED STANDARDS

Guaranteed Standards provided by npower

Electricity account enquiries
If you tell us you believe your electricity bill is incorrect or that you wish to change the way you pay your electricity bills, we will respond within 5 working days. If you are subsequently due a refund we will pay you within 5 working days. If we don't we will pay you £20. This standard only applies to customers in the Central Networks (West) distribution area.

Meter accuracy
IIf you tell us that you believe your gas or electricity meter is inaccurate, we will give you a plausible explanation within 5 working days or contact you within 7 working days to arrange a visit. If we don't we will pay you £20.

Making and keeping appointments
When we, your local electricity distribution company or your gas transporter visit your home you will be offered a timed appointment within a reasonable time and that appointment will be kept. If not you will receive £20.

npower is a leading energy company supplying electricity and gas to both residential and business customers.

npower abides by the Code of Practice of the Association of Energy Suppliers (AES), of which it is a member. This code has been developed in close co-operation with the government, the industry regulator Ofgem and consumer bodies. Its aim is to provide customers with excellent service and advice.

npower has issued its own 'charter', its Guaranteed Standards, which are illustrated above; these reflect the AES Code of Practice.

www.npower.com

The **Banking Code** is issued by the Banking Code Standards Board. Its mission is to ensure that the Banking Code (for personal customers) and the Business Banking Code deliver their promises of fair dealing and standards of good banking practice to the customers of UK banks and building societies.

www.bankingcode.org.uk

Activity 25.1 – internal and external customers

Use your chosen organisation or a large local shop or service provider (eg bus or train company) to carry out the following activities:

1   Investigate to see if the organisation is covered by a code of practice or customer charter. If the documents are available, identify and make a note of the terms relating to customer service standards and the way in which customer complaints are dealt with.

2   Investigate the way in which the organisation deals with customer complaints (eg the return of a faulty product to a shop, or a problem such as a missed job interview caused by a very late train).

3   Where appropriate, suggest ways in which these processes could be improved.

Suggestion: carry out a role play involving a customer with a complaint and a member of staff at the customer services desk to appreciate the ways in which the confrontation can affect both staff and customer.

Monitoring and Improving Customer Service

If an organisation wishes to maintain its established standards of customer service, it will need to monitor those standards. If there is a falling off from the standards, action will need to be taken to prevent customers from leaving. If customer performance is better than the standards, the organisation will have succeeded in its aim of improving its levels of service. The aim of organisations should be that of continual improvement.

Methods of monitoring standards involve people both inside and outside the organisation. The **internal** monitoring includes:

- monitoring the level and content of customer complaints
- using staff feedback from 'team' meetings, quality circles and suggestion schemes
- random visits from senior management, including the MD

Monitoring using **external** sources includes:

- customer suggestion schemes and focus groups
- random customer questionnaires
- using loyalty scheme customers for obtaining feedback
- receiving feedback from visits by external inspectors
- sending in a 'mystery customer'

We will now describe these methods in more detail.

internal feedback – monitoring customer complaints

The seriousness, content and frequency of customer complaints are useful indicators of how well customer service is performing in an organisation.

It is essential that an organisation has a formal system for the logging and managerial analysis of customer complaints, so that action can be taken as appropriate. Details of complaints might be recorded on a special form which remains 'live' until the issue is resolved. The job of the customer services staff in each case is to prevent the problem recurring. Each time a complaint is made, the organisation is in danger of losing a customer.

Typical complaints might be:

- **Problems with goods or services** – here the staff will need to have a good working knowledge of customers' legal rights so that the correct response can be given (see pages 466–467 for more detail). It will normally be a case of a refund or an exchange. If the problem persists, the supplier will need to be contacted for an explanation. The supplier may need to be changed.

- **Problems with customer service** – here the customer may be reporting rudeness, inefficiency, problems with the premises or non-delivery of goods or services. In each case the relevant staff member should be identified where possible, an explanation requested and a suitable apology made to the customer. Remember that although the 'customer is always right', the customer may also be a bad-tempered, miserable individual whom nobody can please. Staff must be given a hearing. If this problem recurs, there will be a case for reinforcing staff training to improve the standard of service.

team meetings, quality circles and staff suggestion schemes

The customer service staff who are constantly in the 'front line' when dealing with customers are perhaps in the best place to sense how well customer service is succeeding. Organisations that appreciate this point will establish a regular routine involving:

- **meetings** of the customer service 'team' – ie everyone involved in dealing with customers – to discuss problems and successes and to make recommendations for improvements, eg to premises layout, staff uniform, merchandising, opening hours and so on

- meetings of **quality circles** – special committees set up to discuss aspects of quality across all the functions of the organisation, including customer service

- **staff suggestion schemes** – welcoming suggestions submitted by staff (confidentially in writing) covering areas such as customer service

You said...we listened...

> Increased award from £10 to £20. A more meaningful and worthwhile individual amount to spend

> Can be awarded to individuals or teams. Teams can and do make a difference and from this year a team award can be made and celebrated together

> Updated badges and certificates. New Making A Difference Award certificates and badges to be worn with pride

The Homebase 'Making a Difference' award

Organisations are more likely to get a response from staff if they offer some form of money incentive for good suggestions and also for good performance, eg a bonus added to wages, or some form of spending tokens. The Homebase 'Making a Difference' award is an example of this.

visits by senior management

Customer service can be kept up to standard if there is the possibility that senior management – or even the Managing Director – will come and see how things are going. This can be taken a step further if the senior management or MD also join in and work alongside the customer service staff. Often the management will see areas for improvement, and staff will appreciate and be motivated by the fact that management are prepared to 'get their hands dirty'.

external feedback – customer suggestion schemes

Organisations will often try to get customer feedback about the success of customer service by providing a customer suggestion scheme. This might involve customers writing formal proposals and putting them in a letter box on the premises, or just writing comments in a book placed at a strategic point, eg on a table in a hotel reception or on the counter of a customer service desk. Experience has shown that customers are far more easily persuaded to write in a book rather than going to all the effort of posting a formal note (see the Sports Centre Case Study on page 465).

Customer comments of this type are a very valuable form of feedback to an organisation. They are voluntarily made – if they are negative they can be acted upon to improve service, and if they are positive they can be passed on to the staff involved who will then be motivated to keep up the high standards. In a Sports Centre, for example 'there is never any paper in the ladies loo' is a problem easily solved and 'Lisa's badminton coaching was brilliant!' will motivate Lisa to keep up and even improve her high standards.

focus groups

Organisations sometimes invite groups of customers or potential customers to come and discuss issues such as new product design or customer service schemes. In return for coffee and biscuits they are able to feed back comments and opinions from these **focus groups** for use by marketing and customer service management.

random customer questionnaires

Customers of an organisation such as a shop can also be encouraged to complete a questionnaire by randomly picking up a card or leaflet and completing it in return for a reward or entry to a competition.

The example below is from Slater Menswear which sells quality men's clothing – including well-known brands – at value-for-money prices. Note the marketing information which will be gathered from the 'Personal Details' and 'Survey' sections, and the customer service information gained from the 'Questionnaire'.

COMPLETE THE DETAILS BELOW AND POST TO US (NO STAMP REQUIRED) & YOU COULD WIN ONE OF FIVE £100 GIFT VOUCHERS IN OUR MONTHLY PRIZE DRAW

1. PERSONAL DETAILS (Please use block capitals)

DATE OF VISIT
FIRST NAME (MR/MS/MRS)
SURNAME
ADDRESS

POSTCODE
YEAR OF BIRTH

LOCATION OF STORE (Please tick box)

GLASGOW ☐ CARDIFF ☐ LEEDS ☐
ABERDEEN ☐ CHELTENHAM ☐ LIVERPOOL ☐
AYR ☐ CHESTER ☐ MANCHESTER ☐
BASINGSTOKE ☐ DUNDEE ☐ NEWCASTLE ☐
BIRMINGHAM ☐ EDINBURGH ☐ NOTTINGHAM ☐
BOLTON ☐ HULL ☐ WORCESTER ☐
CANTERBURY ☐

OTHER (please state)

SLATER MENSWEAR
www.slatermenswear.com

IS THIS YOUR FIRST VISIT YES ☐
TO SLATER MENSWEAR? NO ☐

2. QUESTIONNAIRE (Please tick appropriate box)

	EXCELLENT	GOOD	AVERAGE	POOR
WAS THE SERVICE	☐	☐	☐	☐
WAS THE SELECTION	☐	☐	☐	☐
WERE THE PRICES	☐	☐	☐	☐
STAFF APPEARANCE	☐	☐	☐	☐
ALTERATIONS	☐	☐	☐	☐
COLLECTIONS	☐	☐	☐	☐

PLEASE RATE THE SERVICE YOU RECEIVED FROM OUR STAFF (The names are on your receipt)
ENTER YOUR RECEIPT NO. HERE

NAME	EXCELLENT	GOOD	AVERAGE	POOR
SALES ASS'T	☐	☐	☐	☐
SALES ASS'T	☐	☐	☐	☐
SALES ASS'T	☐	☐	☐	☐
CASHIER	☐	☐	☐	☐

3. SURVEY (Please use block capitals)

HOW DID YOU HEAR ABOUT US? (Please tick)

NEWSPAPER ☐ POSTER ADVERTISING ☐
RADIO ☐ BUS ADVERTISING ☐
PERSONAL RECOMMENDATION ☐ TAXI ADVERTISING ☐
TV ☐ WEB SITE ☐

OTHER (please state)
(If newspaper, please state which one)

ARE THERE ANY OTHER PRODUCTS OR BRANDS YOU WOULD LIKE US TO STOCK?

ANY OTHER COMMENTS?

THANK YOU FOR YOUR HELP
PAUL SLATER, MANAGING DIRECTOR

Slater Menswear customer questionnaire

customer loyalty schemes

Commercial organisations, particularly in the retail sector, are developing customer relationships and encouraging their customers to stay by providing customer loyalty schemes. Examples of these are Boots Advantage, Homebase Spend & Save and Tesco Clubcard. These work by 'signing up' existing customers free of charge to a 'club' which persuades them to continue shopping by providing a wide range of benefits. Typical benefits include:

- a card which gives them points every time they make a purchase
- 'cash back' vouchers against future purchases
- special discount promotions
- air miles

These cards help the marketing function in many ways. Each time a purchase is made, the card is swiped through the checkout terminal, providing details of where the customers shop and what they buy. This builds up for each store a profile of its customer base in terms of lifestyle buying habits and enables it to plan the products it should keep in stock. Additionally, because the organisation has each 'club' customer's home address, it is also able to mail out a customer service questionnaire to each 'loyal' customer. This enables it to monitor customer service standards and make improvements where necessary. An extract from a Homebase questionnaire is shown below.

---

3. Have you had any questions or problems with Homebase during the past three months?

   □₁   Yes   (Please continue)   □₂   No   (Please skip to question 9)

4. Please tick **ONE** box that corresponds to the **most serious** question or problem you experienced

   □₁ Getting information before visiting the store   □₇ Availability of product information
   □₂ Appearance and cleanliness of store   □₈ Getting help from Homebase staff
   □₃ Product too expensive   □₉ Service at Information Desk or Extra Choice Desk
   □₄ Product out of stock   □₁₀ Other in-store services, e.g. board cutting, paint mixing
   □₅ Product range   □₁₁ Service at check-out
   □₆ Product quality   □₁₂ Product delivery and/or installation service

5. Have you contacted anyone at Homebase about your **most serious** question or problem?

   □₁   Yes   (Please continue)   □₂   No   (Please skip to question 9)

6. Who have you contacted **at all** about your **most serious** problem, and which **one** did you have the **most** contact with?

	At all	Most				At all	Most	
a.	□	□	Information desk, in store	d.		□	□	Extra Choice/Ordering/Delivery Desk
b.	□	□	General assistant, in store	e.		□	□	Store, by telephone
c.	□	□	Check-out staff, in store	f.		□	□	Head office/Helpline

7. In total, how many times did you have to contact Homebase before receiving an indication of a final response to your **most serious** question?

   □ 1   □ 2   □ 3   □ 4   □ 5   □ 6   □ 7+   □ Final response still not given

8. Which **ONE** of the following statements best describes your feelings about our response to your **most serious** question or problem?

   □₁ I was completely satisfied   □₄ I was not at all satisfied with the response given
   □₂ I was not completely satisfied, but the response was acceptable   □₅ I was not at all satisfied, no response was given
   □₃ I was not completely satisfied, but some response was given

---

a customer service questionnaire sent to Homebase Spend & Save customers

Activity 25.2 – monitoring customer service

Study the Homebase customer service questionnaire shown above.

1 Describe the aspects of customer service that it is monitoring.

2 Explain the benefit that this information will provide for the customer service management at Homebase.

3 Suggest actions that could be taken by the customer service management at Homebase on the basis of this information.

4 Obtain, if it is available, a copy of a customer service questionnaire from the organisation that you are investigating and note how effective it is in identifying problems with customer service.

external visitors – inspectors and 'mystery customers'

Another technique used by organisations to test out the standards of customer service and pinpoint problems is to use external visitors to make the assessment.

Sometimes the organisation will know that the visitors are arriving. These are often referred to as 'inspectors'. One example with which you may be familiar are the school or college inspectors who examine the resources and standard of teaching of a school or college.

Another example of an external visitor who assesses customer service is the 'mystery customer' who visits unannounced, disguised as a real customer. He or she will give the organisation a 'score' and make comments about various aspects of customer service which are then fed back to management so that action can be taken and improvements made where needed. A mystery customer of a shop, for example, might concentrate on three stages of the service process: being greeted by staff, the transaction itself, and paying at the checkout. An extract from a typical feedback sheet from a mystery customer of a shop is shown below. The area which needs improvement is immediately obvious!

MYSTERY CUSTOMER FEEDBACK: MEREFORD HIGH STREET STORE		visit: 20 July	
area of assessment	comment	points	percentage
Store presentation	Clean, tidy and well presented	68/75	91%
Helping customer	Staff member helpful and enthusiastic	17/25	68%
Electronic goods	Advice given in a confident manner	44/60	73%
Homeware	Staff polite, helpful and friendly	35/40	88%
Paying at till 1	Transaction slightly rushed	24/45	53%
Paying at till 2	Transaction impersonal	20/45	44%

Activity 25.3 – improving customer service

Make a list of the ways in which your chosen organisation monitors its levels of customer service, using both internal and external means.

Compare this list with the methods of monitoring explained on the last six pages of this chapter.

Identify areas in which you think the monitoring process could be expanded or improved.

Now read the Case Study of a Sports Centre on the next two pages and see how the principles of customer service can also be applied to a public sector service provider.

Case Study – Customer Service at a Sports Centre

St John's Sports Centre – the background

St John's Sports Centre is funded by local government. It provides a wide variety of sports facilities and classes to suit all ages and levels. The facilities include a sports hall, squash courts, a fully-fitted gymnasium, a crèche, a bar, an outdoor football pitch, changing rooms and toilets. It offers a wide range of classes, from aerobics to trampolining. It also runs a very successful holiday play scheme for school-age children.

Although the Centre charges for its services, the income from customers is not enough to keep the Centre open, so the local City Council provides the shortfall. A government-funded centre such as this has an obligation to provide high-level customer service. There are many competing facilities in the surrounding area, and the Centre is aware that if it does not attract and retain customers, it may be closed down, as the Council may not be willing to increase its grant.

the staff

The staff are well trained, qualifications including NVQs in Customer Care and Council-run courses such as 'Dealing with Difficult Situations'. The uniform of polo shirt and tracksuit is provided for staff working in the gym areas; employees on the reception desk receive a clothing allowance.

QUEST – quality standards

This Centre has demonstrated continuous improvement in the management of
- CUSTOMER SERVICE
- STAFFING
- FACILITIES
- STRATEGIC PLANNING

through independent on site Assessment, Mystery Visits and regular Reassessment.

QUEST is a national award scheme that monitors and reports on the level of quality being provided at sports facilities. Quest regularly examines the level of staff training, including appropriate qualifications for coaches, the facilities available, and the number and quality of programmes on offer. Quest also measures the extent to which the Centre improves its service over time, using onsite assessment and 'mystery visits'. Visit www.pmpconsult.com/quest/

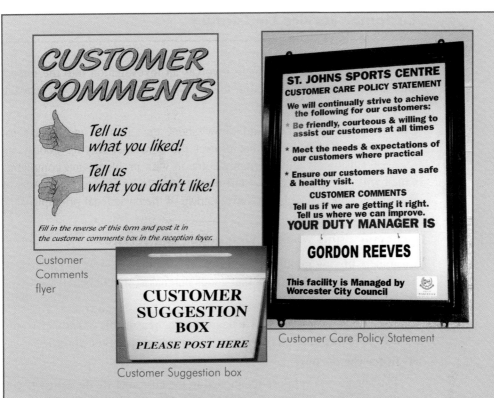

Customer Comments flyer

Customer Suggestion box

Customer Care Policy Statement

monitoring customer satisfaction

All staff are authorised to deal with customer complaints, but if the customer is not satisfied, the manager will deal with the problem. Customer satisfaction is measured in a variety of ways. Customers can write their complaints in the Customer Comments Book on the reception desk, and the manager will reply within seven days. There is also a Customer Comments flyer that customers can complete and put in the 'suggestion box' in the reception area. Experience has shown that customers are far more likely to respond straightaway and write in the book than fill in a separate form. From time to time the manager will run a 'Meet the Manager' session in the bar, where customers are invited to talk over issues relating to the running of the Centre. Finally, focus groups are organised to obtain feedback from key users such as badminton players.

customer retention

All members are sent a letter when their membership is due for renewal to try to get them to rejoin. Likewise, children who have been to the play scheme will be mailed offering them the chance to join in again in the next holidays.

The main method of retaining customers, however, is through maintaining high standards of customer service. This is very much in evidence at this Sports Centre. It was recently awarded a 'highly commended' award by Quest, making the Centre joint top award winner in England.

Customer Service Legislation

The last part of your assessment involves an investigation into the impact and effects of legislation on the customer service of your chosen organisation.

Customer service staff should know about the 'impact and effects' of legislation and regulations that protect the consumer buying goods and services. Customers will inevitably come in with problems and complaints which will raise legal issues. Staff do not have to be able to quote Acts of Parliament – they just need to have a grasp of the basic legal principles.

customer rights when buying goods and services

Customers **buying goods** are protected by a number of Acts of Parliament. The **Sale of Goods Act** states that goods purchased should be:

- **of satisfactory quality**

   The goods must meet the standard that a 'reasonable' customer would accept, taking account of the description and price of the goods.

- **fit for the purpose**

   This means any purpose mentioned to the customer by the seller. If you are buying a computer game and you explain you want one that can be played on a particular machine, the seller must not give you a game that cannot be played on that machine.

- **as described**

   This means described on the packaging or a display sign, or by sales staff. If a customer is told that a shirt is 100% cotton, then it should not be made of polyester and cotton.

If any of these three conditions is not met, the consumer is entitled to a full or a partial refund, depending on how soon the fault appears, how serious it is and how quickly the matter is taken up. Note also:

- the buyer can accept a replacement, but can also insist on a refund if a replacement is not wanted
- the buyer does not have to accept a credit note for spending on other purchases

The **Supply of Goods and Services Act** additionally protects the consumer when a **service** is provided by a business. This Act states that anyone who supplies a service – a haircut, a train journey, a holiday – must carry out the work:

- with reasonable care and skill
- within a reasonable time
- at a reasonable price

The problem here is, how do you decide what 'reasonable' is? The consumer is helped by standards laid down by various bodies – Trade Associations, professional bodies, or one of the official 'Watchdog' bodies such as Ofcom. Service businesses, power companies for example, operate compensation schemes when service standards are not reached (see page 457).

The **Trade Descriptions Act** makes it a criminal offence:

- to make false statements about goods offered for sale
- to make misleading statements about services

This Act affects false or misleading adverts, packaging and labels – for example, making a misleading statement about a service, eg 'our dry cleaning is guaranteed to remove every stain' when it does not.

EU influences on legislation

The **Sale and Supply of Goods to Consumers Regulations**, which came into force in 2003, implement an EU Directive geared towards harmonising consumer law throughout the EU, providing additional remedies to consumers in certain circumstances. In the case of the UK, consumers were already in a strong position, but the following additional rights were granted to UK consumers by this EU-based set of regulations:

- consumers will be entitled to their legal rights wherever they buy goods in the European Union
- UK consumers will have the right to a repair or replacement if goods are faulty
- if goods develop a fault within the first six months and the retailer wishes to dispute the claim, the retailer will be required to provide proof that the fault was not present when the goods were sold – in other words, the shop is unlikely to be able to refuse a claim for faulty goods within six months of purchase

Trading Standards and the Office of Fair Trading (OFT)

Consumers are entitled to take their complaints to their local **Trading Standards** office (www.tradingstandards.gov.uk) If this is threatened, the retailer would be well advised to meet the demands of the consumer because adverse publicity might damage the retailer's reputation.

Another body you should be aware of is the **Office of Fair Trading** (OFT), the UK government's consumer protection agency. The OFT states that it is 'responsible for making markets work well for consumers . . . by promoting and protecting consumer interests throughout the UK, while ensuring that businesses are fair and competitive'. The site www.oft.gov.uk contains a wealth of information and advice on consumer matters.

CHAPTER SUMMARY

■ An organisation needs to maintain high standards of customer service in order to retain its customers.

■ Industry standards – eg the standards of the power supply industry – are set down in Codes of Practice.

■ Individual organisations establish rules and targets in relation to customer service in the form of Customer Service Charters

■ Public sector organisations may apply to the government for a Charter Mark, which indicates compliance with a high standard of customer service.

■ An organisation should monitor its standards of customer service if it is to maintain those standards.

■ An organisation should also aim to continually improve its standards of customer service.

■ Internal monitoring of standards can be achieved by:

- analysis of customer complaints

- feedback from staff and team meetings

- quality circles and suggestion schemes

- visits from senior management

■ External monitoring is carried out through the use of:

- customer suggestion schemes and focus groups

- customer questionnaires

- feedback from 'loyalty' customers

- visits from mystery customers and other external visitors

■ Customer service staff must be aware of the impact and effects of consumer protection legislation (both UK and EU), although they will not be expected to be familiar with individual laws and regulations.

■ Individual consumer complaints may be taken to a Trading Standards office.

■ The Office of Fair Trading is the UK government's consumer protection agency.

KEY TERMS

code of practice   an industry standard for standards of service

customer charter   standards of customer service set out in a document by an individual organisation

charter mark   a mark of excellence for customer service in the public sector

quality circle   a group of employees who meet on a regular basis to analyse issues of quality in an organisation and suggest improvements

focus group   a group of independent individuals who meet to discuss issues such as product design or customer service

loyalty scheme   a scheme in which a customer is signed up free of charge to a club which provides a range of benefits (points on a card, cashback vouchers, special discounts) – the object being to establish the customer's loyalty and continued custom

mystery customer   an individual who tests out the customer service of an organisation by visiting the organisation and pretending to be a real customer

Trading Standards   the local office to which complaints about breaches of consumer legislation can be referred

Office of Fair Trading   the UK government's consumer protection agency which promotes and protects consumer interests

Investigating promotion

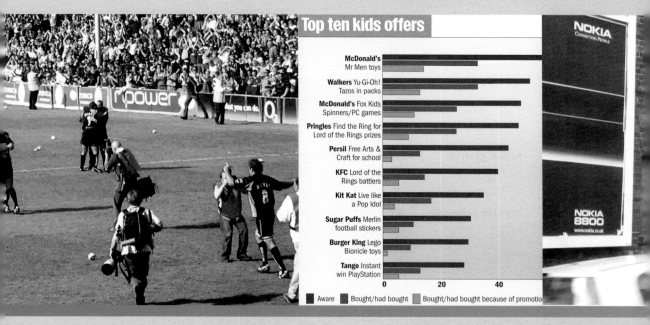

Top ten kids offers

	0	20	40
McDonald's Mr Men toys			
Walkers Yu-Gi-Oh! Tazos in packs			
McDonald's Fox Kids Spinners/PC games			
Pringles Find the Ring for Lord of the Rings prizes			
Persil Free Arts & Craft for school			
KFC Lord of the Rings battlers			
Kit Kat Live like a Pop Idol			
Sugar Puffs Merlin football stickers			
Burger King Lego Bionicle toys			
Tango Instant win PlayStation			

■ Aware ■ Bought/had bought ■ Bought/had bought because of promotion

In this unit you will take your study of marketing further by carrying out a detailed investigation of one of the 4 Ps of marketing – Promotion. This will involve research into:

■ the ways in which promotion supports the objectives of an organisation

■ the different promotional tools used, including advertising and PR

■ the constraints that an organisation faces when planning a promotional campaign in terms of resources

■ the constraints that an organisation faces when planning a promotional campaign in terms of legal rules and regulations

■ the importance of evaluating the success of a promotional campaign so that lessons can be learnt for the future

Unit 6

 Chapters in this Unit...

26

Promotional methods

Starting point

As you will have seen from Chapter 21 in this book, a promotional campaign aims to get a message about an organisation or its products to a carefully selected and targeted market segment – the teenage market, for example.

In your investigations for this Unit you will need to look carefully at the market segments identified by the businesses involved, analyse the promotional methods used and assess their success.

What you will learn from this chapter

- a promotional campaign must support corporate objectives such as maximisation of sales and profit

- a promotional campaign uses a mixture of tools (techniques), all of which must be co-ordinated; these include:
  - advertising, using a variety of media
  - public relations, which supports the advertising
  - sponsorship to raise public awareness of the business or product
  - sales promotions to attract buyers
  - direct marketing attracting an immediate purchase

- a promotional campaign therefore needs to clarify objectives, identify potential customers, and create messages that will attract them to the product or service; customers will need to be given this information through the use of an appropriate 'mix' of promotional techniques

the Promotional Campaign – your Investigations

When you studied the Marketing Mix earlier in the book, you will have been introduced to the concept of 'promotion'. Before you read this chapter, go back to page 352 in Chapter 21 and make sure that you are fully familiar with the section on promotion as far as page 373.

This current chapter guides you through the various methods used in a promotional campaign. It will greatly help your understanding if you become involved in investigating some real campaigns, possibly using local firms. It would be a good idea to divide into small groups and decide on products or services that are of interest to you. You could choose, for example, a retail outlet, a small manufacturer, a hotel or a leisure centre. You will need to ask the organisation if you can be briefed on its products or services, and the market segments involved. It would be a good idea if your school or college can arrange visits and speakers from the organisation.

a Promotional Campaign

preparing for your assessment

A **promotional campaign** is likely to consist of a 'mix' of advertising, publicity, public relations, sales promotions, sponsorship and direct marketing. You should already know all about these from studying for Unit 3 'Investigating marketing' in Chapter 21. You will find the practical aspects of these processes explained further in this and the next chapter. If you study and investigate real-life promotional campaigns, you will be well prepared for your external assessment which requires you to apply your knowledge of promotion in two ways:

- answering questions on Case Studies – which you will not have seen before
- answering questions on organisations which you have studied

the campaign in a nutshell

A promotional campaign consists of agreeing objectives, identifying the target market segment(s), learning how to affect buyer behaviour with appropriate messages, and choosing the right media to deliver those messages. The costs need to be analysed, a total budget agreed and the whole campaign carried out at the right time. At the end of the campaign, all promotional activities must then be evaluated.

the Campaign – Objectives and Overview

The objectives of the organisation promoting the campaign must be clearly understood by the marketing function, and by the chosen external advertising agency if one is used, because the whole approach to later decisions on media choice, message and timing are affected.

The campaign will therefore try to achieve the objectives of the organisation and a whole range of promotional activities will be chosen to have an impact on buyer behaviour – to get the chosen market sector 'to buy'.

The main promotional objectives and promotional techniques are as follows:

- **promoting the business and its products, to sell more products overall, or to maximise profits**

    These are main corporate objectives and therefore must also be supported by marketing objectives. Promotions to consumers will stress the benefits to be gained from buying the product – so increasing sales and profits.

- **creating awareness of a new product**

    This is a basic objective and very necessary in generating the initial sales that decide whether the product will survive in the marketplace. Firstly, the 'trade' (selling outlets) must be made aware of the product's existence. Secondly, the targeted consumers must be informed.

- **raising awareness of existing products**

    It is important to keep consumers aware of existing products, despite the constant stream of new products entering the market.

- **creating a image**

    New products in particular need a 'personality' that consumers can relate to, that suits their own lifestyle and the way that they as individuals wish to be thought of. The concept of image relates to brand name as well as to specific products and much advertising is devoted to giving an identity to specific brand names.

- **changing an image where necessary**

    External influences can affect the impact of brand images built up over many years. The anti-obesity lobby, for example, played havoc with the advertising messages of many businesses. The result was a series of exercises in which 'images' were redesigned: fast food chains became 'healthier' and, as you can see on the next page, the Michelin man advertising car tyres lost weight!

Michelin Man is affected by the anti-obesity lobby

■ **public relations**

Public relations (PR) also relates to image – it aims to safeguard and promote to the public a positive image of the whole organisation and its products. It sets the scene that will allow an advertising message to fall on receptive ears, as well as correcting mistakes and repairing damage as they occur. Loss of reputation – eg a food product which is found to contain toxins – will otherwise destroy the effect of the best adverts.

■ **publicity**

Publicity is different from public relations. It aims to get the main media such as newspapers, TV and radio to feature a company's name and products on news items – for free. Controversy can actually be a good thing: sales of new AA road atlases soared beyond all targets when the the fact that they contained the location of all fixed speed cameras was argued about on TV, radio and in the press. As the saying goes, 'There is no such thing as bad publicity.'

■ **sponsorship**

Sponsorship can also enhance the company image. It provides funds or other means of support in return for publicity. It can operate on a local or national level. Sports and athletics sponsorship by sportswear and drinks manufacturers is an obvious example (Nike, Adidas, Lucozade, Carling, Heineken).

■ **sales promotion**

Sales promotion objectives are similar to those of advertising in that they try to increase sales and draw attention to the product. They specialise in creating interest in the product at the point of sale, getting retailers interested in stocking the product and encouraging consumer impulse buying.

■ **direct marketing**

Direct marketing achieves a sale by advertising and asking for the order at the same time, eg advertising products on the internet and TV. It enables shopping to be carried out from home. It also has the advantage of saving money by cutting out the middle person (eg the wholesaler) and so improving profitability.

■ **communicating effectively to provide information that will satisfy the needs of target customers**

Effective communication might include giving technical specifications, product availability (sales outlets), price ranges, how to use the product correctly, and many other items of helpful advice that make consumers feel better about an organisation.

Activity 26.1 – objectives and techniques

Divide into small groups within the class and choose a local business to discuss. This could either be a national business with a local presence (eg a well-known supermarket) or a local independent business. It could be a manufacturer, service provider or retailer. In your groups:

1 Write down a list of what you consider to be the main objectives of the business (look at Chapter 2 if you want a reminder of what these might be).

2 Write down the ways in which the business promotes itself and how these promotional methods can persuade consumers to buy the products (eg promotion using advertising, PR, sponsorship – look at the list on the previous two pages).

Identifying the Prospects and Target Markets

A **prospect** is a possible buyer of the product, or person who receives the marketing message. Prospects can be grouped into categories, which we know already as **market segments**, according to demography, geography and psychography (see pages 295-300). You also need to appreciate the importance of lifestyle, because buyer behaviour related to lifestyle will also place consumers into categories. The key to getting this right is effective market research.

Market research (see pages 304-320) collects and analyses information about the many markets that exist. A sample of the population should accurately cover social class, age, sex and regionality, all in the correct proportions. Research is undertaken on a regular basis with as near as possible the same type of people, to retain continuity. Typical questions ask about family (size and structure), spending on the home, hobbies and leisure, TV programmes watched, newspapers and magazines read. This provides businesses and advertisers with information about total market sizes and which social groups buy which product types. Equally importantly, it will show which media reach which target groups.

Creating the Message

How do you turn prospects into customers? A suitable message must be communicated to them which stresses the benefits to be gained from purchasing the product or service in question. It must also be persuasive enough to make them take the 'buying decision'. A good campaign has a **USP**, which stands for a 'unique selling point', or a 'unique sales proposition'. This distinguishes a product from the competition, and simplifies the key benefits to be gained by responding to the message.

An effective advertisement follows the simple formula **AIDCA** in trying to achieve its aims. AIDCA stands for **A**ttention, **I**nterest, **D**esire, **C**onviction and **A**ction, and works as follows

- the **Attention** of the prospects (target customers) must be obtained – by use of noise, movement or colour
- **Interest** can be engaged by a headline stressing a particular benefit to be obtained, or the mention of a subject area in which the prospect will be interested
- **Desire** is activated by having one or two key benefits of the product spelt out clearly in the limited time or space available
- **Conviction** can only be achieved if the initial desire is followed swiftly with further facts about the benefits on offer, like 'value for money' or some other benefit; this leads to:
- **Action** – as any professional salesperson will tell you, the whole exercise collapses unless there is some invitation for the prospect to place the order – an address (web or postal) to contact, a coupon, a phone number

Buyer Behaviour

If you understand the psychology of consumers, you can offer the benefits to which they will respond. In marketing, there are two levels at which consumers make their choices: the **factual** (physical) and the **emotional**. Marketing messages must operate at both levels (see page 297).

the factual message

Factual considerations are essentially practical factors which will interest the prospect:

- **features**: how a product is constructed and how it works, its reliability and performance – eg a computer or an MP3 player
- **economic considerations** relating to the budget of the trade buyer or the personal finances of the consumer and his/her disposable income – these determine the importance that product price plays in the buying decision, and the need for value for money; economic considerations ensure that 'price' will always be a key factor in the buying decision, and this is why so many advertising messages feature this basic information

the emotional message

Emotional (behavioural) considerations relate to the psychological approach, and the understanding of what really triggers the choice of product or service purchased. It is based on Maslow's Hierarchy of Needs:

the need . . .	which is achieved by . . .
self-actualisation	personal growth and self fulfilment
Esteem	Recognition
	Achievement
	Status
Social needs	Acceptance/love/friendship
Safety needs	Security
	Freedom from pain and threats
Physiological needs	Food, water, air, rest

The basic point here is that every consumer has a list of priorities in life when deciding what is wanted and what will be bought. Needs start at the bottom of the pyramid with basic instincts: the need to survive, be safe and accepted by your fellow being, Then, with increasing affluence, personal desires such as self-esteem, status and self-fulfilment become more important.

Advertisers appreciate that this appeal to different types of need is the key to message creation. Examples of the types of need include, in order of priority:

physiological needs	food and drink, sleep and clean air
safety needs	car safety and security, insurance, health care
social needs	acceptance by others, happy family life, romance, a partner
esteem	being thought fashionable, having money to spend – the right car, clothes, clubs, credit cards
self-actualisation	personal fulfilment – achieving ambitions, acquiring skills, spoiling yourself 'for a job well done'

Activity 26.2 – sending the right message

Divide into small groups within the class and identify examples of adverts which appeal to the levels of need shown above. In each case establish the 'message' given by the advertiser and the ways in which it is made persuasive by the advertiser.

Discuss areas where there is a combination of 'needs' which is appealed to, for example a fashionable drink that fulfils both a physiological need and also a desire for esteem.

essentials of an effective advert

An effective advert should contain a message. The message can be serious or humorous in tone. If humour is involved, make sure the prospects are laughing with the product and not at it!

A good slogan creates a lasting effect. Some have been adopted as common sayings. What slogans can you recall?

An effective advert should contain a good eye-catching headline offering a key benefit, some form of picture and as much relevant detail as space or time permits. It should encourage the prospect to take action NOW, and provide a coupon or a website/postal address or a telephone number.

In the Activity on the next page you will have the opportunity to create your own advert.

Shown below are details of some advertising campaigns from *Campaign* magazine (courtesy Haymarket Business Publications). Note that the principle of an advertising 'message' applies equally well to a charity.

GETTING THE ADVERTISING MESSAGE ACROSS

Nike | Nice and new

The lowdown

A spot for the new Nike Tuned7 shoe, available exclusively at the footwear chain Footlocker, shows just how far one man is prepared to go to keep his new trainers looking box-fresh.

His route home from the shops involves rolling down hills, crawling across a park and walking on his hands for the final stretch to his front door. (Why he didn't simply wear his old shoes is unclear.)

Footlocker operates some 4,000 stores in 18 countries across North America, Europe and Australia. Last month, the company reported a 15.1 per cent increase in quarterly sales, up to $1.53 billion in the three months to 29 January 2005.

NSPCC | Babies and toddlers 2005

The lowdown

The Government's Children's Act, which outlaws smacking children, should be enough to make most parents think twice about raising an aggressive hand.

The NSPCC is running a new TV spot through Saatchi & Saatchi that focuses on how easily and unnecessarily adults take their daily frustrations out on their children. The ad shows adults in frustrating circumstances; the scenes gather momentum, with a man missing his tube and a woman angry at being stuck in traffic. The final scene shows a woman lunge towards her toddler as if to hit him. The ad ends with the line: "Hit means lost it."

Activity 26.3 – creating an advert

Work in small groups to create a video advert.

Agree a product or service with your tutor, write a script that you can act out in front of a video camera, allocate the parts and get filming.

As this is a TV-type advert, its total length should not be more than 40 seconds. It will take much rehearsal and retaking to get to even a reasonable performance, but you will improve your communication skills in the process.

If you have chosen a physical product, have that product on display, or in use, and stress to your intended audience the benefits that a buyer will gain.

Remember – select your market segment and create the right message.

Advertising Media – an Introduction

a question of choice

There are many methods of promotion available to a business. The problem facing the marketing function – whatever its size – is to decide on which mix of promotional methods to use to achieve its objective in the most effective way. It is precisely this question of choice which will form an important element of your investigations in this Unit and which will feature in your external Unit assessment.

The choice can be made by the marketing function, but if skills are lacking or if the likely campaign is very complex, businesses are more likely to seek additional professional help from an independent advertising agency which can advise on or manage the whole promotional campaign – but at a cost.

using an advertising agency

An **advertising agency** is an independent commercial organisation skilled in organising advertising, normally for larger organisations. An agency's clients are not only businesses, advertising agencies manage the advertising for bodies such as political parties and charities. Investigate the sites some of the famous agency names such as: Publicis (www.publicis.co.uk), Abbott Mead Vickers BBDO (www.amvbbdo.co.uk), JWT (www.jwt.co.uk), and M&C Saatchi (www.mcsaatchi.com)

Why are advertising agencies needed? Because there are many different ways to advertise and many different 'audiences' and media, getting the best out of advertising is a highly demanding task. A typical advertising campaign

Welcome to Publicis

If you believe in brand ideas and world class creativity that unifies every consumer contact point, then welcome to the building.

We're a seamless communications agency that operates under one Profit and Loss account. Our cross-functional teams unite specialists from advertising, relationship marketing and publishing. These teams work together, to develop amazing and relevant creative work that speaks with the customer wherever they connect with our clients and their brands.

Welcome to the world of Holistic Difference.

click to continue

Visit www.publicis.co.uk

might involve input from writers, photographers, designers and TV production companies. The advertising agency finds out what message the business wants to deliver to the targeted consumers, and can then turn it into a piece of artwork for a newspaper or magazine, or into a commercial for TV or cinema, or a poster.

As mentioned earlier, not all businesses will have either the funds or the inclination to use an advertising agency, but you should investigate them and visit their websites. They are the experts in what this Unit is all about.

Useful websites for finding out about the advertising agency industry include:

 www.ipa.co.uk (The Institute of Practitioners in Advertising [IPA])

www.isp.org.uk (The Institute of Sales Promotion [ISP])

The Case Study that follows gives an introduction to what is involved in a successful promotional campaign. Read it and answer the questions that follow. The remainder of the chapter examines advertising media in more detail and shows how they are used in the smaller business, so preparing you for the type of questions you could get in the Unit assessment.

Case Study – Lynx Pulse

This Case Study is based on extracts from an article in *Marketing*.

The text and images are reproduced by kind permission of Haymarket Business Publications Limited.

Lynx: activity for the Pulse campaign included TV, press and poster ads, as well as a dedicated website

The Study shows how Lever Fabergé successfully launched Lynx Pulse, a male deodorant.

Campaign Casebook

Objectives

Lever Fabergé launches a fragrance variant of its market-leading male deodorant Lynx each year. For the introduction of Lynx Pulse in spring 2003, the global brand management team, based in the UK, decided to create a campaign that would tap more closely into the brand's personality, rather than just referring to the nature of the fragrance. The aim was to boost the brand's 17% share of the male deodorant market in the UK. The campaign was also to be used across Europe, as well as in Australia and New Zealand.

Strategy

Lynx campaigns have always been about helping young men achieve greater success with women, so the activity had to focus on Pulse's role in this. The inherent seduction promise led to the idea of using music and dance in a campaign based around a TV ad. This offered the chance to devise a dance, which it was hoped would be emulated by men eager to achieve the 'Lynx effect'. The music was to be a feelgood track with wide appeal and an infectious hook, performed by a little-known artist who would not overshadow the brand.

Media plan

Execution

After an exhaustive selection process, the team chose the track *Make Luv* by DJ Room 5. A choreographer created a series of fairly simple dance moves that the geeky hero of the ad could perform, copied by two women. The track was sent to key DJs ahead of the ad's launch, and the track was released a few weeks later. Other activity included press and poster ads and a website that allowed users to remix the track. There was also extensive field marketing work to encourage consumers to try the dance, including 'Pulse areas' within stores such as HMV.

Budget

£3m

Results

The campaign outperformed its target by 100%. By the end of summer 2003, Lynx's total brand share had risen to 19%. The Pulse variant had managed to capture a 5% share – double that of Lynx Dimension, the fragrance launched the previous year. This success brought some unexpected benefits to the Lynx team by re-engaging people internally, according to Margaret Jobling, Lynx's European brand director. 'Everyone has heard about the Pulse campaign at Unilever; it's been talked about at lots of internal conferences and has given the team new-found confidence in the brand.'

about the dance . . . *The Sun* went so far as to produce a double-page feature illustrating the moves. Media coverage produced about £2m in advertising-equivalent value. Jobling remembers being in a bar, hearing the music start and watching people get up and do the dance. 'That's when I realised it had really taken off,' she says.

Activity 26.4 – Lynx Pulse

1   What market segment did Lever Fabergé identify for its Lynx Pulse brand?

2   What exactly is the 'message' of the 'Lynx effect' and what was the strategy for achieving it?

3   What does the article mean when it states that the campaign was to 'tap more closely into the brand's personality, rather than just referring to the nature of the fragrance'?

4   What practical targets did Lever Fabergé set for its Lynx Pulse brand, and how successful was it in achieving its objectives?

5   What was the budget for the campaign and to what extent did the product receive free publicity?

the Available Media

The main types of advertising media used are:

- **print** – newspapers, magazines, brochures, leaflets and handbills
- **audio** – national and local radio
- **moving image** – TV, cinema, video and DVD
- **ambient** – advertising using posters, plasma and LCD screens, stickers on cars, adverts on pizza boxes ('ambient' = 'surrounding')
- **new media** – internet banners and pop-ups, text adverts on mobiles, teletext

Clearly not all businesses can afford all these media, nor will they all be appropriate to a local taxi service, for example. But some of them will be used, whatever the size of the business. It is the task of whoever is in charge of marketing that the promotion of the business is carried out effectively and efficiently.

choosing the advertising media

The choice of media to use will therefore depend on a number of different factors, all of which you should consider in your investigations:

- the **strengths** of the type of advertising in meeting the target market – for example the ability of TV advertising to reach a national audience
- the **limitations** of the type of advertising in meeting the target market – for example the use of internet pop-ups is limited to the population who have online access
- the **cost** of the media used, based on the budget allocated by the business – for example a taxi driver is unlikely to be able to afford to use an

advertising agency charging £500 a day, but could usefully spend £250 on printing leaflets for local distribution

■ related to the cost of the media used are the **production requirements** of producing the advertising media, for example a full-colour advert in a local magazine – is an outside agency required, or can the company use its own in-house design facilities?

These various types of media, together with their advantages and disadvantages, will be described in detail in the tables that follow on the next few pages. We will examine the costs of the media in the next chapter which deals with various constraints which affect the promotional campaign.

some terminology

We need to explain some terminology used when assessing the success or otherwise of media promotion:

coverage	the percentage of people in the targeted market segment (eg teenagers) who are likely to see or hear the advertising message over a set period of time – eg 50% of teenagers, or
	the percentage geographic coverage of the promotion – eg an advert released in London and the South East 'covering', say, 30% of the UK population
frequency	the number of times ('frequency') that the people in the targeted market segment (eg teenagers) are likely to see (or hear) the advert over a set period of time

Print Media

The traditional advertising media using the printed word are still very common and can be extremely effective. They include:

■ national newspapers

■ local newspapers

■ trade and specialist magazines

■ general consumer magazines

■ directories

■ catalogues

■ leaflets

Now study the table on the next page.

PRINT MEDIA	advantages	disadvantages
national newspapers	■ national coverage (eg the *Sun* sells 3 million daily) ■ they carry authority ■ they can be passed on to other people	■ aimed at a limited market segment (socio-economic) ■ thrown away after a day ■ may lack impact of other media
local newspapers (sometimes free)	■ local interested readership ■ read at home in relaxed surroundings ■ they can be passed on	■ low circulation will limit market ■ socio-economic groups not defined
trade and specialist magazines	■ specific and interested readership ■ technical information possible ■ likely to be retained	■ no major disadvantages
consumer magazines	■ regularly bought by people likely to purchase in specific product areas, eg photography ■ read in consumers' leisure time	■ strong competition ■ limited readership ■ adverts may be grouped, lessening impact
directories (eg Yellow Pages)	■ well-known and regularly used ■ they last for a year	■ message brief ■ many similar adverts ■ often lacking visual impact
catalogues	■ targeted to a specific readership ■ they last and can be passed on to friends and family ■ they are normally in colour and have strong impact	■ message brief ■ relatively costly to produce ■ delivery costs can be high
leaflets (mailed or picked up)	■ can be targeted ■ costs are low ■ a good level of detail	■ likely to be lost or discarded ■ timing has to be right ■ too common to have great impact

Audio Media

Audio media include two important methods of promotion:

■ national radio

■ local radio

There are numerous digital stations (also available on Sky) and the traditional analogue stations. Some are 'general interest' stations; some specialise in areas such as sport and music. The advantages and disadvantages are shown below.

AUDIO MEDIA	advantages	disadvantages
national radio	■ national coverage 24/7 ■ they carry authority ■ people listen to them when doing boring things such as driving and washing up	■ 'airtime' can be expensive ■ market segments not always easily targeted ■ people prefer TV for entertainment
local radio	■ local interested audience ■ good for promotion by local businesses	■ limited geographical coverage

Moving Image Media

Moving image media includes some of the most popular media, but also some of the most expensive to use for promotional purposes:

■ TV

■ cinema

■ video and DVD

The watching of **TV** in today's society makes it an attractive vehicle for promotional messages, but its universality is at the same time its own worst enemy – there are literally up to hundreds of channels available in the growing proportion of households which have both terrestrial and satellite TV. Advertising can be expensive and may lose impact as consumers get weary of commercial breaks. Try watching an action film which is punctuated by frequent and often irritating advertising. Technology has its weapons solutions in the shape of zappers and recorders which enable the consumer to filter out the ads!

The **cinema** is possibly a more immediate and demanding 'in-your-face' medium and can be used both for national advertising and also for local advertising.

Promotional **videos** and **DVDs** are also popular and are used effectively on a national basis by businesses such as holiday companies and car manufacturers.

The relevant advantages and disadvantages are shown in the table below.

MOVING IMAGE MEDIA	advantages	disadvantages
TV	▪ national coverage 24/7 ▪ impact – of colour, movement and sound ▪ low cost per person reached ▪ targeting of time of day possible ▪ repetition of message possible ▪ national events covered attractive to sponsors, eg football matches	▪ high production costs ▪ high total cost of 'airtime' ▪ too many channels to choose from ▪ people 'zap' and change channels during commercial breaks or go off and get a drink
cinema	▪ captive audience ▪ strong visual and sound impact ▪ adverts for specific market segments can be matched to type of film (eg children's film, chick-flik) ▪ also suitable for local advertisers	▪ high production costs ▪ relatively small audience, even when cinema is full ▪ even smaller audience if the film is a flop
video and DVD	▪ can be viewed at leisure when customers are receptive ▪ strong impact	▪ relatively high costs ▪ relatively small audience

Ambient Media

The term 'ambient' means 'surrounding' and **ambient media** therefore refers to media which appear in the immediate surroundings of the consumer and which then attract the consumer's attention. There are very many ways in which these media are used and so it is difficult to generalise about them. Here are some examples:

- you go into a bar and see drinks mats on the tables advertising brands of drink

- you travel by train and see adverts on screens on the station or train

- you buy a take-away pizza and see a product advert on the pizza box

- you walk into a supermarket and the delicious smell of baking bread has been ducted into the entrance and makes you want to buy some cakes

- you walk into a supermarket, see a product demonstration and get a free sample

- you are sitting in a traffic jam and notice the advertising sticker on the windows of the surrounding cars or the advert on the side of the bus

- you see a van belonging to a business and read the details and contact information on the side

- you are going along a road and notice a large poster by the roadside

details on the side of a commercial van

All these examples appear in the consumer's everyday surroundings, they all involve an element of surprise and they are all totally random as far as the consumer is concerned. But they can be effective, as the advantages listed below show.

AMBIENT MEDIA	advantages	disadvantages
a wide variety of promotional messages which are placed where the public can see them at random as part of their 'surroundings'	■ immediate impact as they may be unexpected ■ the person who sees them may be unoccupied at the time and so can give full attention to the message ■ wide coverage to a potentially large number of people	■ they are not targeted to a specific market segment ■ people who have seen them frequently before (eg advertising screens on trains or train stations) may ignore them

New Media

The term 'new media' refers to the opportunities made available to advertisers for promoting their messages on the 'new' electronic media:

- the internet
- mobile phones
- teletext

the internet – websites

The **internet** has seen very significant growth in promotional advertising. When you go online there are many types of advertising that you will see:

- banner advertising – ie a horizontal strip which carries a promotional message, sometimes combined with 'flash' features – animations which attract the eye
- pop-ups – a separate small page which 'pops up' with a specific advertising message

Some of this advertising – particularly pop-ups and flash – can at times prove distracting and irritating. Some computer programs will allow you to prevent pop-ups popping up. To get some idea of the ever-changing advertising techniques available on the web, go to www.wanadoo.co.uk/mediapack and look at the 'Products and Prices' option which will lead you to the different types of web advert format.

Websites and promotion are dealt with in detail in Chapters 22 and 23.

mobile phones

Mobile phone usage is also growing and the SMS system (Short Messaging Service) is increasingly being used to relay brief adverts to targeted customers.

Other techniques are developing along with 3G (3rd Generation) technology, which supports bandwidth-hungry applications such as full-motion video, ideal for advertising purposes.

teletext

3G phone technology

Television information services such as teletext have been established for some time, in technology terms, and remain powerful vehicles for getting across advertising messages.

NEW MEDIA	advantages	disadvantages
internet website	■ worldwide coverage ■ can provide a wide range of product and company information ■ it is a permanent presence which can be accessed 24/7 ■ customers can be directed to the site through keywords on the main search engines ■ maximum impact provided by colour, movement and sound ■ interactive – customers can download information ■ interactive – customers can make instant purchase decisions if there is an online shop	■ high set-up costs for smaller businesses ■ needs constant revision and updating ■ security issues if payment accepted for products online
mobile phones	■ captive audience	■ can be intrusive to customer ■ costly to run ■ reliant on advanced technology which may not be available to all customers
teletext	■ can be viewed at leisure when customers need information ■ widely available on TV	■ not interactive ■ can be difficult to navigate through large amounts of information

Now read the Case Study on the next page and carry out the Student Activity which follows. This Activity will involve you in assessing the various types of media used in the promotional campaign of a small local business. This is the type of task you may be asked to carry out in your Unit assessment.

Case Study – Martine and Aphrodite

Martine is a nationally famous model. She is planning, however, to leave the life of the catwalk and to set up in business in Cardiff where she intends to settle down with her partner and start a business.

She is planning to open a city-centre upmarket beauty salon for women and has decided to call it Aphrodite.

The potential customers that she has identified are the well-off professional classes, many of whom work in central Cardiff. She aims to sign up 250 clients in the first 12 months of trading.

These customers do not have a lot of spare time, but they do like to be pampered and are prepared to pay for the privilege. The main message Martine wants to get across is 'Feel Beautiful!'

Martine realises that she will have to promote the business very strongly if she is to succeed. She does have a major advantage in that she is well-known as a model, and her good looks have appeared in many fashion magazines. She reckons that after she has set up the salon she has a budget of about £30,000 for promotion and advertising.

Activity 26.5 – Martine and Aphrodite

1   What are two of Martine's main objectives in starting Aphrodite? How could effective promotion help Martine to achieve these objectives?

2   What market segment is Martine targeting, and why?

3   Where is Martine planning to locate her business, and why?

4   What is the message that Martine will try and get over to her target market?

5   Martine does not have a large budget for promoting her business. Suggest ways in which she could make best use of any of the following:

   (a)   publicity
   (b)   written media
   (c)   moving image
   (d)   ambient media
   (e)   new media

   In each case explain how her choice of media is affected by her target market and by the strengths and limitations of those media. You do not need to allocate Martine's budget.

CHAPTER SUMMARY

■ A promotional campaign will consist of a 'mix' of advertising, public relations, publicity, sales promotions, sponsorship and direct marketing.

■ A promotional campaign should support corporate objectives such as sales maximisation, profit maximisation or sustainability (care of the environment).

■ The campaign needs to identify the target market – the segment identified by market research as appropriate for the product.

■ The campaign also needs to adopt an appropriate 'message' for the target market – this may well appeal to the lifestyle aspirations of the chosen market segments.

■ The extent of the promotional campaign will depend on the size of the organisation and the size of its budget.

■ The organisation will need to decide whether or not to use the professional skills and organisational know-how of an advertising agency to help promote the product.

■ There is a wide choice of advertising media, some of which may or may not be appropriate in a particular campaign, either because of cost or because of the target market.

■ Print media include newspapers (local and national), magazines, (trade, specialist and consumer), directories, catalogues and leaflets.

■ Audio media include national and local radio.

■ Moving image media include TV, cinema, video and DVD.

■ Ambient media are media with which the target customers come into contact in their everyday surroundings. 'Ambient' means 'surrounding'. Examples include drinks mats, adverts on screens on trains and stations, stickers on vehicles, roadside posters and product demonstrations in supermarkets.

■ The 'new' media include the internet (pop-ups and banners), mobile phones and teletext.

■ Organisations should also make the most of publicity (free features published in the media). This can be achieved by press releases or even through good luck.

KEY TERMS

promotional campaign	an appropriate mix of advertising, publicity, public relations, sales promotions, sponsorship and direct marketing
corporate objectives	statements of what a business wishes to achieve
marketing objectives	statements of what a business wishes to achieve through its mix of marketing activities
public relations	safeguarding and promoting the image of a product or company
publicity	free media coverage obtained through news items about the product being promoted
sponsorship	associating a product or company with a team, event or person
sales promotion	a technique for creating interest in a product using a special offer over a limited time period
direct marketing	persuading the consumer to respond to an advert by placing an order immediately by phone, post or email
advertising agency	an independent business which plans and organises all the media required for a promotional campaign
print media	newspapers, magazines, brochures, leaflets and handbills
audio media	national and local radio
moving image media	TV, cinema, video and DVD
ambient media	'ambient' means 'surrounding' and 'ambient media' means using advertising media which attract attention in everyday surroundings, eg roadside posters, screens, pizza boxes
new media	advertising on the internet, mobile phones and teletext
coverage	the percentage of people in the targeted market segment who are likely to see/hear the advertising message over a set period of time
frequency	the number of times the people in the targeted market segment are likely to see/hear the advertising message over a set period of time

27

Promotion – constraints and evaluation

Starting point

Promotional campaigns involve asking many questions. If you are planning a promotional campaign, you need to deal with a number of constraints: 'How much will an advert or a poster cost? Can we afford it? Will it be worth it?' and 'How do we make sure we do not fall foul of the law with our campaign?' When the campaign is over you will need to ask further questions: 'How effective was it? Would we do the same again? What have we learnt from it?'

In this chapter we investigate a number of practical situations and explain the constraints that are placed on a promotional campaign. We also describe the methods used to evaluate it.

What you will learn from this chapter

- an organisation running a promotional campaign will be constrained by a number of factors, such as the costs involved and the extent of the in-house expertise and technical resources

- an organisation may need to use an advertising agency to deal with the promotional media required

- campaign planners must be aware of the external legal and regulatory constraints which exist to protect the public from being offended, misled or exploited by promotional campaigns:
  - legislation such as the Trade Descriptions Act
  - regulatory bodies for consumer complaints such as the Advertising Standards Authority (ASA)

- campaign planners must also be able to evaluate the completed promotion process – eg using questionnaires, sales statistics

Staff Expertise and Technical Resources Needed

The question that has to be asked by the marketing function of an organisation when planning a promotional campaign is: 'Can we do this ourselves or will we have to call in outside help?'

The answer will, of course, depend on the size of the organisation and whether it has an in-house design facility which can provide the staff expertise and technical resources that are needed.

D I Y (do it yourself) promotion

The type of promotional media that could be dealt with in-house by a small business where the skills and resources are available, include:

- **printed media** – leaflets, simple newspaper adverts and handbills
- **new media** – simple websites with product details and new promotions

This may be all that a small business will require. The media are effective and well within the small business budget.

buying-in promotional media from individual experts

A more ambitious promotional campaign for a small or medium-sized local business could include:

- **printed media** – a full-colour advert in a specialist local 'glossy' magazine which requires a higher level of colour design skills
- **audio** – a local radio advert
- **moving image** – a simple 'slide' advert at the local cinema
- **ambient media** – a full-colour poster, car stickers, drinks mats
- **new media** – a more sophisticated website with pop-ups and video clips

These media will require outside professional help from graphic designers, audio specialists and website experts, and, as we will see in the next section, they will need to be budgeted for. They may not be as expensive as you might think.

employing an advertising agency

In the last chapter we explained the part played by advertising agencies in the promotion process (see pages 480-482). They are expert and professional – but at a cost. You will have seen that the Lynx Pulse campaign was budgeted at £3 million. This was, however, a full-scale campaign using national TV, cinema and press media with website back-up. More modest requirements will, of course, cost considerably less.

the advertising agency brief

Using an advertising agency will help to concentrate the minds of the marketing function – the organisation will have to produce a **campaign brief** for the agency. This will comprise:

- the background to the organisation and the reasons why the promotion is needed
- details of the product and the competition in the market
- the objectives of the organisation – for example capturing a 30% market share within 12 months, increasing sales by 25% and profits by 20%
- the make-up of the target market – in terms of age, gender, socio-economic grouping, lifestyle
- an idea of the type of product message that the campaign will communicate
- the timescale
- the proposed budget

agreeing the budget

The budget is clearly a critical item here; it will have been arrived at after 'negotiation' between the marketing team and the finance team. This can be complex: the marketing team will often want to spend more than the finance team is prepared to budget for! See Chapter 15 for more on budgeting.

In the next section we will describe in practical terms how much it costs to 'buy' promotional media.

the Constraints of Cost

sources of information – BRAD

A good starting point for your investigations is is to obtain a **BRAD** (British Rate and Data) book. You could try a local advertising agency who may have an old copy spare. BRAD is a huge and complex directory which lists nearly all advertising media rates, whether national and local press, journals and magazines, in great detail. Rates change frequently, so any issue quickly goes out of date – but this improves your chances of acquiring a copy. The bad news is its complexity, and the reluctance of TV and radio stations to publish figures. They prefer to negotiate with customers individually, often offering new customers 'starter rates' (see below). Local radio stations and local papers may let you have a 'rate card'. It is a good idea to pool, as a class, all the information you obtain for your research work – including BRAD.

actual cost and cost per prospect

When making media choice decisions based on cost, there are two considerations: firstly, you should look at the actual cost of adverts in any one medium; secondly, consider the **cost per prospect reached** (a 'prospect' is a target customer).

We will now describe the costs of the main promotional media in turn.

the costs of TV advertising

The use of TV may appear to be ruled out for many businesses by 'total cost' considerations. Just to create a television advert is expensive, and to this must be added the cost of buying airtime. The main advantage of TV promotion is that the advert may reach a huge number of prospects, and provided that these are relevant to your product, TV gives a very low 'cost per prospect reached'.

Example costs: a furniture store advertises on Regional TV

How much does it cost for a furniture store to advertise on Regional TV?

Commercial TV is divided into different areas. The packages quoted below were designed for **new customers** of a TV area of 4.5 million people. The word 'spot' refers to an individual showing.

Low option: 10 spots	10 secs	20 secs	30 secs
	£7,600	£12,600	£15,200

This contract is for 3 spots at peak time and 7 spots at off peak time. Peak time is 5.15 pm to midnight. Figures are totals for the 10 spots. To this should be added the commercial production of the advert artwork and the video voice-over.

High option: 25 spots	10secs	20secs	30secs
	£19,000	£31,500	£38,000

The high option contract is for 9 spots at peak time; 16 spots off peak time.

Commercial production is typically a half-day video shoot, edited with digital video effects, voice-over and library music. The likely production cost for this is up to £1M.

Prices for 'spots' for **regular advertisers** are assessed on factors such as the time of day of showing, time of year, length of advert, length of campaign, request for a specific time slot, various discounts that apply, and payment of premium rates for prime-time viewing. An example of premium rates would be the cost of showing one 30 second advert in the middle of Coronation Street – about £7,500 for part of an ITV region.

For national data on the costs of the ITV network, go to www.itvsales.com

the costs of radio advertising

The cost structure of radio advertising is very similar to the TV example on the previous page. There are initial production costs for the creation of a tape, which will be a minimum of £200 using one voice. The addition of more voices and background music will raise this to nearer £500. If the client has requested anything specific such as a musical identity (a jingle), then this would start at £3,000 upwards. The number of prospects reached by local radio is typically 350,000. Radio is a very effective medium because people often listen to it when they are doing something boring, eg driving to work.

Example: local radio advertising for a College Open Day

A local college is planning to advertise a College Open Day in a bid to increase its student numbers on a wide variety of classes. It has negotiated a contract package for 25 spots, each of 40 seconds, from Monday morning through to Friday lunchtime. The local area audience is 200,000.

Timings	Spots
06.00 to 10.00	6
10.00 to 13.00	3
13.00 to 16.00	3
16.00 to 19.00	5
19.00 to 24.00	4
24.00 to 06.00	4
Total cost (of airtime only)	£3,100
Production cost for 40 second tape	£500

Normal advertising rates will vary according to the number of listeners likely to hear the broadcast, and this will vary with the time of day, the day of the week and the time of the year. Special days, such as Mother's Day, and special times, like 'on the hour', will also affect the rates. New customers may be offered an introductory price, and well-established and volume clients can negotiate favourable terms.

The time of day rates, say for a middle of the week 30 second spot, can vary from over £200 for peak times to under £10 for a middle of the night spot. For a peak period at the weekend, this top rate may rise to £250. The most expensive time zone is drive time: 07.00 to 09.00 on weekday mornings.

Activity 27.1 – TV versus radio advertising

Study the costs of regional TV advertising and local radio advertising on the previous two pages.

1 What is the total cost for a new customer of buying twenty five 30 second spots of high option TV advertising? This total should include both airtime and the cost of producing the advert.

2 What is the cost per prospect reached of this TV advertising (to the nearest 'p')?

3 What is the total cost of buying twenty five 40 second spots of local radio advertising? This total should include both airtime and the cost of producing the advert.

4 What is the cost per prospect reached of this radio advertising (to the nearest 'p')?

5 Why is the advertising medium which is more expensive <u>in total</u>, cheaper per prospect?

6 Why might the more expensive medium <u>per prospect</u> be more effective advertising?

7 Give two examples of organisations/businesses that would particularly benefit from advertising on regional TV and two examples of organisations/businesses that would particularly benefit from advertising on local radio. Give reasons for your choice.

the costs of cinema advertising

Cinema advertising ranges from the sophisticated film presentation to the simple 'still' slide, ideal for local advertising. At each main performance a carousel of about 20 local advertisement slides is shown, on a loop that brings each advert back on screen every two and a half minutes, normally for seven seconds. This will occur throughout multi-screen cinemas as well as in single-screen venues. A useful website is www.pearlanddean.com

Example: a local firm of estate agents advertising at a cinema

The cost of showing the advert for a year via the carousel is £85 per week for a 1,400-seater cinema. The amount will vary according to the size of the cinema and its average seating uptake. Lesser periods of time can be booked, but these will take a lower priority to annual campaigns. An equivalent rate to the above, for a six-month campaign, would be £105 per week.

The production cost for a slide is about £300 for one design, £600 for two. The production time required is 4 weeks.

the Cost of Printed Media

advertising in newspapers and magazines

The choice is immense, so when you are investigating paper-based media you should refer to BRAD and also to local sources of advertising space such as local newspapers who will be able to provide you with a rate card.

You should study the circulation and readership figures and information about the target market. You should ask yourself which publications will reach the right prospects? You will need to understand the jargon, such as dps (double-page spread) and scc (single-column centimetre).

Example: advertising in *Top of the Pops* magazine

Top of the Pops
The Magazine
Est Feb 1995. **Affiliations** ABC NRS PPA TGI
URL www.bbcworldwide.com/magazines
Publisher BBC Worldwide Publishing, Woodlands, 80 Wood Lane, London W12 0TT Switchboard: Tel 020 8433 2000. Fax 020 8749 0538. **Circulation Manager** Ceri Jones. **Editor** Peter Hart. **Editorial Director** Corinna Shaffer. (Tel 020 8433 3701.) **Marketing** Helen Nothard. (Tel 020 8433 2748.) **Production** Emma Pym. **Publisher** Alfie Lewis.
Advertising Department Fax 020 8576 2424. **Ad Manager** Gerry Anyanwu. (Tel 020 8433 3549.) **Ad Sales** Jonathan Boakes. (Tel 020 8433 1569.) **Ad Assistant** Juliet Cromwell. (Tel 020 8433 3722.) **Group Ad Manager** Claire Stidwell. (Tel 020 8433 2446.) **Senior Ad Executive** Kate Norum.
Ad Sales Tel 020 8576 3549/2446.
Frequency Fortnightly. **Price** Single copy £2.
Editorial Profile The pop bible aimed at all music loving teenagers. Packed with gossip, posters, lyrics & TOTP backstage stories.
Circulation 1 Jul-31 Dec 2004 ABC 200,907 (UK & Eire 197,874 other 3,033)

	Total	UK	Other
N'Trade and Other Single Copy Sales	200,616	197,648	2,968
Single Copy Subs Sales	289	226	63
At BAR	213	156	57
Below BAR but not < 50%	69	63	6
< 50% BAR but not < 20%	7	7	-
Multi Copy/Sponsored Sub Sales	2	-	2
At BAR	2	-	2
Actively Purchased	200,905	197,874	3,031
Number of Effective Issues in Period	6	-	-

Readership All Adults Total Readership 550,718 (1.9 readers per copy based on Jul 2004 - Dec 2004 ABC 200,907)

	A	B	C1	C2	D	E
Profile Index	18	58	89	96	153	183
Coverage %	0	1	1	1	2	2
Coverage '000	3	69	143	111	136	89

	15-24	25-34	35-44	45-54	55-64	65+
Profile Index	333	102	126	34	14	5
Coverage %	4	1	1	0	0	0
Coverage '000	284	91	130	30	11	5

Source: NRS (National Readership Surveys Limited) 2004 Q4
Target Readership 11-19 year olds who are fanatical about music. 80% female readership. Median Age 13
Rates Received 23 May 2005. Effective 1 Jun 2004. Agencies 10%

Display Rates	Colour
Dps	£19,000
Page	£9,500
Half	£4,750
Quarter	£2,500

Inserts Loose: Accepted By arrangement £30 per thousand. Bound-in: Accepted By arrangement £30 per thousand. **Extras** Bleed 10% Guaranteed 10%.

Ad Sizes	Type area	Trim size	Bleed area
Dps	265 x 400	285 x 420	293 x 428
Page	265 x 190	285 x 210	293 x 218
Half horizontal	130 x 190	140 x 210	144 x 218
Half vertical	265 x 88	285 x 103	293 x 107
Quarter box	125 x 90	135 x 100	139 x 104
Quarter horizontal	59 x 190	69 x 210	73 x 218
Quarter vertical	265 x 40	285 x 50	293 x 54

DTP Quark Xpress supplied on ISDN, CD, Zip disk. **Print Method** Heat set web fed offset litho. **Screen Ruling** 150 lpi Screen angles: C 75°, M 45°, Y 90°, K 15°. **ISDN** Tel: 0208 433 3692. Fax: 020 8433 3236. **Production Note** Pdf files. Digital only. Pass 4 Press.
Deadlines Copy 21 days preceding publication date. **Cancel** 6 months preceding publication date

This extract from BRAD shows the publication details for *Top of the Pops*, a magazine for 'all music loving teenagers' which provides:

'gossip, posters, lyrics and TOTP backstage stories'.

Note the following details which advertisers will look for:

■ publisher and contact details (please see important note below)

■ frequency of publication

■ coverage

■ circulation in numbers

■ circulation by socio-economic grouping

■ circulation by age group

■ rates for adverts

■ rates for inserts

■ deadline for submission of material

This illustration is reproduced by kind permission of BRAD who have requested that, out of courtesy to their client, under no circumstances should the publishers of *Top of the Pops* be approached directly by tutors or by students.

Activity 27.2 – magazine advertising

Study the extract from BRAD on the previous page and answer these questions:

1 What is the total circulation of *Top of the Pops* and what is the total readership? What does this tell you about its effectiveness as an advertising medium?

2 What is the target readership of *Top of the Pops* and how do the targets relate to the gender and age of the readers?

3 What do the readership figures tell you about the socio-economic groups and age groups to which the magazine appeals?

4 What type of products do you think would be most suitable for advertising in *Top of the Pops*? Give marketing reasons for your answers.

5 How much would it cost to place a single page colour advert in *Top of the Pops*? How does this compare with the cost of placing a loose insert in the magazine?

the cost of printing leaflets, catalogues and brochures

The following costs represent what an advertiser might have to pay a local printing firm for printing leaflets, brochures and catalogues. Note that there are normally two printing options:

■ cheap and cheerful **one-colour** printing (eg blue or black) possibly on single-coloured paper

■ **full-colour** (often called 'four colour') printing, which is more expensive but looks more professional

The choice between the two will depend on the effect the advertiser is trying to achieve: one-colour printing is very acceptable for leaflets, but full-colour is more impressive for product catalogues – tropical beaches and food products, for example, look rather disappointing in black and white.

Example: printing costs of leaflets, catalogues and brochures

	1,000 1 colour	1,000 full colour	10,000 1 colour	10,000 full colour
A4 leaflet (one sided)	£100	£330	£260	£530
8 page catalogue/brochure	£230	£940	£400	£1150
64 page catalogue/brochure	£900	£4320	£2200	£6250

the Cost of Ambient Media

The examples below show typical costs of **ambient media** – ie the type of advertising which appears in the 'surroundings' of the prospect's everyday life, for example while the prospect is out shopping, travelling or visiting bars and restaurants.

roadside posters

posters and billboards

- Panels measuring 3m by 6m booked by local advertisers on a single site would be £320 to £460 per panel per fortnightly block The price varies according to the desirability of the site.

- Panels measuring 2m by 1.5m might cost between £100 and £150 per fortnight.

- Bus shelter type panels measuring 2m by 1.5m, back lit, could be £250 to £400 per fortnight. These cost more because they are visible 24 hours per day

transport advertising

Local businesses find advertising on buses very effective, because routes are localised.

- the rear of one bus could cost £25 per week (a minimum of 4 weeks, a minimum number of 5 buses)
- the side of one bus could cost £40 per week (terms as above)

Production techniques usually involve the attachment of a vinyl sheet to the bus, at a minimum but one-off production and placement cost of £50 per bus.

Further examples of transport advertising include adverts on the sides of trains and advertising screens on railway stations.

the organisation's own transport

Many businesses advertise themselves effectively by using the side of cars, vans and lorries. Some will even park an articulated lorry in a field by the side of the motorway with a large advert placed on the side, often showing prominently a contact number or a website address!

The design work on a Ford transit type van, depending on complexity, would range from £200 to £500, with an extra £250 for fitting.

the Cost of New Media

'New' media makes use of websites, mobile phone advertising and teletext. We will concentrate here on websites, which for the small business on a modest budget is a very effective advertising medium. This subject has been developed further in Unit 4 'Investigating electronic business' (see Chapters 22 and 23).

Businesses can use websites for promotional purposes in two distinct ways:

- a website can be set up solely for a business as a means of promoting itself and its products
- advertisements in the form of pop-ups and banners can be placed on the websites of other organisations

a website page – simple and effective product promotion

The basic cost of setting up a website 'from scratch' is between £2,000 and £3,000. Optional costs include extra pages, movement, e-commerce facilities (an internet shop might cost £1,500 to establish) and the cost of updating the site (at about £500 per year).

To have your site contents listed on a search engine like Google, the cost is negotiable and often competitive with other companies using the same 'keywords' as yourself. For advice go to www.google.co.uk/adwords

The cost of placing adverts on other websites, in banner, pop-up and other ever-changing formats, are always under review and mainly negotiable. This is an area where you will need to carry out research, by speaking to website providers locally.

Publicity and Public Relations

Publicity is promotion which occurs because a business or its products appear in news items – an article in the press, a feature or interview on the TV or radio local news.

Publicity is the accountant's best friend because it is normally completely free of charge. For example, a brand of rubber gloves hit the news when a publicity - a gift to the marketing department

pair of gloves saved the life of a woman in Norfolk when she was struck by lightning while washing up the dishes.

Any promotional campaign should therefore encourage as much publicity as possible.

Public relations (PR) also relates to image – it aims to safeguard and promote to the public a positive image of the whole organisation and its products.

In smaller businesses, a lot can be done 'in-house' and without spending too much of the marketing budget. For example, the cost of sending an emailed press release to the local paper is minimal. Larger businesses may employ a public relations agency, who try to keep their client's name in the public eye and create positive images. The agency must also respond to unfavourable coverage when and where needed. This all comes at a cost.

the Cost of Sponsorship

Sponsorship is an arrangement between a business, or a group of businesses, which provide funds for an event or a series of events in return for publicity and benefits such as opportunities for entertaining clients. Sponsorship can be small-scale and local, or it can involve a multi-million pound deal.

Zurich, npower and O$_2$ banners on a rugby ground perimeter

Popular sponsored events include sports leagues and TV series – where the publicity from TV coverage is high profile. The Cadbury's two-year deal for Coronation Street cost £10 million. Perimeter banners on the picture on the left would cost an individual advertiser £3,000.

Sponsorship works well as long as the sponsor has a positive public image. Tobacco companies, for example, because of the health implications, have not proved popular sponsors.

Activity 27.3 – 'there's no such thing as bad publicity'

The saying goes that 'there's no such thing as bad publicity'. Think about this comment and then answer the questions that follow.

1 What is the cost to a business of publicity in the media?

2 What function in the marketing department will deal with the management of the public image of a business and its products? What action might it take if:

(a) the business expands and creates 100 new jobs in the local area?

(b) one of the major products of the business is found to be faulty and has to be withdrawn from sale?

3 A large local employer signs a sponsorship deal for the local team playing in the Rugby Union Premier League. What are the likely benefits which will be offered to the employer? It is revealed that the sponsor is a brewery business. Is this a problem?

External Constraints on Promotion

ethical considerations of advertising

A business that is ethical is one that conforms to accepted standards of social or moral behaviour. It does 'what is right' both for society and also for individuals. Many businesses make this a specific objective, adopting 'corporate social responsibility' policies.

It is important that promotional activity, and advertising in particular, is ethical. The danger is that in order to attract attention and get a message across, advertising will try shock and be unconventional. Adverts may:

- be too 'sexy', 'irreligious' and too 'near the mark' for some people
- contain shocking images which upset people
- mislead people about what the product is or does
- discriminate – against sex, race or age
- intrude where they are not wanted – eg email 'spam'

The government, consumer groups and the advertising industry have worked together over a number of years to make sure that the worst of these practices are either illegal or can be made the subject of official complaint. These bodies have established regulatory **external constraints** on promotion that marketing teams need to be aware of. We will describe these constraints in the section that follows.

legislation

There are a number of Acts of Parliament which have made it a criminal offence to include false descriptions of products and to discriminate against certain groups of people. Advertisers must beware!

The **Trade Descriptions Ac**t makes it a criminal offence:

■ to make false statements about goods offered for sale

■ to make misleading statements about services

This Act affects false or misleading adverts, packaging and labels, eg:

■ making a misleading statement about a service, eg 'our carpet cleaning is guaranteed to remove every mark' when it does not

■ 'clocking' a second-hand car which is for sale, eg changing the mileage indicator from 250,000 miles to 80,000 miles

Infringements of the Trade Descriptions Act should be reported to the local **Trading Standards** office which will look into the complaint. If the complaint is upheld, the offending organisation could be prosecuted.

We have already covered **anti-discrimination law** in Chapter 6 'Recruitment and selection' (pages 108-110). Advertisers must take care that they do not infringe any of the following:

■ **Sex Discrimination Act** – unfairly demeaning one sex, eg suggesting that women are not good at driving or parking

■ **Race Relations Act** – being racist, eg anti-Semitic political advertising

■ **Disability Discrimination Act** – making fun of people with a disability, eg someone in a wheelchair

The government has established a number of bodies which monitor enfringements of the laws mentioned above. They include:

■ the **Office of Fair Trading**, which monitors complaints about false or misleading descriptions of products visit www.oft.org.uk

It is seen as unlawful for a nightclub to advertise free admission to women on the basis that men have to pay. In one reported case it was ruled unlawful to try to get around this problem, as one advertiser did, by bending the rules and advertising 'free drinks to all people wearing skirts'.

sex discrimination?

■ the **Equal Opportunities Commission**, which monitors complaints about sex discrimination – visit www.eoc.org.uk

■ the **Commission for Racial Equality**, which monitors infringements of racial equality – visit www.cre.gov.uk

It must be stressed that while this framework of Acts of Parliament and regulatory bodies has been established to enforce the law, the advertising industry is **self-regulatory**, as we will now see.

Codes of Practice

Advertising in the UK is mainly controlled through voluntary **codes of practice**. The British Code of Advertising, Sales Promotion and Direct Marketing is a body of rules drawn up by the advertising industry. It requires advertisements to be **legal, decent, honest and truthful** and to be prepared with a sense of responsibility to consumers and society at large.

The **Control of Misleading Advertisements Regulations** provides the legislative back-up to this self-regulatory system in respect of all advertisements which mislead or which do not comply with the Code.

regulatory bodies - Ofcom

Ofcom is the independent regulator and competition authority for the UK communications industries. It has responsibilities across the TV, radio, telecommunications and wireless communications industries. Until recently it handled complaints into advertising and sponsorship on both TV and radio, but these are now handled by the Advertising Standards Authority (see below). Visit www.ofcom.org.uk for further information.

Advertising Standards Authority (ASA)

The ASA was set up by the **Committee of Advertising Practice** (CAP) and is now responsible for all of the codes of advertising practice – broadcast and non-broadcast. These are some of the key rules contained in the codes:

- **misleading advertising**

  Advertisers must hold evidence to prove the claims they make about their products and services before an advert appears.

- **offensive advertising**

  Special care needs to be taken on the grounds of sex, race, religion, sexuality and disability. The ASA considers many factors before deciding whether or not the advert. is offensive – including where the advert. appears, the audience, the product and what is generally acceptable conduct at the time.

- **other rules**

  The codes also contain specific rules about sales promotions and direct marketing, including how advertisers can use certain types of personal data, and the non-receipt of mail order items. Other rules cover adverts aimed at children, and adverts for alcohol, health products, financial services, employment and business opportunities, and gambling.

Now study the extracts from the ASA website on the next page and answer the questions that follow.

THE WORK OF THE ADVERTISING STANDARDS AUTHORITY (ASA)

The dos and don'ts of advertising

Every advertisement – whether it appears on the TV, radio, Internet, in a newspaper or on a poster, or if it drops on your doormat – is required to meet certain codes of conduct. Administered by the Advertising Standards Authority (ASA), these codes are there to prevent advertising that is either misleading or offensive.

Religious offence is the predominant theme in complaints to the advertising regulators

The ASA's Annual Report for 2004 reveals the most complained about advertisements for 2004. Reflecting its new responsibility for broadcast advertising, two top ten lists of most complained about ads have been published - one of non-broadcast advertisements; the other for broadcast commercials. All of the ads featured in the broadcast listing attracted complaints to the previous broadcast advertising regulator, Ofcom.

Religious offence was a predominant theme in the complaints received by the regulators. The two most complained about non-broadcast advertisements - a Channel 4 poster for the programme Shameless (which depicted a drunken family scene styled on the Leonardo Da Vinci painting of the Last Supper and attracted 264 complaints) and a poster by Schering Health Care Ltd (advertising the morning-after pill, Levonelle, beneath the headline "Immaculate Conception" and drawing 183 objections) – and the second most complained about broadcast commercial – for Mr Kipling cakes (806 complaints about a nativity play which featured a real-life birth) attracted 25% of the all the complaints sent about the ads featured in both the top ten lists. The ads had attracted complaints that they mocked elements central to the Christian faith. Of these three, complaints about both the Mr Kipling commercial and the Levonelle poster were upheld.

Top of the broadcast advertising complaints list was the teleshopping channel Auctionworld, which attracted 1,360 complaints principally about delays in the delivery of ordered goods, misleading guide prices and poor customer service. Ofcom not only upheld complaints about the channel, but issued a record fine of £450,000. The channel's licence was revoked and Auctionworld has not broadcasted since November.

The advertising codes state that advertisements should not cause serious or widespread offence. Auctionworld was the only advertisement listed in he broadcast list of most complained ads, which was not challenged underneath the offensiveness code. Eight of the ads appearing in the non-broadcast top 10 most complained about ads list generated complaints that their content was offensive.

www.asa.org.uk

How to make a complaint

It only takes one complaint to launch an investigation, and we've made sure the complaints procedure is fast and fair.

First, decide whether your complaint is covered by the ASA – among the types of complaints we look into are those about the content of ads, the administration of sales promotions, the availability of advertised goods and services, the protection of privacy, unwanted mail and the non-delivery of goods, promotional items or refunds.

If it is, send us your complaint – soon afterwards, you'll be given the name of the person who will handle the case and be your point of contact from now on. Use our online complaints form to make a complaint.

We aim to reach a decision on all but the complex complaints within a month, and will keep you informed at regular intervals.

All complaints are anonymous unless you are asking us to get you name taken off a mailing list or you are complaining on behalf of your company. Also there is no charge for making a complaint as all of the ASA's costs are met by a levy paid by advertisers.

Activity 27.4 – making a complaint

1 What was the predominant theme of the complaints received about broadcast adverts? Explain what was thought to be 'wrong' about these adverts.

2 What was the most complained about broadcast advert? What were the grounds for complaint and what action was taken against the advertiser?

3 What was the predominant theme of the complaints received about non-broadcast adverts? Why do you think that this theme is so predominant?

4 What current adverts you have seen might attract complaints, and on what grounds?

5 How would you make a complaint to the ASA?

Case Study – the ethics of healthy eating

Essentials The promotions tightrope

Promoting food deemed unhealthy for kids has become a lot more difficult. Five years ago Walkers created one of its most successful on-pack campaigns by inviting customers to collect tokens to be redeemed for books for their children's school. The activity proved so popular that it was repeated on an annual basis for five years.

Last year Cadbury Trebor Bassett embarked on a campaign along similar lines, but was soon under fire. Its Get Active sports kit for schools scheme, endorsed by athlete Paula Radcliffe (below) and boxer Audley Harrison, encouraged consumers to redeem wrappers from brands including Dairy Milk for free sports equipment.

More than 5000 schools registered with the programme and £9m of sports equipment was to be given away. But the volume of tokens needed to get the equipment prompted a media outcry and Cadbury has since dropped the token collection element.

Edwin Mutton, director-general of the ISP, believes Cadbury's experiences illustrate how promotional activity can become 'subsumed into the obesity debate'. So how can companies that sell products such as crisps and chocolate walk the promotional tightrope? Mutton says that activity that gets parental approval should be safe.

He adds that the Cadbury campaign may have failed where Tesco's Computers for Schools and Walkers' free books campaigns succeeded because 'sport is a bit close to a child's psyche in a way that computers or books are not'.

The ISP is advising members to obey 'the spirit as well as the letter' of its code.

The issue of child obesity and the need for children to eat healthily have become major concerns to food manufacturers and the government watchdog, the Food Standards Agency (www.food.gov.uk).

The question asked is: 'Is it ethically responsible to promote products such as crisps and chocolate and place them by the supermarket checkouts when 'snacking' by vulnerable children is known to lead to obesity?'

The producers of sweets and snacks have 'sweetened the pill' by using promotions which enable parents to obtain tokens which can be exchanged for worthy items such as school books. Is this ethical?

Read the article on the left (reproduced by kind permission of Haymarket Business Publishing) and answer the questions in the Activity that follows.

Note: the ISP is the Institute of Sales Promotion, the trade association for organisations involved in promotional marketing (www.isp.org.uk).

Activity 27.5 – the ethics of healthy eating

Read the Case Study on the previous page and answer the questions that follow.

1 What issue does the title of the article – 'the promotions tightrope' – raise?

2 What was the basis of the Walkers' campaign and why was it so successful?

3 What was the basis of the Cadbury's campaign, and how was it criticised?

4 What is the view of the Institute of Sales Promotion on the campaigns highlighted in the article? Do you agree?

5 What other evidence have you seen in the promotion of food products that businesses are now taking note of the obesity debate?

the influence of the European Union

European Union Directives affect UK legislation and regulatory practice in a number of different of areas, including the use of personal data.

The **Data Protection Act 1998** and the **Freedom of Information Act 2000** are enforced by the Office of the Information Commissioner. This government office regulates the way in which personal information about members of the public is held and how it is used. For example:

■ the compilation of database mailing lists and their use by direct mailing companies to send out promotional material

■ the holding of personal information used in credit assessment (eg applications for loans and credit cards)

The Office has also published guidance on the **Privacy in Electronic Communications (EC Directive) Regulation**. This guidance aims to provide practical advice and guidelines to marketers, to show them what is required by the Directive in relation to unsolicited faxes, email 'spam' and advertising text messaging (SMS). This guidance can be accessed on the Commissioner's website www.informationcommissioner.gov.uk

Another European influence is the **European Advertising Standards Alliance (EASA)**. This is a non-profit making organisation based in Brussels which brings together organisations representing the advertising industry in Europe. It promotes high ethical standards by means of effective self-regulation. You will find more information on the website www.easa-alliance.org

Evaluation of the Promotional Campaign

the need for evaluation

Promotions are important to the future of any business, and can be expensive to carry out, so it is important to conduct research into whether or not they were successful. This means comparing the level of sales before the promotion with the level after the promotion has finished, and conducting research into whether consumer attitudes to the firm have changed as a result of the promotional activity.

what should be evaluated?

Evaluation is an integral part of any business planning process: a plan is made, it is carried out and then evaluated to see what lessons can be learnt.

meeting objectives

All campaigns try to raise buyer awareness of the product or the business, be it through advertising, PR, sponsorship, sales promotion or direct mail. The majority of campaigns will attempt to raise the level of sales, and create awareness of new and existing products and services. All have the survival and prosperity of the business as main objectives.

Internal Methods of Evaluation

There are a number of ways in which data can be gathered directly by the business promoting its product. This is an accurate and cost-effective way of seeing to what extent a sales campaign has reached its target.

- monitor sales figures by looking at the accounts:
  - have sales increased significantly following the promotion?
  - have sales reached the budgeted target?
- use 'keyed replies' – most press adverts carry a code that the buyer will quote when ordering the product; this code will indicate where the advert was seen and which medium was successful in generating the business
- use coding on advertising leaflets – often a tear-off slip on a promotional leaflet will provide the seller with details of how and when the leaflet got to its target
- if you have a website, you can record the number of 'hits' (visits) made to the relevant web page(s) and the number of email enquiries received

■ conduct field research where an audience can be identified, eg after the showing of a cinema advert, after the distribution of leaflets in a defined neighbourhood, after the transmission of an advert on a local radio

These techniques are particularly suitable for local or small businesses which have markets defined either by location or by market niche.

External Methods of Evaluation

Larger businesses, which have larger budgets, may well employ specialist research agencies to gather and assess the information that they need, often on a national basis. The techniques used include:

■ **Field surveys**, using proven sampling techniques. This means making sure that the sample is large enough and the data collection method appropriate. The information gathered can cover any aspect of the campaign the advertiser wishes.

■ **Recall tests** ask consumers to remember what adverts they have seen. They are asked what the message was and where it was seen or heard. **Noting tests** take recall one step further by asking for the details of the advert. They will ask for opinions of the message and test to see if a specific benefit has registered.

■ **Tracking studies** take the simple recall research to the next level. These could be conducted by a single advertiser, but the majority of firms use 'continuous research' agencies for the period of time immediately after a campaign. They can attach their particular questions to one of the 'omnibus' surveys that are conducted. These use large samples from the national population on a regular weekly or monthly basis.

■ The major brand advertisers will find recall tables displayed in the journal *Marketing*, under headings such as Adwatch. Other market research findings are also published in *Marketing* (see left).

■ Focus (discussion) groups formed of relevant consumers will be asked to discuss adverts seen, their opinion of them and whether any changes in their attitude to the brand have taken place.

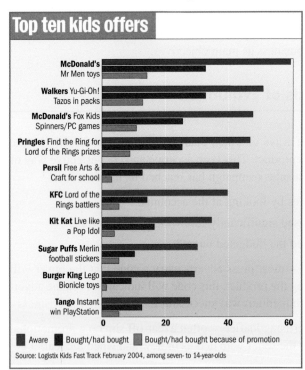

The effectiveness of special promotions for products for 7-14 year-old 'kids'. Reproduced from *Marketing* by kind permission of Haymarket Business Publishing.

Activity 27.6 – advert awareness questionnaire

Your brief is to write a questionnaire which you will use to test the public's awareness of current TV advertising campaigns. The 'public' in this case could be a random selection from the general public (the best option) interviewed in a public place, or from your fellow students (likely to be a more narrow sample).

You should form into small groups within the class and draw up a series of simple questions which should extract the following information:

■ the two most memorable adverts – ranked in order of being memorable

■ the message that each of them gave

■ the way in which the message was conveyed – using humour, shock, being 'way out', being sexy, being irritating, and so on . . .

You should check your questionnaire with your tutor, carry it out at the same time as the other groups and process the answers. Then compare your findings with those of the other groups in the class. A further comparison could be made with the Adwatch feature, which carries out a similar exercise in the journal *Marketing*.

Activity 27.7 – promotional techniques: a summary

You and your partner run a local business, OmniNuptia, offering a complete wedding service – cake, dress, flowers, music, reception. In fact, everything needed for a top-notch wedding. You have decided that you want to increase your sales and profits over the next six months, using the following promotional methods:

■ 10,000 A4 full-colour leaflets, using the strapline 'the Perfect Occasion'

■ a 'still' advert in the local cinema for six months

■ 25 spots on local radio

■ an advert on the back of 5 buses over 4 weeks

■ a new website

1 How much is this promotional campaign going to cost? Use the figures from this chapter as a guide.

2 What are your target market segments for these promotional media?

3 Draw up a table listing the main advantages and disadvantages for OmniNuptia of the five chosen promotional media.

4 Suggest the most effective ways in which the colour leaflets could be distributed.

5 Your annual sales figure of £250,000 increases by 15% as a result of this promotion. Have you achieved your objective of increasing profitability?

6 Suggest ways in which you could evaluate the success, or otherwise, of the different promotional media you have used.

CHAPTER SUMMARY

■ Any organisation running a promotional campaign will need to decide whether to manage the promotional media in-house, to go to individual experts or to employ an advertising agency to manage the campaign.

■ If an advertising agency is used, the organisation requiring the advertising will have to draw up a brief which will set out the background to the organisation, the product, the objectives, the target market, the desired message, the timescale and the budget.

■ The cost of promotional media – which can be a major constraint – is set out in a directory publication known as BRAD (British Rate and Data).

■ TV advertising is expensive but reaches a very large audience, achieving a comparatively low 'cost per prospect reached'.

■ Radio advertising is expensive but reaches a very large captive audience, for example people driving to work, washing the dishes or decorating the house.

■ Cinema advertising can be used for sophisticated moving image adverts and also for 'still' slide images; the latter are useful for local adverts and are comparatively cheap.

■ The source of marketing data for newspaper and magazine advertising is BRAD, which provides details about circulation, market segment and costs.

■ Leaflets, catalogues and brochures are a cheap and effective means of promotion, as long as they reach the right target market.

■ Publicity is free but public relations can be expensive. Sponsorship can provide major benefits for both the sponsor and the organisation sponsored as long as the sponsor has a positive public image.

■ External constraints on promotional campaigns include: legislation (eg Trade Descriptions; Sex, Race and Disability Discrimination); voluntary Codes of Practice and regulatory bodies.

■ The Advertising Standards Agency (ASA) is the body to which breaches of the Codes of Practice – ie complaints about adverts – are reported. These can be on the grounds of being misleading, offensive and contravening the rules relating to advertising to children, and adverts for products such as alcohol and food.

■ European Directives influence UK legislation and regulations, for example in respect of electronic advertising.

■ Evaluation of a promotional campaign – internal and external – is an important part of the marketing planning process.

KEY TERMS

campaign brief	instructions given by an organisation to an advertising agency for a promotional campaign – they include details such as company background, objectives, market, timescale and budget
BRAD	British Rate and Data – the definitive and detailed directory of promotional media
cost per prospect reached	the cost of reaching one target customer (prospect) with a chosen promotional medium
spot	an individual showing (moving image) or hearing (audio) of an advert
ethical advertising	advertising that is 'right' both for society and for individuals and does not offend, shock, mislead, unfairly discriminate or destroy privacy
Trading Standards	the office (part of the DTI) which will investigate complaints about trading irregularities such as false claims and misleading descriptions
Codes of Practice	a voluntary body of rules which regulates the advertising industry, requiring adverts to be legal, decent, honest and truthful
Advertising Standards Authority (ASA)	an independent body set up by the Committee of Advertising Practice (CAP), responsible for the regulation of broadcast and non-broadcast advertising in line with the Codes of Practice
EU Directives	guidance from the European Union that UK legislation must follow
recall tests	asking consumers what adverts they can remember and what the 'message' was
noting tests	asking consumers opinions of the advertising 'message' and details of benefits promised

Unit 7

Investigating enterprise

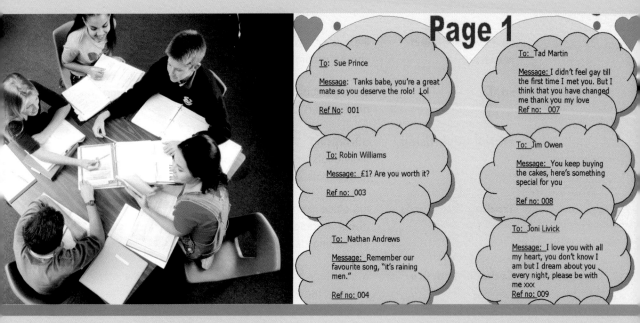

Page 1

To: Sue Prince

Message: Tanks babe, you're a great mate so you deserve the rolo! Lol

Ref No: 001

To: Robin Williams

Message: £1? Are you worth it?

Ref no: 003

To: Nathan Andrews

Message: Remember our favourite song, "it's raining men."

Ref no: 004

To: Tad Martin

Message: I didn't feel gay till the first time I met you. But I think that you have changed me thank you my love
Ref no: 007

To: Jim Owen

Message: You keep buying the cakes, here's something special for you

Ref no: 008

To: Joni Livick

Message: I love you with all my heart, you don't know I am but I dream about you every night, please be with me xxx
Ref no: 009

This unit is a very practical unit which involves you in setting up and running your own company in a student group. This will enable you to appreciate and develop the skills needed to work as a team and to start and run an enterprise. You will research and be actively involved in:

■ the 'nuts and bolts' of starting and running a company – documentation, meetings, and raising of finance

■ the need for a clear purpose: deciding on a product or service, the planning process, and organisation of resources

■ developing teamwork in achieving objectives – the establishment of management and the allocation of roles

■ the way in which a company ceases trading and is 'wound up'

Unit **7**

Chapters in this Unit...

Launching an enterprise 518

29 Running the company and winding it up 538

28

Launching an enterprise

Starting point

Launching an enterprise is a risky business and the start of a long learning curve. For the sole trader the risks are very high, but so is the potential reward. Setting up a limited company has a different range of risks and rewards. The members of the company immediately become a team: they share expertise and ideas, financial resources and a sense of common purpose. But they also have to acquire the skills of working in a team: they need to show commitment, to be able to communicate and cooperate with the rest of the team, to pull their weight and not go off on their own and 'do their own thing'. It is often the best team – as in sport – which achieves the winning result. Working in a team in this way can give a real 'buzz' to an enterprise project.

What you will learn from this chapter

- launching a limited company enterprise involves getting to know about the way a company is established and structured in terms of shares, shareholders and directors, documentation, different types of meeting and voting procedure

- every company member needs to be involved in choosing the right product or service and to be aware of the business issues this raises in terms of marketing, production, finance and sustainability

- when the product has been chosen, the company needs to plan how it is going to achieve its objectives; this is likely to involve a Mission Statement, a Business Plan and an Operations Plan

- a limited company will need directors – all of whom will have particular skills and responsibilities in encouraging teamwork

the Unit Assessment

the demands of running a recognised enterprise scheme

It is likely that you will be taking this Unit in conjunction with a scheme such as a Young Enterprise (YE) Company Scheme. The YE scheme has a very structured approach to setting up a company and provides excellent company documentation, instructions and time schedules. It also includes a review process for individual students to establish how they personally are achieving as a member of limited company. All the Young Enterprise procedures are tried and tested and work very well. They are helpful in structuring a complex process which could otherwise get out of hand and become chaotic! Visit www.young-enterprise.org.uk

But you also have to provide assessment evidence for this Unit. So you have to plan carefully to make sure that the demands of the enterprise scheme your college or school has adopted 'tie in' with what Edexcel, your examining board, requires you to produce.

the work needed for your assessment

There are four main pieces of evidence you need to produce:

(a) your own **diary or journal** showing evidence of what you did in the launch, planning and running of the company – and an evaluation of what you did

   – this can usefully be tied in with the YE review system and Record of Achievement

(b) your own **report** on the roles and responsibilities of the other members of the company – what they did and how well they contributed to the enterprise

   – this is additional to the normal requirements of the YE scheme

(c) a recognised individual contribution to a **group presentation and report** explaining the launch, and assessing the day-to-day running and the eventual 'winding up' of the company

   – this can be tied in with the Annual Report which is presented to the Annual General Meeting (AGM) of a YE company at the end of the year

(d) your own **report** reviewing and evaluating the success of the enterprise

   – this is additional to the normal requirements of the YE scheme

the Secret of a Successful Company

You will be setting up your own limited company enterprise and will want to make a success of it. Your investigations into businesses will have told you that there are a number of ingredients to the recipe of a successful enterprise:

- know who your customers **are** – do your research
- know what your customers **want** – do your research
- keep **listening** to your customers – do your research
- be clear in your **objectives** – maximise your sales, maximise your profit, look after your stakeholders
- make the most of your **people** – encourage the entrepreneurs with a flair for business ideas, use people's technical expertise in product development, use the salesperson who can sell ice to eskimos

You should also find out about well-known **entrepreneurs**. Read about entrepreneurship and Stelios on pages 6-8 of this book. Investigate on the internet other entrepreneurs such as Richard Branson and James Dyson. Find out what makes them 'tick'.

Stelios - founder of easyJet

Limited Companies – the Facts

Before explaining the practicalities of setting up an enterprise in the classroom, we need to cover briefly some of the theoretical aspects of limited companies that you will encounter in your enterprise work. To recap from Chapter 3 'Types of Business'(pages 34-36):

A **limited company** is a business

- owned by shareholders – also called 'members'
- managed by directors, who are appointed by the shareholders
- set up as a body which is separate from its owners, the shareholders

The term **shareholder** simply means that the person has a 'share' in the ownership of the company.

The shareholder will have contributed some capital to the company and should receive a **share certificate** in return (see next page).

In small private limited companies the directors are likely to be shareholders. This is seen clearly in the diagram on the next page which shows a private limited company with five shareholders, two of whom are directors. This business set-up might represent a small family enterprise with husband and wife as directors.

limited liability

The shareholder owner of a limited company stands apart from the business, which is a body in its own right. At the end of the year you will probably be involved in **winding up** your company so that it ceases to exist. This does not affect you as a separate shareholder, except that you should get your money back. Similarly, if a company goes 'bust', the shareholder is protected by what is known as 'limited liability' and does not lose all his or her money – only the money invested.

types of company

A limited company will either be:

- a **private limited company** (abbreviated to Ltd) or
- a **public limited company** (abbreviated to PLC or Plc or plc)

Most small or medium-sized businesses which decide to incorporate (become a company) become **private limited companies**. Your own limited company enterprise is likely to be a private limited company. Public limited companies include well-known names such as Tesco, Body Shop and Boots, the shares of which can be traded on the Stock Exchange.

Company Documentation

share certificates

If you are running a company as an enterprise project, you will doubtless be asked to try and sell shares to friends and family as well as buying some yourself. In return for the money you give them a **share certificate** which states the amount of their investment. The object of this exercise is to raise capital for the company. Each company will issue a set number of shares, eg 500 shares of £1. If these are all sold to investors, the company will then have a share capital of £500.

Certificate of Incorporation, Memorandum and Articles

Before you can formally set up a limited company, you will have to chose a name for it, which will have to be registered. You will need to decide this at an early stage of your project. Setting up a limited company requires careful documentation. Companies are regulated by Companies House, www.companieshouse.gov.uk All companies have to register with Companies House and are issued with the company equivalent of a birth certificate – the **Certificate of Incorporation**, which states the company name. In addition, a company will also need two further documents (often referred to as the 'Mem & Arts'):

- the **Memorandum of Association** – which states what the company can do in terms of trading activities
- the **Articles of Association** – the internal 'rule-book' of the company which regulates what directors can and cannot do and sets out the rules for holding meetings

If you are setting up an enterprise project, you are likely to have these documents already prepared for you.

COMPANY DOCUMENTATION

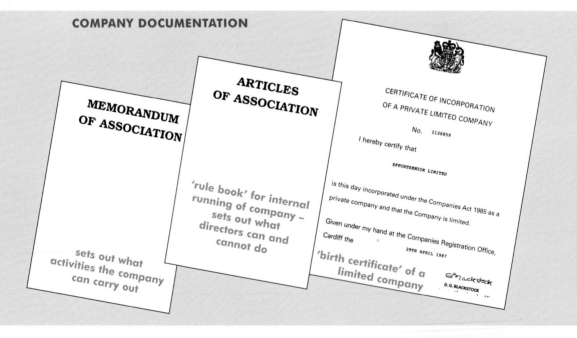

MEMORANDUM OF ASSOCIATION

sets out what activities the company can carry out

ARTICLES OF ASSOCIATION

'rule book' for internal running of company – sets out what directors can and cannot do

CERTIFICATE OF INCORPORATION OF A PRIVATE LIMITED COMPANY

No. 2126859

I hereby certify that

EFFORTSENIOR LIMITED

is this day incorporated under the Companies Act 1985 as a private company and that the Company is limited.

Given under my hand at the Companies Registration Office, Cardiff the 29TH APRIL 1987

D. G. BLACKSTOCK

'birth certificate' of a limited company

company meetings

Enterprise projects inevitably involve meetings at which voting can take place. Normally a simple majority is required to pass a motion. Company meetings might include:

- weekly **company meetings** at which a wide variety of company matters can be discussed and put to the vote by the shareholders

- monthly **board meetings** at which the directors discuss and put to the vote matters of company policy; again a simple majority is required

- the **Annual General Meeting (AGM)** of the company at which the Report and Accounts will be presented to all the shareholders and voted on (a simple majority again required for approval) – this is often the culmination of an enterprise project and is an opportunity for the making of the formal presentation required by your assessment

One of the first meetings you are likely to have when you are setting up a school or college enterprise company is a **company meeting** to elect directors and assistants where necessary. The roles that you will need to allocate are:

- **managing director** – the overall leader of the group

- **company secretary** – dealing with company documentation and managing all the meetings held by company

- **operations director** – who oversees the production of a manufactured item or the organisation of a service

- **finance director** – who oversees the financial management of the company

- **human resources director** – who oversees the workforce management

- **marketing director** – in charge of organising the 4 marketing Ps

- **sales director** – directing the sales force

- **ICT director** – planning and managing the ICT resources (hardware and software) needed by the company

These various roles and responsibilities are explained in more detail later in this chapter (see pages 531-533).

Activity 28.1 – dealing with the red tape

The following questions are often asked when an enterprise project is first set up. How would you answer them?

1   'What is the difference between a director and a shareholder?'

2   'Will it affect my voting rights if I do not get appointed a director?'

3   'What is so special about an AGM?'

4   'What exactly is a Certificate of Incorporation and why is it referred to as a company 'birth certificate'?'

5   'What is the function of the Memorandum of Association and the Articles of Association of a company?'

Getting Started - Choosing a Product

One of the early tasks of a newly-formed school or college enterprise company is to decide on a product. This is a very different order of doing things than you would find in a normal business, where the product idea usually comes first and the type of business adopted (ie sole trader, partnership, limited company) comes next.

This is also a very difficult task because different students will have different ideas and dominant students will often get their way!

Here are some factors that you will need to decide:

- are you going to make a product or provide a service?
- do you know if there is a market for the product or service?
- does it have a USP (Unique Selling Point)?
- can you make it/provide it at a profit?
- can you make it/store it/provide it within your school or college?
- will the product/service be seasonal or can it be modified for use throughout the year? Christmas cards are an old favourite for enterprise companies, but you will need to be flexible in terms of other religions and festivals and annual celebrations such as Valentine's Day
- are you safe to make it/provide it in terms of Health & Safety regulations and the law? – you may find you are not allowed in a school/college environment to make products like fireworks, supply services like dial-a-pizza or an escort agency, or set up an online payment facility

Check it out.

Set out below are some product ideas that have been successfully developed by school and college enterprise companies. Also take a look at the websites that have been developed by Young Enterprise companies nationally: http://www.young-enterprise.org.uk/dynamic/companysites.asp

Have a brainstorm for product ideas.

AN ENTERPRISE PRODUCT BRAINSTORM

candles	clocks	calendars	card games	chess sets
key rings	caps	pencil cases	CDs	cookery books
T-shirts	book markers	aprons	book ends	greetings cards
boxes	bowls	children's books	place mats	parties
clubbing events	knife racks	wallets	valentine messages	talking books
coasters	mouse mats	photo frames	beach bags	trays

Activity 28.2 – brainstorming the product

The object of this Activity is to decide on a product or service for an enterprise company, or at least produce a shortlist for future discussion. One of the problems of trying to do this in a full class session is that people can be reluctant to suggest ideas in case others think they are stupid or the ideas 'naff'.

You should therefore divide into small groups of three or four within the class and 'brainstorm' ideas for products and services in a less formal setting. You can use some of the ideas suggested in this text or, better still, think of some yourselves.

Delegate one of your group members to write down the ideas as they occur. Towards the end of the time given for this discussion, go through the ideas and select a shortlist.

Report your ideas back to the class. It is a good idea if someone writes the ideas on a board or flipchart.

When all the ideas have been written up where they can be seen, they should be discussed by the whole class and narrowed down to form a final shortlist. You should use the questions listed on the previous page (or similar questions) help you make your final choice.

Note: this Activity is based on Activity 10.1 on page 168.

is the product feasible?

Before finally deciding to go ahead with the product or service, any enterprise company must ensure that the product is **feasible** – that it can realistically produce and sell it to make a profit within the given timescale. This is the beginning of the planning process and takes note of a number of the factors mentioned on the previous page:

- **costs**

  How much is it going to cost to produce the product or provide the service? Will the income from sales cover the costs and go on to generate a profit? (See Chapter 13: Financial forecasting – break-even)

- **timescales**

  Is there sufficient time in the calendar to meet production deadlines, eg for the Christmas market or for the Trade Fair at the end of the academic year?

■ **resources**

Do you have what is needed by way of materials and workshop facilities if you are making a product? Do you have enough people in the company to work on the production processes?

How long will it take to make a prototype of your product? Do you or your advisers have the necessary skills?

■ **sustainability**

Have you considered whether the product or service helps protect the environment and does not waste resources such as power? Are any raw materials used sourced from recycled materials? These could be valuable selling points if an environmental policy is in place.

the Planning Processes

The subject of business planning has already been covered in Chapter 10 'Planning and managing a business' (pages 162-181). This explained the overall planning process and described the function of the Mission Statement and the formal Business Plan.

When you are involved in an enterprise scheme such as Young Enterprise, many of the planning processes will be covered by the company documentation, for example the Five Point Risk Assessment carried out by the Operations Department and the budgeted Profit & Loss Statement and Break-even processes carried out by the Managing Director (with help from the Finance Department).

Whatever scheme you are involved in, you will need to plan by drawing up a Mission Statement, a Business Plan, and a separate Operations Plan. Study the diagram on the next page and the read the explanations that follow. They will provide structure to what you are doing in your own enterprise.

Mission Statement

Planning can be said to start in general terms with the Mission Statement. This is a statement by the business setting out in a concise and memorable way what the business does, what it aims to achieve, and also the values it has adopted. For example, an enterprise company called 'Aspect', set up in a school or college to manufacture photo frames, might have the following Mission Statement:

At Aspect we aim to produce photo frames of the best quality to give pleasure to our customers. We want to become well known for excellence in the area.

THE PLANNING PROCESS

Mission Statement	**Business Plan**	**Operations Plan**
a statement of the overall aims of the enterprise	a formal document containing: ■ a description of the business ■ its products ■ its aims & objectives ■ its key people ■ projections of sales ■ the target market ■ financial requirements ■ financial projections	a formal document containing: ■ details of product or service ■ risk assessment ■ Health & Safety provisions ■ legal requirements covered ■ insurance ■ equipment needed ■ premises and facilities used ■ details of suppliers
decide what you are doing and where your company is going	work out what resources you will need, how you will finance the company and market the product	the basic practicalities of how the company will produce the product or service

the Business Plan – the background

The **Business Plan** is a formal written document compiled when a business wants to raise finance, either when it is starting up or when it wants to expand. It is presented to a lender such as a bank or a potential investor and sets out the reasons why lending to or investing in the business is an attractive proposition.

When you are running a mini enterprise such as a Young Enterprise company, you are likely to be financing the business from capital raised by selling shares to friends and family. You may be borrowing by means of an overdraft from a bank. You may have to take part in a simulation exercise involving an interview in which you are applying for finance from a bank lending officer. Completing a Business Plan is a very useful exercise.

Who does it? The Business Plan is normally the overall responsibility of the Managing Director who will call for help from the directors responsible for the various function areas of the business: finance, sales, marketing, human resources and ICT. The Operations (production) Plan may be part of the business plan, or it may, as here, form a separate document.

There is no rigidly set format for a business plan. You can obtain Business Plan formats from the banks and from websites such as www.bized.ac.uk The guidelines which follow are fairly standard.

the Business Plan

The main structure and contents of a typical Business Plan are set out below. If you go on to complete the A2 part of the Applied GCE course, you will compile a business plan as Part of Unit 8 'Business development'.

THE BUSINESS PLAN

the business – a summary

- the name of the business
- the names of professional advisers
- the legal form the business will take (sole trader, partnership or limited company)
- a brief description of the products or service that the business will provide
- a Mission Statement and the short-term and long-term objectives
- the market into which the business will sell (brief details)
- how the business is expected to perform (eg sales, budgeted profit)

key people

- details of main directors or 'key people': name, age, experience and qualifications, role in business, likely salary
- the overall number of employees

products or services

- a more detailed description of what the business proposes to sell
- selling points of the product or service
- costings, proposed pricing and a break-even analysis to show that it is feasible
- sales targets

the market

- a description of the market: the geographical location, market segment(s) of customer
- details of market research carried out
- promotional methods to be used
- methods of distribution

continued ...

---

financing

- funding required for premises, machinery and office equipment
- financing needed for stock and raw materials
- financing needed for administrative expenses
- details of credit provided by suppliers
- requirement for overdraft
- requirement for longer-term loans
- grants available
- money available from issue of shares

financial projections

- budgeted profit and loss account
- break-even calculation (see also 'products or services')
- cash-flow forecast

appendices

- detailed results of market research
- technical information about the product or service

the Operations Plan

The Operations Plan is the plan for the production of a manufactured item or the organisation of a service. It incorporates short-term targets for the operational areas of the business. Sometimes it is incorporated in the Business Plan; sometimes – as here – it is a separate document.

The Operations Plan is normally the responsibility of the Operations Director. When you take part in an enterprise project you will be very much involved from the start with the production process (if you make a product) or the organisational process (if you provide a service). See the next page for the contents of an Operations Plan for a manufactured item.

THE OPERATIONS PLAN

product or service

■ details of the product or service provided

premises

■ details of premises – whether leased or owned

equipment and tools

■ any equipment needed will be listed, together with its possible source and means of financing (eg purchase or leasing agreement)

■ any tools needed in the production process will be detailed, their source and an indication of whether they are purchased or rented

materials

■ details of suppliers of materials and any credit period given

Health & Safety

■ details of Health & Safety arrangements made by the Human Resources Director and Operations Director

■ Risk Assessment carried out

■ insurance cover

■ other employer legal requirements covered

Activity 28.3 – preparing the diary or journal

In the first part of your assessment for this Unit you have to write a diary or journal showing evidence of what you did in the launch, planning and running of the company – and provide an evaluation of what you did.

In preparation for this assessment you should look at the planning and launch stages of the business covered so far in this chapter and draw up notes for your diary. In particular you should record what you achieved in the processes of choosing the company name, influencing the company structure, carrying out market research, dealing with the company documentation and generally helping with running the business. You will need to be able to evaluate your success in all this, using appropriate examples from your diary. If you are on a Young Enterprise scheme, you could link this with the YE review system.

Company Officials – Roles and Responsibilities

preparing for the assessment

A limited company, unlike a sole trader business, involves a whole team of people whose job it is to work together to achieve the common aims and objectives of the business – to make a quality product, to maximise sales and profit, and to do so in a socially responsible way.

In this section we:

- explain the roles and responsibilities of the various company officials
- examine the types of task that they undertake
- identify the skills that they need
- explore the ways in which they interact and communicate with each other

An understanding of the 'business team' prepares you for the second part of your Unit assessment. This requires you to write your own report on the roles and responsibilities of the other members of the company – what they did and how well they contributed to the enterprise.

who runs the company?

The people who run the business are:

- the directors who form the Board of the company
- the Managing Director who heads up the Board
- the Company Secretary who looks after the company administration

There are also external professional advisers – solicitors and accountants – who advise the company on legal and financial matters, and auditors who check the financial records and accounts of the business.

On the next two pages we examine the roles and responsibilities of the company officials. Study the table carefully and read the text that follows.

OFFICIALS	ROLE AND RESPONSIBILITY	
Managing Director	■ responsible for formulating company aims and objectives ■ responsible for staff well-being and identification with company aims ■ responsible to shareholders and other stakeholders of the company	
Company Secretary	■ responsible for company administration and documentation ■ calling and minuting of company meetings ■ ensuring the company completes necessary returns	
Operations Director	■ responsible for actual production process – products or services ■ development of new products or services – Research & Development ■ issues of Health & Safety, quality, costing, purchasing	
Finance Director	■ responsible for financial planning – budgeting and break-even ■ production of year-end profit statement and balance sheet ■ day-to-day financial transactions – buying, selling, payroll	
Human Resources Director	■ responsible for human resource planning – recruitment ■ staff development – training and appraisal ■ staff administration – records, payroll, Health & Safety, discipline	
Marketing Director	■ responsible for marketing planning – new markets, new products ■ co-ordinating marketing mix – product, promotion, pricing and place ■ liaison with other key functions – sales, operations and finance	
Sales Director	■ responsible for sales policy and planning ■ co-ordinating sales teams ■ liaison with other key functions – marketing, finance, production	
ICT Director	■ responsible for ICT systems implementation – hardware and software ■ establishing website and keeping it up to date ■ liaison with other key functions – marketing, finance, administration	

TYPES OF TASK UNDERTAKEN	SKILLS NEEDED	INTERACTION WITH TEAM
heads Board meetings representing company – PR employee liaison	leadership recognising priorities communication	leads Board of Directors motivation of whole company encouraging teamwork
keeping share register arranging and minuting meetings Company Return to Companies House	organisational skills planning ability accuracy	deals with staff share issues involving in meetings obtains information for Return
meetings with production staff monitoring production line production/operations budget	leadership technological organisational	instructing production team seeking opinions requesting information
agrees departmental budgets completion of Report and Accounts deals with accountants and auditors	leadership communication numerical	motivation of staff requesting information monitoring people and systems
interviews senior job applicants managerial appraisals deals with industrial disputes	leadership interviewing negotiating	leads staff planning meetings listens to staff feedback resolves disputes
co-ordinates market research decisions on products and pricing PR co-ordination – press releases	creative thinking planning ability communication	feeds creative ideas to team co-ordinates different teams encourages individual ideas
liaises with marketing – customer feedback liaises with finance – pricing, credit control liaises with production – stock control	personal skills planning ability negotiating	motivation of sales force encouraging communication training of sales force
ICT for sales force – mobiles and laptops ICT for finance – computer accounting introducing company intranet and training	computer skills planning ability communication	negotiation with departments encouraging communication training of sales force

Company Officials and Teamwork

what is a team?

You will appreciate from reading the information on the previous two pages that company officials and directors form a complex team. What do we mean by a 'team'?

Working with others implies the need for teamwork. It is easy to start to define a team by giving examples – a football team, a workplace team – and explaining that they work together – sometimes well and sometimes not quite so well. But what exactly is a team?

A team is a group of people working together to achieve defined objectives

In the case of a football team, the objective is clearly to play skillfully and defeat the other side. The objective of a company team is to work together to achieve the company objectives – maximising sales and profit, making a quality product or providing an excellent service.

the benefits of teamwork

As you will know from working in a team project, you normally achieve better results than if you work on your own. The benefits include:

- **pooling of skills and abilities:** some people are better at some tasks and some are better at others, and so a team will take advantage of individual strengths and overcome individual weaknesses

teamwork

- **creative thinking:** working with other people means that individuals can be stimulated to create and share ideas on a scale that would probably not be possible if they were working on their own

- **motivation:** people get a 'buzz' out of working in a team – it gets people going and brings its rewards when the team is successful

- **help and support:** team members usually support each other when support is needed – this can take the form of advice, moral support and assisting with or taking over tasks which may be causing a problem

We will discuss teamwork further in the next chapter where we examine the running of an enterprise company.

Activity 28.4 – choosing the company officials

Choosing the company officials for an enterprise project is not an easy task. One class has recently started a mini-enterprise, which it has called Insight Out. It wants to manufacture a product but is not sure yet what it will be. It is having a meeting to choose its first group of officials:

■ Managing Director

■ Company Secretary

■ Operations Director

■ Finance Director

■ Sales Director

Five individuals have put themselves forward for election. Read the descriptions carefully and answer the questions that follow.

Tariq is a quiet but responsible student, well-liked and good at maths. He has a part-time job in the cash office of a local business. He wants to get a business studies degree.

Toby is a loud student, popular in the local social scene. He is not hot at academic subjects and wants to get a job. He can usually talk anyone round to his point of view.

Sam is a strong character and captain of a local netball squad. She occasionally imposes her will on people and so is sometimes unpopular. She wants to be a lawyer.

Bex is a popular student who is happy to go along with the crowd and does not have any strong opinions. She is neat and well-organised. If she has a fault, she is too quiet.

Mel is a well-liked student who is very practical and wants to specialise in Design and Technology. She is well organised and has got some imaginative ideas for products.

1   Outline the roles and responsibilities of the five vacant positions.

2   Which company position would you give to each student? You should back up your answer with reasons based on the character of the person, the skills needed for the job and the types of task involved.

3   What do you understand by 'teamwork' and why is it important in a business and an enterprise project?

4   Few people are perfect for a job. Having made your decisions about your choice for the five jobs, do you see any problems that might occur with any of the students you have chosen, in terms of their ability to carry out their tasks and work in a team?

5   Make preparatory notes for your Assessment report and evaluation of the roles and responsibilities of other members of your enterprise group in the launch of the company. How well did they do?

CHAPTER SUMMARY

■ A successful business is one where the employees know and listen to their customers and know what they want; they are clear in their objectives and make the most of the abilities and skills of the people in the company.

■ A limited company is a business owned by shareholders and managed by directors. It is a business legally separate from its owners so that if it is wound up or goes bust, its shareholders can only at worst lose the money they invested.

■ Company documentation includes share certificates (a statement of an amount invested), a Certificate of Incorporation (the company 'birth certificate') and the Memorandum and Articles of Association (which are the 'rule books' of the company).

■ There are different types of meeting held by a company: a Company Meeting is attended by shareholders and directors, a Board Meeting by directors, and the Annual General Meeting (AGM) by shareholders and directors.

■ Choosing a product can be a difficult task. Questions asked include: product or service? Is there a market for it? Will it make a profit? Will it be safe? Is it feasible?

■ The planning process may involve a Mission Statement, a Business Plan and an Operations Plan.

■ There is no set format for a Business Plan, but its main sections often include: a summary of the business, a description of its key people, its products or services, the target market, financing and financial projections.

■ Similarly, an Operations Plan (for a manufacturing company) could include: details of the product, premises, equipment and tools, materials and Health & Safety considerations.

■ The officials who run the company (mainly the directors) include: Managing Director, Company Secretary, Operations Director, Finance Director, Human Resources Director, Marketing Director, Sales Director and ICT Director. They all have very specific responsibilities and need specific skills to carry out their work.

■ Effective teamwork is very important if a company is to achieve its objectives. Officials such as directors must be prepared to be able to communicate and to encourage teamwork.

■ Effective teamwork can result in the pooling of skills and abilities, creative thinking, motivation and help and support.

KEY TERMS

limited company	a business owned by shareholders and run by directors, set up as a body separate from its owners
private limited company	a limited company whose shares are held by the directors and are not for public issue; it must have 'limited' in the name
public limited company	a limited company which is authorised to allow its shares to be sold to the public through the Stock Exchange
shareholder	a person who owns shares in a limited company
share certificate	a document issued to a shareholder giving details of his/her shareholding
director	a person who is responsible for a functional area of a company – a director may own shares in the company
winding up	the process of making a company cease to exist
Certificate of Incorporation	a certificate issued by Companies House when a company is formed – often known as the 'birth certificate' of a company
Memorandum of Association	a document which states what the company has power to do in terms of its activities
Articles of Association	a document which sets out the powers of the directors – often seen as the 'rule-book' of the company
Mission Statement	a public statement by the business stating what the business does, what its values are and what it aims to achieve
Business Plan	a formal written document produced as a presentation to a potential investor or lender
Operations Plan	the short-term (normally one-year) targets for the various operational areas of the business
team	a group of people working together to achieve defined objectives

29

Running the company and winding it up

Starting point

The key words for running an enterprise project are 'team', 'time' and 'commitment'.

Your company must work as a team: company members share skills and ideas, motivate and support each other. The company must manage its time effectively, because, although the project will run for three terms, time is very short if meetings are held only weekly. Commitment must be shown by each team member in supporting other members and in meeting common objectives.

Lastly, at the end of the enterprise project, reports will have to be written, presentations made and the company liquidated. Company members should have profited, both from the experience and also from the final payout of dividends.

What you will learn from this chapter

- running a successful enterprise project involves teamwork, which comes from holding regular company meetings; these should be well-structured and flexible enough to allow changes in the planning process, in product/service design and the allocation of jobs

- the main functional areas are sales and marketing, production and finance; these should be seen as being very much interlinked

- there are two main targets in the company year: a possible appearance at a Trade Fair and, secondly, the Annual General Meeting (AGM) at which the company Annual Report is presented, both in writing and orally in front of an audience

- the final stage is the liquidation of the company after settling of debts and making of payouts; at this point the company ceases to exist

the Company Year: an Overview

Most school or college enterprise projects, such as Young Enterprise, run over three terms. We described in the last chapter how a company is launched. That is obviously only the beginning. The main stages can be illustrated diagramatically – as below. The timings are only an indication.

THE LIFE OF AN ENTERPRISE PROJECT COMPANY

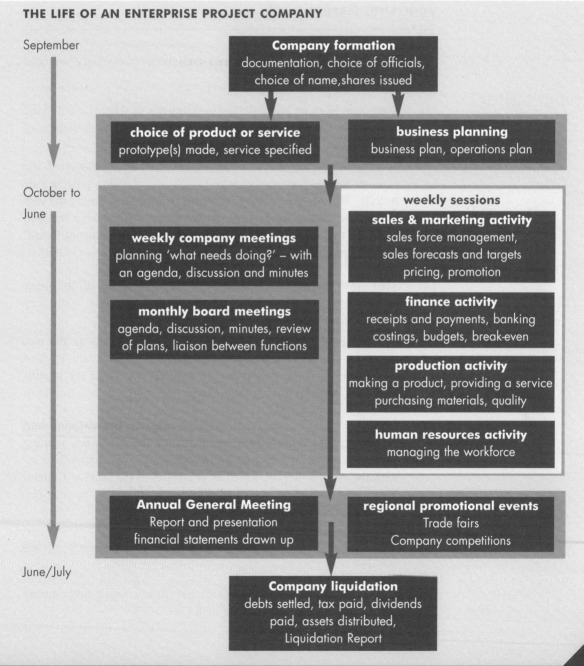

September

Company formation
documentation, choice of officials, choice of name, shares issued

choice of product or service
prototype(s) made, service specified

business planning
business plan, operations plan

October to June

weekly company meetings
planning 'what needs doing?' – with an agenda, discussion and minutes

monthly board meetings
agenda, discussion, minutes, review of plans, liaison between functions

weekly sessions

sales & marketing activity
sales force management, sales forecasts and targets pricing, promotion

finance activity
receipts and payments, banking costings, budgets, break-even

production activity
making a product, providing a service purchasing materials, quality

human resources activity
managing the workforce

Annual General Meeting
Report and presentation financial statements drawn up

regional promotional events
Trade fairs
Company competitions

June/July

Company liquidation
debts settled, tax paid, dividends paid, assets distributed, Liquidation Report

the company year

The first two stages shown on the diagram on the previous page (company formation and product planning) were covered in the last chapter. The remaining stages will be explained further in this chapter. Note that the timescale shown on the left of the diagram is for indication only. The only definite factor about the time is that is in short supply.

your Unit Assessment

As noted in the last chapter, there are four main pieces of evidence you need to produce for this Unit:

(a)   Your own **diary or journal** showing evidence of what you did in the launch, planning and running of the company – and an evaluation of what you did.

You should already have prepared material, or have completed, the diary or journal for the company launch and planning process (see Activity 28.3 on page 530). This should be continued during the year as you take part in the running of the business. Remember that you will need to include an objective evaluation of what you contributed, giving appropriate examples.

(b)   Your own **report** on the roles and responsibilities of the other members of the company – what they did and how well they contributed to the enterprise.

Again, you should by now have started making notes on the part played by others in the launch and planning stages (see Activity 28.4 on page 535). These should now be continued to cover the months leading up to the AGM and liquidation.

(c)   A recognised individual contribution to a **group presentation and report** explaining the launch, and assessing the day-to-day running and the eventual 'winding up' of the company. This can be 'tied in' with the Annual Report which is presented to the Annual General Meeting (AGM) of an enterprise company at the end of the year, just before it enters into liquidation.

(d)   Your own **report** reviewing and evaluating the success of the enterprise.

Clearly it will be a good idea for items (c) and (d) to compile notes during the course, ideally as you also compile item (a).

the importance of meetings

Meetings

Enterprise projects are particularly valuable to students of business because they lay great stress on meetings. They concentrate into one single weekly session all the activities and personal interactions which a normal business will provide over the course of a week. You will know if you do a part-time job that you will probably do the same thing day after day and will rarely, if ever, attend a meeting. An enterprise project, on the other hand, will often start and end with a meeting of all participating students before getting stuck into the processes of production.

weekly meetings

The meetings held during the weekly sessions are more likely to be brief and involve:

■ an Agenda drawn up by the Company Secretary and Managing Director

■ looking to see what needs doing in the various functional areas of sales and marketing, production and finance – action points from previous meetings

■ hearing brief verbal reports from the function directors

■ minutes to be written up by the Company Secretary

Normally people will want to get on with the production, and so these meetings should be brief and to the point. They are valuable because they encourage teamwork – the exchange of ideas – and provide an opportunity for the function directors to involve and motivate the less 'switched on' workers.

monthly Board Meetings

Regular Board Meetings are held – possibly on a monthly basis – so that the Managing Director (MD) and other function directors can:

■ ensure the company is keeping to its Mission and objectives

■ monitor progress against specific targets, eg: 'How well are our sales doing? Are we keeping to schedule? Have we got enough money in the bank?'

■ make decisions which involve different function areas, eg the Sales Director wants to reduce prices to stimulate sales but the Finance Director says that this will reduce profits too much – a decision has to be made

- resolve any specific problems – eg company members not turning up or failing to bring in their money from the sale of shares

- deciding on policy matters – eg how much dividend the company should pay out to its shareholders

Because of the nature of these meetings, it is important that the Company Secretary draws up an Agenda well in advance. A meeting Agenda has a set format (see the numbered items in bold type below).

AGENDA

1 Apologies for absence
(the names of people who have sent in apologies)

2 Minutes of the last meeting approved
(to be signed by the MD when members have agreed that they are correct)

3 Matters arising
(issues in the last meeting's minutes which are not raised in this agenda)

4 Directors' Reports
(reports on the achievement of company aims, progress against targets and performance in terms of sales levels, sales events, production levels, absenteeism, profitability, training, and so on)

5 Specific agreed Agenda items
(eg next month's Trade Fair, changing of job roles between members)

6 Any other business
(any new issues that members want to raise that are not on the Agenda)

7 Date of next meeting

The meeting will normally be 'chaired' by the Managing Director, and the Company Secretary will take the minutes. It is important that meetings are taken seriously and conducted in a formal manner, otherwise they can degenerate into a 'free for all'.

As we will see in the section that follows, group communication through regular meetings is what helps to hold a company together.

Monitoring Company Performance

getting going

When setting up an enterprise project such as a Young Enterprise company, it is important that the business gets going as soon as possible. Time is of the essence. If things drift along from week to week without a decision over a product or with disagreement between directors, the company will be in trouble – no product means no income or profit, and members will become demotivated.

What is needed in an ideal company is:

- an early decision on a product
- an enthusiastic group of directors working very much as a team
- a motivated workforce
- a steady flow of income, firstly from the issue of shares and secondly from sale of the company's product or service

These needs can be defined very clearly by setting targets:

- specific targets for production, eg 50 items a week
- specific targets for sales, eg at least 40 items a week
- specific targets for financing, eg 100 £1 shares sold in the first three weeks

the monitoring process

These various targets must be monitored on a regular basis, and then, if they are not being met, the situation can be investigated and rectified. Alternatively, the target itself can be modified and made possibly more realistic.

Another area of the business which is constantly under review is the performance of the individuals who work in it. Schemes such as Young Enterprise have a system for personal review and a Record of Achievement. Targets that can be set for individuals can include areas such as attendance (to deter absenteeism) and productivity (the number of items produced each session).

The Case Study and Activity which follow investigate how the following functional areas should deal with problems related to performance:

- production
- sales and marketing
- finance

Case Study – monitoring 'smiley' performance

Teknix is an enterprise project company which is in its first few weeks of trading.

The company manufactures 'smileys' – novelty key fobs which have smiley faces embedded in them. They cost £1 each to manufacture and they sell for £2 each. The target market is the adult market – particularly car owners. There are 10 shareholder members in the company, all of them responsible for selling 'smileys'.

The company directors have set a number of targets for the next four weeks of trading:

The **Production** Director, in consultation with the members, has proposed that they should set a target of producing 50 'smiley' key fobs a week, which will be sold, at the suggestion of the **Marketing** Director, to friends and family of the company members.

The **Sales** Director has set a target for each member to sell five 'smiley' key fobs a week, which should result in weekly sales of 50 key fobs.

The **Finance** Director has therefore budgeted on a weekly sales income of £100 against a weekly cost of £50, and has set up a cash-flow forecast based on this. She has asked that the members ensure that they bring in £5 each minimum from the sale of remaining shares by next week as she needs to bank the money to help pay the costs of making the 'smileys'.

The first four weeks of production and trading have not gone too well in a number of function areas of the business, and so a Board Meeting has been called:

Production

- weekly production of key fobs for the first four weeks has been: 48, 41, 36, 32
- there have been quality problems – some of the key fobs have been returned
- production staff are getting fed up – last week only five of the ten members turned up
- the Production Director's assistant is unhappy in his job and is much more interested in working in Marketing

Marketing and Sales

- feedback from customers is that the 'smiley' key fobs are more for children than for adults
- weekly sales of key fobs for the first four weeks has been: 40, 36, 32, 25

Finance

The balance of the bank account is dangerously low for two reasons:

- income from sales is below target because sales are below target
- half the members have failed to raise the agreed £5 from the sale of shares

Activity 29.1 – monitoring 'smiley' performance

Read the Case Study on the previous page, making a note of all the problems that have occurred. Then answer the questions below. The questions are divided into groups relating to the various functional areas of the business.

Production

1   What is the total production target figure for the key fobs for the first four weeks?

2   What is the actual production figure and the shortfall in production for this period?

3   What are the likely causes of this failure to meet the target?

4   What courses of action could the Production Director recommend to remedy the situation?

Sales

5   What is the target number of 'smiley' key fobs to be sold during the first four weeks?

6   What is the actual number of key fobs sold during the first four weeks? What is the shortfall from the target?

7   What is the target sales income for the first four weeks and what is the actual amount received?

8   What could the Sales Director do to improve sales performance?

Marketing

9   What indication is there that the company's market research findings about the target market might be at fault?

10 What courses of action could the Marketing Director recommend to remedy the situation?

Finance

11 The company has failed to reach the targets set in its budgets. What is the total shortfall in money received:

(a)   in sales receipts?

(b)   from the sale of shares?

Which financial forecast would show up this shortage of money in the bank?

12 What courses of action could the Finance Director recommend to improve the deteriorating financial position of the company?

Notes on Financial Management

The person elected to the post of Financial Director in an enterprise project has taken on one of the most complex jobs and will often need an assistant. Documentation is normally provided in the shape of a large number of forms to complete. The notes that follow here are intended to provide a background and a context for all these forms and the work of the finance function.

If you are involved in financial management of any sort, you will always be needing to look in two opposite directions: backwards and forwards.

looking backwards – financial accounting

You will be interested in the transactions that have already taken place, eg sales, purchases, money coming in from the sale of shares; these transactions should be entered accurately into the accounts and form the basis for financial statements such as the profit & loss account and the balance sheet.

This process is known as **financial accounting** and is summarised in the diagram below.

FINANCIAL ACCOUNTING

transactions and documents	financial transactions – eg sales, purchases, wages, paying bills – involving financial documents such as invoices, receipts and cheques
recording transactions	the financial documents – eg invoices and receipts generated from transactions – are listed and summarised ready for entering in the accounts
entering transactions in the accounts	the lists and summaries of the financial documents are entered in a system of double-entry accounts
extracting report information	figures are extracted from the accounts to provide information and reports for the management and other interested parties, eg a profit and loss account (showing profits/losses) and a balance sheets (showing what the business owns and owes)

looking forwards – management accounting

This form of financial management lies more in the area of informed guesswork than in recorded fact, because instead of analysing what has happened in the past, it involves making informed estimates of what is likely to happen in the future. This is known as **management accounting.**

You will probably already have dealt with this area of financial management earlier in this book, when studying for example:

- **break-even analysis** (Chapter 13), ie working out how many items you will have to produce in order to cover your costs and start to make a profit

- **budgets** (Chapter 15), which estimate future costs, incomes and items produced and enable you to monitor actual performance against projected performance so that you can decide what action to take if you need to

- **cash-flow forecast** (also known as a 'cash budget' – see Chapter 16 and the illustration below) which projects all future payments in and out of the bank account and shows whether the business can pay its way or whether it needs further financing, either from the bank or from elsewhere

These financial processes will be required in the running of an enterprise project, and particularly when preparing for the Annual General Meeting and the eventual liquidation of the company.

CASH-FLOW FORECAST

	A	B	C	D	E	F	G
1	DVD EXPRESS						
2	CASH BUDGET for 6 months						
3		JANUARY	FEBRUARY	MARCH	APRIL	MAY	JUNE
4		£	£	£	£	£	£
5							
6							
7	RECEIPTS						
8	Sales	10,000	10,000	10,000	10,000	10,000	10,000
9	Bank Loan	8,000					
10	Capital	12,000					
11	TOTAL RECEIPTS	30,000	10,000	10,000	10,000	10,000	10,000
12	PAYMENTS						
13	Purchases	5,000	5,000	5,000	5,000	5,000	5,000
14	Equipment	14,500	15,250				
15	Rent	575	575	575	575	575	575
16	Insurance	50	50	50	50	50	50
17	Electricity			100			100
18	Telephone	100	100	100	100	100	100
19	Wages	1,000	1,000	1,000	1,000	1,000	1,000
20	Postage	450	450	450	450	450	450
21	Marketing	200	200	200	200	200	200
22							
23	TOTAL PAYMENTS	21,875	22,625	7,475	7,375	7,375	7,475
24	CASHFLOW FOR MONTH	8,125	- 12,625	2,525	2,625	2,625	2,525
25	Opening Bank Balance		8,125	- 4,500	- 1,975	650	3,275
26	Closing Bank Balance	8,125	- 4,500	- 1,975	650	3,275	5,800

Trade Fairs

Enterprise company projects will often get involved in setting up a stall at a some form of public trade fair. Examples of these are Young Enterprise trade fairs held in public venues such as town halls, and also Christmas (Winterfest) fairs which encourage a variety of traders to take a stall.

Fairs of this type are excellent in a number of ways for the development of the skills of individuals running companies:

- **working to deadlines** – the fair will be on a certain date and the company has to produce a stand, sufficient stocks of its product(s) and a competent sales force by that date

- **planning skills** – the function directors will have to set targets to ensure that the event is a success – there will have to be enough money available to finance the event; there will have to be enough stocks of the products; the products will need advertising; the stand will need to be designed

- **quality** – the stand and its products will need to be of a good quality

- **encouraging teamwork** – the event will mean that all the company members will have to work well together

- **motivation** – the company team should get a 'buzz' from working together to meet its targets and then to see its products on display in public

Sometimes a company will have the opportunity of exhibiting twice, once in December and again during the following six months. Lessons learnt at the first event can be put into action for greater success second time around.

Activity 29.2 – the benefits of Trade Fairs

Your enterprise company has been invited to take a stall at the local Christmas (Winterfest) fair.

1 Explain how an event such as this will affect in practical terms the organisation of the area of the company in which you are working.

2 Describe the benefits to the company as a whole of taking part in a Trade Fair.

3 Describe the benefits to an individual company member of taking part in a Trade Fair.

the Annual General Meeting

The **Annual General Meeting (AGM)** of a company is an annual company meeting which involves shareholders and directors and at which the Annual Report and Accounts are presented.

In the case of a large PLC the AGM can receive much media publicity and attract hundreds of shareholders, whereas the AGM of a private limited company may be a very low key affair over a cup of coffee involving the owner directors and shareholders. In the case of an enterprise project company the meeting is the main opportunity for inviting people who have helped the company during the year and to present the company's achievements.

the AGM and winding up the company

For most commercial limited companies, the AGM is just part of the annual pattern of events which occur, and which will be co-ordinated by the directors, eg the Annual Return to Companies House, payment of Corporation Tax, payment of dividends, the drawing up of the Annual Report and Accounts.

For the type of company that you will be running, however, the AGM is very much geared towards the 'winding up' and 'liquidation' of the company which will take place shortly afterwards. The questions that will need to be dealt with are not just 'What assets does the company have?' and 'What profits has it made?' but 'How will the assets be distributed? and 'Who will get the profit?'

These issues are dealt with in full in the section which starts on the next page.

the AGM and your Unit Assessment

Preparing for the AGM is also the time for:

- the writing of a joint report of the company's activities during the year
- the presentation of the report and the financial statements to the shareholders and invited guests

These activities tie in closely with your Unit assessment and help to provide evidence for the following requirements:

- A recognised individual contribution to a **group presentation and report** explaining the launch, and assessing the day-to-day running and the eventual 'winding up' of the company
- your own **report** reviewing and evaluating the success of the enterprise

Preparation for Winding up the Company

'winding up' and 'liquidation'

A limited company is a legal entity which is separate from its owner(s). If the owner directors of a company die, the company carries on. If a company ceases to exist, it will have been 'wound up' or 'liquidated' by legal processes. The terms **winding up** and **liquidation** (which effectively result in the same thing) will therefore always apply to a company, but never to a sole trader or partnership.

Winding up and liquidation occur either because the company has gone bust and suppliers and lenders want to get their money back through the courts, or because, as in the case of your enterprise, the members have to stop trading, and need to distribute the money and resources held by the company.

the processes of winding up

It is important to plan the winding up of your company carefully. It needs to follow the AGM but should not conflict with events such as Trade Fairs which require that the company is operational and trading.

Before you wind up the company you will have to calculate:

- the money that is available in the bank account and as cash held
- money which can be raised from selling any remaining assets, eg stock and materials
- money due to the company, eg customers who may owe money
- any debts that have to be paid, eg invoices from suppliers
- tax due, eg any VAT and Corporation Tax (company tax)

This will enable you to work out the money you will then have available to distribute to the shareholders of the company. If you are running a Young Enterprise company, you will have documentation and forms to help you.

Other processes the company will have needed to carry out before winding up include:

- making sure all outstanding orders have been fulfilled
- counting stock and materials (which the company might be able to sell)
- timetabling the running down of operations
- writing the company report
- drawing up the financial statements – the Profit & Loss Account and Balance Sheet

Now read the Case Study which follows.

Case Study – winding up the company

The enterprise company Musicmaniax has successfuly made and sold CD racks. It has planned carefully in advance for its liquidation. It is now the middle of June and the winding up is complete. The company has ceased to exist, but of course the experience of running it remains a very valuable experience.

It has taken over six weeks in all to complete the process which has involved closing down the production line, returning the tools to the Design and Technology Department and completing all the paperwork. The AGM was held on 1 June and the Annual Report and the financial statements presented and circulated.

Probably the most difficult task was compiling the financial statements (the Profit & Loss Account and Balance Sheet) and working out how much money – the dividend – should be distributed to the shareholders of the company (100 shares of £1 each had been sold).

The calculation was carried out as shown below. Note the adjustments that have been made for outstanding amounts due and received, and for the Corporation Tax that had to be paid on the profit.

The company has been financially successful and the shareholders have made a gain of 44% – they have been paid back £1.44 for each £1 share originally purchased.

MUSICMANIAX: DISTRIBUTION OF FUNDS TO SHAREHOLDERS ON LIQUIDATION		
1 June	Amount in company bank account and as cash at date of AGM	140.00
5 June	Outstanding bill paid to a supplier of materials	10.00
		130.00
8 June	Outstanding amount received from customer	9.00
12 June	Amount received from sale of outstanding stock	21.00
	Final net profit figure	160.00
15 June	Corporation Tax paid @ 10% of net profit	16.00
	Money available as dividend payable on 100 shares	144.00
17 June	Dividend distributed to shareholders @ £1.44 per share	144.00
17 June	Money left in company bank account and cash tin	nil

The final Case Study in this chapter has been written by the Managing Director of a Young Enterprise company in the West Midlands. It is an honest appraisal of a business which has not been without its share of problems, but which eventually hit upon a very successful product which helped motivate the company team. Read it through, as it should provide ideas for the type of issues that you should be raising in your own Unit assessments.

Case Study – MaXXd, a Young Enterprise Company

Osborne Books would like to thank Graham Williams, Sam Hartwell and the members of MaXXd of Worcester Sixth Form College for their help in compiling this Case Study.

A Rolo in a box for your Valentine!

At the beginning of our Business course in September we were asked if we would like to form a Young Enterprise company. We were told that it would help us gain a better understanding of business if we were to form one ourselves. We agreed to participate, and from then on found out that it was harder work than we thought. In our first meeting we decided who was going to play which role in the company. The Managing Director had to chair company meetings and keep the peace!

Initially we had to set up the legal structure of the business up by filling in the company forms. We then had the difficult job of deciding what we were going to be called and what we were going to do. After much head-scratching we decided that we were going to be called MaXXd and sell car air fresheners and other car accessories. This idea was based on the strengths of the individuals in the group. We then carried out some small-scale market research to see if our ideas were feasible. When the results seemed positive we had to set up our bank account so that we could pay money in and send our cheque off to pay the registration fee.

To start off as a company we decided to raise money by selling shares. Every member of the company had to raise £5 in shares within two weeks. At the time there were 12 members in our group and if everyone managed to raise the money, we estimated that we could get enough cash to start trading.

It was coming up to Christmas fast and we still had not produced any products, and we were setting up a stall at the local Christmas Fayre in two-and-a-half weeks. The pressure was on for us to get something to sell. We finally made the decision to make a selection of Christmas cards using 'make your own' packs so that they could be unique in design and even tailored to individual taste. We were not very successful at the Fayre as there was a lot of competition from other schools and colleges. However, we managed to make enough money to cover the cost of making half the cards and the cost of going to the Fayre.

After Christmas we decided that we wanted a new Managing Director. After a vote by all of the directors it was decided that Sam should take over the position.

The new management structure now set its sights on the production of birthday cards, and with Valentine's Day coming up, a secret valentine service. The idea here was that by paying £1 staff and students could send a 'Rolo in a box' to the person they fancied with a secret message. The messages were then posted on the college intranet and for 50p the recipient could find out who sent it. It took us weeks to decide how we were going to promote and set up the scheme and deliver the Rolos. Finally, we decided that we would advertise the event via the college

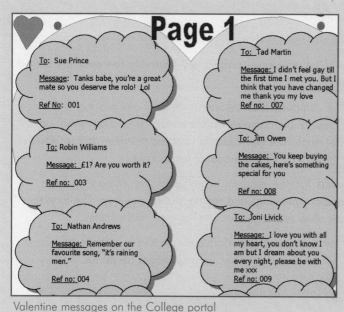

Page 1

To: Sue Prince

Message: Tanks babe, you're a great mate so you deserve the rolo! Lol

Ref No: 001

To: Robin Williams

Message: £1? Are you worth it?

Ref no: 003

To: Nathan Andrews

Message: Remember our favourite song, "it's raining men."

Ref no: 004

To: Tad Martin

Message: I didn't feel gay till the first time I met you. But I think that you have changed me thank you my love

Ref no: 007

To: Jim Owen

Message: You keep buying the cakes, here's something special for you

Ref no: 008

To: Joni Livick

Message: I love you with all my heart, you don't know I am but I dream about you every night, please be with me xxx

Ref no: 009

Valentine messages on the College portal

portal and display the service from outside the canteen, as this was where most people would see us.

During our Young Enterprise lessons the week before Valentine's Day we would deliver the Rolos and messages by finding out where people were at certain times of the day and deliver the Rolos in special boxes to them in class. It was a great success and our biggest money maker, costing us very little to produce and we raised £42.50. The students loved it!

We attended the Young Enterprise Trade Fair later on in the year where we sold our remaining stock of car accessories, birthday cards, home-made handbags and friendship bracelets. Although success was mixed, it was an enjoyable day.

The whole experience was hard work but very rewarding and taught us much about ourselves and let us see how a business works. Probably most importantly of all we learnt that it was important to work as a team, and that if you want to be successful in business you have to be well-organised and look at every situation in a positive way.

Activity 29.3 – MaXXd, a Young Enterprise Company

Read through the Case Study and answer the questions that follow.

1 How much capital was initially raised by MaXXd?

2 What market research was carried out by MaXXd?

3 What products were provided by MaXXd, and why did they vary so much?

4 What was the greatest success of MaXXd and why was the nature of this product also a major problem?

5 What did this Young Enterprise group learn from forming and running MaXXd?

CHAPTER SUMMARY

■ The company year of an enterprise project will normally run over the limited period of three terms.

■ During this period the company must decide on at least one product or service, produce it, sell it, report on company achievement and then wind up the company. There is not much time available for all these activities and so effective time management and teamwork are essential for success.

■ Meetings are required for the efficient working of the company; these will comprise weekly company meetings and regular Board meetings. The formalities of meeting should be observed: agendas, a chairman and minutes.

■ It is important for any business that performance should be monitored. Targets should be set and met wherever possible. Targets should be set for:
  - production volumes
  - production quality
  - sales (by volume and by amount)
  - financing (sale of shares and sales income)
The targets become particularly important when the enterprise company has to take part in a public selling event such as a Trade Fair.

■ If targets are not met, the cause(s) should be identified and rectified where possible.

■ Monitoring performance of a business also involves assessing the contribution (or lack of contribution) of company members. Absenteeism and poor performance affect the company 'team' and should be dealt with. Enterprise company projects often involve a formal system of personal review and the completion of a Record of Achievement.

■ One of the more complex areas of the business is the finance function. It is important that the Finance Director and his/her assistant understand the way financial management works in terms of financial accounting and management accounting. This will provide an understanding of the many complex financial forms that may have to be completed.

■ The Annual General Meeting of the company is in many ways the culmination of the year's work, involving the preparation and presentation of a Report of the company's activities and its financial statements to shareholders and guests.

■ The enterprise company must be wound up at the end of the year. This is a complex process which will result in the effective 'death' of the company. It involves collecting in any money due, paying outstanding bills and tax and then distributing the remaining money – ie the capital and profit – to the shareholders.

KEY TERMS

agenda	a list of items to be discussed at a company meeting, normally drawn up by the Company Secretary
minutes	notes on the items discussed at a meeting, including decisions made and action points raised
monitoring	assessing the performance of a business against set targets so that action can be taken where appropriate
financial accounting	looks backwards – involves the recording of financial transactions and entering them in the account books so that financial statements such as the profit & loss account and balance sheet can be drawn up for the benefit of the managers and owners of the business
management accounting	looks forward – providing financial data to the company management (eg future income and costs) so that planning can take place and decisions made accordingly, eg budgets and break-even analysis
Annual General Meeting	a formal meeting of a company at which the company's annual report and financial statements are presented to shareholders and invited members of the public
winding up	the legal process of making a company cease to exist, either so that its remaining funds can be distributed in the form of dividends to the shareholders, or if the company is insolvent (bust) , to the creditors who are owed money

for your notes

Index